Belgium and the Congo, 1885–1980

While the impact of a colonising metropole on subjected territories has been widely scrutinized, the effect of empire on the colonising country has long been neglected. Recently, many studies have examined the repercussions of their respective empires on colonial powers such as the United Kingdom and France. Belgium and its African empire have been conspicuously absent from this discussion. This book attempts to fill this gap. *Belgium and the Congo, 1885–1980*, examines the effects of colonialism on the domestic politics, diplomacy and economics of Belgium, from 1880 – when King Leopold II began the country's expansionist enterprises in Africa – to the 1980s, well after the Congo's independence in June of 1960. By examining the colonial impact on its mother country, Belgium, this study also contributes to a better understanding of the Congo's past and present.

Guy Vanthemsche is professor of contemporary history at Free University Brussels (Vrjie Universiteit Brussel). Professor Vanthemsche is also secretary of the Royal Commission of History in Belgium. He is co-director of the Belgium-based journal *Revue Belge de Philologie et d'Histoire*.

Belgium and the Congo, 1885–1980

GUY VANTHEMSCHE
Vrije Universiteit Brussel

Translated by
ALICE CAMERON AND STEPHEN WINDROSS

Revised by
KATE CONNELLY

CAMBRIDGE
UNIVERSITY PRESS

CAMBRIDGE
UNIVERSITY PRESS

University Printing House, Cambridge CB2 8BS, United Kingdom

One Liberty Plaza, 20th Floor, New York, NY 10006, USA

477 Williamstown Road, Port Melbourne, VIC 3207, Australia

314-321, 3rd Floor, Plot 3, Splendor Forum, Jasola District Centre, New Delhi-110025, India

79 Anson Road, #06-04/06, Singapore 079906

Cambridge University Press is part of the University of Cambridge.

It furthers the University's mission by disseminating knowledge in the pursuit of education, learning and research at the highest international levels of excellence.

www.cambridge.org
Information on this title: www.cambridge.org/9781107449312

© Guy Vanthemsche 2012

This publication is in copyright. Subject to statutory exception and to the provisions of relevant collective licensing agreements, no reproduction of any part may take place without the written permission of Cambridge University Press.

First published 2012
First paperback edition 2017

A catalogue record for this publication is available from the British Library

Library of Congress Cataloging in Publication data
Vanthemsche, Guy.
  Belgium and the Congo, 1885–1980 / Guy Vanthemsche.
    p. cm.
  Includes bibliographical references and index.
  ISBN 978-0-521-19421-1 (hardback)
  1. Belgium – Relations – Congo (Democratic Republic) 2. Congo (Democratic Republic) – Relations – Belgium. 3. Colonization – Political aspects – Belgium – History. 4. Colonization – Economic aspects – Belgium – History. 5. Belgium – Politics and government – 1830–1914. 6. Belgium – Politics and government – 1914– 7. Belgium – Economic conditions. 8. Congo (Democratic Republic) – Colonization – History. 9. Congo (Democratic Republic) – Politics and government. I. Title.
DH569.C7V26 2012
967.51´02–dc23   2011048650

ISBN 978-0-521-19421-1 Hardback
ISBN 978-1-107-44931-2 Paperback

Cambridge University Press has no responsibility for the persistence or accuracy of URLs for external or third-party internet websites referred to in this publication, and does not guarantee that any content on such websites is, or will remain, accurate or appropriate.

*To my wife Françoise,
who was born in Léopoldville and on whom the Congo has also left its mark*

*In memory of Jean Stengers,
who left his mark on Belgian colonial historiography*

Contents

List of Figures		*page* viii
List of Tables		ix
	Introduction	1
1.	Origin of the Colonial Phenomenon in Belgium	14
2.	The Congo and Belgium's Domestic Policy	33
3.	The Congo and Belgium's External Position	101
4.	The Congo and the Belgian Economy	143
5.	Belgium and the Independent Congo	200
	General Conclusion	268
Annex		273
Index		281

Figures

4.1. Belgian imports from the Congo and Belgian exports to the Congo (value), index 1913=100 *page* 151
4.2. Belgian imports from the Congo and Belgian exports to the Congo in percentage of total Belgian imports and exports 151

Tables

2.1.	Opinion Poll on the Belgian Congo (1956)	*page* 80
4.1.	Share (in %) of the Total Empire (dominions included) (= EMP) and of the sub-Saharan African Colonies (= SA) in the Exports and the Imports of Great Britain, France, Portugal and Belgium (1879–81 to 1945–51)	154
4.2.	Belgian Capital Exports in the Form of Foreign Direct Investments (FDI) 1879–1939 (in millions of current Belgian francs, annual averages)	167
4.3.	Share of Customs Duties on Imports and Exports in Total Tax Revenues of the Congo and in the Total Value of Imports and Exports (in %)	170
4.4.	Net Profits as a Ratio of Capital and Reserves	185
4.5.	The Congo's Share (in %) in Belgian Port Activity (1895–1939)	188
5.1.	The Congo's Share in Imports and Exports of the Belgian-Luxembourg Economic Union (in %)	238
5.2.	The Congo's Share in Belgium's Bilateral Assistance to Developing Countries (1960–1999)	252

Introduction

Empire and Metropole

In the sixteenth century, Western Europe became a presence in the global arena; a presence that would become increasingly dominant throughout the nineteenth century. From then on, no non-European society would be able to escape the profound and long-lasting changes imposed by a number of European powers, which were themselves undergoing great changes, and by young nations such as the United States. Many complex factors contributed to this process of change: the emigration of men and women; the export of capital; the expansion of enterprises; the spread of beliefs, languages, techniques and ways of life; and the introduction of military forces, political structures and repressive, educational and medical systems.

Belgium, a new nation founded in 1830, participated in this great upheaval. Throughout the nineteenth century, Belgian entrepreneurs founded businesses, traded goods and exported capital all over the world, while missionaries spread the Catholic faith. Belgium's global activities also assumed a political dimension when this country colonised vast regions in the heart of Africa, disrupted the indigenous societies and created a new political entity called the Congo. Against all odds, this entity still exists today. Thus a small, newly founded European nation had a profound influence on the enormous continent that – often for the wrong reasons – has been called 'dark'.

But the opposite is also true: The Congo has, albeit unintentionally, left its mark on Belgium. Belgian colonial activity transformed Belgium. It is this transformation that constitutes the subject of this book. An overview of recent international developments in the study of imperialism will help to understand our aim.

Since its beginnings in the second half of the nineteenth century, the historiography of colonialism has been characterised by profound changes.[1] The

---

[1] F. Cooper, *Colonialism in Question: Theory, Knowledge, History* (Berkeley, 2005). See also H. Wesseling, "Overseas History", in P. Burke, ed., *New Perspectives on Historical Writing* (Cambridge, 1991), pp. 67–92.

days when the chronicle of the white man's global expansion was spoken of in laudatory prose are, of course, long gone. Many preconceptions and divisions have been, over time, addressed and dismissed.

First of all, there is the division between eras. Until recently, the pre-colonial, colonial and post-colonial eras were neatly separated, thus neglecting the many complex threads linking societies, people, habits and ideas over these so-called divisions. Currently, analysts are striking a more complex balance between continuity and discontinuity. Next, there were divisions between scientific disciplines. Colonial historiography, originally limited to the domain of high politics, gradually began to integrate theoretical perspectives, specific methodologies and new dimensions, in particular economic history. Over time, colonial historians began to integrate theories and concepts from the fields of sociology, anthropology, literature and cultural studies. Finally, there was the division between the colony and the colonial power. Traditional imperial historical works concentrated almost exclusively on the influence the metropolis or 'mother country' had on its colonies. From the 1960s onwards, this bias was rightly criticised as being Euro-centric. A new generation of works appeared, focused not only on the changes wrought by the European presence, but also on those caused by 'local' structures and the adaptive mechanisms adopted by the colonized. Gradually, the mother country faded out of sight, as if developments in the colony(ies) were of no importance to the metropolis itself. Moreover, the traditional historiography of European nation-states largely ignored the existence of colonial empires, as if those empires had no influence on Europe.[2] Fortunately, over the last twenty years or so, this neglect has been remedied.

Historians have increasingly realised that the imperial situation cannot be understood if the different locations involved in the process are studied in isolation. In the introduction to their well-known volume, Stoler and Cooper posited that "metropole and colony, coloniser and colonized need to be brought into one analytic field".[3] Beginning in the second half of the 1990s, global connexions became the leitmotiv of colonial historiography. Developments and experiences both at home and in-colony were inter-woven, constantly reflecting, shaping and re-shaping themselves in often subtle and complex ways. As a result, historians are now returning to the metropole. They are contributing significantly to the study of imperial processes without falling into the trap of Euro-centrism by asking – and answering – some fundamental questions: What impact did colonialism have on the economic development of Western Europe?[4] How did colonialism mould the experience of European identity?

---

[2] A. G. Hopkins, "Back to the Future: From National History to Imperial History", *Past & Present*, 164 (1999), p. 207.

[3] A. L. Stoler & F. Cooper, "Between Metropole and Colony: Rethinking a Research Agenda", in F. Cooper & A. L. Stoler, eds., *Tensions of Empire: Colonial Cultures in a Bourgeois World* (Berkeley, 1997), p. 15.

[4] B. Etemad, *De l'utilité des empires. Colonisation et prospérité de l'Europe (XVIe – XXe siècles)* (Paris, 2005).

Introduction

Did the colonial system breed totalitarianism and genocide in Europe? (This was the position put forward by Hannah Arendt as early as the 1950s,[5] which has gained new momentum in the last few years.)[6]

Paradoxically, the study of global imperial connexions often remains within a national model, notably the British case. The colonial impact on the metropolis is rarely studied from a truly transnational, comparative perspective.[7] Most historians still take a specific national example as the focal point. Consequently, a survey of the thriving 'empire strikes back' theme cannot escape the juxtaposition of *national* historiographical studies. We shall look at the British and French examples, touching only briefly on the Dutch, German and Italian cases.[8]

The historiography of the British Empire stands out as an impressive intellectual monument, the rich trajectory of which has been mapped out more than once.[9] We will focus on how the metropolitan scene appears in these studies of the imperial process. The oldest studies focused on the domestic political bases of imperial activity. They repeatedly emphasised high politics and diplomatic activity and were rightly criticised for being one-sided. Yet this research laid the solid foundations on which further work, inspired by different perspectives, was built.

Studies concerning the economic dimensions of imperialism came later. Since the 1970s, much groundbreaking research has been devoted to the relationship between the British Empire and the British domestic economy, including the impact of the former on the latter. Trade and the flow of capital have been mapped within and outside the British colonial world and their impact on Britain's position in the world economy dissected. Historians have examined the profitability of colonial investments and evaluated the role of domestic economic interests on starting, maintaining and/or ending colonial dominance. Many authors have tried to answer an apparently simple question: Was the empire profitable, or not, to the British economy? The answers have always been far more complex than the question itself.[10]

More recently still, attention has shifted to the socio-cultural field. In 1984, John MacKenzie broke fresh ground with his classic book on British imperial

---

[5] H. Arendt, *The Origins of Totalitarianism* (New York, 1951), p. 221.

[6] *Revue d'Histoire de la Shoah*, 189 (July-December 2008): "Violences de guerre, violences coloniales, violences extrêmes avant la Shoah", pp. 101–246.

[7] Some notable exceptions: M. Kahler, *Decolonization in France and Britain: The Domestic Consequences of International Relations* (Princeton, 1984); M. G. Stanard, "Interwar pro-Empire Propaganda and European Colonial Culture: Toward a Comparative Research Agenda", *Journal of Contemporary History*, 44, 1 (January 2009), pp. 27–48.

[8] The Portuguese and Spanish cases will not be mentioned, being of a very different nature.

[9] Wm. R. Louis, "Introduction", in R. W. Winks, ed., *The Oxford History of the British Empire. Vol. V. Historiography* (Oxford, 1999), pp. 1–43; R. W. Winks, "The Future of Imperial History", in ibid., pp. 653–68; J. Gascoigne, "The Expanding Historiography of British Imperialism", *The Historical Journal*, 49, 2 (2006), pp. 577–92.

[10] For example L. E. Davis & R. A. Huttenback, *Mammon and the Pursuit of Empire: The Political Economy of British Imperialism, 1860–1912* (Cambridge, 1986); M. Edelstein,

propaganda.[11] Since then, he and many other historians have studied the impact of empire on popular culture, lifestyle, art, consumption patterns, attitudes and perceptions of the empire 'at home'.[12] These historians assert that the mind of the British population was profoundly saturated with imperial ideology. Within the innovative and multifarious currents of the 'new imperial history (or histories)' and post-colonial studies, historians have shown that, in Britain, the empire moulded worldviews, conceptions of race, religious structures, gender roles and stereotypes.[13] Furthermore, historians have identified the colonial phenomenon as a crucial element in the definition and construction of British national identity and the identity of its constituent parts. In other words: We cannot understand the cultural and ideological foundations of Britain without taking into account Britain's imperial structure. The past few years have witnessed impressive academic advances, particularly that it is now impossible to study British history while leaving empire somewhere on the periphery. "Britain was very much a part of the empire, just as the rest of the empire was very much part of Britain".[14] Does this mean that any further research in the field is unnecessary? Certainly not. A number of new insights – or hypotheses – are still debatable. For example, Bernard Porter, one of Britain's leading imperial historians, has recently argued that the colonial impact on large parts of the British population was much more superficial than previously suggested.[15] Porter – the 'king of the sceptics' (as Catherine Hall and Sonya Rose have called him)[16] – has attracted harsh criticism.[17] Simon Potter aptly summarises the debate: "It is relatively clear that imperial influences reached Britain through a number of channels; what historians most frequently debate is whether those influences had a significant impact or not, a question that raises the difficult issue of audience reception".[18] Clearly, the debate on the impact of colonial activity rages on.

Another striking feature of contemporary imperial studies is their sociocultural focus. On the one hand, when studying the colonial impact on the

"Imperialism: Cost and Benefit", in R. Floud & D. McCloskey, eds., *The Economic History of Britain Since 1700. Vol. 2. 1860–1939* (Cambridge, 1994²), pp. 197–216.

[11] J. M. MacKenzie, *Propaganda and Empire: The Manipulation of British Public Opinion 1880–1960* (Manchester, 1984).

[12] See for example the numerous books published in the 'Studies in Imperialism' series published by Manchester University Press.

[13] S. Howe, ed., *The New Imperial Histories Reader* (London-New York, 2010), pp. 1–20.

[14] D. Cannadine, *Ornementalism: How the British Saw Their Empire* (London, 2001), p. XVII.

[15] B. Porter, *The Absent-Minded Imperialists: Empire, Society, and Culture in Britain* (Oxford, 2004).

[16] C. Hall & S. Rose, "Introduction: Being At Home With the Empire", in C. Hall & S. Rose, eds., *At Home With the Empire: Metropolitan Culture and the Imperial World* (Cambridge, 2006), p. 16.

[17] J. M. MacKenzie, "'Comfort' and Conviction: A Response to Bernard Porter", *Journal of Imperial and Commonwealth History*, 36, 4 (December 2008), pp. 659–68.

[18] S. J. Potter, "Empire, Cultures and Identities in Nineteenth- and Twentieth-Century Britain", *History Compass*, 5, 1 (2007), pp. 51–71 (citation on p. 54); J. Thompson, "Modern Britain and the New Imperial History", *History Compass*, 5, 2 (2007), pp. 455–62.

coloniser, proponents of new imperial history and post-colonial studies offer insights into such fields as the representation of the Other and the Self, the (re)creation of racial and sexual stereotypes, gender relations, religious attitudes, migrations, consumption patterns, class relations and daily life. On the other hand, the new imperial historians sometimes neglect aspects they (un-justly) consider old-fashioned, such as political institutions and processes, economic structures and international relations. Naturally, the quasi-monopoly that these 'old-fashioned' subjects previously exerted on historical research has produced a vast amount of knowledge. Moreover, many British historians continue to study the impact of the colonial system on British economic structure and performance.[19] Several interesting monographs have also analysed the colonial dimension of Britain's domestic political scene, but it remains necessary to integrate all these different aspects into a global picture of the empire's impact on Britain's history, cultural and social aspects, politics, foreign relations and economics.[20] P. J. Marshall has published some balanced evaluations of how the empire influenced contemporary British history.[21] But Andrew S. Thompson's recent book *The Empire Strikes Back? The Impact of Imperialism on Britain from the Mid-Nineteenth Century* offers the most balanced overview to date, covering a long time span and encompassing the entire range of thematic issues.[22] As we move more deeply into the Belgian case, we shall return to a number of essential points made by these British historians.

In size and diversity, the British Empire exceeded all the other colonial empires of its time and the same can be said of academic research pertaining to these respective empires. The historiography of other modern colonial systems pales before the vast knowledge that has been accumulated concerning Britain.

---

[19] See for example B. R. Tomlinson, "The British Economy and the Empire, 1900–1939", in C. Wrigley, ed., *A Companion to Early Twentieth-Century Britain* (Oxford, 2003), pp. 198–211; A. R. Dilley, "The Economics of Empire", in S. Stockwell, ed., *The British Empire: Themes and Perspectives* (Oxford, 2008), pp. 101–29; P. J. Cain, "Economics and Empire: the Metropolitan Context", in A. Porter, ed., *The Oxford History of the British Empire. Vol. III. The Nineteenth Century* (Oxford, 1999), pp. 31–52; A. Offer, "Costs and Benefits, Prosperity, and Security, 1870–1914", *Idem*, pp. 690–711; D. K. Fieldhouse, "The Metropolitan Economics of Empire", in J. M. Brown & Wm. R. Louis, eds., *The Oxford History of the British Empire. Vol. IV. The Twentieth Century* (Oxford, 1999), pp. 88–113.

[20] For example D. Goldsworthy, *Colonial Issues in British Politics 1945–1961: From 'Colonial Development' to 'Winds of Change'* (Oxford, 1971); S. Howe, *Anticolonialism in British Politics: The Left and the End of Empire 1918–1964* (Oxford, 1993); S. Howe, *Ireland and Empire: Colonial Legacies in Irish History and Culture* (Oxford, 2001). On the imperial impact on Ireland, see also K. Jeffery, ed., *'An Irish Empire'? Aspects of Ireland and the British Empire* (Manchester, 1996).

[21] For example P. J. Marshall, "Imperial Britain", in P. J. Marshall, ed., *The Cambridge Illustrated History of the British Empire* (Cambridge, 1996), pp. 318–37.

[22] A. S. Thompson, *The Empire Strikes Back? The Impact of Imperialism on Britain from the Mid-Nineteenth Century* (Harlow-London, 2005); A. S. Thompson, *Imperial Britain: The Empire in British Politics c. 1880–1932* (Harlow-London, 2000); A. S. Thompson, "Empire and the British State", in S. Stockwell, ed., *The British Empire. Themes and Perspectives* (Oxford, 2008), pp. 39–61.

This has consequences for our central theme of the colonial impact on the metropolis, a subject that, for many years, has been largely ignored by scholars working on the non-British colonial powers in Europe. Nevertheless, things have changed rapidly in the last decade or so, spurred on by post-colonial studies and new imperial histories published in the United Kingdom.

France is a first case in point. Here, only a small number of studies concerning the imperial impact on the metropolis had been published before the rise of the new British approaches. Forty years ago, Raoul Girardet explored the domestic (political and ideological) sources of French imperial activity.[23] In the 1970s, Charles-Robert Ageron analysed the impact of colonial activity on French politics and – rather ahead of his time – on public opinion and popular perceptions.[24] According to Ageron, the imperial impact on French minds and attitudes was both limited and late. Others – not only renowned French historians such as Claude Liauzu, but also foreign scholars – followed in the footsteps of these two pioneers and continued to study the domestic political dimension of colonialism.[25] At the same time, the specificity of French imperialism engaged many historians. Jean Bouvier, Jacques Thobie and René Girault highlighted some of the domestic economic sources of imperial activity, but mainly focused on French investments and trade in the periphery, of which the colonial empire was just one facet.[26] This growing interest in the economic dimension of imperialism culminated with the publication in 1984 of Jacques Marseille's *Empire colonial et capitalisme français: Histoire d'un divorce*, which revealed how the French economy reacted to imperial activity and was influenced by it.[27]

In the second half of the 1990s, French colonial history underwent revival and re-orientation. This revival was not limited to the purely academic sphere. It originated in and was largely influenced by discussions of the delicate and problematic relationship of French society with its colonial past – a problem existing in other European countries as well.[28] Many aspects of France's colonial

[23] R. Girardet, *L'idée coloniale en France de 1871 à 1962* (Paris, 1972).
[24] Ch.-R. Ageron, *France coloniale ou parti colonial?* (Paris, 1978); Ch.-R. Ageron, "Les colonies devant l'opinion publique française (1919–1939)", *Revue Française d'Histoire d'Outre-Mer*, 37, 286 (1990), pp. 31–73.
[25] C. Liauzu, *Aux origines des tiers-mondismes. Colonisés et anticolonialistes en France (1919–1939)* (Paris, 1982); C. Liauzu, *Histoire de l'anticolonialisme en France. Du XVIe siècle à nos jours* (Paris, 2007); A. Biondi, *Les anticolonialistes (1881–1962)* (Paris, 1992). Among the foreign scholars, Raymond F. Betts, A. S. Kanya Forstner and William B. Cohen were of course outstanding specialists in French colonialism. See also S. M. Persell, *The French Colonial Lobby 1889–1938* (Stanford, 1983).
[26] J. Bouvier & R. Girault, eds., *L'impérialisme français d'avant 1914* (Paris-The Hague, 1976); J. Bouvier, R. Girault & J. Thobie, *L'impérialisme à la française. La France impériale 1880–1914* (Paris, 1982).
[27] J. Marseille, *Empire colonial et capitalisme français* (Paris, 1984).
[28] D. Rothermund, "The Self-consciousness of Post-Imperial Nations: A Cross-national Comparison", *India Quarterly. A Journal of International Affairs*, 67 (March 2011), pp. 1–18 (pdf available on http://iqq.sagepub.com/content/67/1/1.abstract). See also S. Jahan & A. Ruscio, eds., *Histoire de la colonisation. Réhabilitations, falsifications et instrumentalisations* (Paris, 2007); O. Dard & D. Lefeuvre, eds., *L'Europe face à son passé colonial* (Paris, 2008).

past remain controversial: slavery, the use of violence, torture and even mass murder in the colonies. A French law, passed in April 2005, required schools to teach the 'positive effects' of colonialism. This led to many protests and the law was soon abolished. The role of the imperial past in French history and its lasting influence on contemporary French society remains a highly politicised topic. In 2009 and 2010, French authorities launched a public debate on the meaning of French national identity. Colonial heritage was, inevitably, part of that debate in which a number of crucial questions that had been discussed in the public forum for many years were uncomfortably linked to French colonial history. How could France's central values of *liberté, égalité, fraternité* be reconciled with the crimes and oppression in the colonies?[29] What was and is the place of colonial and post-colonial migrants in French contemporary society? Does today's racism relate to the colonial past? What is the meaning of being 'French' in a country where many influences, including some from the former colonies, are at play? Why were imperial matters – at least some of their more disturbing aspects – erased from public memory? What could (and had to) be done to (re)activate these forgotten aspects?[30]

Originally, foreign scholars inspired by post-colonial studies were responsible for the new approach to France's colonial past, but their research did not really enter French consciousness. In the early 1990s, Herman Lebovics started to explore the colonial roots of French cultural traits and the French mentality.[31] Many other (mainly British) authors examined similar themes, highlighting the ways in which empire shaped French arts, worldviews, gender roles, daily life and social attitudes.[32] This revived foreign interest in French colonial history was not limited to the field of post-colonial studies. Other historians, such as Martin Thomas, Martin Evans and Robert Aldrich, also analysed various aspects of the repercussions of empire on the metropolis.[33] Alice Conklin, in her book on the French 'civilising mission' in West Africa, draws attention to

---

[29] G. Manceron, *Marianne et les colonies. Une introduction à l'histoire coloniale de la France* (Paris, 2003).

[30] For example R. Bertrand, *La controverse autour du 'fait colonial'* (Paris, 2006); C. Coquio, ed., *Retours du colonial? Disculpation et réhabilitation de l'histoire coloniale* (Nantes, 2008).

[31] H. Lebovics, *True France: The Wars over Cultural Identity* (Ithaca, 1992); H. Lebovics, *Bringing the Empire Back Home: France in the Age of Globalization* (Durham, 2004) and so forth.

[32] For example A. G. Hargreaves & M. McKinney, eds., *Post-colonial Cultures in France* (London-New York, 1997); A. G. Hargreaves, ed., *Memory, Empire, and Postcolonialism: Legacies of French Colonialism* (Lanham, 2005); T. Chafer & A. Sackur, eds., *Promoting the Colonial Idea in France: Propaganda and Visions of Empire in France* (Houndmills, 2002); E. Ezra, *The Colonial Unconscious. Race and Culture in Interwar France* (Ithaca-London, 2000); D. J. Sherman, "The Arts and Sciences of Colonialism", *French Historical Studies*, 23, 4 (Fall 2000), pp. 707–29; T. Shepard, *The Invention of Decolonization: The Algerian War and the Remaking of France* (Ithaca, 2006).

[33] M. Thomas, *The French Empire Between the Wars* (Manchester, 2005); M. Evans, ed., *Empire and Culture: The French Experience 1830–1940* (Houndmills, 2004); R. Aldrich, ed., *Vestiges of the Colonial Empire in France: Monuments, Museums, and Colonial Memories* (Houndmills, 2005); R. Aldrich, *Greater France: A History of French Overseas Expansion* (New York, 1996), etc.

the effects of colonial ideology in France itself: "[T]he practice of colonialism may well have reinforced and enabled these other forms of discrimination in the metropole in ways that have not yet been recognized".[34]

Finally, after some delay, a new generation of French historians began to (re)explore France's colonial past. By 1995, Alain Ruscio had already analysed the French view of the colonised world and its populations.[35] At the very end of the 1990s, a group of historians (Pascal Blanchard, Nicolas Bancel, Sandrine Lemaire, Françoise Vergès, etc.) began to explore various aspects of colonial influence on French society, originally focusing on the analysis of representation and propaganda, but gradually extending the scope of their research to include political and economic issues as well.[36] Like many of their British colleagues, these authors stress the importance of colonialism in shaping French social habits and mentality. A few recent studies directly tackle the political dimension. Olivier Le Cour Grandmaison analyses the way imperialism has influenced the French state, in particular by creating what he calls 'state racism'.[37] The creation of a French political identity is at the centre of Dino Costantini's work.[38] He analyses the paradoxical relationship between the human rights proclaimed by the French Republic and the colonial 'exception' where these rights were not upheld. These recent publications essentially dwell upon political discourse, representation and ideology, and not so much on political practices and movements, or on the institutional aspects of imperialism. A few exceptions stand out, particularly Marc Michel's studies analysing the influence of the colonial experience on the military and on the rise of right-wing sentiments in French politics.[39] Nevertheless, a global and thematically well-balanced analysis of the colonial impact on French history – the equivalent of Andrew Thompson's work on Britain – still remains to be written.

The other ex-colonial powers on the European continent are also taking a new interest in their imperial pasts. And as in France, the memory of colonialism is a sensitive subject in some countries. Specific dramatic aspects of their

---

[34] A. L. Conklin, *A Mission to Civilize: The Republican Idea of Empire in France and West Africa, 1895–1930* (Stanford, 1997), p. 253.

[35] A. Ruscio, *Le crédo de l'homme blanc. Regards coloniaux français XIXe – XXe siècles* (Brussels, 1995).

[36] P. Blanchard, S. Lemaire & N. Bancel, eds., *Culture coloniale en France. De la Révolution Française à nos jours* (Paris, 2008); P. Blanchard, N. Bancel & S. Lemaire, eds., *La fracture coloniale. La société française au prisme de l'héritage colonial* (Paris, 2005); N. Bancel, P. Blanchard & F. Vergès, *La République coloniale. Essai sur une utopie* (Paris, 2003), etc. A recent study analyses the imperial impact on a particular French region: R.-C. Grondin, *L'empire en province. Culture et expérience coloniales en Limousin (1830–1939)* (Toulouse, 2010).

[37] O. Le Cour Grandmaison, *La République impériale. Politique et racisme d'État* (Paris, 2009) and Id., *Coloniser, exterminer. Sur la guerre et l'État colonial* (Paris, 2005).

[38] D. Costantini, *Mission civilisatrice. Le rôle de l'histoire coloniale dans la construction de l'identité politique française* (Paris, 2008).

[39] M. Michel, "La colonisation", in J.-F. Sirinelli, ed., *Histoire des droites en France. Volume 3. Sensibilités* (Paris, 1992), pp. 125–63. See also J. Marseille, "La gauche, la droite et le fait colonial des années 1880 aux années 1960", *Vingtième Siècle. Revue d'histoire*, 24 (October-December 1989), pp. 17–28.

respective imperial past – for example the use of poison gas by the Italians in Ethiopia, the German *Vernichtungsbefehl* against the Hereros and of course 'red rubber' in the Congo Free State – have caught the attention of a broader public and even of official authorities. This has stimulated interest in the colonisers' role in the colonies *and vice versa*. In Italy and Germany, a new wave of studies explores the impact of colonies on the nation. As is the case in Great Britain and France, most of these publications explore socio-cultural issues such as gender constructions, racial attitudes and stereotypes, literature and the arts, daily life and colonial memory.[40] In the German case, historians raise challenging and crucial political questions, namely the relationship of colonial racism and violence to National Socialism. This is a specific national variant of the larger debate, mentioned earlier, concerning the relationship between colonialism and the rise of totalitarianism, racism and genocide in Europe.[41] In the Netherlands, historians have always been very attentive to the role of the colonial empire in economic development at home – a crucial factor in their national history.[42] According to historian Edwin Horlings, for example, "the financial benefits [from the empire] were used to lay the foundations for a process of modern economic growth in the 19th century".[43] Most recently, Dutch historians have increasingly turned to the study of the post-colonial effects of empire.[44]

---

[40] J. Andall & D. Duncan, eds., *Italian Colonialism: Legacy and Memory* (Oxford, 2005); P. Palumbo, ed., *A Place in the Sun: Africa in Italian Colonialism from Post-Unification to the Present* (Berkeley, 2003). M. Colin & E. R. Laforgia, eds., *L'Afrique coloniale et postcoloniale dans la culture, la littérature et la société italiennes. Représentations et témoignages* (Caen, 2003). N. Labanca, *Oltremare. Storia dell'espansione coloniale italiana* (Bologna, 2002) is a general history of Italian colonialism, but also deals with its domestic aspects and repercussions. E. Ames, M. Klotz & L. Wildenthal, eds., *Germany's Colonial Pasts* (Lincoln-London, 2005); B. Kundrus, *Moderne Imperialisten. Das Kaiserreich im Spiegel seiner Kolonien* (Cologne, 2003); R. Kössler, "Awakened from Colonial Amnesia? Germany After 2004", available online at www.freiburg-postkolonial.de/Seiten/koessler-colonial-amnesia.htm (2006, accessed 4 February, 2010); M. Perraudin & J. Zimmerer, eds., *German Colonialism and National Identity* (New York, 2011).

[41] P. Grosse, "What Does German Colonialism Have to Do with National Socialism", in E. Ames, e.a., eds., *Germany's Colonial Past, op. cit.*, pp. 115–34. See also J. Zimmerer, "Holocauste et colonialisme. Contribution à une archéologie de la pensée génocidaire", *Revue d'Histoire de la Shoah*, 189 (July-December 2008), pp. 213–46.

[42] P. C. Emmer, "The Economic Impact of the Dutch Expansion Overseas, 1570–1870", *Revista de Historia Economica*, 15, 1 (1998), pp. 157–76; E. Horlings, "Miracle Cure for an Economy in Crisis? Colonial Exploitation as a Source of Growth in the Netherlands, 1815–1870", in B. Moore & H. Van Nierop, eds., *Colonial Empires Compared: Britain and the Netherlands, 1750–1850* (Aldershot, 2003), pp. 145–67; H. Baudet & M. Fennema, e.a., *Het Nederlands belang bij Indië* (Utrecht, 1983); P. van der Eng, "Economic Benefits from Colonial Assets: the Case of the Netherlands and Indonesia 1870–1958", research memorandum of the Growth and Development Centre of the University of Groningen, June 1998 (downloadable from http://ideas.repec.org/p/dgr/rugggd/199839.html); M. Wintle, *An Economic and Social History of the Netherlands, 1800–1920* (Cambridge, 2000), pp. 214–25.

[43] E. Horlings, "Miracle Cure (…)", art. cit., p. 167.

[44] G. Oostindie, *Postkoloniaal Nederland. Vijfenzestig jaar vergeten, herdenken, verdringen* (Amsterdam, 2009); U. Bosma, *Terug uit de koloniën. Zestig jaar postkoloniale migranten en*

So how does Belgium fit into this picture? Colonial historiography was a latecomer in Belgium.[45] Belgian universities introduced the first courses on overseas and colonial history at the end of the nineteenth century, but very few academic historians actually specialised in this domain. Most writings on the Congo were blatant eulogies for Leopold II and the pioneers of the Congo Free State. Real historical research into the Belgian colony, especially its origins, only began appearing in the 1950s. One scholar, Jean Stengers, meticulously analysed Leopoldian politics and the birth of the Free State. From the 1960s onwards, he also published many studies on the decolonisation of the Congo. Some other historians did, of course, publish on early Belgian colonial history, but they were rather isolated figures on the periphery of academia. They certainly did not have Stengers's scholarly stature. Moreover, they had not yet freed themselves from the then widespread admiration for Leopold II. In the 1970s, Jean-Luc Vellut started his impressive scholarly activities, which led to real advances in the understanding of Belgian colonial history. For many years, Vellut and Stengers were practically the only Belgian historians specialising in Congolese colonial history. The Congo was studied much more actively abroad, notably by British and U.S. historians; a trend that started in the 1950s and continues until today. Congolese historians, meanwhile, only joined the international research community in the 1970s and 1980s, due to the late development of higher education in the Congo. In Belgium itself two authors, anthropologist Daniël Vangroenweghe and former diplomat Jules Marchal, published several books in the mid-1980s revealing the horrors of the Leopoldian regime in the Congo. These publications revived general interest in the colonial past and may have contributed to a revival of Belgian academic interest in colonial history. From the 1990s on, a new generation of researchers increasingly focused on the Congo. Yet, most of these works, like the numerous publications of foreign historians, deal with the situation in the colony itself. Only very recently have Belgian and foreign historians analysed the colony's impact on the Belgian metropolis, especially in the socio-cultural field. This is entirely in line with the international research trends in (post-)colonial studies.

The Focus of the Present Book

This brings us to the purpose of the present book. The most important gaps in our knowledge of the colonial nexus relate to the political and economic impact of the Congo on the metropolis. Stengers (1960s) focused on the Leopoldian period and decolonisation. The role of colonial activities in Belgian politics from 1908 to the end of the 1950s remains completely unexplored. The

hun organisaties (Amsterdam, 2009); L. Van Leeuwen, *Ons Indisch erfgoed. Zestig jaar strijd om cultuur en identiteit* (Amsterdam, 2008).
[45] G. Vanthemsche, "The historiography of Belgian colonialism in the Congo", in C. Levai, ed., *Europe and the World in European Historiography* (Pisa, 2006), pp. 89–119 (online: www.cliohres.net/books/6/Vanthemsche.pdf).

same can be said of the economic impact of the Congo on Belgium. This is a real scientific *terra incognita*: The most recent work analysing this aspect dates back to 1936![46] The role of the colony in Belgian foreign policy emerges in some studies on international relations (most notably in Jonathan Helmreich's works), but has never been analysed globally. This book aims to precisely fill these gaps.

As usual among former colonial powers, the colonial aspect of history has always been considered peripheral, even irrelevant, to the national history. The time has come to re-integrate the colonial factor into the Belgian history *corpus* and curriculum. Knowing how the Congo has influenced Belgium is not only important for a better grasp of Belgium's past, it is also of great relevance for anyone interested in what happened in the Congo itself. The Congolese imprint on Belgium has reciprocally determined how Belgium has dealt with the Congo. The colonial nexus consists of continuous reverberations, an incessant give and take between colony and metropolis. From this point of view, a synthesis of the colonial impact on the metropolis seems indispensable: To understand what happened in the Congo, it is necessary to know how the colony influenced the metropolis. It is also necessary to examine specifically what the colonial nexus meant for Belgium *after* formal decolonisation. What effect did an independent Congo have on Belgium's political, diplomatic and economic situation?

This focus may seem surprising. In these days of blossoming post-colonial studies, most publications on the colonial influences in other former imperial powers deal with representation, memory, gender roles, social behaviour, mentality and so forth. I nevertheless believe that these aspects only assume their full relevance when they are fully integrated with discussion of the political, diplomatic and economic elements. Andrew Thompson has made the same observation with regard to British imperial historiography: "[C]ultural histories of empire frequently fail to set imperial propaganda activity in any sort of meaningful political context". He further stresses that "our understanding of what the Empire did to Britain has been greatly impoverished by the neglect of the political sphere in recent historiography".[47]

The political and economic dimensions of imperialism in the metropolis are already far better known in Britain or France than they are in Belgium. So in a sense, this book is an attempt to catch up. Since it is crucial, first and foremost, to synthesise the essential political and economic dimensions of Belgian colonialism, this book is not intended as a comparative analysis – that would require an entirely different book! At some crucial points, however, it will be necessary to refer to similar or contrasting foreign experiences.

Although an integrated approach justifies the fact that the political, diplomatic, political and economic aspects are being *brought in*, it still does not explain why the socio-cultural dimensions are being largely *left out*. In my

---

[46] M. Van De Velde, *Économie belge et Congo belge* (Antwerp, 1936).
[47] A. S. Thompson, *Imperial Britain, op. cit.*, p. 3.

opinion, the discussion of socio-cultural aspects would be premature given the state of Belgian historiography. While a general picture of Belgian political, diplomatic and economic history is now fairly well established, the situation is entirely different for the socio-cultural field. Here, global syntheses are painfully lacking. Since the main features of *Belgian* socio-cultural history still have to be mapped, it would be very difficult to integrate and comprehend the far-reaching effects of colonialism. Still, several fine studies have recently explored the socio-cultural effects of the colony on Belgium; they will briefly be presented in due course.

Let us now briefly present the structure of this book and the main sources on which it is built. Logically, we start with the implementation of the colonial system within Belgian society. The first chapter skims over the main developments of the Belgian colonial enterprise and serves as a brief reminder of the essential background necessary for the thematic analyses that will constitute the main part of the book. First of all, we must observe the impact of Belgian colonialism on Belgium's internal political life (Chapter 2). Without giving anything away, I want to immediately point out that this impact was limited. The Congo, apart from its entry into colonialism and its hurried exit in 1960, did not have a great deal of influence on the behaviour and, *a fortiori*, structure of Belgian political players and institutions. The Congo's impact on the foreign policy or, more generally, on the external position of Belgium was far greater. This theme constitutes the subject of the third chapter. On several occasions, owing to its presence in the Congo, Belgium appeared at the forefront of the world scene. In terms of Belgian diplomacy, the Congo has always represented a major stake. Additionally, the Congo has affected the Belgian economy. The fourth chapter will therefore examine the impact of the Congo, before independence, on the structure and economic activity of Belgium. In the fifth and final chapter, we touch upon the relations between Belgium and the Congo following independence, particularly on a political and economic level. Each chapter is preceded by a brief general outline introducing the relevant elements of Belgium's past. With this background in mind, we can better understand the specific colonial effects on the metropolis.

As mentioned, the existing scholarly literature mainly covers 1885 to 1908, and the turmoil of 1960 to 1965, but this coverage is insufficient for a balanced synthesis. Fortunately, archival sources provide some information for the period from 1908 to the end of the 1950s. There are the archives of the former Ministry of the Colonies, of major private companies, and of private persons. Unfortunately, the diplomatic relations between Belgium and the Congo/Zaire are insufficiently illuminated because most diplomatic archives of the 1960s onward are still largely sealed. Thankfully, this obstacle can be overcome through probes into foreign archives and the private papers of a number of important Belgians from 1960 to 1990. The archives of several private companies have also shed new light on the first decade of an independent Congo. Furthermore, we must acknowledge the wealth of information and analyses of Belgo-Congolese relations produced, since 1960, over the course of many decades by the CRISP[48] / CEDAF / *Institut Africain*, now the Contemporary History section at the *Musée royal de l'Afrique centrale*. Their meticulous and incessant work provides a useful guideline for studying the turbulent evolution of Belgo-Congolese diplomacy. For the period of Congo's independence, the bulk of the historical work on the archival sources remains to be done. I hope this book will serve as a springboard for the academic attention this vast, important and fascinating subject deserves.

Throughout the writing of this work, I benefited from Jean-Luc Vellut's numerous suggestions; I thank him wholeheartedly for all his help. I would also like to thank Ms. Françoise Peemans and Mr. Pierre Dandoy for the help they provided during my research into the archives of the Ministry of Foreign Affairs and the African Archives; Mr. Antoine Lumenganeso for having facilitated my research into the Congolese National Archives in Kinshasa; Mr. René Brion for allowing me to consult the Fortis/BNP Group archives; Mr. Etienne Deschamps for his useful suggestions; and the late Mr. André Huybrechts and Mr. Daniel Olivier for their careful reading of the earlier version of this book.

---

[48] For the major role of CRISP (Centre de Recherche et d'Information socio-politiques) in the study of independent Congo, see G. de Villers, "Le secteur africain du CRISP. Apports et héritages", in X. Mabille, ed., *Le CRISP – 50 ans d'histoire* (Brussels, 2009), pp. 65–71. In 1971, CRISP gave birth to CEDAF (Centre d'Étude et de Documentation africaines).

I

Origin of the Colonial Phenomenon in Belgium

Traditionally, histories of Belgian colonisation begin by training the spotlight on one man, King Leopold II. His ambitions and, more broadly, his psychology, are central to most analyses. These elements are undoubtedly essential to an understanding of the beginnings and later developments of colonialism in Belgium, but since the monarch and his actions must be considered within the global context of the era we will begin with a brief overview of Belgium's position in the world in the early to mid-nineteenth century.

Belgium at the Dawn of Colonisation

The first half-century of Belgium's existence was characterised by three particular elements. First, the founding of the nation in 1830–1 constituted a diplomatic issue of primary importance for the major powers at that time.[1] Belgium – from its founding – was required to remain strictly neutral. Nonetheless, its very existence was threatened on several occasions, for instance by French ambitions. The scrupulous respect of this imposed neutrality constituted one of the key elements to the country's survival. Second, Belgium adopted a representative democracy (although highly elitist) – a political system unusual at the time – which severely limited the role of the constitutional monarch. Personal political action undertaken by the king was seen as a threat to the running of institutions in which political parties played an increasingly important role. Third, Belgium occupied a leading position in terms of economic development. It was Europe's second industrial nation: a capitalist economy in full expansion with the majority of its markets in the neighbouring countries. Various free trade agreements (the main concern of the young Belgian diplomacy), as well as other measures designed to liberalise the economy, stimulated and guaranteed this remarkable development.

For Belgium in 1830, distant horizons were only of marginal interest. Owing to the vagaries of its history, it had hardly inherited any connections overseas.

[1] R. Coolsaet, *België en zijn buitenlandse politiek 1830–1990* (Leuven, 1998).

Origin of the Colonial Phenomenon in Belgium

The ephemeral Ostend Company (1722-37) had had neither the time nor the means to leave a durable 'Belgian' trace in Asia. After some initial success, Habsburg emperor Charles VI, under pressure from neighbouring countries that wanted to eliminate him as a trading competitor, disbanded the Ostend Company.[2] While individual inhabitants of the Southern Netherlands (the region that later became Belgium) were travelling the world as seafarers, traders or missionaries in the sixteenth to eighteenth centuries, the Southern Netherlands, unlike England, France, the Netherlands, Spain and Portugal, did not participate as a national entity in maritime commerce and the resulting geopolitical stakes. Then, in 1814-15, the European powers combined the southern and northern parts of the former Low Countries to form the United Kingdom of the Netherlands. This meant that the future 'Belgian' part was, briefly, directly involved in the Dutch colonial possessions (in particular the Dutch East Indies). But then the Belgian revolution of 1830 severed this ephemeral link.

After the birth of Belgium as a nation, the geopolitical stakes intensified, but also changed in nature. Gradually, colonial rivalries became more intense and had an ever-increasing influence on the relations between Belgium's neighbours. The interference of Belgium in this global posturing represented a major risk to both its political position in Europe and its economic prosperity. Any falling-out between Belgium and another European nation could have dire consequences in terms of foreign markets or supplies; at worst, the very survival of the Belgian nation could be called into question. Thus, an active colonial policy would have jeopardised the country's neutrality.

Still, colonisation certainly figured on the agenda of the young Belgian state. Between 1840 and 1850, the political authorities – King Leopold I in particular – supported or incited several colonial initiatives.[3] Once the colonisation of the Congo had begun, Belgian historians eagerly looked for early proof of the country's colonial predisposition.[4] The rare examples of 'Belgian' overseas activity in the Middle Ages and early modern times were therefore exhaustively listed and the colonial or expansionist projects imagined during the first decades of Belgium's nationhood were also extensively studied. These efforts created a standard narrative of the national colonial initiatives that preceded activity in the Congo.[5] One of these was located on the Rio Nuñez, in contemporary Guinea (Conakry). A Belgian trading post had been founded there; the Belgians and the French had clashed militarily with the British in this region in 1849, a very dangerous situation indeed for Belgian neutrality.[6]

---

[2] See H. Hasquin, "Le temps des assainissements (1715-1740)", in *La Belgique autrichienne, 1713-1794* (Brussels, 1987), pp. 82-6; K. Degryse, "De Oostendse Chinahandel (1718-1735)", *Revue belge de Philologie et d'Histoire*, 52, 2 (1974), pp. 306-47.

[3] *L'expansion belge sous Léopold 1er. Recueil d'études* (Brussels, 1965).

[4] H. Kermans & C. Monheim, *La conquête d'un empire (...) Histoire du Congo belge* (Brussels, 1932), p. 13.

[5] M. Huisman & P. Jacquet, *Bibliographie d'histoire coloniale. Belgique* (Paris, 1932), pp. 7-21.

[6] R. Braithwaite, "The Rio Nuñez Affair. New Perspectives on a Significant Event in 19th-Century Franco-British Colonial Rivalry", *Revue française d'Histoire d'Outre-Mer*, 83, 311 (1996),

This enterprise lasted only a few years (1847–55). Its failure was essentially the result of two factors: the government's indecision and "the ambiguous attitude of the business milieus, who were very interested in subsidies, though little inclined to take commercial risks".[7] Another attempt at colonisation ended badly when nearly 200 Belgian settlers lost their lives on the insalubrious coastline of Guatemala, in the poorly managed establishment of Santo Tomas, a domain conceded by the young Central American republic (1841–54).[8]

These resoundingly disappointing forays into colonialism reinforced the opinion of the great majority of the country's political decision makers and economic players that Belgium had little to gain and much to lose from a colonial policy. The numerous colonisation projects envisaged by King Leopold I were often mere fantasies. Traditionally, the country felt little pressure in terms of emigration, until the crisis period of extreme poverty in the 1840s awakened the idea of establishing overseas outlets for the excess population, vagabonds and/or criminals.[9] Furthermore, colonial initiatives involved expenses that the Belgian state was neither able nor willing to support. According to the liberal ideology that predominated in Belgium, colonisation involved 'incidental expenses' that only served to establish monopolies and privileges that would paralyse free trade.[10] For all that distant horizons could offer the world of business (already flourishing thanks to its closest neighbours), Belgian industry and trade would be better served, or so people thought, by discreetly edging their way into the global trading opportunities created, in particular, in the wake of Britain's informal empire. A telling example of Belgium's lack of imperialist ambitions is the disbanding of its small military navy in 1862. The Belgian commercial fleet was also limited, with the result that Belgian overseas exports essentially relied on foreign shipping companies and trading houses.[11] Finally, the remarks made concerning the Southern Netherlands in the sixteenth to eighteenth centuries still applied in independent Belgium's early period. The Belgians were not completely 'locked up' within their own borders.[12] Scientists were gathering information in Latin America and making important contributions to the knowledge of India and the Middle East; missionaries were trying

---

pp. 25–45; Id., *Palmerston and Africa: The Rio Nuñez Affair: Competition, Diplomacy and Justice* (London-New York, 1996), pp. 113–25 and 252–6.

[7] J. Everaert & C. De Wilde, "Pindanoten voor de ontluikende industriële revolutie. Een alternatieve kijk op de Belgische commerciële expansie in West-Afrika (1844–1861)", *Bulletin des Séances de l'Académie royale des Sciences d'Outre-Mer*, 37, 3 (1991), p. 318.

[8] M. Lafontaine, *L'enfer belge de Santo Tomas. Le rêve colonial brisé de Léopold I*^{er} (Ottignies-Louvain-la-Neuve, 1998).

[9] J. Stengers, *Emigration et immigration en Belgique au XIXe et XXe siècles* (Brussels, 1978); Id., "Les mouvements migratoires en Belgique aux XIXe et XXe siècles", in *Les migrations internationales de la fin du XVIIIe siècle à nos jours* (Paris, 1980), pp. 283–317.

[10] J. Stengers, "L'anticolonialisme libéral au XIXe siècle", in *L'expansion belge sous Léopold I*^{er}, op. cit., pp. 404–43.

[11] G. De Leener, *Ce qui manque au commerce belge d'exportation* (Brussels, 1906).

[12] E. Stols, "Kolonisatie en dagelijks leven van de hedendaagse tijd (1830–1940)", *Bijdragen tot de Geschiedenis*, 64, 3–4 (1981), pp. 237–59.

to convert North American, Chinese or Indian 'heathens'; businessmen were trying to make money as far away as Asia and the Pacific. But until just prior to the 1880s, none of these initiatives was systematically pursued with the help of the state. These individual Belgian contacts with the wider world were not the expression of any 'imperialist' dynamic.

The Initiatives of Leopold II and the Foundation of the Congo Free State (1885)

The Essential Traits of the Leopoldian Initiatives

It is within this pre-1880s context that the figure of the crown prince, the Duke of Brabant, the future Leopold II (1835–1909) appeared. He observed the vain efforts of his father to promote the idea and practice of colonisation. A great traveller, the young Leopold rapidly developed an almost obsessive interest in overseas affairs. But was he really the solitary and visionary 'genius' who developed his colonial projects all on his own, as the old hagiographic literature would have it? Recently, historian Jan Vandersmissen has shown that this was not the case.[13] Since the 1840s, other Belgians had been dreaming of Belgian overseas expansion via either scientific exploration or commercial activity. It's true that Leopold was very systematic in tackling the colonial idea: He informed himself thoroughly, read many books and tracked the latest statistics and reports with the help of a few carefully selected collaborators (intellectuals, officers, diplomats or civil servants sharing his ideas). Leopold did not focus on one particular overseas expansion formula. Depending on the circumstances of the moment, he envisaged the creation of a classic colony, based on overseas sovereignty of the state; the founding of a concessionary company with or without support; or even the setting up of an international organisation. He constantly adapted his projects to the local context and the ever-changing opportunities. His motives for undertaking colonial action were complex. Recently, historian Vincent Viaene rightly stressed that Leopold's tenacious pursuit of empire was not solely inspired by greed. Political and social motives were inextricably linked with the material benefits that could be gained from overseas activity.[14] The strengthening of the nation, the symbolic and diplomatic affirmation of its grandeur, the reconciliation of contending social groups, the stimulation of national energies; all these elements were present in his expansionist ideas. But all were undeniably linked with and resulted from Leopold's basic motive: wealth. Wealth created from colonial activities would support the more noble ideals. It was within this context that Leopold saw forced labour as one of the possible and legitimate methods of squeezing profits out of the overseas domains. Finally, expansionist projects also had a

---

[13] J. Vandersmissen, *Koningen van de wereld. Leopold II en de aardrijkskundige beweging* (Leuven-The Hague, 2009).
[14] V. Viaene, "King Leopold's Imperialism and the Origins of the Belgian Colonial Party, 1860–1905", *Journal of Modern History*, 80 (December 2008), pp. 741–90.

personal dimension. Leopold was an astute businessman, looking after his own financial 'portfolio'. More than once, when envisaging or effectively setting up a colonial or commercial project, he was personally financially involved. Other elements, such as humanitarian considerations, never played a role in his inner thoughts, though when circumstances required, they were used as instruments to reach his essential goals.

Belgian authorities and most business circles were, and remained, highly sceptical and even hostile towards the numerous projects Leopold proposed. But after his ascension to the throne in 1865, he continued his efforts to unearth 'the good deal' that would, in his eyes, be extremely profitable to himself and to the country. Some ideas were merely touched upon, while others were pursued tenaciously for years: the Philippines, Formosa (Taiwan), Tonkin (North Vietnam), Crete, Cyprus, Borneo, Morocco, Angola, Mozambique, Cameroon, the Fiji Islands, the Solomon Islands, the New Hebrides, Ethiopia and so forth.[15] Leopold sounded out those who held the 'legitimate rights' to these territories and attempted to establish some system or other that would allow him to realise his goals either in the form of a privileged trading company or a territory he could lease or buy, or even an 'independent state' that could be placed under his personal sovereignty, as in the case of the Philippines. None of these projects were successful; few people, both inside and outside the country, took the king's hare-brained schemes seriously.

Towards the middle of the 1870s, European penetration into the heart of Africa once again allowed the Belgian sovereign to launch into one of his apparently unrealistic enterprises.[16] This time, however, a combination of extraordinary circumstances made success unexpectedly possible. Jean Stengers's detailed research revealed the hidden motives of this process.[17] A number of observations immediately stand out.

First, the end result: At the start of the enterprise the king did not conceive of the foundation of the 'Congo Free State'. This idea took shape little by little, according to circumstances, through a series of sometimes unexpected reversals. Originally, Leopold II did not have in mind the 'colony for Belgium' that certain historians later attributed to him.

Second, the first observation can be more easily understood in the context of the broader background to the king's initiative. Paradoxically, the concrete creation of the Congo Free State owed less to the strength of the sovereign than to his relative weakness. Of course, the importance of the king's tenacity cannot be denied. His uncommon understanding of the diplomatic game and the strength of his dreams, like his 'Pharaonic' ambition of establishing his hold on the banks of the Nile, played a decisive role in the development of his plans.

---

[15] It should be noted that a number of these projects were pursued even after the Congolese venture had begun.
[16] H. Wesseling, *Le partage de l'Afrique 1880–1914* (Paris, 1996); R. Anstey, *Britain and the Congo in the Nineteenth Century* (Oxford, 1962).
[17] J. Stengers, *Le Congo, mythes et réalités* (Gembloux, 1989).

But in the end, the formation of the Congo was above all a result of the rivalry between the major powers of the time; in particular, Great Britain, France and Germany and, to a lesser degree, Portugal.

Third, the king deployed a whole range of unusual methods to launch, and then to keep, his Congolese enterprise afloat. No cost was too great: Leopold made use of smoke screens, straw men and humanitarian and philanthropic alibis. He corrupted journalists and launched propaganda campaigns aimed at manipulating national and international public opinion. He manipulated official texts, and even lied to his own government and to foreign authorities. He often went back on his word, improvised impulsively and made unexpected turnarounds. Traditional historiography – for a long time, pure hagiography – rarely highlighted details of these activities. When they were discreetly mentioned, they were justified by the fact that the king always acted 'for the good of Belgium', and only wanted to endow his 'beloved homeland' with a colony. It is true that Leopold continuously considered the ultimate aim of his initiatives, in the Congo or elsewhere, to be the greatness of Belgium. But in the end, this colonial 'gift' to Belgium had to be ripped from him in a fierce battle that plunged the political class and Belgian society into turmoil.

Fourth, while Leopold II was indeed the source of Belgian colonial activity, it should also be emphasised that little by little, his initiative was taken over by forces within Belgian society. Well before the Congo officially became a Belgian colony in 1908, ties were created between Belgium and Africa. Belgium gradually produced colonial interest groups that, on the one hand, were brought into being by the king's initiative but that, on the other hand, felt themselves in opposition to it.

The Foundation of the Congo Free State

In a matter of years, the king's pet project morphed into a Belgian colony. How did this happen? Leopold's initiative took form during an extraordinary window of opportunity. In the middle of the 1870s, central Africa was only known in Europe through the work of a handful of explorers. Leopold II endeavoured to take advantage of these initial explorations in an attempt to launch a profitable scheme. The first step, in 1876, was Leopold's call for an International Geographic Conference to be held in Brussels. As a result, the Association internationale africaine (International African Association), draped in humanitarian and scientific finery, was founded and led by the king.[18] The struggle against slavery was an essential alibi to facilitate the royal projects. The next step was Stanley's return to Europe after his spectacular trans-African expedition (1874–7) and his vain attempts to interest Great Britain in the Congo River region. Leopold secured the explorer's services. Stanley agreed to return to the Congo to set up stations on behalf of the Comité d'Études du Haut-Congo (Committee for Studies of the Upper Congo), a new organisation backed by the Belgian sovereign. By 1879, Stanley and his team had penetrated

---

[18] *La Conférence de géographie de 1876. Recueil d'études* (Brussels, 1976), p. 551.

the region surrounding the Congo River, reaching present-day Kisangani. They set up posts, first under the aegis of the Committee, which was rapidly dissolved, then under that of the Association internationale du Congo (AIC, International Association of the Congo), the organisation that succeeded it. Leopold, monitoring these activities from Brussels, willingly maintained the confusion that reigned between these various organisations in the eyes of the national and international public. He was, therefore, able to hide his purely commercial motives. The king was unquestionably seeking to establish trade monopolies though (as yet) he had no thoughts of establishing some form of political sovereignty.

Around 1882, the rapidly changing international context forced Leopold to adopt new tactics.[19] Brazza, an explorer who, like Stanley, was active in the region at the mouth of the Congo, made agreements with African chiefs who acknowledged French sovereignty in the region. Clearly, a purely commercial scheme like Leopold's had no weight when compared with a European power established in the region. The king therefore had a change of heart and determined to found a sovereign political entity that would protect his commercial activities. From that moment on, the AIC sought recognition from both the African chiefs and (especially) the Western powers as a 'state'. But Brazza's political initiative, supported by France, led to other concerns. Britain, particularly, could not tolerate such French advances, nor could Portugal which, considering its own secular establishment on the African coast, also claimed territorial rights in the region.[20] In 1884, the British and the Portuguese made an agreement in which Britain acknowledged Portugal's sovereignty rights over all the territory surrounding the mouth of the Congo River. This meant the end of access to Africa via the Atlantic and hence an end to Leopold's dreams.

Leopold reacted immediately. Although he was in search of trading monopolies, he now proclaimed, especially to the British and the Americans, his willingness to establish and maintain free trade in the current and any potential future territories of the AIC. In 1884, to counter French fears that the Association's territories might fall into the hands of the British, Leopold granted France a preemptive right over the Congo, a move that would have serious consequences for the future. This essentially meant that if Leopold were ever to give up his schemes in the Congo, France would recoup the territory – if France wanted to. This was a clever move. On the one hand, France would condone the activities of the AIC (which it hoped would soon fall under French control). On the other hand, this move encouraged Portugal to moderate its territorial ambitions and to leave Leopold some scope, lest he abandon the territory, thereby handing it to the French, far more fearsome neighbours than the Belgians would ever be. Britain, naturally, was not at all pleased that pre-emptive rights had been granted to France, though the British could only applaud the promise of free

---

[19] J. Stengers, "Léopold II et la rivalité franco-anglaise en Afrique, 1882–1884", *Revue belge de Philologie et d'Histoire*, 47, 2 (1969), pp. 425–79.
[20] F. Latour da Veiga Pinto, *Le Portugal et le Congo au XIXe siècle* (Paris, 1972).

trade. Germany, the new European power with growing interest in the great colonial game, accepted Leopold's arrangement with France and was, additionally, willing to grant France some external satisfaction in order to distract the French from their recent losses to Germany in Alsace-Lorraine.

This brief overview of the diplomatic conflicts surrounding the establishment of the Congo is essential to our understanding of Belgian colonial history. All the elements were in place: on the one hand, great powers who were mutually preventing each other from occupying a sought-after piece of land; on the other hand, a seemingly frivolous and ephemeral player who would temporarily maintain a precarious balance. Finally, there was the possibility of creating a free trade zone. Thus, in 1884–5, several nations successively acknowledged the sovereignty of the AIC. This acknowledgement occurred prior to, and on the periphery of, the International Conference of Berlin. During that conference, certain terms governing European involvement in black Africa were fixed. One of these terms stipulated that the so-called Conventional Congo Basin was and would remain an area of free trade and free navigation. No right of entry could be levied there; everybody would be able to trade freely and on equal footing. This decision played a key role in Belgian colonial history and was at the centre of the controversial activities of the Congo Free State (État indépendant du Congo) created at the beginning of 1885, with Leopold as absolute ruler.[21] Theoretically, Belgium had no link with this new African political entity.

Main Characteristics of the Congo Free State (1885–1908)

Conquests and Financial Needs

Although unusual in its beginnings and nature, the Congo Free State nevertheless had the same needs as any other state: the need to obtain financial means and the need to occupy and manage the territory. The establishment of Congo's borders is a story that combines the audacity of the king who, with a simple pencil line on a map, included Katanga in his 'state'; the inexorable laws of *Realpolitik* in Europe; and finally, the pure luck that Great Britain had to recognise the proposed borders of the Congo following a true diplomatic 'blunder'.[22] By agreeing with the proposed borders, Britain recognised the Congo Free State's possession of land that was in no way part of the territory effectively occupied by the former Association internationale du Congo.

To establish its authority over this vast acknowledged territory, the Congo Free State either opposed or allied itself with (depending on the circumstances and the eras) the 'Arabized' authorities that had been established before its arrival. Officially, military force was used to end the age-old slave trade. In this struggle the Force publique (the Congo's military force) was supported by large numbers of native auxiliary troops having no modern organisation

---

[21] *Le centenaire de l'État indépendant du Congo. Recueil d'études* (Brussels, 1988), p. 533.
[22] J. Stengers, "Léopold II et la fixation de frontières du Congo", *Le Flambeau*, 46 (1963), pp. 153–97.

or discipline. For the king, the fight against slavery was nothing more than a blind aimed at hiding his material ambitions. Leopold's anti-slavery campaigns were simply a means of establishing trade and political domination in the heart of Africa. It is true that, following this struggle, the traditional slave trade was eliminated, but the Congo Free State authorities immediately introduced other forms of coercion and forced labour. They either seized and diverted traditional trading activities to serve their own advantage or established new ones. The new white power was confronted with numerous challenges: It had to break the resistance of the recalcitrant traditional African authorities and bloodily repress the revolts of its own black troops. It also had to outstrip the English, who were eying Katanga from southern Africa, which meant having to occupy the territory at any cost. Finally, the king was still obsessed with his desire to reach and occupy the banks of the Nile, so he continued to interfere in the great European colonial race. This led to heavy costs and severe loss of human life. It was dangerous because the Congo Free State faced military confrontation with European nations. As a result, the king attracted diplomatic enmity that endangered Belgium's neutrality.

Expeditions and military campaigns require a lot of money. Moreover, a governing body, however basic, had to be established and a transport infrastructure created where none had previously existed: in particular the famous railway line between Léopoldville and Matadi (where the Congo River was not navigable). Without a railroad, it would be impossible to move trade goods or raw materials. The financial challenge was enormous. Between 1885 and 1895, the Congo, which was supposed to be a profitable affair, turned out to be a bottomless financial pit. The personal fortune of Leopold, which had always been an essential source of financing for the Congolese venture, was no longer sufficient to keep the Congo Free State going. This financial need is what ultimately made the Congo an official part of Belgium's political life.[23] To save his enterprise from failure, the king requested and obtained financial aid from the Belgian state.

In 1891-2, Leopold took several measures that, in the short term, saved the Congo Free State but, in the long term, had repercussions that would last for decades. Through a series of legal and statutory provisions, Leopold introduced the so-called domain system (*système domanial*) in the Congo. This meant that any land not directly cultivated by the indigenous population was considered 'vacant' and declared the property of the state. This way, the natural resources found there belonged to the state by right, and only the Congo Free State had the right to acquire them, trade them or grant concessionary rights to private companies. As a consequence of this measure, the free trade promised by Leopold before the foundation of the Congo Free State, and solemnly proclaimed by the Berlin Act in 1885, was circumvented.

---

[23] With the exception of two aspects: the law authorising the king of the Belgians to take charge of another state and the 'detachment' of Belgian soldiers enlisting in the service of the Congo (see Chapter 2).

Exploitation and Massacres in the Leopoldian Congo

The domain system had severe consequences. At home in Belgium, it caused a rupture between Leopold and a number of his initial supporters who accused him of killing off free enterprise. This immediately led to political difficulties. In the Congo, dramatic repercussions provoked an international outcry, which finally led to the end of the Free State. Around 1895, the gathering of ivory, and especially the harvesting of wild rubber, became highly profitable, thanks to the *système domanial*. The Congo Free State (i.e. the king) and concessionary private companies did everything they could to increase the production and sale of these raw materials on world markets that couldn't get enough of them. The profit from the sale of goods belonging directly to the state, as well as the taxes levied on exports, inflated the national budget.

In order to maximize profit, both the Congo Free State authorities and the concessionary companies set up a particularly harsh system of exploitation.[24] The Congolese were not only subjected to a merciless work regime, but also to acts of violence aimed at breaking any vague ideas of resistance. The destruction of villages, summary executions, hostage taking and various types of corporal punishment were common practice in many parts of the Congo Free State. Not all the regions of the Congo were affected in the same way, but when these events did occur, they were not simply the uncontrolled actions of a few brutal individuals, but were part of a systematic value system that encouraged those in charge to deliver ever-increasing quantities of product at almost any human cost. The harsh exploitation of the Congolese population was not merely a consequence of Leopold's greed; it was a consequence, an essential and specific feature, of this unusual 'private' style of colonisation. Since the military and initial administration costs could not be paid for by the metropolis (as they had been by other colonial empires), the financial burden of conquest necessitated a particularly severe and exploitative regime.

This is a crucial episode in Belgian colonial history, not only because the facts themselves are important, but also because of the impact they would have on the entire course of Belgian colonial history. The Belgian and international public were, quite rightly, vexed by this issue, which aroused heated reactions. Though other scholarly works have dealt with the atrocities of Leopold's regime,[25] Adam Hochschild's book, *King Leopold's Ghost: A Story of Greed, Terror and Heroism in Colonial Africa*, has re-opened the controversy. Hochschild's book tells of a 'holocaust' perpetrated in the Congo, setting the number of victims at ten million. The term *holocaust*, associated in the public mind with genocide, seems inappropriate in this case.[26] No one sought to systematically exterminate

---

[24] D. Vangroenweghe, *Rood rubber. Leopold II en zijn Kongo* (Brussels-Amsterdam, 1985); Id., *Voor rubber en ivoor. Leopold II en de ophanging van Stokes* (Louvain, 2005); A. M. Delathuy (pseudonym of J. Marchal), *E. D. Morel tegen Leopold II en de Kongostaat* (Berchem, 1985) and many other works by this author.

[25] M. Ewans, *European Atrocity, African Catastrophe. Leopold II, the Congo Free State and its Aftermath* (London, 2002).

[26] Used only in the title of the French translation of the work, this term does not feature in the original title in English or in the Dutch translation. A. Hochschild, *King Leopold's Ghost. A Story*

the native population; who, then, would have provided the labour on which the exploitation was based?[27] Hochschild's estimate remains conjectural. No one knows the exact figure of the population of central Africa at the end of the nineteenth century. The first, rather unreliable, population statistics only go back to 1924. These put the figure at approximately ten million inhabitants. The figure of ten million victims was suggested by combining this data with an estimate given by Jan Vansina that "between 1880 and 1920 the colony's population was probably reduced by half"[28] – an estimate Vansina has, himself, recently called into question, as we shall soon see.

We should tread cautiously. Percentage estimates of population reduction vary enormously from one region and source to another. For instance, historian Léon de Saint-Moulin points out that in some regions the death rate may have been as high as eighty per cent; in other regions, the percentage seems to be much lower.[29] It is therefore risky to suggest a single percentage for population loss that is valid for the entire Belgian colonial territory. Nevertheless, the creation of the Congo Free State certainly had gruesome consequences for the Congolese population. We can certainly state that during the first four decades of Belgian presence in the Congo, the number of Congolese fell dramatically. Certain regions were well and truly de-populated, but what was the total result? Currently, no one contests the fact that several hundred thousand, even millions, of people perished under white power. No self-respecting historian,

---

of Greed, Terror and Heroism in Colonial Africa (Boston-New York, 1998); French translation: *Les fantômes du roi Léopold. Un holocauste oublié* (Paris, 1998). However, the ambiguity persists. An article by the same author, published in the Japanese newspaper *Yomiuri Shimbun* on 15 March 2005, bears the following title: "Genocide: Belgium's Monument to Denial" (however, the author says, in the above-mentioned publication, that this term was used without his consent). The praise written by Nadine Gordimer concerning the book by Hochschild featuring on the fourth page of the cover, speaks of "King Leopold's holocaust of the Congolese people". In an article published in the *New York Review of Books*, 12 January 2006, p. 57, Hochschild points out that *holocaust* written 'with a small "h" means a 'widespread massacre'. Considering the proximity with the Holocaust (with a capital letter), indicating the genocide of the Jews during the Second World War, I believe it is necessary to use this term with extreme caution. In any case, it would be unfortunate to situate the debate concerning the Leopoldian period on a semantic level. However, there is absolutely no doubt that there were 'widespread massacres' in the Leopoldian Congo, as we shall see later on. An analysis of the stirs caused by this controversy can be found in M. Dumoulin, *Léopold II un roi génocidaire?* (Brussels, 2005).

[27] Historian Robert Weisbord also explicitly uses the term *genocide* to designate the Congo atrocities and notes: "On this matter it is worth noting that the UN Convention on the Prevention and Punishment of Genocide does not require that there be an attempt to kill every single person in a given population" (R. G. Weisbord, "The King, the Cardinal and the Pope: Leopold II's Genocide in the Congo and the Vatican", *Journal of Genocide Research*, 5, 1 [2003], p. 35).

[28] J. Vansina in his introduction to D. Vangroenweghe, *Rood rubber, op. cit.*, p. 8. This evaluation is explained more extensively in J. Vansina, *Sur les sentiers du passé en forêt. Les cheminements de la tradition politique ancienne en Afrique équatoriale* (Louvain-la-Neuve, 1991), p. 307. Original English edition: *Paths in the Rainforest* (Madison, 1990).

[29] L. de Saint-Moulin, "What is Known of the Demographic History of Zaire Since 1885?", in B. Fetter, ed., *Demography From Scanty Evidence* (Boulder, 1990), pp. 299–325.

Belgian or otherwise, is calling into question the horror of the work regime imposed by Leopold II. The works of Jean Stengers himself, dating back to the 1960s, leave no doubt whatsoever with regard to this subject. After clarification concerning the infamous practice of cutting off hands, which shocked the world following the wide distribution of photographs, Stengers described the punitive expeditions against villages 'guilty' of not having provided enough rubber: "The horror was that people were killed for rubber".[30]

The incontestable dramatic decrease in the Congolese population was due to a set of factors. World history is strewn with demographic catastrophes. These occur when indigenous societies, isolated from the rest of the world and lacking technological potential, are brutally subjected to European contact (pre-Columbian America, the South Sea Islands, etc.). Population collapse in such cases is due to a combination of deadly elements. Similarly, in the case of central Africa in the period from 1880 to 1920, numerous factors apart from the compulsory work regime combined to provoke the dramatic de-population: military operations, the 'maintenance of law and order', porterage, the decline in fertility and malnutrition (each partially linked to the rubber regime) and, last but not least, epidemics (caused or facilitated by all the previous elements) that wiped out entire regions either through the introduction of new bacteria or through the increase and spread of endemic diseases. Jan Vansina recently returned to the issue of quantifying the total population decline; he has revised his earlier position and even concludes that "[C]ontrary to expectations, the Kuba population [admittedly only one of the many Congolese populations] was actually rising rather than falling during the first two decades of the colonial era". In this area, there was ultimately a population decline of approximately twenty-five per cent, but this occurred between 1900 and 1919 and was mainly due to sickness.[31] The current impossibility of establishing a *precise* count of the deaths caused by the Leopoldian work regime (and of isolating the losses due to other causes) does not, in any way, mitigate the incontestable atrocities of 'red rubber' which became the subject of an international protest campaign.

The acts of violence committed in the Congo did not go unnoticed. A few isolated voices (especially those of American journalist George W. Williams and Protestant missionary William Sheppard) sounded the first cries of alarm. Next, a British citizen, Edmund D. Morel, set up a campaign of protest against the Congo Free State that aroused a great deal of emotion in Britain and abroad.[32]

---

[30] J. Stengers, *Congo, op. cit.*, p. 142 (original edition of this essay in Wm. R. Louis & J. Stengers, *History of the Congo Reform Movement*, Oxford, 1968). Concerning the practice of cutting off hands: To avoid wasting ammunition, soldiers had to bring back the cut off hand of their victim as 'proof'; some soldiers even cut the hands off people who were left for dead but who were simply injured. Sometimes they even inflicted the same fate on a living person to justify wasted cartridges.

[31] J. Vansina, *Being Colonized: The Kuba Experience in Rural Congo, 1880–1960* (Madison, 2010), pp. 127–49 (quotation p. 147).

[32] Wm. R. Louis & J. Stengers, *E. D. Morel's History of the Congo Reform Movement* (Oxford, 1968).

The British government ordered its consul in the region, Roger Casement, to make an inquiry. His report confirmed the reality of the accusations and set in motion a whole series of political consequences, both inside and outside of Belgium.[33] Then, at the beginning of 1904, Casement and Morel founded the Congo Reform Association, which pursued an anti-Congolese campaign. British authorities threatened to call into question Leopold's domination in the Congo.[34] With the help of his liegemen, the king launched a counter-propaganda campaign maintaining that the claims of Morel and his men were to a large extent groundless; nothing more than another manoeuvre of perfidious Britain in its bid to seize the long sought-after Congo. But the campaign against the Congo Free State gained impetus and the king's policies raised an increasing number of questions, even in Belgium. In 1904, giving in to pressure and desirous of arresting the allegations, Leopold set up a commission of inquiry composed of eminent jurists, including a Belgian and two foreigners. Against all expectations, its report confirmed, in cautious terms, the abuses committed in the Congo. From this moment on, the question of Belgium taking over the Congo Free State gained prominence. The Congo had become a Belgian political problem of primary importance. After a fierce struggle between Leopold and the government, Belgium annexed the Congo in 1908: This marked the beginning of actual Belgian colonisation.

Official Belgium in the Face of the Leopoldian Episode: Denials and Repression

This new episode of Belgian colonisation initially began with a programme of collective amnesia. Leopold II died in 1909, shortly after Belgium took control of the Congo. Those in political and economic circles spouted their undisputed worship of Leopold, who was honoured more after his death than during his reign. The king's argument to justify his management of the Congo immediately became the official Belgian position. To the world and to their own citizenry, Belgian officials willingly admitted to a number of abuses in the Leopoldian Congo, all the time emphasising that they had been eliminated immediately. Over time, however, these admissions of abuse were watered down. A whole range of arguments was found to 'justify' or lessen the 'blunders' that had occurred in Leopoldian Congo: the work regime was not harder than elsewhere; the king had to find money somewhere, since the Berlin Act of 1885 forbade raising the entry rights and so forth. In the end, the abuses were flatly

---

[33] *The Casement report. (...) Introduction et notes de Daniel Vangroenweghe. Préface de Jean-Luc Vellut* (Louvain-la-Neuve, 1985).
[34] Nevertheless, the 'hard' attitude of British authorities was not so much driven by Morel's action, but rather based on original information collected by British diplomat W. Thesiger. J. O. Osborne, "Wilfred G. Thesiger, Sir Edward Grey, and the British Campaign to Reform the Congo, 1905-1909", *Journal of Imperial and Commonwealth History*, 27, 1 (January 1999), pp. 59-80.

denied. The whitewashed vision of the Leopoldian past was officially adopted and spread by the Belgian diplomatic service, especially after the First World War and during the rest of the twentieth century.

During the entire colonial period and well beyond, official Belgium never really faced up to the truth about the Leopoldian episode. The colonials, along with the political and economic officials who had never experienced the dark years of the Congo Free State, sincerely believed in the official version. They fiercely rejected the criticism directed at the Congo Free State and, as an indirect result, at the Belgian Congo and themselves. The Belgian colonials who had actually been in the field and had seen what went on in the Leopoldian Congo with their own eyes kept quiet and modestly veiled anything that might damage the Great King's image. We only need to read the revealing text written by Octave Louwers, an influential figure of the Belgian colonial milieu. Louwers was a magistrate in the Congo Free State who returned to Belgium to pursue a brilliant career as an advisor in colonial matters at the Ministry of Foreign Affairs. In 1933, he made this eloquent confession in a private letter:

> (Leopold II) can be praised for his initiative, he was the creator, but in certain respects he was a bad administrator. Affected by megalomania at the end of his life, overly dominated by material considerations, he entered into ventures from which he only extricated himself thanks to a miracle. The horrors of the rubber business are not a legend; I experienced them; it is one of the darkest stories of all colonial history, which in itself is already very dark. We must also be careful not to allude to all this and especially not to [(...) remind the existence] of those who, at the time, denounced the abuses of the Free State [i.e. Morel and Casement].[35]

After the king's death, the memory of the rubber episode was repressed. Leopold became a cult figure and Belgium assumed, for over half a century, the multifaceted heritage of the Congo Free State.

Rapid Overview of the Belgian Colonisation of the Congo Between 1908 and 1960

Organisation of the Belgian Colonial Institutions

Upon assuming official control of the colonial territory, Belgian authorities had to create a new institutional framework for the Congo.[36] The law commonly known as the 'Colonial Charter', adopted by parliament in 1908, dictated the fundamental mechanism of the Belgian colonial empire. The aim was to put an end to the absolutism of the Leopoldian state. The Belgian legislative chambers would, in theory, become the supreme authorities for the management of the

---

[35] Archives générales du Royaume, Brussels (AGR), Louwers Papers, n° 367, Louwers to former colonial minister Paul Crokaert, 5 October 1933, p. 4.
[36] J.-L. Vellut, F. Loriaux & F. Morimont, *Bibliographie historique du Zaïre à l'époque coloniale (1880–1960). Travaux publiés en 1960–1996* (Louvain-la-Neuve-Tervuren, 1996); I. Ndaywel è Nziem, *Histoire générale du Congo* (Paris-Brussels, 1998).

Congo, in particular through the approval of the budgets. Another decisive element of the charter was the rigorous financial separation of Belgium and the Congo. Belgian finances were not to be used for expenses relating to the colony. The minister of colonies, a full member of the government, was also granted legislative power to make decrees since parliament could not manage all the details of colonial policy. The minister was accountable for the management of the Congo and his draft decrees, before being officially enacted, had to be submitted to the colonial council. The council was a new, purely consultative organ. Parliament appointed six of its members and the king eight. The colonial charter specified that certain rights enjoyed by the Belgians at home, such as the freedom of association or the freedom of the press, did not apply to populations in the Congo, both black and white. Moreover, no representative form of government was introduced. The representative of Belgian central authority in the Congo was the governor-general, who had strictly limited power to make decisions.

The territorial structure of power in the colony itself was organised in the form of subordinated entities whose number varied over the years: provinces, then districts and finally territories; led by governors, commissioners (*commissaires*) and local administrators (*administrateurs territoriaux*) respectively. At an even lower level, authority was exercised by 'indigenous chieftainships'. Belgium opted for a form of *indirect* rule by which compliant indigenous chiefs became auxiliaries of the colonial power.[37] In general, colonial power was characterised by its centralised nature: Brussels decided all the important matters. In the Congo itself, the successive capitals, first Boma, then Léopoldville, clearly dominated the subordinate powers. It is important to note that, throughout the history of Belgian colonialism, tensions existed between the central power and the 'GG' (governor-general) and, more generally, between metropolitan (i.e. Belgium) and colonial (i.e. the Congo) structures of government. Furthermore, centralisation within the Congo itself led to recurring discussions and several reorganisations of the subordinated powers that continuously demanded more autonomy.

The Catholic Jules Renkin, first in a long series of ministers of the colonies, had the cumbersome task of addressing the numerous deficiencies in the Leopoldian administration. Not only did he have to put an end to the international difficulties, he also had to reform internal management. The Belgian authorities abolished the *système domanial* and re-introduced free enterprise and trade. The harsh Leopoldian work regime was suppressed – though forced labour did not actually disappear. Throughout the history of colonial Belgium, compulsory work remained in force, either for porterage and the development or maintenance of public utility work or for certain productive activities, for instance the growth of so-called educational crops introduced in order to stimulate commercial farming by the native population.

[37] A. Zajaczkowski, "Belgian Congo: Between Indirect and Direct Rule", *Hemispheres: Studies on Cultures and Societies*, 1 (1984), pp. 259-70.

The Congo under the Belgian Colonial Regime

Belgium is a small country, but the Belgian Congo was a huge territory. The difference in size between the metropolis (31,000 km^2) and the colony (2,350,000 km^2) was striking: The Congo was seventy-five times the size of Belgium. Only in the British Empire was there a larger disproportion: The total British colonial territories, including the Dominions, were 132 times bigger than Britain itself. The Dutch, French and Portuguese colonial empires were, respectively, fifty, seventeen and nine times bigger than the metropoles. The difference between the populations of Belgium (with 7.4 million inhabitants in 1910) and its colony (with c. 11 million before the First World War) is less striking. In this case, the ratio of the colonial population to the metropolitan population is 144 per cent: a less spectacular figure than in the case of the British and the Dutch empires (865 per cent and 804 per cent respectively), but somewhat comparable to the French (120 per cent) and the Portuguese (94 percent) situations.[38] In short, Belgium's newly gained empire was far from negligible, and foreign observers, politicians and diplomats wondered if this colony was not 'too big' for small and inexperienced Belgium to handle.

The inclusion of the Congo in the world economy did indeed pose a great challenge to the Belgians. After the plunder that had characterised the Congo Free State, it was now necessary to 'develop' the immense Congolese territory. The railways already constructed under the preceding regime had to be modernised and extended, as did the port and river infrastructures.[39] In these sectors, the Belgian state and the colonial authorities provided a significant boost at the beginning of the 1920s, a decade also marked by a significant and renewed flow of private Belgian capital into the Congo. Compared to other colonies, the Belgian colony was at the top of per capita capital investment. No other overseas territory (outside the British Dominions) had attracted such amounts of capital. By 1938, the Belgian Congo had received forty-eight dollars of foreign capital per inhabitant; in British India (including Burma and Ceylon), this sum amounted to eight dollars; in the Netherlands Indies, thirty-six dollars; in the French African colonies, twenty-five dollars; in the British African colonies, thirty-two dollars; in Portuguese Africa, eighteen dollars.[40] Belgian colonisation was very capital intensive – a fact of great importance for the colonial impact on the Belgian economy.

It was first thought that the Congo would be an agricultural powerhouse. Around the time of the First World War, it became increasingly apparent that the Congo would be a major producer of mineral riches. Belgium took over the mining activity, only recently started in the Congo Free State, which grew significantly in the 1920s. The Congo became one of the main global producers of copper, cobalt, industrial diamonds, uranium and many other minerals

---

[38] B. Etemad, *La possession du monde. Poids et mesures de la colonisation* (Brussels, 2000), pp. 185, 231, 236, 241, 247, 311 (figures relate to 1913).
[39] A. Huybrechts, *Transports et structures de développement au Congo* (Paris-The Hague, 1970).
[40] J. Frémeaux, *Les empires coloniaux dans le processus de la mondialisation* (Paris, 2002), p. 48.

such as gold and tin. Congo played a leading role in the global arena due to the mining industry – a situation that would have major repercussions for Belgium. Between 1921 and 1948, minerals, as a percentage of the total value of Congolese exports, fluctuated between fifty-two and seventy-two per cent.[41] Between 1938 and 1951, the Congo's share in Africa's total exports increased from 4.7 per cent to 7.4 per cent.[42] The agricultural sector (palm oil, cotton, coffee, etc.) was certainly significant, but ranked second to minerals in the colony's exports. Agricultural produce came either from European plantations or from African farmers. From then on, these African farmers had to maintain sufficient production for export while simultaneously producing enough for their own needs – quite a difficult task. The Congolese countryside experienced great hardship. In addition, the Congolese people had to provide labour, recruited by force, for the big mining concerns that were often far from areas of high demographic density. Masses of workers, who were victim to a high death rate, were recruited far away from the mines, transported and ended up living as displaced populations in their own country. Labour shortages and the nagging fear of de-population finally led to a turnaround in production policy. From the 1920s onwards, major companies such as the Union minière du Haut-Katanga devised a 'stabilisation' policy.[43] They reinforced mechanisation and introduced social protection measures for their black workers.

This paternalistic concern gradually became generalised in the colony. The colonial state endeavoured to establish basic education, health and medical networks. This work was left to the care of the religious missions (with Catholic missions favoured over Protestant) that had been active in the Congo since the beginning of the colonial enterprise. However, the extent of this educational and medical effort remained modest until the Second World War. The economic crisis of the 1930s followed by the enormous boost in productive effort from 1940 to 1945 caused great social upheaval and labour unrest in Congo and in many other sub-Saharan colonies.[44] The harsh living conditions of the native populations only began to improve in the second half of the 1940s.

The last fifteen years of Belgian domination in the Congo were characterised by a set of exceptional factors: the takeoff of mining and agricultural production boosted by high prices on world markets; a significant increase in both public and private investment; rapid development of Congolese processing industries; considerable improvement in community facilities and infrastructures; increases in the purchasing power of black workers; improvement in black living conditions, housing and consumption, at least in urban centres; the influx of populations towards these so-called extra-customary centres (to the

---

[41] *Industrie. Revue de la FIB*, 3, 5 (May 1949), p. 302.
[42] E. Hickmann, *Belgisch-Kongo. Struktur und Entwicklung einer Kolonialwirtschaft* (Bremen, 1952), p. 76.
[43] This policy seems to have been introduced somewhat earlier in the Belgian Congo than in other African colonies. See F. Cooper, *L'Afrique depuis 1940* (Paris, 2008), p. 56.
[44] See F. Cooper, *L'Afrique, op. cit.*, p. 60.

point where the rural exodus and the rise in urban unemployment, at the end of the 1950s, began to worry colonial authorities); mass schooling of young people (in this area, the Congo held a leading position in black Africa); the extension of social and medical services to the countryside (to which the creation of the Fonds du Bien-Être indigène (Indigenous Welfare Fund) in 1947 largely contributed).

Just before the sudden collapse of the colonial system, the Belgian authorities boasted of these undeniable achievements to justify the validity of their sovereignty in the Congo to the rest of the world. Still today, former Belgian colonials – precisely those who knew and built the Congo of the 1940s and 1950s – refer to these positive results in reaction to what they perceive as unjust attacks against colonialism. They quite rightly underline the striking contrast between the progress of 'their' Congo and the race to the depths of despair in the decades after 1960. But is it really justifiable to project these peak years onto previous decades when the track record reads differently? Shining the spotlight unilaterally on the social and economic advances from 1945 to 1960 puts the darkest facets of the colonial picture firmly in the shadows. Moreover, at the dawn of independence, the Congolese rural sector encountered serious difficulties. Food production was in crisis and food shortages became common. Paradoxically, the Congo, the great exporter of agricultural produce, was forced to import foodstuffs in increasing quantities just to feed its own population. Despite the relative material well-being that certain strata of the black population enjoyed, Congolese society was marked by heavy and threatening imbalances. Compared to other African countries, the Congo had a large urban and industrial proletariat, but it consisted quasi-exclusively of executants. The strata above were extremely underdeveloped. In addition, employees and civil servants, already relatively few in number, were restricted to inferior tasks. The famous 'Africanisation of the executives' that the Belgian coloniser launched into suddenly and belatedly just before his hasty departure was rather limited at the time of independence. The Congolese lower middle class, middle class and, *a fortiori*, business class were practically non-existent. The colonial authorities had always prevented access to property and autonomous economic activity. The colonial educational policy was designed to create a large literate base, from which a cultural 'elite' could be moulded in some distant future. This policy largely contributed to a dangerous distortion within Congolese society. Who would lead this independent nation?

It is true that the Congo of the end of the 1940s and the beginning of the 1950s seemed calm and relatively trouble-free. But was it? Such a conclusion ignores the social upheavals that shook the colony during the decades before the 1950s. Several revolts and strikes had to be repressed by the armed forces, most notably in the 1890s, in the 1930s (e.g. the Pende revolt of 1931) and immediately after the Second World War. The authorities also ignored or hushed up the latent and diffuse grievances within the black population. Before the final years of colonisation, the discontent of the black population had no 'modern' expression, especially in the countryside. It was voiced collectively through syncretistic or traditional religious movements (e.g. the Kimbanguist religion, still vivid in the Congo; the Kitawala; etc.) – a phenomenon that the authorities endeavoured to control and even quell. An undoubtedly different kind of discontent also affected urban circles. Only a minority of Congolese people benefitted from Western education and assimilated European values and lifestyles. These 'evolved', Westernised Congolese (*évolués*) were often frustrated by the lack of possibility for promotion and even more so by the daily expressions of racism inflicted upon them by some whites. Other whites, it should be said, showed respect, consideration and sincere friendship towards the native Congolese. While these 'bright' facets of the complex prism of colonial life should certainly not be forgotten, the darker facets must also be remembered. Although it was never subjected to a South African-style apartheid system (something the Belgian authorities explicitly rejected), the Belgian Congo did indeed have a colour bar that only began to break down shortly before independence.

It is precisely at this point that popular discontent found a more traditional, political expression. Beginning in 1956, newly-created Congolese political associations expressed very cautious and moderated nationalist views. Over time, these organisations were gradually radicalised; finally leading, in 1959 and 1960, to demands for immediate and complete independence. These demands were formulated by a multitude of rival political factions that suddenly appeared – an aspect of one-upmanship that certainly cannot be denied. The local and metropolitan Belgian authorities were caught off guard. They were woefully unprepared for the possibility of Congolese independence. The atmosphere became even more tense due to a sudden burst of violence in January 1959, followed soon afterwards by other bloody incidents and a campaign of civil disobedience. After a few tentative steps, Brussels succumbed. At the beginning of 1960, after a conference with all the Congolese political forces, Belgium suddenly decided to put an end to its sovereignty in the Congo on 30 June 1960. And so, for a couple of years between 1958 and 1960, the Congo returned to the forefront of Belgian political life, a place it had not occupied since 1908. The following chapter is dedicated to the impact of the colony on Belgium domestic politics: a long (apparent) silence between two outbursts.

2

The Congo and Belgium's Domestic Policy

In 1896, publicist Alphonse de Haulleville, a zealous propagandist of the Congolese venture, published an ample volume titled *Les aptitudes colonisatrices des Belges* (*The Colonising Aptitudes of the Belgians*). At the time, there was much discussion about the innate abilities of different peoples to succeed in the noble enterprise known as colonisation. For Haulleville, there was no doubt: The Belgians definitely had what it took. But then how could he explain the Belgians' obvious lack of colonial achievements before the 1880s? He pointed to historical circumstances (foreign 'domination'); to the fact that highly prosperous Belgium had been 'spoilt' by fate; and also to the eternal domestic political struggles: "We were hypnotised by amateur politicians!" Politicians have always suffered from bad press among Leopold's partisans and hagiographers. The politicians' "vain quarrels" and "timorous, shopkeeper attitudes" were polar opposites of the king's visionary character. Luckily, Leopold II and the Congo venture prevented the country from being "stuck in the rut of mediocrity".[1]

Less than thirty years later, Belgium was managing a huge colonial empire. What caused this turnaround? In this chapter, we examine how the Congo was integrated into the country's domestic policy, as well as the results of this integration.

Brief Outline of Belgium's Domestic Policy

Representative liberal democracy had been introduced quite early in Belgium compared to most other European countries.[2] The members of both the house of representatives and the senate were elected, but the electorate was extremely restricted. Only the richest taxpayers, approximately one per cent of the Belgian

---

[1] A. de Haulleville, *Les aptitudes colonisatrices des Belges et la question coloniale en Belgique* (Brussels, 1898), pp. 139 and 414.

[2] See E. Witte, J. Craeybeckx & A. Meynen, *Political History of Belgium: From 1830 Onwards* (Brussels, 2009); J. C. H. Blom & E. Lamberts, eds., *History of the Low Countries* (London, 2006).

population, had the right to vote. The voting system led to the formation of two parties, the Liberals and the Catholics, which alternated in winning the parliamentary majority. Between 1847 and 1884, the Liberals were in power most of the time; from 1884 to 1914 – the decisive period for the Congo affair – a Catholic government dominated by conservative politicians ruled the country. In the nineteenth century, Belgium's political struggles mainly concerned the position of the Catholic Church. The Liberals persistently attempted to roll back religious influence in both the state and society. This contentious posturing did not fade in the twentieth century. It flared up again as late as the 1950s during the so-called School Wars, in which successive governments promoted either the Catholic or the official state schools until a compromise, the School Pact, satisfied the advocates of both sides on essential points.

The position of the monarch in the Belgian political structure deserves some consideration. According to the constitution of 1831, the king could not take his own political initiatives: Executive power was in the hands of the ministers. In practice, though, the first king, Leopold I, decisively influenced the domains of foreign policy and defence. He also had an important impact on ministerial careers. Consequently, a tradition of 'royal political activism' was present in Belgian politics right from the start and became particularly important with regard to colonial policy.

From the 1880s onwards, decisive steps were taken towards the introduction of mass democracy. The Socialist Parti ouvrier belge (Belgian Workers' Party) was created in 1885. Within the Catholic Party, a progressive Christian-Democrat faction gradually challenged conservative domination until the Catholics finally agreed to create a new centre party in 1945. The new party, the Parti Social Chrétien, had both left and right wings, but was considered 'Christian-Democrat'. Social movements such as trade unions, co-operatives and mutual benefit societies were intimately linked to both the Socialists and the Christian-Democrats. The gradual entrance of the general populace into politics went hand in hand with the long and protracted creation of a welfare state from about 1886 to 1944.

Long-lasting political agitation, including general strikes, led to three successive electoral reforms. Universal manhood suffrage was introduced in 1893, but with a system of multiple votes: Certain criteria provided the richest electors with two or even three votes. In 1900, the majority voting system was replaced by proportional representation. The divisions within the electorate were now neatly reflected at the parliamentary level. Universal manhood suffrage was finally achieved in 1919. These last two reforms in particular had a profound influence on Belgian politics. The 'one man, one vote' system of 1919 combined with the proportional representation granted in 1900 meant that after the First World War none of the three major parties[3] succeeded in gaining

---

[3] After the First World War, other parties were created: a Communist party, whose parliamentary representation was negligible (expect for a few years after the Second World War); in Flanders, there were some successive (small) Flemish nationalist parties.

an absolute majority in parliament.[4] Henceforth, in order to form the inevitable coalition governments, two of the three leading parties – the Catholics/Christian-Democrats, the Liberals and the Socialists – or even all three, had to make compromises. This led to the development of a specific political culture of 'pacification democracy' in which party elites negotiated encompassing and complicated deals to solve delicate issues, including the decolonisation process (1959–60).

One of Belgium's particularities is, of course, its multi-lingual character. Both Flemish- and French-speaking people inhabit the country, each linguistic group residing in a specific region. But in the nineteenth century and until well into the twentieth, a tiny minority, especially the social and intellectual elite, also spoke French in Flanders. Moreover, when the Belgian state was created in 1830, French was always used for public and administrative affairs. A struggle against French language domination began a few years after the creation of Belgium. Its significance has changed over time. In the beginning, a number of Flemish middle-class citizens requested the recognition of the Flemish language in Flanders and that Flemish should be on an equal footing with French. Later on, towards the end of the nineteenth century, a growing number of people joined the Flemish movement, which gradually radicalized its demands. The moderate wing demanded unilingual Flemish administration in Flanders, while a radical fringe dreamt of breaking up the Belgian state and either making Flanders an independent state or creating an official link between Flanders and the Netherlands. During the inter-war period, several important laws were passed to establish Flemish as the only official language in Flanders.[5] Two crucial laws passed in 1962 and 1963 defined the linguistic border and the limits of the bilingual Brussels area. The next fundamental step – the gradual transformation of the unitary state into a federal state – was taken in 1970. In short, the nascent Belgian identity had to cope, from the late nineteenth century onwards, with the gradual rise of an alternative Flemish identity.

The Congo venture evolved when the transition towards mass democracy and a welfare state was already well on its way. We have to question whether the colonisation of the Congo influenced this transition. Furthermore, did the Congo affect the way political affairs were dealt with in Belgium? The king's special role in Belgian politics is especially relevant in the colonial issue; this aspect will of course be examined carefully. And, finally, was there any relationship between Belgium's colonial activities and the complex problem of national identity?

---

[4] This happened only once, in 1950, when the Catholic Party gained the absolute majority in both chambers. In 1958, the same party again obtained the absolute majority, but only in one of the two chambers.
[5] French of course was the only official language in the southern part, Wallonia. The country's centre region, Brussels, became a bilingual entity.

The Congo Free State and Belgium's Domestic Policy (1885–1908)

The Introduction of the Congo into the Belgian Political Arena

The Congo entered the Belgian political arena very unobtrusively through discreet contacts among the political elite. Little by little, awareness of the Congo extended to other circles until it became the subject of open controversy. When Leopold II was manoeuvreing in Africa at the end of the 1870s, he knew he could not rely on the support of the Liberal head of government, Walthère Frère-Orban, who believed that the king's *private* initiatives in Africa were of no concern to Belgium.[6] But then in 1884, Belgian politics was radically altered by the electoral victory of the Catholic Party, which would remain in power for the next three decades. This new order was a godsend for the king's African enterprise. The opposition of the former Liberal leader no longer mattered. The new prime minister, Jules Malou, was no more in favour of granting official support to Leopold II's Congolese venture than Frère-Orban had been, but he was certainly interested in the Congo as a private affair.[7]

Then, just at the right moment for the king's Congolese ambitions, the political situation changed again. Malou's cabinet was dissolved in the aftermath of the School War, which had divided the Catholics and the Liberals for a long time. The king, by demanding the resignation of two 'ultra-Catholic' ministers, played a decisive role in this event. Was the Congo part of Leopold's political agenda when he dismissed Malou's government, a government that did not support his colonial initiatives? Historians remain divided on this subject.[8] Certainly, the new Catholic prime minister, Auguste Beernaert, proved to be extremely supportive of the king's African ambitions. His support was a decisive factor in the success of the Congolese enterprise. Beernaert facilitated the royal enterprises on a diplomatic level at the Conference of Berlin. When the Congo Free State was officially founded, Beernaert brought the subject of the Congo to the forefront of Belgian politics.

Meanwhile, Belgium was gradually forming ties with the Congo Free State. Belgian soldiers were made available to the Congo. Volunteers supposedly seconded to the Institut cartographique militaire actually entered Leopold's service. This practice, inaugurated before the foundation of the Congo Free State, increased after 1885. That same year, Leopold received authorisation to become the sovereign of the Congo Free State, a separate political entity. The Belgian parliament unenthusiastically voted in favour of this law. Although the Belgian king had become the head of another state, Belgium theoretically was in no way responsible for the latter.

---

[6] N. Lubelski-Bernard, *Léopold II et le cabinet Frère-Orban (1878–1884). Correspondance entre le Roi et ses ministres* (Brussels, 1983), pp. 70–81.
[7] A. Roeykens, *Jules Malou et l'oeuvre congolaise de Léopold II (1876–1886)* (Brussels, 1962), p. 94.
[8] J. Stengers, "Léopold II et le cabinet Malou (juin-octobre 1884)", in E. Lamberts & J. Lory, eds., *1884: un tournant politique en Belgique* (Brussels, 1986), pp. 165–75 and 199–200.

Financial ties were created when, from 1885 onwards, the Congo experienced enormous financial difficulties. The king, constantly short of money, asked for financial support from the Belgian state and Beernaert supported these ever-increasing demands for money. A law dated 29 April 1887 authorised the issuing of a loan of 150 million francs from Belgium to the Congo Free State, but this initiative had only very limited success. On 29 July 1889 things went a step further: The Belgian state participated in the foundation of a Congolese company, the Compagnie du Chemin de Fer du Congo (CFC), which would be responsible for the construction and exploitation of the railway between Léopoldville and Matadi. This was not a trivial decision: The authorities invested ten million francs in a risky affair for which a handful of reticent private investors were only providing fifteen million. The authorities had, probably without knowing it, inaugurated a system of collaboration between the private and public sectors that would play a crucial role in the history of the Congo. In 1890, the Congo asked Belgium for another twenty-five million francs in an interest-free loan to be repaid over a period of ten years. In comparison, the total tax revenues of the Belgian state for the same year amounted to just 115 million francs. In order to ward off the MPs' negative reactions, and with the king's agreement, Beernaert revealed Leopold's will, in which the king bequeathed the Congo to Belgium after his death. The loan was approved by law on 4 August 1890. The terms were that, if the Congo had not repaid the debt after ten years, Belgium would be authorised to annex the Free State. Another clause forbade Leopold from undertaking any new financial commitments without the agreement of the Belgian state.

In the meantime, other forces were supporting activities in the Congo. During the 1880s, the first 'Congolese networks' essential for the realisation of Leopold's project were founded in Belgium, mainly by the king himself. Most of the colonial interest groups owed their existence (or at least their origin) to Leopold II. The essential point, stressed by historian Jean Stengers, is that without the king's personal involvement, colonialism would never have taken root in Belgium. Only Leopold's symbolic, political and financial leverage could achieve this outcome.

Leopold encouraged, not without some difficulty, the creation of the first private Belgian companies in the Congo. Colonel Albert Thys, his collaborator from the beginning, mobilised a number of financiers to found the Compagnie du Congo pour le Commerce et l'Industrie (CCCI) in 1886. Many other organisations would spring from the CCCI. The chambers of commerce, particularly in Antwerp, also began to support colonial activity. Nevertheless, the country's main capitalist forces, the major banks, kept their distance from the colonial movement for many years.

The church also supported the colonial venture. Leopold distrusted the foreign Protestant missionaries already present in the Congo; in order to maintain the Belgian character of his enterprise, he encouraged Catholic missions to evangelise the region. Finally, numerous associations such as friendly societies, study circles or lobby groups were created to defend and propagate colonial ideals. There were, for example, the Cercle africain (1890), the Société d'Études coloniales (1894) and the Comité d'Action pour l'œuvre nationale africaine (1895), among others. A press network was created, with the Congo as the principle subject. Among numerous publications, *Le Mouvement géographique* stands out as the unofficial mouthpiece of the group founded by Colonel Thys. Various authors, sometimes paid from the king's private funds, wrote newspaper articles and numerous, often repetitive brochures extolling the virtues of the Congo Free State. They tried to arouse enthusiasm for a royal initiative that, until now, had at best met with indifference; at worst, with sarcasm, distrust or hostility.

Belgian Political Struggles with the Congolese Question before the Takeover of 1908

Two events were soon to shake the political world and the young Belgian colonial lobby. In 1892, the king introduced the domanial system described earlier. He thereby contravened the spirit of the Berlin Act and seriously disrupted the activities of private companies. The Belgian colonial milieu was divided. One part disassociated itself from the king and began to pursue its own objectives. The Thys group, under threat, acted against the royal initiative. Politicians such as Prime Minister Beernaert disagreed with the king's policy and other faithful collaborators followed suit. The king was inflexible: He mercilessly cast aside his former right-hand men and continued to move forward. The financial problems rapidly returned.[9] Overwhelmed by a chronic lack of money, the king failed to respect his commitment of 1890. In 1894, without the knowledge of the Belgian government, he elaborated new financial structures that would allow him to bail out the Congo Free State. However, the government (at that point led by Jules de Burlet) got wind of these manoeuvres. The ministers were opposed to royal projects that might compromise the Congo, since it could very well be handed over to Belgium in the near future. The government therefore proposed to take over the Congo in advance. An agreement was prepared for this purpose and the king, forced into a corner, accepted.

Then suddenly, through one of those reversals at which he was so adept, Leopold had a change of heart that embarrassed the pro-colonial pressure groups that had been leading the campaign for the annexation of the Congo. The domanial system (based, as we have seen, on forced labour) had, in the meantime, become extremely profitable. The king no longer wanted to let go of 'his' Congo. Through a number of skilful manoeuvres, he orchestrated a complete reversal in the government. The ministers renounced the idea of an early takeover of the Congo Free State. They submitted a new bill to parliament that would grant a new loan of 6.8 million francs to the Congo and at the same time abandoned their right to examine the Congo Free State's financial activities

---

[9] J. Stengers, "La première tentative de reprise du Congo par la Belgique (1894-1895)", *Bulletin de la Société royale belge de Géographie*, 73, 1-2 (1949), pp. 43-122.

(Law of 29 June, 1895). Only one minister, Henri de Mérode Westerloo, minister of foreign affairs, balked at this reversal and resigned.

From then on, the Congo Free State was financially viable and the king no longer intended to relinquish it even after the ten-year period provided for in the law of 1890. Belgium was entitled to take back the Congo in 1901 if the loan had not been repaid. Since the loan never was repaid, part of the Belgian colonial milieu once again brought up the subject of recovery. They wanted to put an end to a royal policy in the Congo that was both uncontrollable and dangerous. Beernaert, former ally of the king, submitted a private bill to the legislative assemblies concerning the annexation by Belgium of the Congo Free State within two years. By methods that aroused great agitation within political circles, the king torpedoed this initiative. During the parliamentary commission's session, Charles Woeste, a great adversary of Beernaert within the Catholic Party, read publicly a letter he had received from Leopold in which the king announced that he would refuse to collaborate in any transition between the former Congo Free State regime and the new Belgian colonial regime. The king justified his refusal to entrust the Congo to Belgium by arguing that the country was not 'mature' enough to manage a colony and take over the Congo Free State. Beernaert was forced to withdraw his bill and Belgium's second attempt to annex the Congo failed. There were still many fierce political battles to come before the successful third attempt at annexation.

In the course of fifteen years (1885–1900), the Congo had become an increasingly important issue in Belgian politics. The colonial problem, which had initially only affected relations between top politicians, the king and a handful of his collaborators, was now discussed in parliament, among the political parties and by the general public. The establishment of laws gradually required the mobilisation of parliamentarians, the party machinery and the press. Leopold II and his close collaborators skilfully exploited the divisions and ambitions of the deputies and senators in an attempt to win public opinion favourable to their cause. The groups they had set up directly or indirectly (economic interests, scientific societies, etc.) began to gain influence and the colonial 'spirit' created by Leopold began to infiltrate Belgian society. When these pro-colonial circles divided and opposed each other, even in the parliamentary arena, the Congolese question led to even greater repercussions.

The major Belgian political movements reacted in very different ways and the highly politicised press reflected this high level of diversity. The Socialist Party, present in parliament beginning in 1894, was clearly opposed to colonialism, believing that this militaristic capitalist venture was nothing more than a huge waste of money when the Belgian working classes were suffering. Their criticism included a humanitarian dimension, as shown by the parliamentary interventions of the great Socialist leader, Émile Vandervelde, who attacked the inhumane practices of the Congo Free State.[10] The Radicals (progressive Liberals) were also opposed to colonialism along similar arguments. They too

[10] J. Polasky, *The Democratic Socialism of Émile Vandervelde* (Oxford-Washington, 1995), pp. 53–82.

rejected the annexation of the Congo.[11] A 'congophobe' or anti-Congo current appeared in Belgian politics and public opinion. However, a *congolâtre* or pro-Congo movement was also developing and eventually became dominant, at least among the political, social and intellectual elites.[12] Some conservative Liberals espoused traditional liberal anti-colonialism, but the great majority gradually adopted a positive attitude towards the Congo, even if they did not actually support the king. Some sided with the colonials who opposed the Congo Free State. The Catholic Party was also divided: The Belgian Catholic Church supported King Leopold's venture, but some Christian-Democrat politicians did not; not only for similar reasons as those of the other progressive forces, but also for electoral reasons. The Congo was not popular among the working classes. In an election, these voters would likely abandon an overtly pro-colonial Catholic Party and join the Socialists or Radicals. Historian Vincent Viaene stresses the fact that "[In] reality, the rank and file of the [Catholic] party were often hostile to the Congo".[13] However, the majority of Catholic politicians followed the party leaders who were favourable to colonialism. They fluctuated according to the balance of power between the pro- and anti-Leopoldist camps. This political situation explains why the different Congolese financial laws of 1889, 1890 and 1895 received a large majority of votes with, in the end, very little Catholic and Liberal opposition.

Between 1876 and 1908, Leopold invested a great deal of energy and money in his African enterprise. At certain moments, he became very discouraged. In 1886, for instance, vexed by his personal financial difficulties and distressed about the lack of support from Belgium's politicians, he considered abdicating. But the Congo also affected Belgian politics in more subtle ways. Inevitably, Leopold's role as head of the Belgian state was influenced by his Congolese activities and this may well have played a particular role in affairs that, at first sight, had nothing to do with the Congo. The king actively intervened in defence policy and in economic and transport matters. He also arbitrated constantly between parties, party factions or key political figures. While doing so, it is likely that he kept the Congolese dimension in mind. Gaining the support of any minister or party (or party faction) for the Congo could require concessions in another domain. Defence is a good case in point for, at crucial moments, in order to safeguard support for his Congo policy, Leopold did not push military reform, although he was in favour of it.[14] Of course, this also worked the other way round: Politicians would give in to Leopold's colonial whims in order to obtain royal support in other matters.

---

[11] A. Lumenganeso, "La question du Congo et les libéraux progressistes belges (1895–1896)", *Études d'Histoire africaine*, 4 (1972), pp. 243–73.

[12] V. Viaene, "King Leopold's Imperialism and the Origins of the Belgian Colonial Party, 1860–1905", *Journal of Modern History*, 80, December 2008, pp. 764–71.

[13] Ibid., pp. 771–2.

[14] L. De Vos, *Het effectief van de Belgische krijgsmacht en de militiewetgeving, 1830–1914* (Brussels, 1985), pp. 261, 275.

Towards the Annexation of the Congo by Belgium in 1908

Between 1885 and 1900, the Congolese issue flared up at key moments. But at the beginning of the new century, the atmosphere changed as the international campaign against Leopold II increased. This had repercussions in Belgium. Some factions of the Belgian press and, increasingly, public opinion, were strongly opposed to the Congo Free State policy. Parliamentarians protested against inhumane practices in Leopold's African state and the Congo became a divisive issue in Belgian domestic politics. According to the government, only a takeover by the Belgian state could solve the problem. The ministers therefore pressed the sovereign to agree to the transfer of the Congo. But the ageing and stubborn king dug in his heels. Finally, in December 1906, he accepted the annexation, but only after foreign powers had threatened to convene an international conference on the Congo.

The Belgian parliament started to elaborate basic legislation for the future Belgian colony, a long and difficult process.[15] A first draft of the so-called Colonial Charter had already been written in 1901, but with an overtone of royal absolutism. As the situation evolved at the end of 1906, this absolutist slant had become unacceptable. Parliament therefore established a special commission responsible for preparing a new bill concerning the government of the Congo. This Commission des XVII gradually excluded all the provisions relating to royal domination. At the end of a fierce battle, Leopold II finally relinquished the crown domain that he had intended to keep for himself in the Congo. He wanted to exclude vast regions of the Congo from the government's control in order to sustain his fortune, which he used, among other things, to enrich Belgium. Congolese funds were already being used and would continue to be used, as far as he was concerned, to finance urban planning and the monumental projects that he tirelessly pursued. But, in the end, the colonial institutions created in the Colonial Charter well and truly constituted a break with the Leopoldian institutional system, much to the king's frustration.

At the time of the 1908 vote on annexation, the political divisions were almost identical to those we have just outlined. The political parties and the press influenced public opinion one way or another; meetings and pamphlets for or against the Congo increased. During the legislative elections in 1908 – the only Belgian vote in which the Congo truly represented a political stake – the Socialists who, with the Radicals, still firmly opposed annexation of the Congo, reaped the electoral gains from their anti-colonialist campaign. However, a number of Socialists did agree to annex the Congo. Their leader, Émile Vandervelde, believed that the country could (and should) play a humanitarian role with regard to the native population. This, in his opinion, justified Belgium in taking over the Congo. For the time being, however, he remained isolated within the party.[16] Only two Catholic MPs and half of the Liberals joined with the Socialists to reject the draft Charter (forty-eight votes against).

[15] J. Stengers, *Belgique et Congo: l'élaboration de la Charte coloniale* (Brussels, 1963), p. 253.
[16] J. Polasky, *The Democratic Socialism of Émile Vandervelde, op. cit.*, chapter 3.

Nearly all the Catholics and the other half of the Liberals approved it (ninety votes for, seven abstentions). On 15 November 1908, the Congo officially became a Belgian colony.

The Belgian Congo and the Belgian Domestic Political Scene (1908–1958)

The impact of the Belgian Congo on Belgian political life can be researched on a number of levels: first, within the structural framework of the Belgian political institutions; second, within the government, parliament and the parties – the 'everyday life' of the politicians; and finally, within the electoral struggles and public discourse. While these distinctions appear somewhat artificial, they will, nevertheless, make it easier to define the Congo's impact on Belgium. The colony left minimal structural traces on the country's institutional landscape (first level) and it barely touched the political conscience and behaviour of the broader categories of the Belgian population (third level). The Congo was present mainly at the second level, in the everyday political practice of the major players. But even at this intermediary level, the Congo occupied only a marginal place in Belgian domestic politics from 1908 to 1958 – with one major exception: At the beginning of the Second World War in 1940, the colony played an essential role in the continuity of governmental power.

The Colonial Institutions in Belgium
The annexation of the Congo required the construction of a new governing body. In the Congo itself, the colonial civil service was being set up. Though the administrative machinery in Africa was quite modest, employing only 1,885 civil servants in 1922 and 3,208 by 1947, it obviously played an essential role in the colony itself. In Belgium, however, the ministry of the colonies had little influence on the administrative structure. This situation was similar to the British and French experiences; even in these powerful imperial nations the colonial ministries did not carry much weight.[17] The metropolitan civil service of the former Congo Free State only had some dozen employees. Gradually, the new Belgian ministry of the colonies grew, but even by the 1950s, it only employed approximately 500 civil servants.[18] Transformed in 1958 into the 'Ministry of the Belgian Congo and Ruanda-Urundi', it served as the starting point for the new co-operation administration set up in the first half of the 1960s. This, together with the National Lottery, created in 1933 as the 'Colonial Lottery', along with a handful of scientific institutions, is one of the rare lasting traces of the Congo on the Belgian institutional landscape.

---

[17] R. Aldrich, *Greater France: A History of French Overseas Expansion* (New York, 1996), p. 109; A. S. Thompson, *The Empire Strikes Back? The Impact of Imperialism on Britain from the Mid-Nineteenth Century* (Harlow-London, 2005), p. 126.
[18] J. Van Hove, *Histoire du Ministère des Colonies* (Brussels, 1968), p. 94.

Contrary to the situation in France, where the turmoil in colonial Algeria played a key role in the foundation of the Fifth Republic, the Belgian constitutional structure was left untouched by colonialism. The only mark the Congo left on Belgium's fundamental legislation dated from 1893, many years before the takeover of the Congo by the Belgian state, but in preparation for this possibility. At that time, the constitution was undergoing modification to introduce plural universal suffrage, but a clause was added to Article 1 stating: "The colonies, overseas possessions or protectorates that Belgium might acquire are ruled by separate laws. The Belgian troops intended for their defence can only be recruited on a voluntary basis". This provision reflected Belgium's vivid defiance of colonial ventures at that time. In 1953 and 1954, Belgian political circles envisaged revising the constitution to make the Congo an integral part of Belgium (as Algeria had been considered as part of France prior to 1962, not as a 'colony'). This plan was conceived in the context of the growing international criticism of colonialism, but it was thwarted due to legal problems.[19] Soon afterwards, as the political situation changed rapidly at the end of the 1950s, the idea was abandoned altogether. Stressing the unity of Belgium with the Congo had become untenable by then.

With the annexation of the Congo, a new cabinet post of minister of colonies was created. Within the government, his status was identical to that of his colleagues. Between 1908 and 1960 – the Belgian colonial period lasted exactly fifty-two years – twenty-three different people occupied this post (see Appendix 1). On average, there was a new minister every twenty-six to twenty-seven months! However, these averages hide widely divergent situations. Several ministers of colonies were truly ephemeral: They only occupied their post for a few months, weeks or even days. Others stayed in office for many years. Jules Renkin managed the department for a decade (1908–18); Louis Franck for almost six years (1918–24); Albert De Vleeschauwer for seven years (1938–45); and André Dequae for four years (1950–4), a similar tenure to that of his political adversary Auguste Buisseret (1954–8). It should be emphasised that exceptional circumstances such as setting up the management of the colony or the outbreak of the two World Wars partially explain these variances. On the other hand, the race for independence created a different situation: Beginning in May 1960, no less than three different men simultaneously oversaw the colony's destiny.

Generally, the post of colonial minister did not carry much political clout. The colonial portfolio was not considered as the zenith of a ministerial career. It was often entrusted to a new, relatively young figure put there to prove his worth. However, there are nuances. Some of these junior ministers did indeed go on to fine careers after serving their time in the ministry of the colonies, among them Pierre Wigny and André Dequae in the 1950s and 1960s. In other cases, key figures were called in to manage the colony. Henri Jaspar, for

---

[19] AGR, Minutes of the Cabinet Meetings (MCM), 19 June 1953, p. 19 (available through the website of the state archives in Belgium at http:// extranet.arch.be/lang_pvminister.html).

instance, held the post while simultaneously serving as prime minister between 1927 and 1931. Auguste Buisseret, already a member of the cabinet many times over between 1945 and 1950, served as minister of colonies between 1954 and 1958. Finally, August De Schryver, an old sage from the Christian-Democrat Party, led the Congo to independence in 1959 and 1960. Still, a number of the incumbents were 'technicians', people who did not belong to the political seraglio and did not hold an elected post. These ministers, supposedly above the party fray, never lasted long but were replaced after a few months.[20] The majority of colonial ministers were thus thoroughbred politicians, party men. But to which party did they belong? In total, the Catholics were in charge of colonial policy for 487 months, the Liberals for 133 months and the Socialists for ... a week. This Catholic domination was reflected in the appointment of governors-general, the representatives of central power in the Congo. Only a handful belonged to a non-Catholic party or were 'neutral'.[21] The administration of the ministry of the colonies in Brussels was also considered a bastion of Catholicism.

Decision Making in Colonial Matters
Compared with other issues in Belgian political life, the colony stood out owing to the significant weight of the private players, especially the major business circles and the Roman Catholic Church. This particularity was linked to the situation in the Congo. The Catholic missions and big companies played a crucial role in the colony; they often found themselves in a sub-contracting situation vis-à-vis the public authorities. The church, for instance, was in charge of education and healthcare. Furthermore, the state and business interests were connected through numerous personal ties.[22] In Brussels, colonial decision making was the privilege of a limited number of people who moved in informal circles.[23] A handful of top officials, businessmen, politicians and clergymen had privileged access to the elaboration of colonial policy, which mostly took place behind closed doors. This did not prevent friction: The minister of colonies, big business and the church did not always agree. Far from it! Some disagreements were the focus of often tenacious struggles.

This fundamental situation explains the relatively modest role played by traditional institutions and political parties. The Colonial Charter did, however,

[20] Paul Charles (minister for a few months in 1931 and from 1934 to 1935) was a high-ranking civil servant at the ministry of the colonies; Gaston Heenen, former vice governor-general of the Congo, became minister in 1939 for less than eight weeks; Léo Pétillon, a former governor-general, managed the department in 1958 for barely four months; Walter Ganshof van der Meersch was present in the government, with two colleagues, to lead the Congo to independence between May and July 1960.
[21] Félix Fuchs (1912–16); Maurice Lippens (1921–3); Eugène Jungers (1946–52). Hendrik Cornelis was labelled a 'Socialist' (1958–60).
[22] Colonial businesses were grouped together in an organisation founded in 1915, the Association des Intérêts coloniaux belges.
[23] J.-L. Vellut, "Hégémonies en construction: articulations entre État et entreprises dans le bloc colonial belge (1908–1960)", *Revue canadienne d'Études africaines*, 16, 2 (1982), pp. 313–30.

provide an essential role for parliament. In 1908, democratic control over the executive power – at the time, over Leopold II's policy – was of great concern. But it soon appeared that the Congo did not play a big part in parliamentary debates. Only a few colonial 'specialists' participated in these rare discussions, which were essentially devoted to the examination of the colonial budgets. Was the subject too technical? Was there a lack of interest among the majority of elected members? Possibly. But there was also the more fundamental reason that the government wanted to keep parliament at a safe distance. Colonial matters, it was thought, should not be discussed along party lines.[24] A few MPs complained about this attitude.[25] Sometimes, when a fiery interpellation was held, the Congo indeed caused a stir in parliament; but these incidents were rather exceptional. Parliament was clearly not the place to elaborate the colonial policy. A similar situation existed in France and Great Britain, where colonial matters were also not a prominent topic of parliamentary discussion.[26]

Yet even within the government, the Congo did not get a great deal of attention. Before the end of the 1950s, there are few written records of lengthy fundamental discussions dedicated to colonial problems.[27] This confirms the preceding claim that colonial policy was, above all, a domain that involved only a few select circles within the periphery of the cabinet of the minister of colonies. Of course, the government ultimately took decisions on the issues under discussion, but by the time these ended up on the cabinet's table, the most important part of the decision making process had already taken place elsewhere.

The relative lack of interest of parliament and the government in colonial affairs both determined and reflected the very modest role of the Congo in political programmes and party activities. The organisation of a 'colonial section' during the 1923–4 congresses of the Catholic Party met with very little success.[28] In 1930, the Liberal Party created a colonial commission that functioned for several months before petering out. Within the Socialist Party, a similar organ was set up in 1929. Shortly thereafter, its activity was severely reduced, but it was revived and took a more active role after the Second World War.[29] The former Catholic Party was replaced by the Parti Social Chrétien – Christelijke Volkspartij (PSC-CVP, the Christian-Democrat Party) in 1945. The new party immediately established a colonial commission responsible for drawing up its Congolese policy.[30] Even the small Belgian Communist Party had its own

---

[24] AGR, MCM, 25 May 1951, p. 11.
[25] K. Van Nieuwenhuyse, *Tussen buit en baat. Congo in het interbellum* (Leuven, 2009), pp. 77, 80.
[26] M. Michel, "La colonisation", in J.-F. Sirinelli, ed., *Histoire des droites en France. Volume 3. Sensibilités* (Paris, 1992), p. 141, 150. A. S. Thompson, *The Empire, op. cit.*, p. 127.
[27] AGR, MCM, 1915–59.
[28] Kadoc (Documentatie- en Onderzoekscentrum voor Religie, Cultuur en Samenleving, Leuven), L. Delvaux Papers, n° 1.5.3.3 and 1.6.2.12/1.
[29] G. Vanthemsche, "De Belgische socialisten en Congo 1895–1960", *Brood en Rozen*, 4, 2 (1999), pp. 31–65.
[30] Kadoc, Cepess Archives, n° 1.8.4, 2.4.7, 2.4.12.

colonial commission (created circa 1946).[31] Clearly, once the Second World War ended, the various Belgian parties had a renewed interest in the Congo.

In Britain and France, the colonial impact on domestic politics seems to have been greater. Andrew Thompson, in particular, has pointed to some structural effects of empire on British politics. Even if, at first sight, the colonies were barely present in Britain's parliament, they did have some influence on the dynamics of party politics, on the rise of new forms of political mobilisation and participation and even on electoral reform. Empire also played a role in the process of social reform and the introduction of a welfare policy at the turn of the twentieth century.[32] In France, the colonies impacted party life, the institutional architecture and its functions.[33] Colonial expansion was one of the ideological tools used by the young Third Republic to justify its legitimacy.[34] In political life, the so-called *parti colonial* brought together MPs with different perspectives along with several organisations, all lobbying for a more active colonial policy; though their influence was on the wane during the inter-war period.[35] The colonial question played an essential role in the political life of the Fourth Republic, and the painful Algerian war ultimately contributed to a regime change – the creation of the Fifth Republic.[36]

In Belgium, things were quite different. Party structures and programmes were never affected by colonial questions. Before 1908 there was a pro-colonial current in Belgian politics. Afterwards, many extra-parliamentary, pro-colonial organisations came into being, but no equivalent to the French 'colonial party' ever took form in Belgium. The few MPs who specialised in colonial matters did not constitute a specific political current in any sense due to the façade of colonial consensus. According to a generally accepted slogan, "politics had to be kept out of the colony". Before the 1950s, the Congo was never politicised by the traditional parties. Disagreements on specific policy issues existed, but most of the time they were kept inside the inner political circle.

In the great reforms of Belgian political life, the colonial dimension played no part. When the heated debates regarding suffrage flared up in the 1880s and 1890s, the issue of the Congo slowly began to creep into the political debate. Indeed, both problems evolved simultaneously until they were resolved

---

[31] T. Masschaele, *De activiteiten van de Communistische Partij van België m.b.t. Belgisch Congo (1945–1960)* (Brussels, 2002) unpublished master's thesis in history, Vrije Universiteit Brussel (VUB), p. 185.

[32] A. S. Thompson, *Imperial Britain, op. cit.*, esp. pp. 59, 189–95; A. S. Thompson, *The Empire, op. cit.*, chapter 6; C. Hall, K. McClelland & J. Rendall, *Defining the Victorian Nation. Class, Race, Gender and the Reform Act of 1867* (Cambridge, 2000).

[33] C. Liauzu, ed. *Dictionnaire de la colonisation française* (Paris, 2007), p. 20.

[34] O. Le Cour Grandmaison, *La République impériale. Politique et racisme d'état* (Paris, 2009), pp. 8–21.

[35] S. M. Persell, *The French Colonial Lobby 1889–1938* (Stanford, 1983), pp. 140–58; Ch.-R. Ageron, *France coloniale ou parti colonial?* (Paris, 1978); M. Lagana, *Le Parti colonial français. Eléments d'histoire* (Québec, 1990).

[36] J. Thobie, G. Meynier, C. Coquery-Vidrovitch & Ch.-R. Ageron, *Histoire de la France coloniale 1914–1990* (Paris, 1990), chapters 19–27.

without having any connection to each other. Likewise, the gradual introduction of the Belgian welfare state from the 1890s to 1944 was never influenced by the colonial problem[37], contrary to what happened in Britain.[38] In Belgium, the political and ideological struggle for or against social legislation never referred to the colonial dimension. There was only one marginal exception: Before 1908, anti-colonialist politicians sometimes argued that it was scandalous to squander money in the Congo when so many social needs existed at home.

The Consensus on the Basic Principles of the Belgian Colonial Policy

With regard to the main principles of the colonial doctrine, there was great consensus between the various political factions. All the parties accepted the validity of Belgian sovereignty in the Congo. Moreover, as this civilising mission was a strictly *national* undertaking, it had to be defended against any foreign interference. This point was particularly important in Belgium's foreign policy. Official Belgium wanted to absolutely prove its 'colonising aptitude', which was often questioned abroad. Being able to teach the others a lesson in good colonial practices was one of the *leitmotifs* of Belgian political leaders. This attitude left little space for internal doctrinal debates, but plenty of room for pragmatic considerations. From 1908 until 1940, attention was above all focused on the establishment and the deepening of Belgian colonial order in the Congo. The notion of a possible post-colonial order was non-existent before the Second World War. The problem of the institutional dynamics of the Congo and its relations with Belgium only arose after 1945.

The task of colonising the Congo was enormous, a common viewpoint being that the Congolese populations, whose heavy burden Belgium had assumed, were among the most primitive on the planet. But Belgium lacked neither ambition nor confidence in its own abilities. The results, gained little by little, inspired Belgian nationalism. The Congo rapidly began to occupy a prime position in official patriotic discourse. The Belgian coloniser wanted to reach out to broad categories of the population before he envisaged the creation of a Congolese elite. In this, the missions played an essential role: In the field, they managed the education, spiritual and corporal welfare of the natives. Therefore, their activities were an integral part of the Belgian colonial system. In principle, these activities were even accepted by those in Belgium who labelled themselves as anti-clericals. Finally, the Congo was presented and promoted as a source of enrichment for Belgium. The spectacular Belgian economic achievements in the heart of Africa reinforced this perception.

This consensus may appear strange considering the fierce opposition of the Socialists to the annexation before 1908. In fact, the Socialist Party rapidly abandoned its opposition to colonialism and came to accept and support the existence of the Belgian Congo. At the very most, the Socialists defended a

---

[37] G. Vanthemsche, *La sécurité sociale. L'origine du système belge* (Brussels, 1994).
[38] A. S. Thompson, *The Empire, op. cit.*, p. 144.

'reformist' version of colonial policy, placing greater emphasis on the necessary 'social progress' of the indigenous populations. Some Socialists even went a step further in accepting colonialism. Under the auspices of the Banque belge du Travail, a financial institution founded by the Ghent Socialists in 1913, a group of 'red factories' had been created, for example, in the textile sector. This group also developed enterprises in the Congo, especially plantations. Thus a faction of the Belgian labour movement had become a colonial entrepreneur! On rare occasions, humanitarian concerns rose to the surface, especially between 1930 and 1932, when Émile Vandervelde yet again raised his voice in parliament to denounce the labour policy and the bloody repression of revolts in the Congo. Left-wing members of the Socialist Party sometimes criticised Belgium's involvement in the Congo, but they were only on the fringe. In fact, the Congo was the least of the Socialist Party's worries. At regular intervals, however, the party did discreetly insist (mostly unsuccessfully) on better representation of the Socialists within the Belgian colonial machinery.

The small Communist Party, created in 1921, was clearly anti-colonial, criticising Belgian oppression of the Congolese people.[39] It tried, unsuccessfully, to foment trouble among black sailors working on the maritime line between Belgium and the Congo. These efforts, of course, aroused mistrust among the political authorities but their fear was totally disproportionate to the true influence – that is, none whatsoever – of the Communists both in the Congo and on Belgium's colonial policy. Between 1945 and 1950, the Communists temporarily changed their attitude – even referring to the colony as 'our' Congo, as did the other parties – before switching, once again, to unambiguous anti-colonialism in the 1950s.

The Flemish nationalist parties were not particularly enthusiastic about the Belgian Congo because French was the dominant language in the colony. On the whole, they were only very marginally interested in colonial issues. When they mentioned the Congo, it was essentially to criticise discrimination against Flemings in colonial administration and public life, or to depict discrimination against the Flemish in Belgium as a form of internal colonialism.

Did anti-colonialism exist in Belgium outside the realm of party politics? In both Britain and France there were political and ideological currents critical of empire. Progressive intellectuals and artists, certain Labour leaders and (far) left-wing politicians and organisations actively opposed colonial rule via press organs, meetings, writings and so forth, but they were only a minority and their impact was not particularly significant.[40] This fringe group had some presence in British and French politics, but none whatsoever in Belgium where active

---

[39] T. Masschaele, *De activiteiten, op. cit.*; B. Verhaegen, "Communisme et anticommunisme au Congo (1920–1960)", *Brood en Rozen*, 4, 2 (1999), pp. 113–27; J.-L. Vellut, "Épisodes anti-communistes dans l'ordre colonial belge (1924–1932)", in J. Gotovitch & P. Delwit, eds., *La peur du Rouge* (Brussels, 1996), pp. 183–90.

[40] S. Howe, *Anticolonialism in British Politics: The Left and the End of Empire 1918–1964* (Oxford, 1993); C. Liauzu, *Histoire de l'anticolonialisme en France* (Paris, 2007); A. Biondi, *Les anticolonialistes (1881–1962)* (Paris, 1992).

Discreet Political Struggles Surrounding the Colonial Policy

Belgian political leaders agreed that the Congo had to remain outside Belgian political struggles. It would, nevertheless, be wrong to conclude that there was no controversy surrounding colonial policy. To start, the labour problem raised serious concerns in official Belgian circles in the 1920s. The incredible development of major capitalist companies had required the forced recruitment of a considerable number of black workers. When, between 1880 and 1920, the Congo seemed threatened by depopulation, official commissions examined the problem and, after mature reflection, created rules relating to the management of the labour force. But the problem didn't go away. Was the Congo developing too rapidly? Was the industrial option the best option? Wouldn't another, less brutal method of colonisation be preferable? A more agricultural option would leave the Congolese in their natural environment and would allow the foundations of Christian civilisation to be instilled in them. In the field, this 'indigenist' current was strong among missionaries and certain colonial civil servants, and it found an echo in Belgium. A Christian-Democrat inspired movement, including a number of Liberal and Socialist elements, opposed the powerful economic interests of the big private companies.

There were serious social abuses going on in the Congo. When news of these abuses arrived in Belgium, it fuelled the confrontation already taking place in the official and unofficial networks of Brussels. This confrontation re-emerged several times in Belgium's public sphere and evoked a number of seemingly disparate elements. Brochures and press articles advocated a reorientation of the colonial policy. Dissensions arose during the Colonial Council's debates. In 1933, Crown Prince Leopold gave a famous speech at the senate in which he acted as the defender of African agriculture and pleaded in favour of the creation of indigenous small holdings (*paysannats indigènes*). Questions were raised in parliament, especially by Vandervelde. Around 1933, Catholic politician Paul Crokaert undertook a campaign against the '*mur d'argent*' (wall of money) that was peripherally linked to his brief role as head of the ministry of the colonies (1931–2), during which time he came up against the great capitalist conglomerates. In 1934, Catholic senator Daniel Leyniers published a sensational parliamentary report in which he, too, attacked the all-powerful financial holdings in the colony. These frictions were in the background of 1930s politics but disappeared in the 1940s.

Another quarrel that continued throughout the history of the colony but which, instead of dying out, actually grew after the Second World War, related to the position of religious institutions, especially the Catholic missions, in the Belgian colonial system. In the Congo Free State, King Leopold wanted to both

---

[41] L. Kottos, *L'anticolonialisme de gauche en Belgique durant l'entre-deux-guerres (1917–1939)* (Brussels, 2006), unpublished master's thesis in history, ULB.

guarantee and reinforce the Belgian nature of his colony by sending over *Belgian* Catholic missionaries. They played an important role in colonial life and were strongly supported by the authorities at the time, and also after the annexation of the Congo by Belgium. This privileged position was a source of continuing friction between Catholics and anti-clericals in Belgium and the Congo. After 1908, tensions grew between the missions and Jules Renkin, the Catholic minister of colonies. Despite a certain understanding between the church and the colonial government, there were still clashes. Between 1921 and 1923, the so-called anti-missionary policy of the Liberal governor-general of the Congo, Maurice Lippens, was subject to public obloquy by the Belgian ecclesiastical authorities. His successor, Martin Rutten, disavowed Lippens's policy.

The balance always seemed precarious. Between 1945 and 1947, Liberal minister Robert Godding endeavoured to end the unfavourable position of the Protestant missions in the Congo; moreover, he laid the foundations for official philosophically and religiously neutral education for the whites in the colony. These measures sparked the hostility of the Belgian Catholic Church. A few years later, in 1953, the Belgian government (led by the PSC-CVP) developed a draft agreement between Belgium and the Vatican (a new concordat). This draft created problems with the Belgian anti-clerical movements on the basis that the text was too much in favour of the Roman Catholic Church. In 1954, the change of parliamentary majority prevented the adoption of this agreement *in extremis*. Revenge was not far behind: That same year, the Socialists and the Liberals formed a most unusual governmental coalition and drove the Christian-Democrat Party back into the opposition. In Belgium itself, numerous anti-clerical measures inflamed Catholic opinion, and this internal Belgian struggle extended to the Belgian Congo. Auguste Buisseret, the Liberal minister of colonies, reduced the subsidies for the missions and established a network of official schools for the Congolese. This time, the reaction was intense: a 'School War' started in the colony.[42]

Another bone of contention would arise in the Congo: the linguistic problem. In global colonial policy, this issue was not as important as those previously mentioned, but it nevertheless had a certain impact in Belgium and the Congo. In the nineteenth century, the Flemish language still suffered considerable discrimination in Belgium. By the beginning of the twentieth century, some advances had been made, but many more Flemish demands remained unfulfilled, which explains the particular linguistic situation in the Congo.[43] During

---

[42] J. Briffaerts, "De schoolstrijd in Belgisch-Congo (1930–1958)", in E. Witte, J. De Groof & J. Tyssens, eds., *Het schoolpact van 1958* (Brussels, 1999), pp. 331–58; M. Depaepe & L. Van Rompaey, *In het teken van de bevoogding. De educatieve actie in Belgisch-Kongo (1908–1960)* (Louvain, 1995), chapter 5; P. M. Boyle, "School Wars: Church, State, and the Death of the Congo", *Journal of Modern African Studies*, 33, 3 (September 1995), pp. 451–68.

[43] See B. Ceuppens, *Congo Made in Flanders?* (Ghent, 2003), pp. 175–238; E. Kets, *Kuifje & Tintin kibbelen in Afrika. De Belgische taalstrijd in Congo, Rwanda en Burundi* (Leuven, 2008); W. Geerts, "Kongo-Vlaanderen", in *Encyclopedie van de Vlaamse Beweging* (Tielt, 1973), vol. 1, pp. 798–801; W. Geerts & M. Ruys, "Kongo", in *Nieuwe Encyclopedie van de Vlaamse beweging* (Tielt, 1998), vol. 2, pp. 1741–4; P. Delforge, "Congo et mouvement wallon", in P. Delforge, Ph. Destatte & M. Libon, eds., *Encyclopédie du Mouvement wallon* (Charleroi, 2000), vol. 1, pp. 327–31.

the Leopoldian period, public life and communications were conducted exclusively in French. In 1908, when the Congo came under Belgian jurisdiction, the Colonial Charter provided for Flemish and French parity in the colony. In practice, though, Flemish was never used in public and administrative life in the Congo. Consequently, Flemish-born civil servants or employees had to use French in the administrations or enterprises where they worked. In the schools for expatriated Belgian children, French dominance was only gradually eroded. Within the civil service and among staff in the large private companies, the Flemings were underrepresented in the high-ranking positions. In the Congo, the use of Flemish was restricted to the sphere of family life and to friendly contacts between expats.

It is hard to know how many Flemings living in the Congo felt frustrated by this discrimination. After all, in the early years of colonisation, the same linguistic adjustment was more or less happening in Belgium. But gradually, as things began to change in Belgium, the continuing linguistic discrimination in the Congo became all the more visible – and intolerable – to a number of Flemings. It was actually during and after the Second World War that some of them began to react. First, they created associations and founded periodicals in order to stimulate the use of their language in cultural activities. It nevertheless remained a delicate issue to stress one's Flemish profile in the Congo, since this was generally seen as introducing Belgian 'quarrels' into the colonial setting, a domain where Belgian unity was not to be questioned. But by the end of the 1950s, some actions were indeed undertaken to create the linguistic equality in public and administrative life that had been proclaimed in the 1908 charter. In 1957, an official commission was created in order to prepare new linguistic rulings for the Congo. But opting for general (Flemish/French) bilingualism in administration and public life was seen as creating a major problem with respect to the Congolese. Would they have to learn *two* European languages in order to be admitted into the public services and administrations? This idea caused some opposition within the native population, who saw the Flemish demands as a new obstacle to their (already all too slow) admission to the public sphere.

The linguistic situation in the colony also had repercussions in Belgium. Flemish organisations criticised the discrimination in the Congo. Some politicians complained in parliament. Flemish-born ministers of colonies, such as Rubbens, De Vleeschauwer and Dequae, admitted that things had to change, but these complaints and declarations remained unheard until the very last years of colonial rule.

Clearly, consensus regarding a number of fundamental elements of the colonial doctrine did not prevent dissension concerning specific issues. The way in which these struggles were conducted did, however, differ from those concerning domestic problems. Silence and conformity reigned supreme among the white population in the Congo. Diverging opinions, judged to be 'dangerous', were not at all appreciated, particularly when they centred on anti-clericalism or progressivism. This attitude existed in Belgium, too, where divergences on the subject of colonial policy were rarely debated in public.

The political expression of Congolese problems did change after the Second World War. As we have just seen, the Belgian political parties set up or revived their internal colonial commissions. From then on, the Congo occupied a slightly more important place in the party activities. Hence, this politicisation of the colonial issue, although still marginal and late in coming, nevertheless represented a new challenge to the informal corridors of power and decision making occupied by private players such as the church and private capital. The extent of the anti-clerical and Flemish requirements after 1945 can therefore not be attributed to the 'export' of internal Belgian quarrels to an idyllic Congo, where these problems did not exist, but rather to the emergence in Belgium of political concepts and practices that gave new meaning to the Congolese problems.

The Impact of the Congo on the Belgian Monarchy, the Army and National Identity

Leopold II played a crucial role in the birth of the country's colonial adventure. Any analysis of the impact of the Congo on Belgium must therefore question the backlash colonialism had on the monarchy and on other key elements such as the army and Belgian nationalism. This question is at the centre of international research concerning the impact of the colony on the metropole. David Cannadine stressed the fact that, in Britain, the empire reinforced the hierarchical aspect of society; the monarchy played an important symbolic role in the empire.[44] By granting the British monarch the imperial crown of India, and through the crown's symbolic role in the commonwealth and many other mechanisms, the prestige of the monarchy was reinforced.[45] In the Netherlands, another colonising monarchy, the royal family was also identified with colonial empire.[46]

The situation was similar in Belgium. King Leopold was a highly controversial figure, even during his lifetime. Apart from his Congolese activities, many aspects of his personality invited criticism: his clear-cut character, his family difficulties, his private life and even his sexual habits. These negative aspects have never truly disappeared from the collective memory but, after the king's death, his 'great Congolese enterprise' served as a means of glorification. Official Belgium, including the royal family, used the Congo to restore and reinforce the image of the monarchy. Monuments, speeches, books and school curricula all turned the colony into a stepping stone for royal prestige.

The Congo was beneficial to the monarchy from a symbolic, but also from a material point of view. At the beginning of his Congolese adventure, King

---

[44] D. Cannadine, *Ornementalism: How the British Saw Their Empire* (London, 2001) p. 122.
[45] P. J. Marshall, "Imperial Britain", in P. J. Marshall, ed., *The Cambridge Illustrated History of the British Empire* (Cambridge, 1996), pp. 325–6; A. S. Thompson, *The Empire, op. cit.*, pp. 191–2; A. S. Thompson, *Imperial Britain, op. cit.*, p. 7.
[46] G. Oostindie, *De parels en de kroon. Het koningshuis en de koloniën* (Amsterdam, 2006).

Leopold II drew considerably on his vast personal fortune, causing him great financial difficulties.[47] However, the Congolese financial godsend, resulting particularly from the rubber boom, completely reversed the situation. His financial interests in the many private companies active in the colony, as well as the income from his private domain in the Congo, rapidly and considerably replenished the king's personal coffers. Leopold II not only restored but also *increased* his fortune thanks to the exploitation of the Congo.[48] Part of this money was used to finance major monumental and urban works in Belgium[49] and in 1901 he also donated considerable property (palaces, land, etc.) to the Belgian state. This property would be put, forever, at the disposal of his successors for free.[50] A special institution, the Donation royale (Royal Trust), was created to manage these properties. While Belgium's current royal family did not directly inherit the private fortune Leopold II accumulated from the Congo, it has benefitted indirectly through the properties bequeathed to the state.

The successors of Leopold II have always been concerned by his colonial legacy. His nephew Albert I (1909–34), Albert's son Leopold III (1934–40) and finally Leopold's son Baudouin (1950–92) all considered the Congo a fundamental element of Belgium's grandeur. This interest in the colony was first expressed through successive visits made by the sovereigns to the Congo, yet the founder of the Congo never actually went there himself. Shortly before Leopold's death in 1909, his nephew and successor, Prince Albert, had already undertaken a grand tour in the Congo.[51] He returned there in 1928 and again

---

[47] Towards the end of the 1870s, this fortune was estimated at FB 50 million, representing approximately FB 7 billion to 8 billion in 2000 (i.e. EUR 200 million in 2002). He invested approximately FB 10 million in Congolese activities between 1879 and 1885: Following the foundation of the Congo Free State, an appreciable share of his private fortune, FB 20 million, was used to form a 'Special African Fund'; a large part of this sum was spent on covering the expenses of the Congolese state.

[48] In 1908, just before his death, his *personal* fortune amounted to FB 50 million (excluding property, but including the deductions already made for urbanistic expenses and property donations to the Belgian state mentioned hereafter).

[49] See L. Ranieri, *Léopold II, urbaniste* (Brussels, 1973); L. Catherine, *Bouwen met zwart geld* (Antwerp, 2002); L. Catherine, *Promenade au Congo. Petit guide anticolonial de Belgique* (Brussels, 2010).

[50] Leopold II, who had no surviving son, just two daughters, only wanted to leave them a small part of his inheritance – the FB 15 million that he himself had inherited from his father, Leopold I. In fact, he wanted to avoid the dispersion of his increasing patrimony abroad. Clauses in his will, as well as obscure legal financial constructions (the so-called Fondation de Niederfullbach), led to lengthy lawsuits between the Belgian state and the daughters of the late king. J. Stengers, "Léopold II et le patrimoine dynastique", in *Bulletin de l'Académie royale de Belgique*, 58, 2–4 (1972), pp. 63–134; G. Kurgan, "La fortune privée de Léopold II", in G. Janssens & J. Stengers, eds., *Nouveaux regards sur Léopold Ier et Léopold II* (Brussels, 1997), pp. 171–85; G. Vanthemsche, "Le Congo et la fortune privée de Léopold II", in *Idem*, pp. 187–99; M. Reynebeau, *Het nut van het verleden* (Tielt, 2006), pp. 204–10 (he estimated the net profit of Leopold II in the Congo to be approximately worth half a billion euros by current standards).

[51] R. Buren, *Journal de route du prince Albert en 1909 au Congo* (Brussels, 2008).

in 1933.[52] His son, the future Leopold III, travelled there twice: in 1925 when he was twenty-four years old and again in 1933. Later, following his abdication in 1950, he visited the Congo on many occasions as a private citizen.[53] At the tender age of twenty-five – already king – his son Baudouin made his first visit to the colony. Another trip took place in the middle of the decolonisation crisis, in 1959. These princely and royal visits were a form of personal training, but they were also an opportunity to establish social contacts that were important to the colonial policy in general. Finally, they emphasised, to the world and the population of Belgium, the links between Belgium, the Congo and the monarchy.

Was the royal interest also of a more directly political nature? Did the kings intervene in actual colonial policy? Between 1885 and 1908, Leopold II obviously played a driving role in the Congo, since he was the absolute monarch. Clearly, his successors did not conduct such an active policy; constitutional rules prevented them from doing so. Nevertheless, they did have some room to manoeuvre, for example, playing a major role in nominating key figures to the colonial administration. In 1920, King Albert I took the initiative to organise a major Colonial Congress (Congrès colonial national), which brought together the lifeblood of national colonialism to glorify the Congolese enterprise and discuss colonial policy. In the following years, several other national colonial congresses were held. It is likely that the monarchs also influenced colonial decision making, but considering the highly restricted circle in which such decisions took place, little evidence remains. It is also difficult to form an idea of royal opinions concerning the colony. Thanks to his travel notes, we know that Albert, at least, was relatively critical of the living and working conditions of the Congolese population.[54] Several months before acceding to the throne, the future Leopold III also created a bit of a stir in colonial circles: The big companies did not appreciate his senatorial speech of 1933, which was mentioned previously. But his brief term as king (1934–40) did not allow him to leave any personal mark on colonial policy.

There is no doubt that the political and especially the symbolic position of the Belgian monarchy was strengthened by colonisation. Was the same true of the other major institution, the army? The dynasty and the armed forces had maintained special relations since Belgium's birth. Since then, successive sovereigns always considered defence as a domain in which they had a special role to play. But the army was not particularly cherished in Belgian politics. Its compulsory neutrality, imposed upon it by the great powers in 1831, was often used as an excuse for the meagre means allocated to the defence budget. And by force of circumstance, the Belgian army had few opportunities to

---

[52] P. Clement, "Het bezoek van Koning Albert aan Belgisch Congo, 1928. Tussen propaganda en realiteit", *Revue belge d'Histoire contemporaine*, 37, 1–2 (2007), pp. 175–221.

[53] Prince Regent Charles, the king's brother, who reigned in lieu of the king while the latter was unable to do so, visited the colony in turn in 1947.

[54] See R. Buren, *Journal, op. cit.* and P. Clement, "Het bezoek", art. cit.

shine on the battlefield. So did the Congo influence the somewhat confined position of the Belgian army? Yes, the activities in the Congo had a definite, though indirect, influence on the Belgian army right from the beginning. To please the king, the Belgian state set up a system that allowed Belgian soldiers to be brought into the Congo on an unofficial basis. Any officers and non-commissioned officers (active or reserve) who wanted to serve the Congolese enterprise of their own free will were temporarily assigned to the Institut cartographique militaire. This body, part of the army, made volunteers available to the king's African venture: They were enlisted in the Force publique, the colonial military apparatus responsible for both conquering and defending the country and maintaining internal law and order.[55] After one or more tours in the Congo, these men returned as members of the Belgian army – unless they decided to leave the ranks definitively to engage in another career, often linked to the colony. The Force publique also included a fair number of foreigners, primarily Scandinavians.

An essential fact is that this separate military force was maintained after the Congo was taken over by the Belgian state. In other words, the Belgian army was never involved as such in the Congo, even after 1908; the conquest of the Congo, the so-called pacification, the maintenance of law and order and the defence of the colonial territory were always managed by a special military apparatus. Furthermore, it is necessary to remember that the constitution (modified in 1893) forbade the use of Belgian soldiers in the colonies unless they were volunteers. This clear separation between the Belgian and Congolese military services had several major consequences. First of all, the Congo never had any impact whatsoever on Belgium's defence budget. Belgian taxpayers never had to assume the expenses associated with the military aspects of colonialism.[56] It was only during the Cold War that the Belgian army built military bases in the Congo, in Kamina and Kitona. The first Belgian soldiers – as, strictly speaking, representatives of the Belgian army – only arrived in the colony in 1953! This was completely different from the experiences of other colonial powers. In Great Britain, for instance, budgetary expenses incurred by the vast military apparatus aimed at conquering, then defending, the immense British Empire constituted a very important element in the evaluation of the global cost of colonialism.[57] A second element that makes the Belgium military experience different from that of other colonial powers is that Congolese troops were never called upon to undertake military operations outside Africa.[58] Hence

---

[55] *La Force publique de sa naissance à 1914. Participation des militaires à l'histoire des premières années du Congo* (Brussels, 1952), pp. 45–9.

[56] Besides the payment, by the Belgian state, of officers assigned to the Institut cartographique militaire during the Leopoldian period.

[57] A. S. Thompson, *The Empire, op. cit.*, p. 175; A. S. Thompson, *Imperial Britain, op. cit.*, chapter 5; A. Clayton, "'Deceptive Might': Imperial Defence and Security", in J. M. Brown & Wm. R. Louis, eds., *The Oxford History of the British Empire. Vol. 4, op. cit.*, pp. 280–305.

[58] With the minor exception of some Congolese soldiers (of the medical service) serving in Burma during the Second World War.

Belgian colonialism in the Congo did not produce the equivalent of the British Empire's Gurkhas or France's Tirailleurs sénégalais, troops who served in many theatres of operations.[59]

These elements obviously played an important role in the colony's impact on the Belgian army. Indigenous troops never served in the Belgian army,[60] and only a minority of its numbers – and exclusively volunteers – had any direct contact with the colony. Some, as we have said, used their colonial assignment as a springboard for other activities, for instance in the world of big business; others returned home to continue their Belgian military careers. Between 1877 and 1908, about six hundred officers and sixteen hundred non-commissioned officers served in the Congo; twenty-nine per cent of them died there. The overall total for the 'Belgian' period, from 1908 to 1960, has unfortunately not yet been established. Towards the end of the colonial era, the white officers of the colonial army – approximately thousand men out of a troop of some twenty-four thousand men (in 1960) – were almost exclusively Belgian. The majority of these officers and non-commissioned officers were reserve cadres in the Belgian army. In 1959, this category represented approximately fifty per cent of the total number of officers in the Force publique. Another share of the officers in the Force publique came directly from the Belgian army's active list. These soldiers temporarily interrupted their Belgian military career, with the approval of the metropolitan authorities, to serve a term in the colony.[61] Historian Louis-Ferdinand Vanderstraeten noted that during the 1950s, more white officers left the Force publique than were recruited. Was this due to a loss or a lack of interest in a colonial military career?

Nevertheless, the Congo played an important role in the imagination of the metropolitan armed forces, in its propaganda and its symbolic identification. The Congo could offer Belgian soldiers that which had been so cruelly lacking in the past: action and a field of operations where they could achieve glory. From the beginning of the 1880s, the army found an outlet for its energy in the Leopoldian enterprise, a backdrop against which it could cultivate heroism and virility. The campaigns against the 'Arabs' at the outset of the Congo Free State, followed by the campaigns against the German colonial territories during the First World War and, finally, the victory over the Italians in Ethiopia in 1941 all attested to the virtues of the Belgian military – even if, strictly speaking, they were not due to the Belgian army itself. The Belgian military press reported on Congolese events right from the beginning of the Leopoldian adventure. Ceremonies marked the departure of soldiers for the Congo or their return to Belgium afterwards; soldiers returning from Africa gave conferences across the country to raise awareness of the Congo, especially at the beginning of the

---

[59] V. G. Kiernan, *Colonial Empires and Armies* (Phoenix Mill, 1998); J. Frémeaux, *De quoi fut fait l'empire. Les guerres coloniales au XIXe siècle* (Paris, 2010), pp. 121–152.
[60] Apart from a few individual exceptions.
[61] L.-F. Vanderstraeten, *De la Force publique à l'Armée nationale congolaise. Histoire d'une mutinerie juillet 1960* (Brussels-Gembloux, 1985), p. 64.

colonial period. They formed associations of colonial veterans that engaged in propaganda activities. Commemorations reminded the public of events deemed important for national honour, even if they took place half a world away from Belgium. Heroic figures were created and young Belgium was sorely in need of such exemplary men.[62]

In short, the Belgian army, faithful to the memory of King Leopold II, was the exalter of colonialism and linked colonialism to Belgian patriotism. What was the relationship between the Congo and Belgian nationalism? Colonialism unquestionably played an important role in forming the national identity of several European powers. The well-analysed case of Great Britain is exemplary in this respect.[63] In France, there is still a wide-ranging debate on the contribution of empire to the definition of what it means to be 'French'.[64] In Belgium, this relationship seems to be dominated by the following elements.

Originally, the link between colonialism and national identity was rather weak. The actual creation of Belgium took place without any colonial component. Furthermore, this new European state did not take any initiative to launch the construction of an overseas empire. The colony was in effect imposed on politicians who, at the beginning, did not really want it. Belgian colonialism was therefore not 'invented' by the authorities to reinforce national prestige, as was the case in Italy – even if this element was very likely present in Leopold II's mind.[65] Nevertheless, as the king's wild dream took shape and wormed its way into the public sphere, a certain number of journalists, politicians and ordinary citizens took pride in being able to link the Congolese enterprise to Belgium.

As long as the Congo Free State remained a private affair, the Belgian authorities could not exalt this link overtly. But after 1908, colonialism was certainly used as an official instrument of national glorification. In bombastic terms, Robert Reisdorff, the private secretary (*Chef de cabinet*) of the ministry of the colonies, exclaimed that "the Belgian soul", naturally borne towards "a noble and perpetual spirit of adventure", found in Leopold II's venture an incomparable means to prove that Belgium was not, as some insisted, "an artificial creation of history":

Here is the Congo, which thanks to [the heroes who colonised this land], has asserted itself as the most wonderful and most grandiose of Belgium's achievements, the Congo which 'IMPERIALLY' [*sic*] bears witness, as Leopold II desired, to the nationality, grandeur and generosity of the BELGIAN SOUL [*sic*].[66]

---

[62] E. Wanty, *Le milieu militaire belge de 1831 à 1914* (Brussels, 1957), pp. 231–3.
[63] P. J. Marshall, "Imperial Britain", art. cit., p. 319. A. S. Thompson nevertheless warns us that we should not overestimate the influence of the empire on the shaping of British identity: It is just one formative factor among others. A. S. Thompson, *The Empire, op. cit.*, pp. 200–1.
[64] D. Costantini, *Mission civilisatrice. Le rôle de l'histoire coloniale dans la construction de l'identité politique française* (Paris, 2008); P. Blanchard, N. Bancel & S. Lemaire, eds., *La fracture coloniale. La société française au prisme de l'héritage colonial* (Paris, 2005).
[65] N. Labanca, *Oltremare. Storia dell'espansione coloniale italiana* (Bologna, 2002), pp. 49, 54.
[66] R. Reisdorff, "L'Âme belge et l'œuvre coloniale", *Bulletin de la Société belge d'Études et d'Expansion*, 80 (April 1931), pp. 131, 136, 139.

These images and clichés, crucially important to the creation of a Belgian identity, were widely disseminated in official propaganda.[67] By 1830, a whole range of heroes and events had been mobilised to construct a national past – a classic phenomenon in the nineteenth century. Thanks to the colonial adventure, the gallery of national glories was further extended with a number of new figures.[68] The Congolese contribution also compensated for the country's modest size. In classrooms, pupils were proudly reminded that the colony was eighty times bigger than Belgium. It was sometimes called the 'tenth province', though without any constitutional basis. However, the image gave substance to the idea of a 'greater Belgium'. The link between the colony and Belgian identity was all the more necessary since Belgium was divided by serious internal dissensions, in particular the growing dissensions between the linguistic communities. These struggles began to increase at the exact moment when the colony erupted onto the domestic scene at the beginning of the 1880s. The Flemish demands for equality peaked first in the inter-war period, shortly after the annexation of the Congo. The Belgian-Congolese flag was willingly brandished to assert Belgian national identity in response to the threat of an ever-increasing rift. A great colonial propagandist, Major Alphonse Cayen, made the following comment in 1932:

In our country where petty linguistic quarrels are causing fratricidal conflicts, the colonial idea is acting as a cement. Whether he originates from the fields of Flanders or industrious Wallonia, the colonial is quite simply a colonial, conscious of serving not only the Congo, but also his homeland.[69]

For approximately half a century, from 1908 to 1960, the Congo, linked to the worship of the monarchy, served in some way as a crutch for Belgian nationalism. The colony was an unforeseen but welcome element in the assertion of Belgian identity both internally and *externally*. Indeed, Belgium was now acquiring greater visibility and legitimacy on the world stage. Furthermore, national honour was at stake: The country had to prove that it was worthy of the much-coveted distinction of being a colonial power. Considering the nefarious Leopoldian heritage, this was not a given. Belgium therefore overcompensated for this lack of legitimacy in the face of international attention by putting even more effort into its colonial enterprise and making it an exclusively national affair.

Nevertheless, we must not lose sight of the opposite effect. The Congo also fanned the fires of criticism directed at the Belgian nation. In Belgium itself, the Flemish movement was opposed to the dominance of the French language in the public life of the colony. To the Flemish nationalists, the Congo represented

---

[67] J. Janssens, *De Belgische natie viert. De Belgische nationale feesten 1830–1914* (Leuven, 2001), pp. 227–9.
[68] T. Verschaffel, "Congo in de Belgische zelfrepresentatie", in V. Viaene, D. Van Reybrouck & B. Ceuppens, eds., *Congo in België. Koloniale cultuur in de metropool* (Leuven, 2009), pp. 63–79.
[69] A. Cayen, *Au service de la colonie* (Brussels, 1938), pp. 126–7.

further proof of the grip of the French-speaking upper-middle classes on the machinery of the state. Thus, in this minority faction of Belgian public opinion, the Congo did not act as a unifying, but rather as an additional dividing force. Some Flemings even used the term *colonisation* to describe the oppression of Flemings within the Belgian state. In the inter-war period, they claimed that Flanders, like the Congo, had been 'colonised' by the French-speaking bourgeoisie.[70] Strangely enough, a few rare supporters of the Walloon movement also used this image of 'internal' colonisation. They claimed that Wallonia was being 'colonised' and exploited by the Flemish, as economic activity faced increasing difficulties.[71]

Considering the real, if elusive, role of colonialism in Belgian national identity, it is tempting to establish a causal link between the independence of the Congo and the profound crisis of the unified state. According to some scholars, the sudden disappearance of the colony contributed to the disintegration of the united Belgian state.[72] The repertoire of Belgian nationalism and propaganda was undoubtedly diminished by the loss of the colony, but I do not believe that this factor had any influence on the move towards federalism after 1960. In fact, this process had already begun much earlier. After fermenting for some decades, starting in the 1890s, community tensions increased during the second half of the 1950s, at a time when the Congo was still firmly anchored to Belgium. The great language laws of the beginning of the 1960s were a direct result of these long-standing confrontations. Milestones leading to the state reform of 1970 had already been laid during the years preceding the sudden independence of the colony. The crisis of Belgian unity and identity was stimulated by internal Belgian factors, especially spatial shifts in Belgium's economic structure. This evolution had begun long before decolonisation. The colony played no role at all in the federalisation process.

Glimpses of the Socio-Cultural Impact of the Congo on the Metropole

The Human Dimension: Belgians in the Congo and Congolese in Belgium

The social dimension of the Congo's impact on Belgium depends, first of all, on the human contacts that existed between the colonisers and the colonised. Table 4 in the Appendix shows the number of Belgians living in the Congo from

---

[70] O. Boehme, *Greep naar de markt. De sociaal-economische agenda van de Vlaamse Beweging en haar ideologische versplintering tijdens het interbellum* (Leuven, 2008).
[71] P. Delforge, "Congo et Mouvement wallon", art. cit.
[72] M. Van Spaandonck, "Belgium: A Colonial Power Becomes a Federal State", *Itinerario. European Journal of Overseas History*, 20, 2 (1996), pp. 64, 75; D. Lesage, "Federalisme en postkolonialisme. Over de natie als museum", in H. Asselberghs & D. Lesage, eds., *Het Museum van de natie, van kolonialisme tot globalisering* (Brussels, 1999), pp. 97–118; M. G. Stanard, *Selling the Tenth Province: Belgian Colonial Propaganda 1908–1960* (unpublished Ph.D. thesis, University of Indiana, 2006), p. 311; N. Tousignant, *Les manifestations publiques du lien colonial entre la Belgique et le Congo belge (1897–1988)* (unpublished Ph.D. thesis, Laval University, 1995), p. 19.

1890 to 1959 and the social and occupational profile of this expat population, and leads to the following observations.[73]

First: For many years, the number of Belgians residing in the colony was very limited. During the period of the Congo Free State, there was a maximum of approximately fifteen hundred people. After the annexation of the Congo, this number gradually increased to seventeen thousand in 1930. The crisis in the 1930s led to a significant drop in the number of Belgians remaining in the colony; there were barely eleven thousand left in 1934! After the Second World War, the Belgian population in the Congo expanded to twenty-four thousand in 1947 and to nearly eighty-nine thousand in 1959.

Second: Initially, the proportion of Belgians relative to the entire white population of the Congo was relatively modest. At the beginning of the Leopoldian period, the Belgians (forty per cent in 1890) were actually in the minority compared with other whites. Many Scandinavians, for example, participated in the construction of the Congo Free State.[74] Afterwards, the proportion of Belgians varied between fifty-six and sixty-five per cent. Not until the inter-war period would they represent approximately two-thirds of the total white population. After the Second World War, the growth in the number of Belgians was accompanied by an increase of their proportion of the total. On the eve of independence, nearly four-fifths of the whites living in the Congo were Belgians.

Third: Not surprising, the white population in the colony consisted, in the beginning, of mainly young male adults (single or married but long-separated from wives who remained in Belgium). By 1925, after four decades of Belgian domination in the Congo, women and children of both sexes under the age of eighteen still represented, respectively, only twenty-one per cent and nine per cent of the white population. Their number and their proportion gradually increased, especially after 1945, to twenty-nine per cent and thirty-five per cent in 1958. Not until the 1950s did the Belgians in the Congo have a family profile similar to that in Belgium.

Fourth: The occupational distribution of the white population shows that civil servants and missionaries were the two major groups. The number of employees in public service fluctuated significantly in the inter-war period between a maximum of twenty-five hundred in 1931 and a minimum of eleven hundred in 1934. Their presence strongly increased after the war, from thirty-two hundred in 1946 to ninety-three hundred in 1958, but their relative proportion fell (from twelve per cent of the total white population in 1925 to 7.3 per cent in 1959). The absolute number of missionaries did not suffer from such fluctuations. It continued to grow, from fourteen hundred in 1925 to seventy-five hundred in 1959 (respectively, eleven per cent and 6.7 per cent of the total). Between 1932 and 1951, the Congo had more missionaries than

---

[73] J.-L. Vellut, "Les Belges au Congo (1885–1890)", in *La Belgique. Sociétés et cultures depuis 150 ans* (S.l., 1980), pp. 260–5.
[74] On the role of the Norwegians, see B. Godøy, *Solskinn og død. Nordmenn i kong Leopolds Kongo* (Oslo, 2010).

civil servants! The rest of the colony's adult male population was essentially made up of employees of private companies. In 1947, these numbered 10,087 compared with the 3,945 self-employed individuals who were 'colonists' in the strict sense of the term.

Of course, the sheer number of Belgians present in the colony does not tell the whole story. The length of their stay must also be taken into account. Few Belgians settled in the colony for the long term. In general, they went for a few years, sometimes for a good part of their career as civil servants or private employees, but they usually returned to Belgium. Unfortunately, there are no statistics on the turnover of colonial staff; for example, we are unaware of the average duration of a stay in the Congo. A relatively short average amount of time would imply that in total, more Belgians came into contact with the colony than the low figures of the white population in the Congo might suggest.

The previously mentioned figures must, of course, be compared with the total Belgian population. The latter grew from 6 million in 1890 to 7.4 million in 1910 and to 9.1 million in 1961. The number of Belgians living in the colony in 1910 and in 1959 thus represented, respectively, 0.02 per cent and 0.9 per cent of the population of Belgium. A second point of comparison must be made with the total Congolese population, estimated at 9.5 million in 1925 and 13.8 million in 1959.[75] During these years, the Belgians represented 0.08 per cent (1925) and 0.6 per cent (1959) of the total Congolese population. If we include all non-Belgian white settlers, these figures rise to 0.13 per cent and 0.8 per cent. Compared to other colonial territories, these figures are on the low side, especially if the Belgian expats alone are taken into account and if we leave aside the final phase of colonial rule, when more Belgians resided in the colony. In 1913, the total white communities represented 0.6 per cent of the colonised population in the Portuguese African colonies, 0.4 per cent in the Italian African colonies, 0.2 per cent in the French African colonies, 0.3 per cent in the Dutch Indies and so forth. The percentages for the Belgian Congo were somewhat comparable with the figures for the British colonies (0.1 percent in the British African colonies and in British India). One last international comparison: The total white community in the Belgian Congo numbered twenty-three thousand individuals in 1938; whereas whites numbered two hundred and sixty thousand in the Dutch Indies – eleven times more, even though the populations of Belgium and the Netherlands were more or less similar.[76]

This was no matter of coincidence. The Belgian authorities scrupulously monitored the social composition of the foreign population in the Congo. They pursued an elitist colonisation: Poor whites were not welcome in the colony

---

[75] L. de Saint Moulin, "La population du Congo pendant la Seconde Guerre mondiale", in *Le Congo belge durant la Seconde Guerre mondiale. Recueil d'études* (Brussels, 1983), p. 25.
[76] In 1938 also, the percentages for the Belgian Congo were lower than for all other black African colonies. See B. Etemad, *La possession du monde. Poids et mesures de la colonisation* (Brussels, 2000), p. 264–5.

and, therefore, mass emigration to Africa was never encouraged.[77] The world of high finance, which dominated economic activity in the Congo, was also opposed to the introduction of small colonial entrepreneurs (in French: *colons*). Large-scale mining and agricultural enterprises often struggled with indigenous labour shortages; the arrival of large numbers of *colons* would only exacerbate the problem. During the 1930s and the 1950s, however, some people raised their voices in favour of (white-run) small, independent businesses, particularly in the farming sector.[78] In their opinion, only a major immigration movement from Belgium would maintain Belgian domination in the Congo. These pleas had barely any influence in practice. Only during the last fifteen years of Belgian rule did the Belgian authorities take measures to facilitate the establishment of small entrepreneurial concerns in the Congo. The Commission du Colonat was created in 1946 and the Société de Crédit au Colonat et à l'Industrie was founded in 1947. The number of these independent economic agents rose from less than five thousand in 1950 to 9,362 in 1956. But this did not change the fundamental imbalance. The *colons* felt that they were neglected and despised; in their eyes, the government and the major companies joined forces to govern the colony as they pleased, certainly to the detriment of small entrepreneurs.[79] In short, Belgium's colonial enterprise never led to the important emigration movement that took place within the British and French imperial territories – to the Dominions and the Maghreb, respectively.[80]

For some Belgians, the Congo represented a wonderful opportunity for upward social mobility, especially at the beginning of the colonial venture. Servicemen, often from a modest background and rank, sometimes succeeded in making a dazzling social breakthrough thanks to their activity in the Congo. Engineers or lawyers from lower middle-class backgrounds successfully entered the economic elite, thanks to a fruitful career in the Congo. But in general, these spectacular successes were limited in time – the time it took to establish colonial society. As soon as the Belgian Congo was established, young people who were ambitious, entrepreneurial and sometimes even quite adventurous discovered interesting career prospects there and gained appreciable material benefits. But does this mean that the structure of Belgian society was profoundly affected by colonialism? All in all, the modest number of colonists, especially before the Second World War, raises doubts. The missionaries certainly had a

---

[77] V. Foutry, "Belgisch-Kongo tijdens het interbellum: een immigratiebeleid gericht op sociale controle", *Revue belge d'Histoire contemporaine*, 14, 3–4 (1983), pp. 461–88.

[78] B. Jewsiewicki, "Le colonat agricole européen au Congo belge 1910–1960", *Journal of African History*, 20 (1979), pp. 159–71.

[79] E.g. V. Jacobs, *La déficience des colons au Congo* (Brussels, 1938), p. 36.

[80] S. Constantine, "Migrants and Settlers", in J. M. Brown & Wm. R. Louis, eds., *The Oxford History of the British Empire. Vol. 4*, op. cit., pp. 163–87; J. Frémeaux, *Les empires coloniaux dans le processus de la mondialisation* (Paris, 2002), pp. 168–9. Contrary to the Belgians, the Italian colonial authorities tried to stimulate mass emigration towards the colonies (especially Libya) but this policy met with little success: J.-L. Miège, *L'impérialisme colonial italien de 1870 à nos jours* (Paris, 1968), pp. 184–6.

particular social and motivational profile. They had no material aims; often, they left Belgium never to return except for short stays. The great majority of them came from Flanders, and many were of rural origin, whereas the majority of civil servants and private employees may have been urban dwellers.[81]

Of course, colonialism was never a one-way system. White people went to the colonies but gradually colonial subjects also came to the metropole. This movement was already very perceptible in Great Britain and in France at the beginning of the twentieth century, when many thousands of non-Europeans arrived in Europe.[82] This aspect of the colonial nexus was almost non-existent in Belgium.[83] The first Congolese were brought to Belgium for a series of exhibitions. On these occasions, a few dozen of them were put on display for European visitors for a number of weeks or months. They were, of course, expected to return to Africa. In the early days of the Congo Free State, educational exchanges were organised and some Congolese children were brought to Belgium but this experiment was soon discontinued owing to the opposition of public authorities.[84] Very exceptional, some of these Congolese students continued their education in Belgium. One of them was Paul Panda Farnana (1888–1930), who had come to Belgium as a child. He graduated from an agricultural high school and worked as an employee at the ministry of colonies, alternating between Belgium and the Congo. He is considered the first Congolese intellectual and played a public role in the Panafrican Congresses (1919 and 1921) and in the First National Colonial Congress, an official event organised by the Belgian colonial authorities in 1920. Farnana stands out as an absolute exception; he was in no way representative of the fate of the other Congolese in Belgium.

Indeed, most Congolese only came to Belgium under particular circumstances. Some black servants were brought to Belgium when their white employers returned home. The same applies to mixed-race children taken to Europe by their fathers. Finally, some Congolese sailors jumped ship upon arrival in Antwerp and stayed on. They generally managed to survive through marginal

---

[81] In 1948, only 16.4 per cent of all missionaries were Walloon. J.-L. Vellut, "Les Belges", art. cit., p. 263.

[82] One figure mentions more than two hundred thousand people coming from the colonies and working in France during the First World War; in Great Britain, census data for 1891 mention more than one hundred thousand colonials living in England and Wales. B. Porter, *The Absent-Minded Imperialists: Empire, Society, and Culture in Britain* (Oxford, 2004), pp. 171 and 258; L. Tabili, "A Homogenous Society? Britain's Internal 'Others', 1800-Present", in C. Hall & S. Rose, eds., *At Home With the Empire: Metropolitan Culture and the Imperial World* (Cambridge, 2006), pp. 68–70; J. Thobie, G. Meynier, C. Coquery-Vidrovitch & Ch.-R. Ageron, *Histoire de la France coloniale 1914-1990* (Paris, 1990), pp. 78–9.

[83] Zana Aziza Etambala, *In het land van de Banoko. De geschiedenis van de Kongolese/Zaïrese aanwezigheid in België van 1885 tot heden* (Leuven, 1993); A. Cornet, "Les Congolais en Belgique aux XIXe et XXe siècles", in A. Morelli, ed., *Histoire des étrangers et de l'immigration en Belgique* (Brussels, 2004), pp. 375–400.

[84] B. A. Yates, "Educating Congolese Abroad: An Historical Note on African Elites", *International Journal of African Historical Studies*, 14, 1 (1981), pp. 34–64.

activities such as working as vendors at fairs or in the entertainment industry, and some were employed by institutions or organisations linked to the colony. Associations were created to help and 'protect' them. Some of these Congolese, mostly single men, married white women and special associations were set up for the mixed-race children who resulted from these marriages.[85] All in all, during the colonial era, very few Congolese actually lived in Belgium: between 400 and 500 in 1953![86] This low figure was due to a government policy designed to restrict, as much as possible, the Congolese population's contact with the outside world (including Belgium). Absolute control of the minds of the colonised population was considered essential for the safeguarding of law and order in the Congo. This control is noticeable in the use of black soldiers, who were deliberately kept outside of Europe. The Belgian authorities never considered bringing Congolese workers to Belgium. In any case, there were often labour shortages in the colony itself and, meanwhile, Belgium regularly had to cope with mass unemployment at home. Only during the 1950s did the ministry of colonies organise meticulously managed excursions to Belgium for a handful of carefully selected Congolese. These *évolués* – only a few dozen of them – were shown the beauties of Belgium, but then had to return to the Congo after a few weeks. During the World Exhibition of 1958, the number of people participating in these excursions grew to approximately 700. During the same period, the first Congolese students came to Belgium for the purpose of higher education, especially at the University of Brussels or Louvain. In short, the physical presence of colonial subjects in the metropole was far from overwhelming; on the contrary, it was clearly marginal.

The Colonial Impact on Religion in Belgium
At the crossroads of the political, social and cultural aspects lies the vast domain of missionary history. In the Congo, as in the other colonies, the missions played an essential role both in the ideological justification of the imperial enterprise and in the control of the colonial terrain, even if relations between the authorities and religious agents were not always free from friction or conflict.[87] But did missionary activity also have an impact on the metropole, in this case Belgium?

One crucial fact should be emphasised from the start: the importance of the missionary movement in Belgium *even before* the Leopoldian enterprise in the Congo had taken shape. Indeed, in early modern times many people from the Southern Netherlands played a significant role in the evangelisation of non-European lands. The famous phrase of Saint Francis Xavier, *Da mihi Belgas* ("Give me Belgians"), has often been repeated, illustrating the missionary vigour of

---

[85] B. Ceuppens, "Een Congolese kolonie in Brussel", in V. Viaene, e.a., eds., *Congo in België*, op. cit., pp. 231–50.
[86] Zana Aziza Etambala, *In het land van de Banoko*, op. cit., pp. 26, 85–6.
[87] K. Hammer, *Weltmission und Kolonialismus. Sendungsideen des 19. Jahrhunderts im Konflikt* (München, 1978); R. Habermas, "Mission im 19. Jahrhundert – Globale Netze der Religion", *Historische Zeitschrift*, 287, 3 (2008), pp. 629–79.

this profoundly Catholic land. It also served as a mobilising call for new vocations, though these were certainly not lacking in nineteenth-century Belgium.[88] Along with France, Belgium was on the front line of this missionary awakening. Some Belgians with evangelical vocations joined foreign, especially French, religious institutions; but several specifically Belgian congregations were also founded during the nineteenth century, such as the famous Congrégation du Cœur immaculé de Marie (CICM – Congregatio Immaculati Cordis Mariae), commonly called the Scheutists and founded in 1862. Furthermore, an apostolic school for the training of young missionaries was founded in the Belgian city of Turnhout in 1872. These developments took place within the framework of the powerful Catholic awakening in Belgium. Numerous religious houses were founded, vocations were increasing and public devotion was gaining momentum.

In the nineteenth century, Belgian missionaries were active worldwide: in Latin and North America, India, Sri Lanka, China, Mongolia, the Philippines and the Pacific islands. They left a considerable mark, the memory of which sometimes lives on today; for instance, Saint Damien among the lepers of Molokai, Father Constant Lievens in Bengal or Pieter De Smet, the evangeliser of the North American Indians. Right from the start of his Congolese adventure, Leopold II was aware of the importance of religion in the construction of the colony. The anti-slavery crusade of Cardinal Lavigerie was the perfect means of mobilising Belgian Catholic energies in favour of the Congo, and Leopold II certainly did not deprive himself of this efficient instrument to expand the foundation of his enterprise within Belgian public opinion. The missionaries also played an important role in the occupation of the Congolese territory. Foreign Protestant missionaries, mostly American and British, were active in the Congo right from the beginning. Foreign Catholic missions, particularly the French Pères blancs, were also established.[89] From the king's point of view, these developments were potentially dangerous. The foreign missionary presence – whether Catholic or Protestant – risked compromising the Belgian character of the colony. Furthermore, the king could not sufficiently control missionary organisations established outside the borders of his own country. This was painfully demonstrated during the campaign against the horrors of the 'red rubber' trade. The foreign Protestant missionaries were among the first to sound the alarm. Obviously, this did not please the sovereign of the Congo Free State.

Leopold endeavoured to conclude settlement agreements solely with *Belgian* orders and missionary organisations. However, his initial efforts did not meet with much success. The Belgian orders and organisations that were contacted refused to follow the king to the Congo: the Scheutistes in 1876, the Jesuits

---

[88] D. Vanysacker, "Les missions belges et néerlandaises au cours des 19e et 20e siècles", *Neue Zeitschrift für Missionswissenschaft*, 53, 1 (1997), pp. 241–70.
[89] R. Kinet, *'Licht in die Finsternis'. Kolonisation und Mission im Kongo, 1876–1908* (Münster, 2005), pp. 24–31.

in 1879, the Franciscans the same year and so forth. The African seminary in Louvain, established in 1886 with the king's financial support, quickly turned out to be a bitter failure owing to a lack of candidates. The Belgian Catholics were wary of the Congolese enterprise, which they believed was subject to the harmful influences of Freemasons and Protestants. Initially, the Vatican itself kept its distance from Leopold's African enterprise, but the king finally succeeded in convincing the papal authorities.[90] His close collaborator, Edmond Van Eetvelde, clearly expressed the aim of this charm offensive on the Holy See: "The main objective is to change the almost hostile indifference of many Catholic Belgians into active sympathy".[91] This strategy turned out to be fruitful: Vatican support did indeed cause a subsequent change of heart in Belgian Catholic opinion regarding the Congo. Under pressure from Rome, the Scheutistes finally agreed to join the Congolese adventure in 1887, the Jesuits signed on in 1893 and many other orders and congregations followed suit.[92] In exchange for this commitment, the Congo Free State awarded important material privileges such as land. The Protestant missions, on the other hand, while not expressly forbidden, as this would have contravened the provisions of the 1885 Berlin Act, were discriminated against in various ways. Although Belgian Protestant missionary activity existed, there was little of it; the Protestant missions in the Congo originated primarily in North America and Britain.[93]

The Belgian and Roman Catholic authorities had thus become faithful supporters of Leopold's colonial policy, even during the campaign against the Congo Free State. When the horrors of 'red rubber' were revealed to the world, the Catholic Church kept quiet.[94] Later, the church felt betrayed by the critical remarks of the Commission of Inquiry of 1904–5, set up by Leopold II to stave off international criticism. Among other things, the Commission pointed a finger at certain brutal and inhumane practices of the Catholic missions in the Congo: ill treatment of children, exploitation of workers, abductions and so forth. Following this inquiry, certain ecclesiastics distanced themselves from Leopold's policies. This controversy also resulted, in 1906, in the conclusion of a concordat between the Congo Free State and the Holy See that determined the major material benefits awarded to the Catholic missions, primarily in exchange for their involvement in teaching in the Congo. This concordat

---

[90] V. Viaene, "La religion du prince: Léopold, le Vatican, la Belgique et le Congo (1855–1908)", in V. Dujardin, P.-L. Plasman e.a., eds., *Léopold II, entre génie et gêne* (Brussels, 2009), pp. 163–89.

[91] Cited in V. Viaene, "La religion du prince", art. cit., p. 179.

[92] F. Bontinck, "Het begin van de Congomissie", in D. Verhelst & H. Daniëls, eds., *Scheut vroeger en nu 1862–1987. Geschiedenis van de Congregatie van het Onbevlekt Hart van Maria C.I.C.M.* (Leuven, 1991), p. 121.

[93] J. Pirotte, *Périodiques missionnaires belges d'expression française 1889–1940* (Louvain-la-Neuve, 1973), pp. 19–24.

[94] R. G. Weisbord, "The King, the Cardinal and the Pope: Leopold II's Genocide in the Congo and the Vatican", *Journal of Genocide Research*, 5, 1 (2003); Zana Aziza Etambala, "De houding van het Belgische episcopaat tegenover het Kongo van Leopold II, 1885–1908", *Wereld en Zending*, 17, 2 (1988), pp. 113–23.

continued after Belgium's takeover of the Congo. But there was another aspect to this debate: The Belgian Church thought that Freemasons and non-believers had inspired the accusations formulated against it by the Commission of Inquiry. The Catholic hierarchy claimed this proved the grip these diabolical forces had on the colonial authorities and on Belgian society in general. In other words, the Congolese conflict intensified the already complex dispute that existed between clericals and anti-clericals in the metropole.

Did colonisation have other repercussions on religion in Belgium? In particular, did it influence Belgian religious practice and ecclesiastical organisation, and if so, how? First of all, the 'nationalisation' of the missions initiated by the king led to a growing commitment of the church to the Congo. In 1908 there were still very few Catholic missionaries in the colony; barely 335 religious men and women were active there. The great leap forward took place between the mid-1920s and the end of the 1940s when the number of missionaries more than quadrupled in just twenty-five years, from 895 in 1924 to 4,607 in 1959. This considerable growth coincided with the feminisation of missionaries. In 1908, nuns represented a third of total missionary staff, in 1959, a little less than half.[95] According to historian Jean Pirotte, "Nearly three-quarters of the Belgian missionary efforts were absorbed by the Congo".[96] An enormous and growing part of the Belgian missionary energy was therefore directed towards the colony.

But did the growing involvement of Catholic missions in the colony occur to the detriment of their commitment in other parts of the world? If *relative* share of the latter certainly diminished, we do not know the exact *absolute* number of missionaries outside the Congo. In any case, the peak of missionary fervour coincided with the colonial period.[97] In the twentieth century, the total number of Belgian missionaries grew continuously, from 2,686 in 1922 to 10,070 in 1961, while other religious vocations (in the priesthood and in metropolitan religious orders) began to decrease after the Second World War. After Congo's independence, the number of missionary vocations began their inexorable decline: In 1988, there were only 3,710 Belgian missionaries left, of which only seventeen per cent were under fifty years old.[98] Considering this data, it is justifiable to formulate the following hypothesis: The colonisation of the Congo did indeed stimulate missionary ardour among the Belgian Christian population.

---

[95] B. Cleys, J. De Maeyer, C. Dujardin & L. Vints, "België in Congo, Congo in België. Weerslag van de missionering op de religieuze instituten", in V. Viaene, e.a., eds., *Congo in België, op. cit.*, p. 152.

[96] J. Pirotte, *Périodiques missionnaires belges, op. cit.*, p. 16.

[97] L. Vints, "De Belgische katholieke missiebeweging in de 19ᵉ eeuw ten tijde van Gezelle", in L. Vandamme, ed., *'Reizen in den geest'. De boekenwereld van Guido Gezelle* (Bruges, 1999), p. 36.

[98] C. Dujardin, "Van pionier tot dienaar. Profiel van de Belgische missionaris in historisch perspectief (1800–1989)", in R. Boudens, ed., *Rond Damiaan* (Leuven, 1989), p. 145; J. Pirotte, *Périodiques, op. cit.*, pp. 12–3: 3,663 missionaries in 1934, 4,930 in 1940.

Other elements point in the same direction. A whole network of propaganda developed around missionary activities in the form of publications and associations that were often very active. "In 1870, there were only three associations [in Belgium] in favour of missions. Twenty-five were set up between 1881 and 1914. Between 1880 and 1914, twenty-three periodicals were added to the five that were published before 1885".[99] In the inter-war period, numerous initiatives essential for the intellectual, moral and material support of the missions were set up. 'Missiology', which endeavoured to give missionary activity a scientific basis, was firmly established in Belgium with the organisation of missiological weeks and the creation of the Missiological School in Louvain. Jesuit Pierre Charles played an essential role in this movement. Specialised associations, such as AUCAM (Association des Universitaires catholiques pour l'Aide aux Missions) in 1925 or the Missiebond, its Flemish equivalent, were founded. Numerous charity appeals and campaigns to collect funds were organised in the most far-flung parts of the countryside. They were often accompanied by conferences or sessions about the religious activities undertaken in the far-off colony. As a result, the Congo began to penetrate the minds of Belgian believers. We should remember that the great majority of missionaries were recruited from Flanders. We can therefore assume that missionary propaganda was more active or more efficient in the northern part of the country.

The colonial missions also had an impact on ecclesiastical organisation. Missionary activity in the Congo influenced the mentality, attitudes and functioning of the religious institutions. The rules established in the beginning were not really adapted to the colonial terrain, which required greater flexibility and adaptation; hence, the Congolese experience in some ways emancipated the missionary agents and eased the day-to-day functioning of the missions. It also stimulated their internationalisation (especially through the incorporation of Congolese priests and nuns), opened wider horizons and increased local autonomy.[100]

Belgian Colonial Propaganda through Exhibitions, Schoolbooks, Monuments and Films

All the colonial powers endeavoured to promote their empires, not only in the eyes of the outside world, but also among the population at home. Numerous historical studies have asserted that imperial ideology deeply influenced the minds, worldviews, ideologies, unconscious attitudes and the daily life of a broad spectrum of the metropolitan population.[101] John MacKenzie introduced this idea in the second half of the 1980s by meticulously analysing the

---

[99] E. de Moreau, s.j., "Histoire de l'Eglise catholique en Belgique", in *Histoire de la Belgique contemporaine 1830–1914* (Brussels, 1929), vol. 2, p. 586.
[100] B. Cleys, J. De Maeyer, C. Dujardin & L. Vints, "België in Congo", art. cit., pp. 164–5.
[101] T. Chafer & A. Sackur, eds., *Promoting the Colonial Idea in France: Propaganda and Visions of Empire in France* (Houndmills, 2002), p. 4.

multiple ways in which imperial ideology affected the British population: commemorations and public events celebrating the glory of the empire; large-scale spectacular exhibitions; educational programmes and pro-colonial schoolbooks; extracurricular activities for the youth; film, theatre and music hall productions; popular literature; pictorial arts, music, architecture and monuments.[102] In France, a similar re-discovery of imperial propaganda took longer to develop. In the 1970s, Charles-Robert Ageron raised doubts about the depth and intensity of the colonial fervour of the great majority of the French.[103] Since then, however, the current generation of Anglo-Saxon and French historians has put forth a new interpretation. The numerous publications by Pascal Blanchard, Nicolas Bancel and Sandrine Lemaire, in particular, show that the colonial reality has profoundly influenced the structures and mentalities of French society up until the present day.[104]

As a young colonial power, Belgium did not escape this general movement. Propaganda was even all the more necessary since the Belgian population had almost no prior colonial links. It was, therefore, necessary to set in motion some sort of crash course in colonial spirit.[105] There has never been a specifically *colonial* great exhibition in Belgium, but starting at the end of the nineteenth century, special sections of universal exhibitions were devoted to the Congo. The Antwerp fairs of 1885 and 1894 opened the market: In 1885, the fair hosted a dozen Congolese, while the 1894 expo featured about 100 of them presented to the Belgian visitors in a mock 'indigenous village'. The colonial exhibition at Tervuren in 1897 also featured a Congolese village inhabited by 267 Congolese who had been brought to Belgium especially for this purpose. The Belgian public was, thus, introduced to the Congo before it was featured in the additional propaganda channels mentioned earlier. Leopold II initiated these introductions and used these public events to bring the Congo to the attention of a Belgian public that had no previous affinity with the region. After the Congo was taken over by the Belgian state in 1908, the tradition of colonial or Congolese pavilions was maintained. The universal

---

[102] J. M. MacKenzie, *Propaganda and Empire: The Manipulation of British Public Opinion 1880–1960* (Manchester, 1984). As mentioned in the Introduction, Bernard Porter, while not rejecting the (undeniable) existence of propaganda channels, calls into question the real impact of these propagandist efforts (B. Porter, *The Absent-Minded Imperialists, op. cit.*).

[103] Ch.-R. Ageron, *France coloniale, op. cit.*, pp. 267, 297–8.

[104] N. Bancel & P. Blanchard, "Avant-propos. Culture post-coloniale: le temps des heritages", in P. Blanchard, N. Bancel & S. Lemaire, eds., *Culture post-coloniale 1961–2006. Traces et mémoires coloniales en France* (Paris, 2005), p. 12.

[105] L. Vints, *Kongo, made in Belgium: beeld van een kolonie in film en propaganda* (Antwerpen, 1984); M. G. Stanard, *Selling the Tenth Province: Belgian Colonial Propaganda 1908–1960* (unpublished Ph.D. thesis, Indiana University, 2006); M. G. Stanard, *Selling the Congo: A History of European Pro-Empire Propaganda and the Making of Belgian Imperialism* (Lincoln, 2011); M. G. Stanard, "Selling the Empire between the Wars: Colonial Expositions in Belgium, 1920–1940", *French Colonial History*, 6 (2005), pp. 159–78; M. G. Stanard, "'Bilan du monde pour un monde plus déshumanisé'. The Brussels World's Fair and Belgian Perceptions of the Congo", *European History Quarterly*, 32, 2 (2005), pp. 267–98.

expositions in Brussels (1910), Ghent (1913) and again in Brussels (1930, 1935 and finally 1958) showed visitors an exotic and optimistic image of the Belgian colony.[106]

Besides these great public celebrations of Belgian colonialism, there were many other more modest and temporary exhibitions. The Colonial Office, a department of the Ministry of the Colonies, was in charge of organising some of these exhibitions (the *Quinzaines coloniales*) in order to promote economic links between the colony and the metropole. They did not, however, always arouse a great deal of enthusiasm among the economic circles. Additionally, private associations, including missionary organisations, initiated and organised small, local colonial exhibitions, often with the support of the Colonial Office.

The propaganda machines of the various colonial powers, including the great exhibitions, had certain traits in common.[107] First of all, propaganda created the image of a unified colonial empire. Second, it depicted the colonial territories as a geographic and demographic extension of the metropole. Third, the colonies were considered as inexhaustible sources of wealth. Fourth, propaganda confirmed that the conquest brought freedom to the colonies, delivering them from internal wars and barbaric violence. Finally, it introduced the idea of an extreme contrast between the 'before' and 'after'. All of these general characteristics were, of course, present in Belgian propaganda. The Congo was depicted as nature's treasure chest, a land abundant with minerals and plants. One of the most commonly used clichés referred to the 'geological scandal' of Katanga, an area packed with minerals. Unfortunately, this land was inhabited by 'some of the most primitive populations in the world' (another commonly repeated cliché) who suffered from endemic disease, tribal wars and the 'Arab' slave trade. The arrival of the Belgians was represented as a beneficial rupture with this sombre and violent past. The Congolese, now peaceful and free from slavery and superstition, could be guided towards civilisation. The Congo was thus presented in a stark before-and-after scenario. Towards the end of the colonial period, a particular emphasis was placed on the material and economic progress of the Congo, represented as a remarkable example of modernity in the tropical world. Furthermore, the propagandist machine underlined the exclusively *Belgian* character of this adventure. These

---

[106] M. Wynants, *Van hertogen en Congolezen. Tervuren en de Koloniale Tentoonstelling 1897* (Tervuren, 1997); K. Guldentops, "Congo als clou van het moderne België. De kolonie op de Belgische Wereldtentoonstellingen (1910–1935)", in V. Viaene, e.a., eds., *Congo in België, op. cit.*, pp. 81–93; S. Van Beurden, "'Un panorama de nos valeurs africaines'. Belgisch Congo op Expo 58", in Ibid., pp. 299–311; H.-J. Lüsebrink, "Images de l'Afrique et mise en scène du Congo belge dans les expositions coloniales françaises et belges (1889–1939)", in P. Halen & J. Riesz, eds., *Images de l'Afrique et du Congo-Zaïre dans les lettres françaises de Belgique et alentour* (Brussels, 1993), pp. 75–88.

[107] M. G. Stanard, "Inter-war pro-Empire Propaganda and European Colonial Culture: Toward a Comparative Research Agenda", *Journal of Contemporary History*, 44, 1 (January 2009), pp. 27–48.

magnificent material and moral achievements were uniquely due to the effort of the Belgians, and proved them to be exemplary colonisers. The depiction of the Congo as a 'model' colony was an essential element in the political, diplomatic and psychological mechanism of the Belgian colonial enterprise. The Congo enabled the glorification of Belgium and contributed to the glorification of Leopold II and his 'colonising genius'. All the players – the government, the church and big business – had a part in the propagandist machinery. Everyone played a special and well-defined role, but they all worked hand in hand to build a new Congo that would remain a part of Belgium for many decades to come. Belgian colonial activities were represented as homogenous and harmonious. This hand-in-hand collaboration is the origin of the 'Belgian colonial trinity', another constantly repeated cliché that ignores the tensions within the triumvirate.

In short, the colonial propaganda inculcated by the exhibitions was a veritable production line for clichés. We should underline two further characteristics of this propaganda. First, and in contrast with the other colonial powers, the Belgian authorities did not have to integrate different colonial situations within a single homogenous empire. The Belgian colonial domain, reduced to one African territory, did not include regions such as north Africa, India or southeast Asia where ancient civilisations, although considered 'inferior', had nevertheless been capable of producing written literature and durable architecture. This in some way simplified the task of Belgian colonial propaganda, the contents and mechanisms of which was not burdened with the nuances present in the experiences of France or Great Britain. Second, the Belgian colonial propagandist view was remarkably static. From the beginning, when the Belgians took possession of the African land, the same motives were employed over and again, with no great alterations during the half century that separated annexation from independence. At the very most, in the 1950s, it was possible to discern a particular emphasis placed on economic achievements and modernism, but the other clichés remained.

These aspects are also present in later channels of colonial propaganda. The schools were obviously a major channel for the distribution of colonial ideology, but it was not until 1908 that Belgium officially included the colony in the national history curriculum. The image conveyed in schoolbooks reflected the elements we have just described. They strongly underlined heroism and the adventurous aspects of the Congolese conquest, themes likely to strike young imaginations. But these history books only covered the Leopoldian era, while presentation of the 'Belgian' period was reduced to a minimum. Historian Benoît Verhaegen, who analysed the Congo's place in secondary school history books, observed that the homogeneity and stereotyping of their contents "may be partly explained by the lack of information available to the authors of these books, who copied from each other owing to a lack of anything better".[108] This

---

[108] B. Verhaegen, "La colonisation et la décolonisation dans les manuels d'histoire en Belgique", in M. Quaghebeur & E. Van Balberghe, eds., *Papier blanc, encre noir. Cent ans de culture*

undoubtedly has something to do with preventing access to knowledge and information concerning the colony, which was organised and systematically maintained by the Belgian authorities. These pre-1960 characteristics even survived decolonisation: Belgian history books continued to repeat the same clichés for more than twenty years after Congo's independence.

Public space was another traditional vehicle for colonial propaganda, both abroad and in Belgium, yet few prestigious buildings clearly bore a colonial stamp. The famous triumphal arch in the Parc du Cinquantenaire in Brussels was certainly built using Leopold's Congolese profits, but this monument bears no reference to the colony. Most of the monuments are distinctly more modest: several statues of great figures from the colonial era, busts of key figures and commemorative plaques. Historian Matthew Stanard has counted approximately 250 monuments directly or indirectly linked to the colony. The great majority were erected during the inter-war period and most are located in the French-speaking part of the country and in the capital: forty-two per cent in Wallonia and thirty per cent in Brussels and Tervuren. Flanders, almost half of the country in surface area, only has twenty-five per cent of the inventoried monuments.[109] Does this imbalance reflect a difference of opinion in the country's two main communities in relation to the Congo? It is difficult to confirm, but this can perhaps be related to previous observations concerning the reserved attitude of at least a part of Flemish public opinion towards the deeply francophone nature of colonisation.

Film was another powerful means of propaganda, but it took a while before the Belgian authorities really took an interest in it.[110] Some films on the Congo were indeed shown in Belgium before the First World War, but for a long time the ministry of the colonies neglected this propaganda channel.[111] A number of filmmakers were certainly active in the colony in the inter-war period and continued their work after the Second World War. They were particularly seeking aid and subsidies from the authorities or from large private organisations. Interest in film did not begin to increase until the second half of the 1940s, primarily because cinematographic production consisted essentially of documentary films or educational films aimed *at* the Congolese. Works of fiction inspired by the colony and aimed at a European audience were extremely rare. The Belgian cinema going public therefore formed an image of the colonial world essentially through American, French or British films.

francophone en Afrique centrale (Zaïre, Rwanda et Burundi) (Brussels, 1992), pp. 333–79 (quotation pp. 349–50); A. De Baets, *De figuranten van de geschiedenis* (Berchem-Hilversum, 1994), pp. 102–12.

[109] Rest: undetermined location. M. G. Stanard, *Selling, op. cit.* (thesis), pp. 213–24.
[110] M. G. Stanard, *Selling, op. cit.* (thesis), chapter 5; G. Convents, *Images et démocratie. Les Congolais face au cinéma et à l'audiovisuel* (Kessel-Lo, 2006); P. Van Schuylenbergh & M. Zana Aziza Etambala, eds., *Patrimoine d'Afrique centrale. Archives films Congo, Rwanda, Burundi, 1912–1960* (Brussels, 2010).
[111] M. G. Stanard, *Selling, op. cit.* (thesis), pp. 268, 300.

The Colonial Impact on Belgian Arts and Sciences

With the sudden opening of central Africa by explorers, soldiers, civil servants, businessmen and Belgian missionaries, links were also created in the artistic domain. Great numbers of African objects rapidly arrived in Belgium. Some were put on display in museums, others formed private collections of 'negro' artefacts.[112] Exhibitions were dedicated to African art; art and cultural reviews devoted attention to the subject. A whole new art market was also created, mainly around statues, masks and everyday objects from the various populations of the Congo and the surrounding areas. These objects were enthusiastically purchased not only by colonials, but also by affluent groups and individuals in Belgium. The trade or transfer of these objects was accompanied by a transfer of meaning: Practical objects became works of art and allowed Belgian homes to be enhanced by the exotic.

Congolese forms and materials influenced certain aspects of Belgian artistic creation at the end of the nineteenth century, particularly in the use of ivory in the sculpture of decorative pieces. Both the Art Nouveau and later the Art Deco movements were influenced by the Congolese experience.[113] After the Second World War, an original and modernist architectural and urbanistic trend developed, underpinned by fascinating parallels and reciprocal influences between the metropole and the colony.[114] The Congo rapidly began to captivate several Belgian artists. A number of sculptors and painters went to the colony to create works in a new style, and the Belgian Africanist movement was born with artists such as Pierre de Vaucleroy, Fernand Allard l'Olivier and Auguste Mambour.[115] However, it must be said that the true Africanist artists do not feature among the most powerful or original Belgian artists of the first half of the twentieth century. The great Belgian surrealists, including René Magritte and Paul Delvaux, were not at all influenced by the Congo.

This artistic activity also had an important propagandist dimension. Like filmmakers, painters and sculptors sought public support to organise, facilitate and/or subsidise their journeys and visits. They were aware, as painter Fernand Allard said, of "constructing a colonial propaganda work". The colonial authorities had established a system of grants for artists because they

---

[112] P. Van Schuylenbergh & F. Morimont, *Rencontres artistiques Belgique – Congo 1920-1950* (Louvain-la-Neuve, 1995).

[113] J.-P. Jacquemin, "L'art colonial à pile ou face: exotisme et propagande", in J. Guisset, ed., *Le Congo et l'Art belge 1880-1960* (Brussels, 2003), p. 69; P. Van Schuylenbergh, *Rencontres, op. cit.*, pp. 49-50; S. Cornelis, "Koloniale kunst. Een herontdekking van gedeeld cultureel erfgoed", in V. Viaene, e.a., eds., *Congo in België, op. cit.*, pp. 215-30; F. Aubry, "L'exposition de Tervuren en 1897: scénographie Art nouveau et arts primitifs", in R. Hoozee, ed., *Bruxelles carrefour de cultures* (Antwerp, 2000), pp. 179-84.

[114] J. Lagae, "Aller/retour? Bouwen en plannen in Kinshasa en Brussel", in V. Viaene, e.a., eds., *Congo in België, op. cit.*, pp. 95-113.

[115] S. Cornelis et al., *Artistes belges dans les territoires d'outre-mer 1884-1962* (Tervuren, 1989); J. Guisset, ed., *Le Congo et l'Art belge 1880-1960, op. cit.*; J.-P. De Rycke, *Africanisme et modernisme. La peinture et la photographie d'inspiration coloniale en Afrique centrale (1920-1940)* (Brussels, 2010).

used the works produced to introduce and promote the colony to the Belgian and foreign public. An Association des Écrivains et Artistes coloniaux belges (Association of Belgian Colonial Writers and Artists) was set up in 1926; the following year, it enjoyed the patronage of the ministry of the colonies. Thus, a network including civil servants, writers and artists was formed with the aim of promoting artistic expression concerning the colony.[116]

As the title of this association suggests, the Congo also exerted an influence on Belgian literature.[117] The colony naturally inspired a certain number of travelogues and memoirs, but also fictional works. Again, however, the authors of fiction do not feature among the most important names of national literature: In Belgium there is no equivalent of such literary giants as Albert Camus, Rudyard Kipling or Multatuli, whose works were profoundly marked by the experience of empire. Nevertheless, the Congo sometimes makes cameo appearances in the work of well-known writers whose main literary activity had nothing to do with the colony. So what is the overall significance of Belgian colonial literature? According to Pierre Halen, the great specialist on the subject, "[The] spectre of the colony haunts [French-speaking] metropolitan literature".[118] Although the quality of this colonial literature varied considerably, "[these books] determined vocations, enthusiasm, peaceful assurances …".[119] The impact on Flemish literature in Belgium seems to be less significant; few original works explicitly adopted the colony as a theme.[120] The content of these (French or Flemish) texts varied quite a lot. They often accentuated the exotism of the colonial setting and underlined the otherness of African society and people. Racial clichés were of course present, as was eulogy for the civilising role of whites. Another common theme was the disorientation or physical and/or moral degeneration of the white man when confronted with this strange world and debilitating climate. Finally, some works

[116] T. Lobbes, "De artistieke reisbeurs in dienst van de koloniale propaganda. Het Ministerie van Koloniën en de koloniale kunstenaars tijdens het interbellum", *Cahiers d'Histoire du Temps présent*, 21 (2009), p. 145.

[117] An old inventory appears in G. D. Périer, *Petite histoire des lettres coloniales en Belgique* (Brussels, 1944); major recent studies were carried out by P. Halen, *Le Petit Belge avait vu grand. Une littérature coloniale* (Brussels, 1993); P. Halen & J. Riesz, eds., *Images de l'Afrique et du Congo Zaïre dans les lettres françaises de Belgique et alentour* (Brussels, 1993); P.-P. Fraiture, *Le Congo belge et son récit francophone à la veille des indépendances* (Paris, 2003); P.-P. Fraiture, *La mesure de l'autre. Afrique subsaharienne et roman ethnographique de Belgique et de France (1918-1940)* (Paris, 2007); M. Quaghebeur, ed. *Papier blanc, encre noire, op. cit.*

[118] P. Halen, "Littératures viatique et coloniale", in C. Berg & P. Halen, eds., *Littératures belges de langue française. Histoire et perspectives (1830-2000)* (Brussels, 2000), p. 327.

[119] P. Halen, "1908. Le roi Léopold II cède la colonie du Congo à la Belgique. Une littérature coloniale", in J.-P. Bertrand, ed., *Histoire de la littérature belge francophone 1830-2000* (Paris, 2003), p. 233.

[120] A. Verthé & B. Henry, *Geschiedenis van de Vlaams-Afrikaanse letterkunde* (Leuven, 1961), pp. 47-9; L. Renders, "Nikkerke en ikkerke. Nederlandstalig proza over Kongo", in T. D'haen, ed., *Europa buitengaats. Koloniale en postkoloniale literaturen in Europese talen* (Amsterdam, 2002), vol. 1, p. 309: "During the period before independence, colonial literature is of mediocre quality".

adopted an outright critical attitude towards colonisation and the colonists' motives and behaviour. This was the case, for instance, in the novel *Kufa* by Henri Cornélus, dating from 1954, and in some Flemish works. Specialist Luc Renders notes that "a strong anticolonialist current flows through the whole of Dutch-speaking Congo literature" – some novels "completely undermined the colonizing myth".[121]

Perhaps more influential was a particular form of literature that lies at the crossroads of textual and visual production, that is, comic strips.[122] Thanks to the huge and often young audience, the impact of this artistic and literary genre may exceed other forms of creative expression. The audience for *Tintin au Congo* (1931), by the famous comic strip writer Hergé, endures to this day. The clichés Hergé conveyed (or created) concerning the Belgian colony and its native inhabitants have been the subjects of numerous exegeses. This work, whose symbolic meaning by far exceeds the limits of the Belgian imperial domain, is a typical example of racial stereotyping. For this very reason, it continues to be controversial.

The impact of the Congo on Belgian science was undoubtedly more distinct and more extensive than on the literary domain. From the beginning of the Congo Free State the sciences were mobilised to support colonial activities, and geography took pride of place. The geographical societies that existed prior to the Leopoldian enterprise enthusiastically participated in the establishment of European domination in central Africa.[123] At the beginning of colonisation, geography was the rallying point for various facets of the intellectual grasp of the Congo. But very quickly, the way opened for a wide range of scientific approaches and several sciences acquired legitimacy.[124] Hence, a range of scientific specialities was created, all focusing on central Africa, an uncharted territory in the minds of the Belgian scientific milieu. Anthropologists and linguists classified the indigenous societies and languages and began to study colonial and traditional laws and local customs.[125] Geologists, climatologists and hydrologists examined the inanimate environment, while zoologists, botanists,

---

[121] L. Renders, "Nikkerke", art. cit., p. 319.

[122] See N. R. Hunt, "Tintin and the Interruptions of Congolese Comics", in P. S. Landau & D. D. Kaspin, eds., *Images and Empire: Visuality in Colonial and Postcolonial Africa*, Berkeley, University of California Press, 2002, p. 90–123; M.-R. Maurin, "*Tintin au Congo* ou la nègrerie en clichés", in P. Halen & J. Riesz, eds., *Images de l'Afrique, op. cit.*, pp. 151–62; Ph. Delisle, *Bande dessinée franco-belge et imaginaire colonial. Des années 1930 aux années 1980* (Paris, 2008).

[123] J. Vandersmissen, *Koningen van de wereld. Leopold II en de aardrijkskundige beweging* (Leuven-The Hague, 2009).

[124] M. Poncelet, *L'invention des sciences coloniales belges* (Paris, 2008); the parts on "overseas sciences" in R. Halleux, e.a., eds., *Histoire des sciences en Belgique 1815–2000* (Brussels, 2001), vol. 2, pp. 235–65.

[125] M. Couttenier, *Congo tentoongesteld. Een geschiedenis van de Belgische antropologie en het museum van Tervuren* (Leuven, 2005); M. Couttenier, "Anthropology and Ethnography", in P. Poddar, R. S. Patke & L. Jensen, eds., *A Historical Companion to Postcolonial Literatures: Continental Europe and its Empires* (Edinburgh, 2008), pp. 12–13.

physicians and tropical agronomists studied the living. In just a few decades, all these sciences underwent massive development. Belgian researchers accumulated an impressive mass of knowledge on the Congo. Belgium, which until the 1870s had almost no scientific affinity with the sub-Saharan region, raised itself to the rank of a world centre for Africanism.

In the beginning, these various scientific disciplines focusing on the Congo were true agents of colonialism; they provided the intellectual instruments to appropriate and dominate the environment and the local populations.[126] After the Second World War, the scientific approach to the Congo began to change. Economic sciences began to show an interest in the Congo; gradually, they adopted developmentalist and sometimes even critical tones towards colonial reality. Anthropology also began to follow other paths, moving further and further away from the protection of the colonial apparatus and adopting completely new methods and theoretical frameworks.

Scientific efforts became institutionalised, first through the creation of specialised institutions and then in the universities. In the wake of the Tervuren exhibition in 1897, Leopold II founded the Congo Museum.[127] It had many functions. It was a warehouse for objects collected in the vast colony, a showcase for the most remarkable artefacts, a permanent platform for colonial propaganda, a place to initiate the Belgian population into colonial 'realities' and a scientific research centre covering the whole of Congolese experience. The museum rapidly attracted numerous visitors: An excursion to Tervuren was a feature of the school curriculum. The museum undoubtedly aroused a great deal of enthusiasm among a broad spectrum of the population. It was (and still is) one of the country's most visited museums. After independence, the museum left its former propagandist stage almost intact; it was not until the beginning of the twenty-first century that a new management team, spurred on by the present curator, Guido Gryseels, endeavoured to finally elaborate a museographic scenario more in keeping with the radically modified awareness of our time. But the Royal Museum of the Belgian Congo (renamed the Royal Museum of Central Africa in 1960) was not only a platform for propaganda and exhibitions, it was also a research centre. Several generations of Belgian Africanists spent more or less their entire careers there; they featured (and still feature) among the world's experts on Africanism. This scientific speciality was also created, accommodated and distributed in other institutions specially created for this purpose. For instance, there is the Institute of Tropical Medicine, which immediately became a global leader in research in this domain.[128] Tropical agronomic research was stimulated by the creation of the Institut national pour l'Étude agronomique du Congo (INEAC) in 1933, which played

---

[126] M. Poncelet, *L'invention, op. cit.*, passim.
[127] *Africa Museum Tervuren 1898–1998* (Tervuren, 1998); B. Wastiau, *Exit Congo Museum* (Tervuren, 2000); M. G. Stanard, *Selling, op. cit.* (thesis), pp. 107–59.
[128] R. Baetens, *Een brug tussen twee werelden. Het prins Leopold Instituut voor Tropische Geneeskunde Antwerpen 100 jaar* (online: www.itg.be/internet/geschiedenis/index.html).

an important role in the agricultural development of the colony.[129] A special foundation, the Institut pour la Recherche scientifique au Congo (IRSAC), was created in 1947 to promote scientific research in and on the colony. And the colony was a godsend for the Botanical Garden in Brussels, founded in 1826. The collection and classification of the astounding variety of Congolese plants gave the institution a scientific credibility that it had previously lacked.[130] The Institut royal colonial belge, founded in 1928 (which became the Académie royale des Sciences coloniales in 1952) occupied a special place. It was not a research institution in the strict sense, but a forum bringing together important scientists specialising in the Congo, leading colonial civil servants, businessmen and missionaries.[131]

Universities represent the second way by which the Belgian colonial sciences were institutionalised. From the start, Leopold II succeeded in mobilising individual support in university circles. Eminent professors became the intellectual and administrative auxiliaries of the Congo Free State. The integration of the colonial element in university structures began a few years before the takeover of the Congo by the Belgian state. However, this process encountered a number of difficulties. Detailed research on the Catholic University of Louvain shows that the measures taken to integrate the colony into research and teaching were disorganised and often inefficient.[132] The university rectors did not always show a great deal of interest in the subject and colonial subjects had mixed success among both teachers and students. Outbursts of enthusiasm certainly existed, but these initiatives, aimed at promoting the Congo among academics, often fizzled out or were rapidly dropped.[133] Special courses leading to a diploma focusing on the colonial domain were created both in the universities and in the polytechnical colleges, but in the social science faculties, in particular, "at the very most, [the] colonial sciences were taught, not produced".[134]

The presence, organisation and vivacity of colonial university sciences somewhat improved shortly before and mainly after the Second World War. Inter-university competition played a role in the development of colonial sciences from the beginning, and also contributed to renewed academic interest in the Congo in the 1940s and 1950s. It was indeed a question of 'occupying' the Congolese terrain through original initiatives. In 1926 and 1932, the Catholic university set up two institutes aimed at establishing medical and agronomy units in the Congo. In 1938, the Université libre de Bruxelles retaliated by

---

[129] V. Drachoussoff, e.a., eds., *Le développement rural en Afrique centrale 1908–1960/1962* (Brussels, 1991).

[130] D. Diagre-Vanderpelen, *Le Jardin botanique de Bruxelles (1826–1940)* (Brussels, forthcoming), manuscript pp. 218, 220, 230.

[131] M. Poncelet, *L'invention, op. cit.*, pp. 264–77.

[132] R. Mantels, *Geleerd in de tropen. Leuven, Congo en de wetenschap, 1885–1960* (Leuven, 2007); J.-L. Vellut, "L'Afrique dans les horizons de l'Université Catholique de Louvain (XIXe – XXe siècles)", in J. Roegiers & I. Vandevivere, eds., *Leuven/Louvain-la-Neuve. Aller Retour* (Leuven, 2001), pp. 205–23.

[133] R. Mantels, *Geleerd, op. cit.*, pp. 32–145.

[134] Ibid., p. 103.

launching a centre focused on medical aid.[135] After the Second World War, this university also engaged in the study of social and political problems in the Congo. In the 1950s, the two movements, Catholic and anti-clerical, were also engaged in a fight to create the first university in the Congo.

The final aspect of the colonial impact on higher education in Belgium is the colonial university.[136] In 1904-5, Leopold II thought of creating a 'world school', an idea that never came to fruition. After Belgium's takeover of the Congo, however, the authorities deemed it necessary to create an institution of higher education for the training of future colonial civil servants. In 1920, the Ecole coloniale supérieure was founded in Antwerp, renamed the Université coloniale in 1923, then INUTOM (Institut universitaire des Territoires d'Outre-Mer) in 1949. The four-year curriculum was essentially oriented towards practical matters. Before the Second World War, between ten and twenty students enrolled every year; after the war, this number rose to around forty or fifty a year. All in all, 997 young Belgians graduated from the Université coloniale between 1920 and 1960. However, this number was not sufficient to cover all the needs of colonial administration. Graduates from other universities were therefore recruited by the colonial service. The established universities looked down on the institute in Antwerp because it only provided practical training and was in no way a scientific research institute.

The Problem of the 'Colonial Spirit' in Belgium
This rapid survey has shown that the Congo influenced different domains of Belgian socio-cultural life to varying degrees. But did these undeniably important propaganda efforts affect the public's attitudes? Were the Belgians 'empire-minded'? The same question has been asked in Great Britain, and is still hotly debated; the answers are rather contradictory.[137] Much research would be needed to make this assessment in Belgium. Nevertheless, many clues seem to indicate that the colony did not arouse great popular enthusiasm.

In a funeral oration delivered in 1934 upon the death of the first minister of colonies, Jules Renkin, the following words were pronounced by a fervent colonial:

The Nation only took over the Congo through duty and following a painful conflict with the inspired Sovereign (…) its heart was not in it. The majority of the Nation did not believe in the continuity of the Congo. Even the minister's immediate colleagues doubted the success of the enterprise.[138]

---

[135] A. Uyttebrouck & A. Despy-Meyer, eds., *Les 150 ans de l'Université libre de Bruxelles (1834–1984)* (Brussels, 1984), pp. 328-31. For the Ghent university and the Congo, see A. Eerdekens, *Ganda-Congo, 1956–1970* (Ghent, 2010), unpublished master's thesis in history, Universiteit Gent.

[136] See *Middelheim. Mémorial de l'Institut Universitaire des Territoires d'Outre-Mer. Gedenkboek van het Universitair Instituut van de Overzeese Gebieden* (S.l., 1987); M. Poncelet, *L'invention, op. cit.*, pp. 278-81.

[137] See B. Porter, *The Absent-Minded Imperialists, op. cit.*

[138] "Discours prononcé par M. O. Louwers à l'occasion du décès de M. J. Renkin, membre titulaire", *Bulletin des séances de l'Institut royal colonial belge*, 5, 2 (1934), p. 363.

The Congo and Belgium's Domestic Policy

Throughout the history of colonial Belgium, somewhat disillusioned remarks illustrated the mixed feelings of the Belgians in relation to its overseas possession. For instance, this is what Albert De Vleeschauwer, minister of colonies, said in 1939:

> [A]ll those who love the Congo are often dismayed when they see to what extent ill-informed opinion expresses little enthusiasm for our wonderful colonial empire. These words are no exaggeration. On the contrary. This ill-informed opinion is not the exclusive feature of the man in the street. In its crudest form – and you have heard it just like me – it is the question that I often hear: 'What use are colonies to Belgium?'[139]

There are many such quotes. They even form a sort of theme in Belgian colonial rhetoric. In Belgium, the Congo was misunderstood and even disliked. Of course, allowances must be made: In the mouth of a skilful orator, such bitter observations could serve as a springboard for more enthusiastic perorations. But other actors, who did not have such a high rank in public hierarchy, have also made many similar comments. Let us cite some examples. In 1920, a brochure praising the Congo as the "most beautiful colony in the world" justified its publication by saying that "the majority of Belgians are, indeed, in almost complete ignorance of what our colony may one day become".[140] Such a statement might be considered normal, since the Congo had only been 'Belgian' for twelve years. But more than fifteen years later, another propaganda booklet also opens with the message that this initiative will hopefully "contribute to giving our Belgian audiences a 'taste for the colony'".[141] At the beginning of the 1920s, André Van Iseghem, a former district commissioner in the Congo, estimated that approximately fifty per cent of the former colonials who had returned to Belgium were indifferent to the colonial ideal. Some even harboured a negative opinion: "They have returned full of resentment towards their colonial life; they confuse their hate towards the venture in the Congo with their hate for the men who run it". Only ten per cent of these ex-colonials were pro-colonists, according to the author.[142] A report dedicated to colonial careers presented during a Catholic Party congress in 1923 also contained signs of disillusionment: "We are unfortunately forced to state [that] despite the laudable efforts of a number of convinced propagandists, (...) deep down, the population remains entirely foreign to this movement [in favour of the colony]. Their appeal has virtually no influence on them".[143]

Such statements are of course anecdotal. It was not until 1956 that a scientific opinion poll was carried out.[144] A carefully selected panel of 3,000 Belgians answered the following questions (answers in percentages).

---

[139] A. De Vleeschauwer, *Belgique-Congo. Conférence (...) à la SBÉE, le 20 novembre 1939* (S.l., 1939), p. 1.
[140] *Le Congo. La plus belle colonie du monde. Ce que nous devons faire* (Brussels, 1920), p. 1.
[141] P. Coppens, *Veillées congolaises* (Brussels, s.d. [ca. 1936]), p. 5.
[142] Cited by L. H. Gann & P. Duignan, *The Rulers of Belgian Africa, 1884–1914* (Princeton, 1979), pp. 186–7.
[143] Kadoc, L. Delvaux Papers, n° 1.5.3.3, "La carrière coloniale".
[144] G. Jacquemyns, *Le Congo belge devant l'opinion publique* (Brussels, 1956), pp. 63–5.

TABLE 2.1. *Opinion Poll on the Belgian Congo (1956)*

	Yes	No	No opinion
Are you interested in the Congo?	76.9	N.A.	N.A.
Do you know white people who are in or who have been to the Congo?	80.5	N.A.	N.A.
Should the white population in the Congo increase?	56.2	21.7	22.1
Is it necessary to stimulate the establishment of small *colons*?	54.9	19.0	26.1
Are you ready to take on a job in the Congo?	19.3	69.6	11.1
Is the Belgian presence in the Congo legitimate?	80.5	5.4	14.1
Is the Belgian presence in the Congo useful for the Congolese?	83.2	4.0	12.8
Is the Belgian presence in the Congo useful for Belgium?	86.3	3.1	10.6

At the end of the colonial period, most Belgians seemed interested in the Congo. In fact, they thought Belgian domination was legitimate *and* useful for both the metropole and the colonised population (about eighty per cent). Only three to five per cent had a clear anti-colonialist attitude. Nevertheless, about two-thirds were not willing to live in the colony. But when other, more precise questions were asked (not featured here), the percentage of 'no opinion' responses rose to about a quarter of all responses and contradictory answers were given. In short, shortly before independence, many Belgians had only vague and general notions about the Congo, and they more or less believed the messages disseminated through official discourse and propaganda.

My hypothesis, which should of course be verified, would be as follows: The colonial enterprise was not supported by a great wave of popular fervour, except in very specific and somewhat limited segments of the population. Five categories stand out in this respect: former or actual colonial civil servants, businessmen, soldiers, scientists and missionaries. They were often fervent colonialists and proclaimed their love of the Congo loudly and clearly. But what did the masses think? Thanks to lessons in school, a few visits to the Congo Museum, several large-scale exhibitions and a profusion of official speeches, Belgians were certainly aware of the Congo. For many, the colony was even perceived as an almost natural extension of Belgium. It had perhaps become the subject of a certain interest, even a sort of pride. Vague ideas, based on personal encounters with former colonials or the use of decorative Congolese objects at home, may have contributed to a certain presence of the colony in daily life.[145] But, in Belgium, there was no attitude similar to British jingoism, which exalted the homeland through the prism of the colonial empire; nor did Belgium experience its own variant of the *mission civilisatrice* with which France identified.

[145] D. Van Reybrouck, "Congo in de populaire cultuur", in V. Viaene, e.a., eds., *Congo in België*, op. cit., pp. 169–81.

How can this be explained? Apart from the modest physical presence of the Belgians in the Congo and of the Congolese in Belgium, a number of structural aspects allow us to support the hypothesis of the weakness of the 'colonial mind' in Belgium. First, there is the ambiguous destiny of Belgian patriotism, often tinged with scepticism and undermined by divided loyalties. A growing number of Flemings struggled against the dominant position of French speakers in their region, and a few radicals dreamed of Belgium's demise. This sector of the public was not particularly enthused by the Congo, which was not only closely linked with the Belgian unitary state but was also completely dominated by the French language and the elite. Second, the absence of prior colonial tradition and geopolitical ambitions also helps to explain the relative lack of colonial passion in Belgium. Normally, it takes some time to mould people's minds, time that was lacking in Belgium. The colonial experience only lasted fifty years, during which Belgium experienced two world wars and foreign occupations for no less than nine years total. That left only a few years in which to build strong imperial minds! Third, the origin of colonial activity did not reside in a multitude of businesses and projects embraced by society. It was the result of an artificial introduction by King Leopold – a most uncommon personality, but nevertheless an *individual* player, with all the limitations this involves. Between 1885 and 1905, part of Belgian colonial enthusiasm was purely and simply mercenary or arose from within a group faithful to the king and was, therefore, only the tip of the iceberg.

Finally, the attitude of the Belgian authorities also played a role. When it came to the Congo, they were always obsessed with controlling the flow of information. There was no freedom of the press in the colony and news from the colony was carefully managed by a state information agency. Only the elite travelled to these distant lands or resided there for some time. Very few Congolese ever visited Belgium. A static image of the Congo, consisting of a handful of clichés, was constructed and promoted by official propaganda channels such as exhibitions and schoolbooks. Public discussion of colonial matters by political actors was reduced to a minimum. When it came to the Congo, conformism and silence were the norm. Dissenting voices in the colony itself were silenced simply by sending the culprits back home where they rarely had any opportunity to express themselves publicly except through personal contacts. All these elements explain why the average Belgian had little direct and spontaneous contact with colonial reality. It is therefore not surprising that the Belgian imperial mind was rather low key.

The Congo's Independence and Belgian Internal Politics (1958–1960)

Adapting the Ties between Belgium and the Congo?
A few months prior to independence, the Belgian colonial authorities still seemed to have an eternity ahead of them. A Belgian diplomatic letter of August 1959 indicates: "The autonomy [the term 'independence' was not even used] of the Congo will only be achieved at the end of a gradual, long term

development".[146] But just ten months later, the Congo was an independent country! The decolonisation of the Congo was quite rightly qualified as precipitous. This country did not acquire its independence at the end of a long, armed struggle like Indonesia, Vietnam, Algeria or elsewhere. And contrary to what had happened in India or in the British dominions, the end of colonial rule was not the result of a long process of political reforms. In 1960, the political ties between Belgium and the Congo were suddenly severed, with no institutional precedent.

Was the nature of the ties between Belgium and the Congo the subject of no prior reflection whatsoever? Such a conclusion would be incorrect. In reality, since the 1940s, this problem had troubled some people, but the debates did not follow the same lines as those in 1960. They must be put into a broader context. Frictions existed between the ministry of the colonies and the ministry of foreign affairs; other tensions were perceptible between the Belgian and Congolese authorities. Furthermore, some colonists dreamed of greater autonomy for the Congo. In the end, all these conflicts revolved around three fundamental questions: Who was running the Congo, for which reason and within what limits? The nature of the ties between Belgium and the Congo did not really allow for the pure and simple independence of a Congo run exclusively by its black inhabitants. Independence under such terms was only the extreme case of a very wide range of nuanced possibilities.

In 1945, the relationship between Belgium and its colony was called into question from two sides: on one side by certain colonial circles in the Congo and on the other by major players on the international scene. Let us begin with the first group. During and after the Second World War, voices were raised in the Congo demanding greater autonomy for the colony (though always within the framework of Belgian sovereignty) or, rather, for the *whites* in the colony – since there was of course no question of granting political rights to the Congolese. Liberal senator and businessman Robert Godding, who had sought refuge in the Congo during the occupation of Belgium by the Germans, pleaded in favour of the participation of the Belgians in the colony's government; he even recommended setting up a permanent legislative council, with consultative powers, in the Congo.[147] Even the highest spheres of the colonial political world seemed favourable to an increase in the colony's autonomy. In 1943, Governor-General Pierre Ryckmans and his close collaborators studied a reform of the existing, purely consultative colonial organs, that is, the government council (the central authority situated in Léopoldville) and the provincial councils.[148]

---

[146] Archives of the Belgian Ministry of Foreign Affairs, Brussels (AMAE), AF-I-26 (1948–60), Van Meerbeke to Wigny, Minister of Foreign Affairs, 12 August 1959.

[147] Musée royal de l'Afrique centrale (MRAC), CSK archives, note "L'évolution de la Colonie. Résumé des informations captées pendant l'occupation", by the CCCI, 1 September 1944, pp. 61–2.

[148] These consultative bodies had been created by the decree of 28 July 1914 and reformed by the decree of 29 June 1933. Ryckmans's point of view in Archives africaines (AA) (kept at AMAE) Pétillon Papers (PP), n° 19, weekly report of the GG to the Minister of Colonies, n° 71 of 28 June 1943.

As soon as Belgium was liberated from the Germans, the governor-general and the new minister of colonies, Edgar De Bruyne, began discussing possible institutional reforms in the Congo. Both of them agreed that it was too early for an elective system, but Ryckmans "pointed out that, in the opinion of many of those in the Congo, this [Government] Council should deliberate on all things". However, this possibility was rejected after discussion.[149] Finally, the decree of 31 July 1945 broadened the composition of the government council and the provincial councils. Minister De Bruyne did not seem hostile to a form of self-government for the Congo in the future.[150] Godding, his Liberal successor, observed in 1946 that "a spirit of independence had developed in the colony" during the war. Among other things, this was because the colonists compared the situation in the Belgian Congo with that of other colonies, where local power of decision was more extensive. He was willing to increase decentralisation, both within the Congo and in relation to Brussels.[151]

The idea of increased autonomy for the Congo continued to trouble minds in the Congo itself. Max Horn, a financier of great influence in colonial circles, recommended the gradual creation of a Congolese nation because "the colonial sense of identity is not incompatible with Belgium's sovereignty". He, however, considered it impossible to imagine the Congo as the 'tenth province of Belgium' because of its particularities.[152] In 1946, an article published in the Congolese newspaper *Courrier d'Afrique* hoped and prayed for the future declaration, in Léopoldville, of "the Independent State of Congo within the Belgian Union".[153]

Shortly afterwards, however, the Belgian political class put an end to these ideas because it feared the autonomist tendencies of some of the white colonists. Colonials favoured autonomy throughout the 1950s, but the metropolitan authorities remained firm: They wanted to prevent the emergence of a white minority in the Congo with power over a black majority without any political rights. The Belgian politicians did not want another South Africa in the Congo! An institutionalised apartheid system was completely unacceptable but, in their view, it was too early to grant voting rights to the black population. The Congolese could only be granted suffrage at the end of a long educational process. This is why it took so long to develop representative authority in the Congo. The first appearance of the electoral process dates from the decree of 26 March 1957 that reorganised the local authorities and introduced, in three towns only, the election of local councillors by the white and black

---

[149] AA, PP, n° 20, "Conférences entre le Ministre De Bruyne et le GG Ryckmans avril-mai 1945", "Séance du 12 avril 1945", pp. 2–3.
[150] J. Van Hove, *Histoire du Ministère des Colonies, op. cit.*, p. 104.
[151] AGR, MCM, 3 October 1946.
[152] M. Horn, "La naissance de la Nation congolaise", *Revue générale belge*, 20 (March 1947), pp. 628–39 (p. 634).
[153] Quoted in *Revue coloniale belge*, 2, 21 (15 August 1946), p. 118.

communities (election of 8 December 1957 in Léopoldville, Élisabethville and Jadotville).[154]

The colonial ties unifying Belgium and the Congo also came under the fire of international criticism. The UN, the Communist bloc, newly independent countries and, to a lesser degree, the United States, pointed an accusing finger at colonialism. In light of these attacks, Belgium reaffirmed its sovereignty rights over the Congo. This element was the cornerstone of the country's international policy. A revealing anecdote of the state of mind in 1945 was when Liberal MP Ernest Demuyter proposed changing the national flag, which, from then on, would combine the Belgian 'black, yellow, red' with the Congolese blue and golden star. This suggestion was abandoned, as were the plans to modify the constitution, which were intended to emphasise the structural link between Belgium and the Congo.

A New Colonial Policy Prepared by the PSC-CVP: The Concept of the 'Belgian-Congolese Community'
Behind this apparent firmness some Belgian political circles nevertheless truly questioned the future of the Congo, and it is from this angle that we return once again to Belgian internal politics. In 1946, the Christian-Democrat Party PSC-CVP set up a colonial commission responsible for elaborating the party's colonial policy. In the beginning of the 1950s, it elaborated a new colonial strategy.[155] The commission believed that, confronted with UN criticism, Belgium should adapt its ties with the Congo. They recommended bringing the colony's black and white communities closer together and seriously examined the possibility of reforming domestic Congolese institutions. They wanted to generate a gradual and controlled political process in the Congo. Ultimately, they believed that this process would guarantee the durability of the bond between Belgium and the Congo, in whatever form it might take. At the same time, in July 1952, the Catholic governor-general of the Congo, Léo Pétillon, introduced the notion of 'Belgian-Congolese community'.[156] This notion crystallised much of the desire for reform, but remained rather vague. In fact, it covered two different aspects of the issue. On the one hand, it referred to the creation of a 'mixed' society in the Congo itself; on the other hand, it referred to the unbreakable tie supposed to exist between Belgium and the Congo. In any case, these two aspects were linked; the creation of new social ties in the colony was considered as *sine qua non* for the maintenance of a special relationship between the two territorial entities, based on a form of internal differentiation. The Belgian-Congolese community could have developed into a modest Belgian variant of the British Commonwealth, the Union française (1946)

[154] A. Beyens, "L'histoire du statut des villes", in *Congo 1955–1960. Recueil d'études* (Brussels, 1992), pp. 15–70.
[155] Kadoc, Cepess Papers, n° 2.4.12.1/4, "Note sur la situation juridique du Congo Belge", 4 November 1952.
[156] A. Stenmans & F. Reyntjens, *La pensée politique du gouverneur général Pétillon* (Brussels, 1993), p. 123.

or the Nederlands-Indonesische Unie (1947-56) and managed the transition from traditional colonial domination to a new kind of privileged relationship between the metropole and the former colony.[157] In reality, this concept never had time to develop; Congo's decolonisation erupted too brutally.

In the wake of the PSC-CVP committee's recommendations, the other Belgian political parties were also beginning to come out of their inertia regarding colonial matters. In 1953, the Belgian Socialists made the bitter observation that "currently, the Belgian Socialist Party has no colonial programme, hence the incoherence in colonial matters".[158] In June 1956, the party finally organised a colonial congress; institutional reforms were recommended that, at the end of a process lasting several years, would lead to the Congo's autonomy. In October 1956, a congress of the Liberal Party also mentioned the concept of 'Belgian-Congolese community' and pronounced itself in favour of a certain institutional evolution in the colony.[159] Towards the middle of the 1950s, the Belgian Communist Party abandoned its conciliatory attitude towards colonialism. It no longer wanted to redefine the ties between Belgium and the Congo, but instead asked for total independence. Around 1958-9, the Belgian Communists attempted to establish ties with the Congolese without, however, succeeding in notably influencing the political struggle in the colony.[160]

The 'Politicisation' of the Belgian Congo (1954-1958)

In terms of colonial policy, the PSC-CVP seemed to be one step ahead of the other parties. But in 1954, the Christian-Democrats suffered a serious electoral defeat. For the first time since 1884,[161] the Catholics found themselves in the opposition. A government composed of the Socialist and the Liberal Parties took over the country's destiny until 1958. The original coalition government conducted an innovative colonial policy. The minister of colonies, Auguste Buisseret, introduced reforms that the Christian-Democrat opposition deemed anti-clerical. He granted official schools a more important position and reduced the impact of the Catholic missions. Buisseret's measures triggered a 'School War' in the Congo that had repercussions even in the domain of higher education. Originally, all Belgian universities had agreed upon the creation of a university in Léopoldville that they would administer jointly. But in 1953, Buisseret's predecessor, Christian-Democrat minister of colonies, Dries Dequae, had authorised the creation of the University of Lovanium in Léopoldville under the sole aegis of the Catholic University of

---

[157] J. Thobie, e.a., *Histoire de la France coloniale, op. cit.,* p. 366-70; H. W. van den Doel, *Het Rijk van Insulinde. Opkomst en ondergang van een Nederlandse kolonie* (Amsterdam, 1996), pp. 282-3, 296, 299.

[158] G. Vanthemsche, "De Belgische socialisten", art. cit., p. 43.

[159] P. Menu, ed., *Congresresoluties van de Vlaamse politieke partijen. 4. De Liberale Partij-PVV 1945-1992* (Ghent, 1994), p. 61.

[160] T. Masschaele, *De activiteiten, op. cit.;* B. Verhaegen, "Communisme et anticommunisme au Congo", art. cit.

[161] Except for a short period between August 1945 and March 1947.

Louvain.[162] This move made a pluralist solution in the university education sector impossible. In order to counter-act this Catholic hegemony, the new minister Buisseret created the official University of the Belgian Congo in 1955 and 1956, situated in Élisabethville.

At the same time, Belgian political parties, in particular the Socialist and the Liberal Parties, also founded *amicales* or 'friendly societies' in the Congo that were types of (future) Congolese satellites of their own parties. Conservative Belgian public opinion deplored this politicisation of the Congo and the exportation of Belgian political quarrels to the colony.[163] The Belgian trade unions also founded Congolese chapters that competed against each other and it was during this period that labour union rights developed in the colony.[164]

In the face of these developments, the Christian-Democrat Party felt as though it had been caught off guard. It hesitated as to which attitude to adopt in relation to the burgeoning political activism in the Congo and finally refused to create a party satellite in the Congo.[165] Nevertheless, Catholic organisations increased their action in the Congo with a view to creating a network of Christian-Democrat organisations. The Catholic Church itself prepared for the development of an independent or autonomous Congo.[166] Two initiatives are situated within this context; both created a great stir and both came from the progressive Catholic sphere. In 1955–6, a Belgian professor at the colonial university of Antwerp, Jef Van Bilsen, published a widely discussed article titled "Un plan de trente ans pour l'émancipation politique de l'Afrique belge" ("A thirty-year plan for the political emancipation of Belgian Africa").[167] The colonial establishment was scandalised, because the problem had never been expressed in such explicit terms. In 1956, a group of Catholic Congolese *évolués* published another famous text, the "Manifeste de Conscience africaine". In rather moderate terms, this document raised the question of the political links between Belgium and the Congo.[168] Progressive Belgian Catholics supported this initiative and soon Congolese groups also raised their voices. They published their own manifestos and adopted increasingly radical stances. Around 1958 and 1959, the number of Congolese political groups increased.

[162] P. Bouvier, "Le rôle des enseignements universitaire et supérieur dans le processus de la décolonisation congolaise", in *Congo 1955–1960. Recueil d'études* (Brussels, 1992), pp. 81–93.
[163] A. De Vleeschauwer, "Constatations et réflexions autour de la politique au Congo Belge", *Revue politique*, 6, 5 (December 1956), pp. 412–4.
[164] R. Poupart, *Première esquisse de l'évolution du syndicalisme au Congo* (Brussels, 1960).
[165] A. De Vleeschauwer, "Constatations…", art. cit., pp. 414–15; Id., "Réflexions sur l'évolution politique du Congo belge", *Bulletin des Séances de l'IRCB*, 3, 2 (1957), p. 221.
[166] L. Vandeweyer, "Paternalisme versus ontvoogding. Een katholiek emancipatieproject voor de Belgische kolonie Kongo (1955–1960)", *Trajecta. Tijdschrift voor de geschiedenis van het katholieke leven in de Nederlanden*, 3, 3 (1994), pp. 252–71.
[167] A. A. J. Van Bilsen, *Vers l'indépendance du Congo et du Ruanda-Urundi* (Kinshasa, 1977), p. 296; J. Van Bilsen, *Congo 1945–1965: la fin d'une colonie* (Brussels, 1994).
[168] J.-M. Mutamba, *Du Congo belge au Congo indépendant 1940–1960. Émergence des 'évolués' et genèse du nationalisme* (Kinshasa, 1998), p. 688; N. Tousignant, ed., *Le manifeste* Conscience Africaine *(1956)* (Brussels, 2009).

The politicisation process of the black population had well and truly begun; the race for independence was under way. All these developments were closely watched by the Belgian monarchy, which still considered the Congo as an essential part of Belgian grandeur.

Viceroyalty in the Congo?

The Belgian monarchy had developed a strong symbolic and political relationship with the colony. This was not to change in the years preceding decolonisation. In 1950, following the Royal Question mentioned in the introduction to the next chapter, King Leopold III was forced to abdicate. His twenty-year-old son, King Baudouin I, succeeded him amidst a violent political crisis. The abdication did not immediately solve the tensions between the court and that part of the political world that distrusted the influence the former king and his second wife, Princess Liliane, exercised over the young king. Within this rather tense context, Baudouin visited the Congo in May and June 1955. This trip was considered particularly successful, and even 'triumphant'.[169] It greatly enhanced the sovereign's prestige, but it may also reflect an active royal involvement in colonial policy. On 1 July 1955, as soon as he returned to Belgium, Baudouin gave a speech in which he pleaded for a 'Belgian-Congolese community' situated within the perspective of a new status for the colony.[170] Note that this concept originated in the circles of the Christian-Democrat PSC-CVP, which was in the opposition.

During the same year, the notion of viceroyalty for the Congo also emerged. A journalist at an Élisabethville weekly, *Congo-Soir*, enthusiastic about the success of the royal visit, asked the sovereign to send his brother, Prince Albert (the current Belgian king Albert II, then aged twenty-one), to the Congo as the viceroy. According to the journalist, this was the best means of maintaining the ties between Belgium and the Congo.[171] During the 1950s, the notion of viceroyalty for the Congo did indeed circulate in the Congolese press and in the autonomist colonist circles, which criticised Belgium's 'amateur politicians' and worked towards more self-government for the whites in the Congo.[172] Was it simply a wild imagining thought up by a handful of ultras? Or did this idea enjoy a wider audience, maybe even the favour of the monarchy?

There is no conclusive evidence that this idea stemmed from or was favourably received by the court. The inaccessibility of the royal archives prevents us from having a clear view. However, various clues allow us to conjecture that the concept of viceroyalty for the Congo was not limited only to marginal circles. First, this system was far from unknown in other colonial empires. A

---

[169] Zana Aziza Etambala, *Congo '55-'65* (Tielt, 1999), pp. 17–38.
[170] Quotation taken from G.-H. Dumont, "Positions et affrontements antérieurs à la Table Ronde Belgo-Congolaise", in *Liber Amicorum August De Schryver, minister van Staat* (Ghent, 1968), p. 362.
[171] *Congo-Soir*, 27 August, 17 September, 15 October, 29 October and 19 November 1955, p. 1 (articles by A. Peclers).
[172] AA, AE-2, n° 1801ter (3283), "La Vice-Royauté nécessaire en Afrique", by Gilbert Hellin, s.d.

viceroy, representing the sovereign of the United Kingdom, ran British India. Prince Amedeo of Savoy (1898–1942), Duke of Aosta, who was related to King Leopold III through family ties (his sister was married to the Italian heir to the throne), had been the viceroy of Ethiopia during the occupation by Mussolini's troops. But how was this notion introduced into Belgium?

This idea had already been circulating in the colonial press prior to the Second World War: Some people wanted Leopold, then the crown prince, to become the viceroy of the Congo.[173] It is not known who came up with this proposal, but perhaps it had been at the back of the royal mind since then. The idea was possibly re-activated in an internal note from the PSC-CVP's colonial commission, dated 1953, which explicitly mentioned the concept of 'diarchy'.[174] The Belgians from the homeland and the Congolese would therefore have two distinct 'nationalities' within the same international entity. Did this idea reach the ears of the royal palace, where it would have been interpreted in a specific manner, that is a Belgian-Congolese structure led by two sovereigns, one for Belgium and one for the Congo? Or might the Belgian king simultaneously become the king of the Congo, a separate entity (on the former Austro-Hungarian model)? In the second half of the 1950s, the idea of a viceroyalty for the Congo was mentioned and discussed regularly in high-ranking political circles.

Moreover, King Baudouin remained actively concerned with the Congolese issue. In November 1957, he incited the then prime minister, Socialist Achille Van Acker, to introduce political reforms in the Congo. According to the sovereign, it was necessary "to plan a new structure in favour of the Belgium-Congo association".[175] But it was all in vain; there were no fundamental changes. When the tensions between the Catholic governor-general, Léo Pétillon, and Buisseret, the Liberal minister, were at their peak at the end of 1956, the king successfully insisted that the mandate of the governor-general be prolonged.[176] In July 1958, when the following government was formed – a minority cabinet consisting only of Christian-Democrats led by Gaston Eyskens – the king *imposed* him as the minister of colonies. This choice did not please the traditional political class, not even the PSC-CVP.[177] Pétillon advocated extensive political reforms, including the gradual introduction of a legislative body in the Congo and the loosening of metropolitan control. These ideas were not received very well by his colleagues.[178] Isolated within the government and the political circles in general, Pétillon appeared, to well-informed observers, to be the king's

---

[173] J. Vanderlinden, *Pierre Ryckmans 1891–1959: coloniser dans l'honneur* (Brussels, 1994), p. 249.
[174] Kadoc, Cepess Archives, n° 2.4.12.1/4, "Considérations sur l'avenir politique du Congo belge", by K. Van Cauwelaert, 9 January 1953.
[175] Letter from the king to the prime minister, 4 November 1957, published in *Documents Parlementaires de la Chambre des Représentants*, session 2001–2002, n° 50 0312/007 of 16 November 2001, vol. 2, pp. 616–18.
[176] AGR, MCM, 16 November, 7, 14 and 19 December 1956, pp. 10–1, 19–20, 5–7, 6–7.
[177] G. Kwanten, *A.-E. De Schryver 1898–1991* (Louvain, 2001), p. 502.
[178] AGR, MCM, 19 and 22 September 1958, pp. 1–5 and 1–5.

'liegeman'. At that moment, in October 1958, the idea of entrusting the Congo to a viceroy surfaced once again. According to diplomatic circles, the 'Pétillon plan' had the king's support. And, as it had been in 1955, this news was also circulated in the local Congolese press.[179]

The Hurried Race to Independence

In the meantime, events gathered pace. The Congo made a dramatic return to the centre stage of Belgian political life.[180] For many months, from the end of 1958 until 1961, the question of the Congo was a major concern of Belgian politicians. Though barely established as the minister of colonies, in July 1958 Pétillon set up a working group composed of representatives from the three major Belgian political parties, along with senior colonial civil servants, to study the political problem in the Belgian Congo. It was the working group's responsibility to outline the country's new Congolese policy. However, Pétillon only remained at the head of the ministry of the colonies for four months. In November 1958, Gaston Eyskens formed a coalition cabinet composed of the PSC-CVP and the Liberal Party. At the end of December 1958, the working group's final report was handed to the Christian-Democrat minister, Maurice Van Hemelrijck, the new head of the ministry – a ministry no longer 'of Colonies' but 'of the Belgian Congo and Ruanda-Urundi'. The report recommended a more accelerated reform policy in the Congo. Without using the term *independence* or setting any specific deadlines, it proposed an evolution towards an autonomous Congo associated with Belgium, but with a democratic regime including the participation of the indigenous population.

Official Belgium was therefore on the point of re-defining its colonial policy. But from that moment on, Belgian political circles were constantly caught short by events. On 4 January 1959, just a few days before the government revealed its new policy plan for the Congo, serious riots broke out in Léopoldville. They were quickly and bloodily repressed, but they had a major psychological impact on both the black and white populations. Uncertainty, concern and a sense of urgency arose in both Belgium and the Congo. These factors would influence political management up until the final act: independence on 30 June 1960.

A few days after the riots, the government prepared to reveal its new African policy. Within the government, conservative ministers (both Liberals and Christian-Democrats) opposed the use of the term *independence* but, after a heated discussion, it was nevertheless accepted. Then came a dramatic turn of events. Before the government could present its declaration to parliament, the king took the *personal* initiative of addressing the nation without the knowledge

---

[179] AMAÉF (Archives du Ministère des Affaires étrangères de France) (branch office in Nantes), collection of the Consulate General of France in Léopoldville, 1934–59, n° 5, Raymond Bousquet (French ambassador in Brussels) to MAÉF, 7 November 1958.

[180] P. Bouvier, *L'accession du Congo belge à l'indépendance* (Brussels, 1965); C. Young, *Introduction à la politique congolaise* (Brussels, 1968); J. Vanderlinden, *La crise congolaise* (Brussels, 1985); Zana Aziza Etambala, *De teloorgang van een modelkolonie: Belgisch Congo (1958–1960)* (Leuven, 2008).

of any of the ministers, except for Prime Minister Eyskens, who protected the crown. In this radio speech of 13 January 1959, Baudouin I announced that the Congo would definitely be given its *independence*. The use of this term by the king himself diffused any possible opposition within the political world, within Belgian public opinion or among the 'implacable' whites in the Congo.[181]

Nevertheless, there was still a great deal of uncertainty at the beginning of 1959. What did the term *independence* actually mean? A government statement of January 1959 proposed certain precise deadlines for the gradual establishment of representative institutions in the Congo, a process ultimately meant to lead to a form of independence. But numerous concrete aspects remained unresolved. In fact, the frantic search for a policy plan for the Congo dominated all of 1959. The government was confronted with an increasingly difficult climate, both in the Congo and in Belgium. In the colony, incidents increased and civil disobedience grew. Congolese political parties proliferated and engaged in ardent political battles. Nationalism increasingly gained favour among the native populations. Discouragement seized the colonial administrative machinery. The political climate in Belgium also became increasingly tense. Among the governmental parties and even within them, there were many divergences. The Socialist Party, in opposition, was equally helpless. Everyone feared taking a false step. Were they going too far too quickly? Or not far enough and too slowly? Furthermore, the political parties had to take into account the palace's policy – yet another complication.

The king and his entourage were unquestionably pursuing their own objectives. The fact that the speech of 13 January was elaborated and given upon the king's initiative and without the government's knowledge is in itself revealing. This initiative was a direct follow-up to the feelers that had been put out in 1955 concerning viceroyalty. In Belgian political circles, it soon became clear that the palace had not given up on this idea. In April 1959, a new incident occurred in the Congo. Since the riots in January that same year, the governor-general, Hendrik Cornelis, had been the target of extensive criticism and was accused of weakness. While the government was getting ready to appoint a new governor-general, the king vetoed the nomination and demanded that Cornelis remain in office. The government yielded.[182] Then, in December 1959, King Baudouin decided on his own initiative to make an impromptu visit to a Congo in complete turmoil, thereby catching the government off its guard. Nevertheless, the cabinet endorsed the royal initiative. In the coming months, the court remained an important factor in the Congolese issue.

Apart from royal interventions, the new minister of the Belgian Congo, Maurice Van Hemelrijck, was confronted with many other problems. He was considered too daring by some of his colleagues. He was rejected, even loathed, for the same reason by a proportion of Belgian public opinion and a group of whites in the Congo. He created a dialogue with Congolese nationalist leaders

---

[181] J. Stengers, "Notre nouvelle politique coloniale", *Le Flambeau*, 42, 7–8 (1959), p. 471.
[182] AGR, MCM, 10 and 13 April 1959, pp. 15–6 and 1–4.

but soon some of them also opposed him. The structure of the future Congolese institutions was an impressive stumbling block. Should the Congo be a unitary state or should it adopt a more or less advanced form of federalism?[183] This question divided Congolese political forces. The party of charismatic leader Patrice Lumumba, the Mouvement national congolais (MNC) (Congolese National Movement) opted for a united Congo. Other influential parties were clearly against a centralised state. Abako in particular, led by Joseph Kasavubu, dreamt of a 'federal' Congo, even a (semi-)independent Bas-Congo. In Katanga, a rich mining province in the east of the country, the Conakat party, led by Moïse Tshombe, also wanted to sever the links between this region and the Congolese central authorities.

Official Belgium generally tended towards unitarianism, but some people thought otherwise. Notes written on 24 and 26 August 1959 by Alain Stenmans, a senior civil servant in the colonial civil service in Léopoldville, and by the vice governor-general of the Congo, André Schöller, recommended a federalist approach.[184] Minister Van Hemelrijck also chose this option and wanted to accelerate the march towards independence, but the majority of his colleagues refused to follow him down this road.[185] Van Hemelrijck had been falling into disrepute in his party for some time.[186] Additionally, the minister for the Congo felt disowned because Prime Minister Eyskens sent his assistant private secretary (*Chef de cabinet adjoint*), Harold d'Aspremont Lynden to the Congo without prior announcement, but upon the king's instigation, to inquire about the situation in the Congo and the impact of the Schöller/Stenmans notes.

In September 1959, Van Hemelrijck resigned and an old hand at Belgian politics, August De Schryver, replaced him.[187] De Schryver had a reputation as a wise and reliable man who could oversee the successful outcome of the difficult Congolese issue. In November of the same year, he was assisted by a new minister, Christian-Democrat Raymond Scheyven, who was responsible for managing the economic and financial issues of the Congo. In October 1959, the Cabinet still opted for a restrictive vision of Congolese independence. Despite the planned existence of Congolese executive power and a Congolese legislative assembly, numerous 'reserved' domains would remain in the hands of the Belgians: defence, foreign affairs, telecommunications, executive management of the economy and transport and currency.[188] The colonial administration always had in mind the creation of a community consisting of Belgium and

---

[183] R. Yakemtchouk, *Aux origines du séparatisme katangais* (Brussels, 1988), pp. 63–157.
[184] A. Schöller, *Congo 1959–1960* (Gembloux, 1982), pp. 61–101; G. Eyskens, *De memoires* (Tielt, 1994), pp. 535–46.
[185] AGR, MCM, 28 August and 2 September 1959.
[186] Kadoc, Lefèvre Papers, n° 1.3.1.1, Lefèvre to Eyskens, 27 August 1959 ("strictly personal and confidential").
[187] G. Kwanten, *A.-E. De Schryver, op. cit.*, pp. 514–5.
[188] AMAÉ, AF-I-1 (March-June 1959), Pierre Deschamps (ministry of the colonies advisor) to M.-H. Jaspar, ambassador in Paris, 13 October 1959.

the Congo – not only an economic, but also a *political* community. An official document added rather cynically that:

> In the present circumstances, the administration has to refrain from proclaiming this intention all too openly; otherwise it would be suspected of wanting to impose this idea on the Congolese populations, notwithstanding the freedom of choice that has been guaranteed to them by the governmental declaration [of 13 January 1959].[189]

At the end of 1959, this solution did not suit the Congolese nationalists at all. They were taking a firmer line and demanded complete independence more vociferously than ever. The Congo risked sinking into chaos. Could Belgium engage in an operation to maintain law and order at the risk of an outright colonial war? The Belgian constitution allowed the use of Belgian troops in the colony only on a voluntary basis. At some point, the government thought of bypassing this provision. It envisaged sending conscripts to the Congo without their consent. In the end, however, this plan was not carried out.[190] It would of course have been possible to use the colonial troops, the Force publique, or to send volunteers from Belgium. However, all the Belgian political and social movements rejected the military option. The Left, in particular, was opposed. The shadow of the Algerian war hung over Belgium.

Not everyone, however, shared this opinion. In a confidential conversation with the French ambassador, Grand Maréchal de la Cour Gobert d'Aspremont Lynden, one of the king's closest collaborators, expressed a very distinct opinion (and his interlocutor took care to note down, for the authorities in Paris), that:

> His words obviously reflect the king's feelings.... As soon as the government abandoned the idea of this dispatch [of troops to the Congo], it fatally condemned itself to the policy of general relinquishment that it has adopted since the beginning of the 1960s. And yet, (...) this fear of an Algerian war in the Congo by sending over several thousand Belgian troops (...) was not based on any foundation. In fact, a complete ignorance of the true situation in the Congo, as shown by the minister [De Schryver], a lack of knowledge of the nature of the Bantous and the radical difference between these populations, which have remained very primitive (...) and the Arab populations of Algeria (...) was necessary in order to believe or pretend to believe in such a childish 'slogan'. However, it was useful to refer to this 'slogan' to prevent the Cabinet from any dynamic action and to justify a policy of relinquishment.[191]

Clearly, in this twilight of the Belgian colonial empire, the court and government circles were not on the same wavelength. At the end of 1959 the government found itself at a crossroads. Having refused the military option, the remaining option was dialogue at any cost. This path was taken from the beginning of 1960. The Socialist Party first launched the idea of a roundtable conference bringing together the Belgians and the Congolese. The government then took up the idea.

---

[189] AGR, MCM, 2 September 1959, p. 2.
[190] AGR, MCM, 25 March and 10 April 1959, pp. 12–3, 5–6.
[191] AMAÉF (Nantes), archives of the French consulate general in Léopoldville, correspondence (received) with the French Embassy in Brussels 1957–9, n° 3, Raymond Bousquet (French ambassador in Brussels) to MAÉF, 8 September 1960.

The Congo and Belgium's Domestic Policy

All the Congolese and the three major Belgian parties were thus invited to a major conference held in Brussels from January to February 1960. The Belgian political leaders were attempting to solve the Congolese problem by applying a pacification policy that had recently allowed other explosive issues to be defused, in particular the School Question (elaboration of the 'School Pact' in 1958).[192]

The roundtable conference was a decisive turn in Belgian-Congolese history.[193] The Congolese parties immediately formed a common front with the result that the Belgians were not faced with divided interlocutors, but with a united bloc demanding immediate independence. The date for the Congo's independence was set for just six months later on 30 June 1960, and the Belgian parties dropped any vague desires for institutional control of the Congo. Hence, there was to be no Belgian-Congolese union or any 'reserved' domains. The idea, initially proposed by the Belgian government, to make the Congo a monarchy and King Baudouin its sovereign was also abandoned. An end was finally put to the palace's dream of continuing to assume the destiny of an 'independent' Congo.[194] The new Congolese institutions were largely modelled on those in Belgium. The Congo was therefore conceived as a unitary state based on a representative democracy with a bicameral system. At the head of the state, a president would be appointed by the two chambers; but the main political post was that of prime minister. The first Congolese institutions were formed after the general elections that took place in May 1960.

Towards the end of the conference, the king called a meeting of the Crown Council. This had great symbolic value, because this organ was only convened under exceptional circumstances. Along with the Cabinet ministers, it also included the ministers of state, an honorary title reserved for particularly worthy politicians. Under the presidency of the king, active ministers and former notables from political life met on 18 February 1960 to assess the situation created by the roundtable. A few isolated voices criticised the way the Congolese question was developing and denounced the government's policy. In his introductory speech, the king himself set out the reasons for his discontent concerning the hesitations of the successive governments since 1955. This Crown Council took on a very specific meaning, especially in relation to a new royal intervention in governmental life that was to take place in August 1960, right in the middle of the Congolese crisis.

And yet, the agreements made at the roundtable allowed a certain hope, since all parties had reached a consensus. In order to ensure a smooth and rapid transition between the colonial system and the independent state, a new minister was appointed within the Belgian government: Walter Ganshof van der Meersch. He mainly focused on setting up the new Congolese institutions.

---

[192] Analysis of the mechanisms of political decision making as regards Congolese politics in J. Meynaud, J. Ladrière & F. Perin, *La décision politique en Belgique* (Paris, 1965), pp. 345–61.

[193] G.-H. Dumont, *La Table ronde belgo-congolaise (janvier – février 1960)* (Paris, 1961), p. 308. An 'Economic Round-table conference' was also held in April-May 1960; we shall return to this in Chapter 5.

[194] Note in Kadoc, De Schryver Papers, n° 11.3.2.2.

The poll of May 1960 revealed the profound rifts in the Congolese political landscape. Ethnic parties such as the Abako and the Conakat obtained good results in their respective regions; however, the unity party, Lumumba's MNC, won the most seats in the Chamber of Deputies and thus emerged victorious from the elections. Joseph Kasavubu became the president of the republic and Patrice Lumumba was appointed prime minister. In just a few months, the Congo seemed to have taken a giant step. Complete independence, unthinkable at the end of 1958, was a reality just eighteen months later. Had Belgium succeeded in its Congolese venture?

The Impact of Congolese Independence on the Belgian Political Scene

In theory, this chapter should end here: On 1 July 1960 Congolese affairs became a foreign policy issue, a subject dealt with in Chapter 5. However, the first months of Congolese independence had such an impact on Belgian internal politics that it is logical to analyse it here, especially since the previously created political tangle was now unravelling dramatically on the Belgian domestic scene. Hence, we shall briefly outline the influence of the Congolese crisis on Belgian political life – 'crisis' being the operative word: The events in the Congo had worldwide repercussions.

On 5 July, a few days after the official declaration of the country's independence, certain units of the new Congolese army, the heir of the Force publique, mutinied. One of the main problems was the insufficient Africanisation of the officers. The Belgian commander of the Force publique, General Janssens, had obstructed the acceleration of this policy months before independence; the price paid for this obstruction was high. The Belgians present in the Congo were subjected to rape and pillage. The Belgian government unilaterally decided to send troops to the Congo, claiming its desire to protect the property and lives of its fellow citizens. From the point of view of the Congolese authorities, however, this was a flagrant violation of the country's sovereignty. Furthermore, on 11 July, Katanga Province declared its independence with the clear support of the Belgians. Then, at the beginning of August, the diamond-rich Kasai Province followed suit, also with Belgian support. The government in Léopoldville felt the rug being pulled from under its feet and called upon the United Nations to put an end to both the secessionist movements and Belgian military intervention. Diplomatic relations between Belgium and the Congo ended on 14 July. In mid-July, the first UN 'blue berets' arrived in the Congo. The country slid into chaos. Contrary to the expectations of Prime Minister Lumumba, the intervention of the UN led to the stagnation of the existing situation rather than to the defeat of the rebel provinces. A difference of opinion arose between the head of the Congolese government and the upper echelons of the United Nations. In Western capitals, Lumumba was already considered a dangerous, unpredictable and even crypto-Communist leader. It was feared that he would lead the Congo towards the Communist bloc.

An internal Congolese crisis thus occurred in the middle of the international crisis; both aspects were obviously closed linked. Western powers encouraged

President Kasavubu to dismiss his prime minister, which he did on 5 September 1960; Lumumba reacted immediately by, in turn, dismissing the president. There seemed to be complete political deadlock. Finally, on 14 September, a coup led by Colonel Joseph-Désiré Mobutu, chief of staff of the Congolese National Army, and inspired by Belgium and the United States, temporarily put the legal institutions out of service; they did not start up again until February 1961. At this point, Lumumba was definitively excluded from the Congolese political scene. He was first imprisoned by the authorities in Léopoldville and then handed over to the Katanga secessionist authorities that executed him on 17 January 1961. For many years his supporters were an important faction on the Congolese political scene; among other things, they formed a separate ephemeral government, established in Stanleyville. As soon as Lumumba had been eliminated, reconciliation between the rebel Katanga authorities and those in Léopoldville could begin; however, the division of the Congo into rival entities finally ended only in January 1963 after a military operation led by the UN. Congo's unity was re-established after enormous losses in human life and years of chaos. But soon, this ravaged country was to be confronted with other bloody crises.

Here, in brief, are the dramatic events experienced by the Congo in 1960 and 1961. Their repercussions on Belgian public opinion were significant but, in the end, relatively limited with regards to the structure and action of the Belgian parties. All the nuances of the Belgian political spectrum, except for the small Communist Party, supported Belgian military intervention in the ex-colony. In the face of the Congolese events, all the other parties formed a bloc. The various political movements abstained from using the Congo as an internal political weapon. Despite the fears of the political players, in fact there was barely any sign of the Congolese debacle being used for electoral or party purposes. All the major parties had been involved in the roundtable; furthermore, the atmosphere of national catastrophe created by the Congolese events was not favourable to a petty settling of scores. Belgium had no real tradition in terms of colonial political struggles: Usually, the parties did not confront each other on Congolese issues except during the colonial 'School War'. Former colonials, repatriated settlers and royalist and anti-political elements did, however, express particularly harsh opinions in relation to the political class. The politicians were pilloried: Their lack of firmness, or rather their 'cowardice', had ruined the colonial venture. However, this wave of opinion never managed to crystallise and form a political force of any significance. Far-right groups appeared soon after the Congolese events, and because of them. These groups unsuccessfully tried to exploit events with the goal of launching an attack on the legal institutions, but they remained very marginal.[195] Despite the extent of the Congolese crisis, it did not leave a long-lasting mark on the Belgian political scene. Belgium did not adopt the French model, where the

---

[195] F. Balace, "Le tournant des années soixante", in *De l'avant à l'après-guerre. L'extrême droite en Belgique francophone* (Bruxelles, 1994), pp. 107–211; R. Pasteger, *Le visage des affreux. Les mercenaires du Katanga (1960–1964)* (Brussels, 2005), pp. 11–4, 192–202.

defence of l'Algérie française galvanised the extreme right movement and gave birth to the terrorist group Organisation Armée secrète (OAS).[196]

Even though decolonisation had no long-term effects on Belgian politics, internal discord was rife during the Congolese crisis itself. Cracks appeared within the government and between the government and the palace. Belgium's attitude to the Katanga secession was one of the essential elements in these rivalries. The independence of the rich mining province was impossible without the military, administrative, logistical and financial support of Belgium, or rather of *certain* Belgian players. Among these were the big conglomerates, particularly the all-powerful Union minière du Haut-Katanga (UMHK).[197] This enterprise absolutely wanted to retain its production plants that, thanks to the existence of the Katanga authorities and with the support of the Belgians, maintained an oasis of calm and prosperity in the middle of a chaotic Congo. This was also the goal pursued by a number of political players, some of whom were actually in the government. For them, Katanga represented an African state where Belgium's hold was guaranteed. Within the government itself, and the state apparatus, other elements opposed what they considered to be a dangerous option. For them, it was necessary to preserve the Congo's unity and not to cut itself off from the rest of the world by acting alone with a Katanga artificially created and kept at arm's length. Therefore, during the events of July 1960 to March 1961, there was not just one Belgian policy for the Congo; there were several conflicting policies, even within the government.

A particularly obscure aspect of the Belgian authorities' Congolese policy lay in the controversial role they played in the elimination of the legitimate Congolese prime minister, Patrice Lumumba. The exact circumstances of this event remained unclear for a long time until the question was recently raised again. In 1999, a book by Belgian sociologist Ludo De Witte concluded that the Belgian government was directly involved in the *physical* elimination of Lumumba.[198] This led to political commotion in Belgium and, in 2000, the Belgian Chamber of Representatives created an enquiry commission to shed some light on Belgium's role in the murder of Lumumba.[199] In the eyes of the expert historians appointed by the commission there is no doubt whatsoever that Belgium well and truly interfered in the internal politics of independent

---

[196] A. Chebel d'Appollonia, *L'Extrême Droite en France* (Brussels, 1996), pp. 298–308; M. Michel, "La colonisation", in J.-F. Sirinelli, ed., *Histoire des droites, op. cit.*, pp. 153–62.

[197] R. Brion & J.-L. Moreau, *De la mine à Mars. La genèse d'Umicore* (Tielt, 2006), pp. 310–25.

[198] L. De Witte, *The Assassination of Lumumba* (London/New York, 2001).

[199] *Documents Parlementaires de la Chambre des Représentants*, session 2001–2002, n° 50 0312/007 of 16.11.2001, 2 volumes (available online www.lachambre.be) (quoted hereafter as *Rapport*); L. De Vos, Ph. Raxhon, E. Gerard & J. Gérard-Libois, *Les secrets de l'affaire Lumumba* (Brussels, 2004). Debates and critical remarks on the work of the enquiry commission in *Bijdragen en Mededelingen betreffende de Geschiedenis der Nederlanden*, 122, 3 (2007), pp. 357–410; F. Reyntjens, "Omgaan met het verleden? Recente parlementaire onderzoekscommissies over Midden-Afrika", in B. Peeters & J. Velaers, eds., *De Grondwet in groothoekperspectief. Liber amicorum disciplorumque Karel Rimanque* (Antwerp, 2007),

Congo; that the Belgian government endeavoured (as did the United States government) to eliminate Lumumba as a political factor; that the Belgian authorities did nothing to ensure the physical safety of the imprisoned prime minister, even when they knew he was in mortal danger; and that they were therefore morally responsible for the murder of Lumumba, even if no document can clearly confirm that this assassination was unambiguously ordered by the Belgian authorities.

This parliamentary enquiry commission clearly showed the existence of *different* and sometimes opposing policies within the government itself at the time. On the one hand, there was a hard line that recommended the use of force and more or less openly supported the Katanga secession. The politicians who were part of this trend include Prime Minister Gaston Eyskens, the Liberal minister Omer Vanaudenhove, and the Catholic defence minister, Arthur Gilson. A more moderate faction hoped to avoid a break with international opinion, in particular with the United Nations, and was opposed to any territorial divisions within the Congo. The minister of foreign affairs, Pierre Wigny, the minister of African affairs, Auguste De Schryver, and minister Raymond Scheyven were part of this second group.[200]

In 1960, things became even more complicated due to the special strategy pursued by the king and his entourage. Throughout this chapter, we have been witness to the sovereign's attempts to impose himself as a direct player in the Congolese question. At the beginning of August 1960, events took a dramatic and potentially dangerous turn when the king attempted to dismiss Eyskens's government, which was considered weak and was discredited by the failure of its Congolese policy. The king wanted to replace the government with an extraordinary cabinet favourable to a hard line and led by two non-parliamentary ex-prime ministers: Socialist Paul-Henri Spaak and/or Catholic Paul Van Zeeland.[201] Belgium seemed to be on the verge of a serious political crisis, because the normal workings of the Belgian institutions risked being seriously disrupted by the advent of a government with a hitherto unheard of structure in the history of Belgian politics. The prime minister in office, Gaston Eyskens, initially appeared to have envisaged supporting the idea of such an extraordinary government, but in the end, he refused to support its implementation. His attitude and that of his government led to the failure of the royal attempt.

A cabinet reshuffle linked to the aforementioned tensions took place a few weeks later, in September 1960. Harold d'Aspremont Lynden replaced De Schryver and Scheyven as the minister of African affairs on 2 September 1960. This was a significant choice. The new minister was the nephew of the Grand Maréchal de la Cour who, as we have seen, harshly criticised the Belgian

---

pp. 457–82; L. De Witte, "Impérialisme nouveau, colonialisme ancien, négationnisme renaissant", *Cahiers marxistes*, 236 (October-November 2007), pp. 125–46.
[200] V. Dujardin, *Pierre Harmel* (Brussels, 2004), pp. 290–1; *Rapport*, pp. 63–5.
[201] M. Dumoulin, *Spaak* (Brussels, 1999), pp. 583–91; V. Dujardin & M. Dumoulin, *Paul Van Zeeland 1893–1973* (Brussels, 1997), pp. 243–6.

political class. When he was called to office, d'Aspremont was in charge of the management of the Technical Belgian Mission (Mistebel) that supported the Katanga secession. He also played a controversial role in the assassination of Lumumba. Had the government's hard line won? In the wake of this reshuffle, both government parties agreed on drastic budgetary cuts and tax increases. It was said that the loss of the Congo contributed to economic and financial difficulties and the government wanted to remedy these problems by passing an austerity law, presented to parliament in November 1960. The painful social effects of this so-called Unique Law led, in December 1960 and January 1961, to one of the biggest general strikes in Belgian history. Hence, the Congo was indeed one of the indirect causes of this major social protest movement.

In reality, the ups and downs of political life would cut short the new structure of the Eyskens cabinet. The legislative elections of March 1961 brought in a new government composed of Christian-Democrats and Socialists. It was presided over by the PSC-CVP's leader, Théo Lefèvre, while the Socialist, Spaak, became the minister of foreign affairs. This new governmental team reoriented the country's African policy. Henceforth, it clearly opted for the reunification of the Congo, thereby putting an end to Belgium's isolation on the international scene. Over the ensuing years and decades, central Africa would remain a crucial problem in Belgian diplomacy. However, even though it continued to divide men and parties at various moments, the Congo was not a central issue in Belgium's internal politics.

Conclusion

A number of striking elements emerge from this analysis. The introduction of colonialism in Belgian politics and society was clearly due to the political action of a very particular character: King Leopold II. Despite his constitutional role, which forbade him any public action not endorsed by a minister's signature, Leopold imposed the Congo on the Belgian political scene. This was a unique occurrence both from an international point of view and from the point of view of Belgian internal politics. The personal action of the sovereigns has been felt throughout Belgian political history in numerous domains, but in no other area has a sovereign's action been as significant as it was in the colonial affair.

After the death of Leopold II, his successors adopted a more low-profile attitude with regard to the Congo. Nevertheless, both the beginning of colonialism and its final years were marked by a king's actions. Many elements bear witness to the role played by Baudouin I between 1955 and 1960, or at least to the role he would have liked to have played. We should not overestimate the king's impact on the final phase of Belgian colonial history, since the main part of the action took place elsewhere. It is necessary, however, to highlight this aspect of the events because it is revealing of the place the Congo occupied in the imagination and attitude of the Belgian monarchy. Without a doubt, the prestige of the monarchy was greatly enhanced by the colony; the worship organised around the controversial figure of Leopold II was one of the essential instruments in this symbolic inflation.

Furthermore, the colonial impact was much greater at this level than in other political arenas such as parliament, the government and the parties. We have observed the relatively marginal effects of the Congo on the structuring and running of these institutions. The colony only exercised any real influence over governmental life and policies on three occasions: the first time episodically between 1890 and 1908, during the annexation of the Congo; a second time during the Second World War (we shall return to this in the following chapter); and a third time during decolonisation from 1958 to 1960. Apart from these three crucial moments, the influence of the colony on Belgian internal politics was not very significant. Contrary to what happened in Britain, the Belgian empire did not play a role in important processes such as electoral or social reforms, or in the formation of national identity. And contrary to events in France, where the switch from the Fourth to the Fifth Republic was partly due to the colonial crisis, Belgium's colonial involvement did not trigger constitutional changes. It is true that the Congo was used as a new and exciting element to enhance Belgian national identity and propaganda. The colony was also a welcome element in strengthening the military's rather weak position and self-image. But there is no convincing evidence to argue that the loss of the colony accelerated in any significant way the crisis of the Belgian unitary state and the rise of federalism in the 1960s.

Two factors can explain the small role of the colony in Belgian political life. First, the origin of colonialism in Belgium was relatively external to the political circles. It was not the politicians who took the initiative to conquer overseas territories. Some leading politicians supported Leopold's enterprise from the mid-1880s, mostly to attain other goals in domestic Belgian politics. Some were in favour of its takeover from the mid-1890s because the Congo was now a fait accompli with increasing Belgian human and economic involvement. But the fact remains that the Congo was imposed upon the Belgian political world by the king's expansionist obsession. It is therefore correct to say that Belgium was a 'reluctant imperialist' at least in the beginning.[202] Once the Congo Free State was annexed by the Belgian state, the authorities and the overwhelming majority of political forces quite paradoxically endorsed the colonial situation with great enthusiasm. In their eyes, Belgian grandeur was dependent on the fate of the new and unexpected colony.

Second, private interest groups such as the church and big business played a major role in Belgian colonial policy. This aspect explains why conglomerates occupied such an exalted position compared with the other elements of Belgian political life, which were dominated by the issues and methods typical of a mass democracy. The muffled nature of colonial policy in Belgium gave

---

[202] The term was used to characterise the Belgian situation by M. Ewans, "Belgium and the Colonial Experience", *Journal of Contemporary European Studies*, 11, 2 (November 2003), pp. 167–80 (p. 167).

this domain quite a different profile in terms of political decision making. The attempt, in 1960, to manage decolonisation by applying the typical Belgian pacification policy of the roundtable conference provided a short-term solution for this tangle. But its practical application rapidly fell apart when it came to the complexities of Congolese life.

3

The Congo and Belgium's External Position

Among the common subjects of Belgian political discourse, the Congo occupies a particular position. Due to its ties with this part of Africa – so the story goes – Belgium benefitted (and still benefits) from a sort of diplomatic advantage. The colonial empire allowed Belgium to play an international role that far exceeded its intrinsic capacities. In other words, 'little' Belgium became great through its colony and was able to take its place in international politics, making the colony a significant factor in Belgian national rhetoric. But this is not the whole story. For Belgium, becoming a colonial power had many unintended side effects. The Congo was a source of concern for Belgian politicians and diplomats, both boosting and tarnishing Belgium's fortunes. It is, therefore, necessary to understand the history of the colony and how it influenced Belgium's international position. It is also necessary to understand how the *external* aspects of Belgian colonialism influenced and partly shaped *internal* politics in the Congo.

Brief Outline of Belgium's External Position

The Belgian revolution of 1830, which led to the founding of the nation and threatened the balance of power on the continent, did not pass unnoticed on the international scene.[1] The 1831 Treaty of London recognised Belgium's independence, imposed neutrality on the Belgians and precluded the development of privileged relations with any other country. The conditions of this treaty certainly influenced colonial matters. For example, Belgian diplomats kept a low profile on the international scene, since any false step could endanger the country's very existence. During the nineteenth century, Belgian diplomats tried to promote national economic interests by concluding commercial treaties with the main trading partners, essentially the neighbouring countries. At that time, paradoxically, Belgium's peculiarity of being small and having no

---

[1] R. Coolsaet, *België en zijn buitenlandse politiek 1830–1990* (Leuven, 1998).

imperialist ambitions sometimes enhanced its international influence. During the final decades of the nineteenth and the beginning of the twentieth century, Belgian experts (lawyers, administrators, engineers, etc.) played supporting roles in countries such as Persia and Siam and in some Latin American republics.

The first king, Leopold I, Europe's 'wise man', developed a parallel diplomacy based primarily on his family ties with monarchs all around the world. He was anxious, above all, to preserve the political equilibrium on the old continent, an essential element for Belgium's prosperity and survival. This personal policy was, of course, conducive to the idiosyncratic attitude of his son and heir, Leopold II, when it came to grand international schemes.

Belgium's neutrality did not, however, prevent its involvement in the First World War. The German armies, on their way to Paris, brutally invaded the country in August 1914. During four long years, Belgian troops clung to a tiny fraction of the national territory in West Flanders. They fought alongside the Allied forces on the Western Front, but also in central Africa. 'Poor little Belgium's' courageous attitude during this conflict was rewarded after the war: The imposed neutrality was lifted and Belgium immediately aligned itself militarily with France, though this active foreign policy was soon abandoned. In 1936, Belgium chose to return to neutrality. With this decision, the Belgian authorities hoped to stay out of any possible further war, but to no avail. Neutral Belgium was invaded once again by the Germans in May 1940. Eventually, the Belgian government sided with the British and continued the fight against the Nazis. King Leopold III unconstitutionally refused to follow his ministers' advice and stayed in the country. Though officially a prisoner, he tried to set up a new regime in occupied Belgium under German aegis. This caused a severe political crisis in post-war Belgium. Many politicians and a large proportion of public opinion did not accept his return to the throne after the country's liberation. This resulted in his abdication in 1950 when his son, Baudouin, who was just twenty years old, became king.

After the war, Belgium became adept at different forms of international co-operation. Belgians took an active part in building new global institutions such as the UN and IMF, and Belgium was also a fierce advocate and an essential pioneer of the European unification process. Finally, the country unambiguously sided with the United States during the Cold War and fully participated in NATO.

In short, owing to its origins, its economic characteristics and its small size, Belgium had developed a tradition of discretion, compromise and *bons offices* on the international scene. Belgian diplomats fostered a low-profile attitude and international co-operation rather than an aggressive and nationalist stance. This makes the eruption of colonialism on the Belgian scene all the more puzzling. Belgium considered itself as an element of peace and stability within Europe, especially prior to 1940, an age of fierce nationalism and intra-European tensions. How, then, did the Congo influence the main currents of Belgian foreign policy and the country's global position?

The Congo Free State on the International Political Scene (1885–1908)

The Shadow of the Conference of Berlin

The particular circumstances surrounding the creation of the Congo Free State left an indelible mark on the history of the Leopoldian project as well as on the Belgian Congo.[2] The birth of this new political entity in the heart of Africa took place on the sidelines of the international Berlin Conference (1884–5). It resulted from the successive bilateral recognition of the Association internationale du Congo by the other nations. A few days before the end of the conference, at the end of February 1885, the Association internationale du Congo accepted the Berlin Act. The conference *took note* of the existence of a new 'Congo Free State' but, in the minds of many, the existence of the Congo was *decided by* the Berlin Conference – an error that continues to appear, even in some history books.[3]

Following the annexation of the Congo Free State in 1908, this perception was not simply inaccurate, it became dangerous: It endangered Belgian sovereignty in Africa because from "the affirmation 'we, the Powers, have conceded the governing of the Congo' to the declaration: 'we are forced to seize it from you for reasons of the greatest importance', there is only one step".[4] Throughout the colonial period, "the shadow of the Berlin Conference and Act" hung over the Congo.[5] During the campaign against the abuses of the Leopoldian regime, in particular in 1903, Great Britain threatened to convene a new African conference to examine the fate of the Congo. After the Congo was taken over by Belgium, Belgian diplomats feared that the British would undertake new steps in this direction.[6] Between 1914 and 1918, when the Belgian authorities wondered about the future international status of the Congo, they wanted to avoid being "dragged into a new African conference which would result in a new general act that could be as dangerous as the [Berlin Act]".[7] In 1945, at the end of the Second World War, the British House of Commons discussed the possibility of a new international conference to examine the status of the Conventional Congo Basin.[8] Even in 1959, when

---

[2] P. Van Zuylen, *L'échiquier congolais ou le secret du Roi* (Brussels, 1959).

[3] J. Stengers, *Le Congo, mythes et réalités* (Gembloux, 1989), pp. 79–90; J.-L. Vellut, *Un centenaire: 1885–1985. Les relations Europe-Afrique au crible d'une commémoration* (Leiden, 1992), special issue of *Intercontinenta*, 12.

[4] AA, AE-II, n° 1802bis (3283), "Note pour Monsieur le Ministre – Au sujet des origines de l'État indépendant du Congo", by Director General Halewyck de Heusch, 20 October 1936, pp. 2–3.

[5] J.-L. Vellut, "L'ombre de la Conférence et de l'Acte de Berlin sur l'histoire internationale du Zaïre à l'époque coloniale", in *L'Afrique Noire depuis la Conférence de Berlin* (Paris, 1985), pp. 71–89.

[6] AMAE, AF-I-1, vol. XII, confidential note of 15 March 1909, from Giers to the secretary-general of the MAE.

[7] AA, AE-II, n° 293 (2901), "Conversations [franco-belges] relatives à la révision de l'Acte de Berlin. Séance du 24 octobre 1917", p. 8 (intervention of Pierre Orts).

[8] AMAE, AF-I-1 (1943–1945), E. de Cartier de Marchienne (Belgian ambassador in London), to P.-H. Spaak, minister of foreign affairs, 17 March 1945.

decolonisation was accelerating, some dreamed of a great international conference that would solve the Congolese problem. In Léopoldville, nationalist leaders Kasavubu and Gizenga approached the consuls general of the Berlin Act's signatory powers to request "that a new Berlin Conference be convened" in order to prevent Belgium from introducing "a rigged independence allowing the colonialist regime to be maintained in the Congo in other forms".[9]

Even though the Congo Free State did not *owe* its existence to the Berlin Act of 1885, the Act nevertheless imposed major political and economic constraints, constraints inherited by the Belgian Congo in 1908 which, in terms of freedom of trade and navigation, will be dealt with in the following chapter. For the moment, we shall limit ourselves to the political aspects. First: The territories situated in the so-called conventional basin of the Congo River, a region more vast than the Congolese state itself, were required to maintain strict neutrality. Second: In certain domains, the Act restricted the designs of the authorities that exercised their sovereignty there. It recommended watching over "the preservation of the indigenous populations and the improvement of their moral and material state of existence" with the goal of respecting religious freedom and not imposing any restrictions on or obstacles to any form of worship (Article 6). All these measures, accepted by Leopold II in 1885 in an effort to succeed in his audacious project, seemed, to the Belgian authorities, to be an insufferable attack on national sovereignty in the Congo. One of their main concerns prior to 1919 was to free the Belgian Congo from these externally imposed constraints and hence put an end to the 'special regime' as constituted by the Berlin Act.[10] However, the 'internationalisation' of the colonies, a grand theme at the birth of the Congo Free State, continued to underpin the perception of the Congo and resurfaced from time to time.[11] It was therefore perceived as a silent threat to the Belgian colonial empire.

The Relations of the Congo Free State with other Colonial Powers
The Berlin Act was not the only diplomatic legacy from the Leopoldian Congo left to the Belgian Congo. The establishment of the borders of the Congo Free State, combined with Leopold II's tireless pursuit of the Nile dream, caused many tensions between the other colonial powers and the new African state and its sovereign.

There were tensions with Portugal. This experienced coloniser claimed 'historical rights' in the area at the mouth of the Congo River and consolidated its control over both the left bank of the estuary and the enclave of Cabinda. Later, the Portuguese hold over these areas would be a major concern for Belgian colonisers who endeavoured, through intense diplomatic

---

[9] AA, AE-II, n° 299 (2902), F. Waleffe to A.-E. De Schryver, minister of the Congo and Ruanda-Urundi, 23.09.1959; telex (6).11.1959.
[10] AA, AE-II, n° 293 (2901), minister of foreign affairs to the prime minister, 10 March 1931.
[11] In 1908, Belgian industrialist Henri Lambert proposed the internationalisation of the Congo: J.-L. Van Belle, *Henri Lambert (1862–1934)* (Braine-le-Château, 2010), pp. 124–33.

negotiations, to substitute Belgian sovereignty for Portugal's in this strategic region. A few years later, however, Portugal was forced to abandon its designs on the Kwango region, which went to the Congo Free State under the agreement of 1891.[12] The frictions with the Lusophone Empire almost turned into a military incident when Portuguese war ships threatened Boma, the first administrative capital of the Congo Free State.

There were tensions with France. Border disputes with the French colonies risked nipping Leopold II's ambitions in the bud. In 1887, which was "an extremely critical period, a fight nearly broke out".[13] Frictions between the Congo Free State and the French Republic worsened when Leopold II interfered in the Franco-British rivalries in the Upper Nile region. The king was prepared to take any risks to extend his hold right up to the banks of the mythical river, well beyond the borders of the Congo Free State acknowledged in 1885. Through the treaty of 12 May 1894, the British authorities leased an area to the west of the Nile (Bahr-el-Ghazal) to the king. This treaty hindered the ambitions of the French, who protested loudly and had it nullified. The French Republic still hoped the Congo would fall into its grasp under the famous preemptive right mentioned in Chapter 1. Indeed, when Belgium first attempted to take over the Congo in 1895, French authorities made clear the scope of this right. France kept an eye open for trouble until the Congo was granted independence in 1960![14]

Finally, there were tensions with Great Britain. In 1891, the Congo Free State beat the British to the mark and under the agreement of 1894 established its presence in Katanga. Although this was only a mild source of tension in the beginning, it increased over the subject of the Nile. After the failure of the treaty of 1894, the king persisted in his Sudanese ambitions, but then had a change of heart. From that moment on, he encouraged French enterprises in Africa, such as the famous Marchand expedition to Fachoda in 1898, thereby attracting British hostility.[15] "Under these circumstances, the Congo Free State once again ran the risk of war".[16] Leopold II even envisaged signing a treaty with France to protect the Congo from possible attacks from abroad.[17] As a result, around the turn of the century, relations between the Congo Free State and Great Britain turned sour. Added to this already somewhat tense

[12] I. Brownlie, *African Boundaries* (London-Berkeley, 1979), p. 1355; J.-L. Vellut, "Angola-Congo. L'invention de la frontière du Lunda (1889–1893)", *Africana Studia. International Journal of African Studies*, 9 (2006), pp. 159–84; F. Latour da Veiga Pinto, *Le Portugal et le Congo au XIXe siècle* (Paris, 1972).
[13] AMAE, AF-I-1, "Note pour Monsieur le Ministre", by O. Louwers, 24 January 1922.
[14] AMAEF (Paris), Europe 1956–1960 series, Belgium sub-series, n° 122, R. Bousquet (French ambassador in Belgium) to MAEF, 8 and 10 March 1960.
[15] AMAE, AF-I-1 (DGS – Colonial Section 1950–1953), "Note pour Monsieur le Ministre", by O. Louwers, 10 January 1952.
[16] Ibid.
[17] Kadoc, De Cleene/De Jonghe Papers, n° 352, handwritten note from Leopold II (1892 ?), "Avant projet d'entente".

situation was the humanitarian campaign against Leopold's management of the Congo, which was a great success in Great Britain, even at the highest level of the British state. However, we cannot consider these events as some kind of Machiavellian plot on the part of 'perfidious Albion' to seize the much sought-after Congo from the hands of Leopold and the Belgians.

Leopold II continued to gamble and to take significant risks and his manoeuvres seriously endangered the neutrality of the Congo Free State declared in the Berlin Act. These events had repercussions on the international position of Belgium. Belgian neutrality was inevitably threatened by the incessant royal initiatives in Africa. The problem became even more complicated because the king was constantly calling upon Belgian diplomats to further his Congolese cause. Moreover, Belgian military seconded to the Congo Free State were fighting in the Congo. In the eyes of international opinion, the Congo Free State was de facto 'Belgian' – or at least was increasingly becoming so. In the European capitals, there was emphasis on the fact that this ambiguous situation could be dangerous for Belgium.[18] How would Belgium respond if the Congo Free State were to be dragged into a conflict? For Belgian politicians, the problem of taking over the Congo also involved an eminently international dimension. Peace in Belgium was likely to depend on it. In 1906, pressure from the European powers played a decisive role in the decision to annex the Leopoldian state.

Structural Aspects (1908–1960): Was Belgium Capable of Colonising the 'Coveted and Threatened' Congo?

This annexation became reality in 1908. The Congo Free State bequeathed a legacy with numerous consequences to the Belgian Congo and Belgium. Leopold's past influenced the attitudes of the powers towards the new colony and towards Belgium. Foreign perceptions, in turn, influenced the behaviour of the Belgians on the international scene and in Congolese internal politics.

'Threats' to the Belgian Congo

The enmities and the alliances created by the king's impulsive behaviour affected the destiny of the Belgian Congo and Belgium itself for a long time. Right after the takeover of the Congo, Great Britain was extremely distrustful of the Belgian colony, demanding the eradication of the former Leopoldian system and thus attentively scrutinising the Belgian policy in the Congo.[19] London did not even officially recognise the Belgian Congo until 1913. British distrust weighed heavily on the Belgian leaders. In the eyes of the Belgians, Britain's

---

[18] J. Willequet, *Le Congo belge et la Weltpolitik (1894-1914)* (Brussels, 1962), p. 15; J. Stengers, "La première tentative de reprise du Congo par la Belgique (1894-1895)", *Bulletin de la Société royale belge de Géographie*, 73, 1-2 (1949), p. 55.

[19] Wm. R. Louis, "The philosophical diplomatist Sir Arthur Hardinge and King Leopold's Congo, 1906-1911", *Bulletin des Séances de l'ARSOM*, 6 (1965), p. 1426.

attitude verged on interference in the internal affairs of the colony. It confirmed and illustrated a fear that far exceeded the problems with Great Britain: a fear related to the very foundations of the Belgian presence in Africa that coloured the country's entire colonial history. Was little Belgium capable of assuming the destiny of this vast colony? Did it have sufficient financial and human means? Was its morality up to the task? Hadn't the Belgians discredited themselves as colonisers – in the 'noble' sense of the term – through the inhuman 'red rubber' practices?

These last two questions have continued to haunt international and, in particular, British public opinion. During the inter-war period and the 1950s, and even up until the present day, they have given rise to press articles, books and pamphlets. The political impact of these questions was central at the beginning of Belgian colonisation; later on, this impact gradually faded. Even though these issues have become depoliticised over the years, this emotionally and politically charged context illustrates why the Belgian authorities have always minimised and even bluntly denied the atrocities of the Leopoldian regime. The moral and political foundations of Belgian colonisation were at stake. Inevitably, the attacks on the Congo exacerbated the sensitivity of Belgian diplomats. For the Belgian authorities, this so-called slander not only undermined national honour, but also hid malevolent intentions. The Belgian Congo was well and truly threatened, coveted by other countries.

The intangible colonial borders were a founding element in the geopolitics of independent Africa, but it would be a mistake to cast this principle into the colonial past itself. For decades, the imperial powers continued to call into question the spatial delimitations of their respective empires. The exact outlines of the borders, often vague and sometimes contested, were the subject of numerous, mostly minor, adjustments. Far more important was the fundamental problem of redistributing or redefining the boundaries of the colonies. Quid pro quo practices, offensive action and all sorts of territorial bargaining formed the web of colonial domination in Africa, at least until the end of the Second World War. In this game, modest colonial powers were more prey than predator; Portugal and Belgium were particularly vulnerable. Great Britain, France and Germany did not hesitate to lead negotiations to the detriment of the smaller powers. Belgian political leaders were thus confronted with the problem of maintaining territorial integrity and, at some points, the very survival of their recently acquired colony. Suddenly thrust onto the forefront of the international scene upon becoming a colonial power, Belgium perceived its direct neighbours as possible or real colonial rivals. These countries were not equally distrusted but, nevertheless, its new status as a colonial power influenced the attitude of Belgium, in one way or another, towards other European nations active in Africa.

Doubts about the Colonising Abilities of the Belgians
The artificial introduction of colonialism in Belgium and the particularities of the Leopoldian legacy explain certain fundamental characteristics of Belgium

as a colonising nation. The Belgian colonial circles did not doubt their moral ability to face the challenge of colonisation. Those who had experience of the Leopoldian abuses endeavoured to put an end to the fundamental deficiencies of the Congo Free State. Those who had not experienced these events, and honestly believed that the accusations against Leopold's regime were slanderous, were incited to practice morally irreproachable colonisation. Despite the continuation of forced labour and other injustices, Belgian colonial activity was underpinned by the axiom that, in the face of such criticism, it was crucial to prove the superiority of Belgian colonisation. This became a commonplace of Belgian colonial rhetoric: The fate of the indigenous Congolese was better than that of their fellow creatures in other colonies. After the Second World War, the image of the 'happy Congolese' would influence both the international positioning and the internal colonial policy of Belgium.

This image also illustrates Belgium's success in the face of another challenge: Was Belgium *materially* capable of making the enormous effort required by colonisation in the Congo? Official Belgium was not very enthusiastic when the Congo was annexed. Some feared that the Congo would become a heavy financial burden for Belgium. To avoid this, the Colonial Charter established a clear separation between metropolitan and colonial finances. Still, doubts did not disappear immediately. In 1914, a somewhat unconventional businessman, Jules Gernaert, published two brochures recommending the sale of part of the Congo because, in his opinion, Belgium did not have sufficient means to develop its African domain. The Belgian authorities – who never had any intention of selling off bits of the Congo – suspected Germany of having financed this publication, because the Reich appeared to covet the Congo.[20] In 1913, a German politician did indeed inform the French ambassador in Berlin that in his opinion, "Belgium is not wealthy enough to develop this rich domain: this enterprise is beyond its financial means".[21] And this scepticism was not limited to a few marginal figures or malicious foreign powers. In 1915, right in the middle of the war, key Belgians such as Émile Vandervelde, the Socialist leader, and Émile Francqui, a top businessman and banker, expressed their doubts about "Belgium's ability to bear the weight of the administration of [the] colony".[22] Even after the First World War, leading politicians and businessmen "raise[d] doubts about the possibility of finding the necessary sums to endow the colony with essential means of communication".[23]

[20] J. Gernaert, *Le Congo belge. Le fond du sac* (Brussels, 1914?); J. Willequet, *Le Congo belge*, op. cit., pp. 334–6, 366–8.
[21] Conversation of German secretary of state von Jagow with Paul Cambon, French ambassador in Berlin in April 1914, reported in *Correspondance diplomatique et politique relative à la guerre en Afrique* (Brussels, 1919), pp. 21–2.
[22] AA, AE-2, n° 364, Paul Hymans, Liberal MP, to Davignon, minister of foreign affairs, 29 March 1915.
[23] AA, AE-2, n° 1801 (3283), E. de Gaiffier d'Hestroy (Belgian ambassador in Paris) to Hymans, minister of foreign affairs, 21 May 1920.

The idea of Belgium possibly 'selling' the Congo continued to circulate in diplomatic conversations throughout the duration of the First World War.[24]

In the end, these fears turned out to be unfounded. From a budgetary point of view, the Congo actually cost Belgium very little. Private capitalists overwhelmingly turned their attention towards the Congo, investing more in the colony than in other foreign countries and fuelling a formidable economic expansion. The fear of not having enough financial and economic resources to succeed in colonisation disappeared – at least in Belgium. Until the Second World War, while many foreigners continued to think that Belgium did not have the stature for such a colonial empire, the top Belgian politicians and opinion leaders did their utmost to prove the contrary.

Foundations of Belgian Colonial Policy: No Foreign Interference; Do Better than the Others

These perceptions shaped the attitude of the Belgian colonisers in relation to the outside world and influenced their internal colonial policy. In short, the Belgian authorities believed that the Congo was a coveted and threatened colony. The presence of the Belgians in Africa was regularly called into question; and doubts were expressed regarding their ability to produce positive results concerning the colony, both from a moral and material point of view. In response, the Belgian authorities remained steadfast. Their goal was to show that Belgium was well and truly up to the task and did not need help from anyone to succeed. The Belgian authorities were extremely wary of any foreign presence in the Congo, whether political, economic or social in nature. This paradoxical and consequence-laden distrust allowed the Belgians to, first, isolate the Congo from the outside world and, second, to reinforce the purely Belgian character of the enterprise. In this way, they defeated misperception and prevented any foreign influence – which could potentially undermine Belgian sovereignty – in their colony.

This distrust was paradoxical because, in fact, both the Berlin Act and the Saint-Germain-en-Laye Convention of 1919 forbade any preferential treatment in economic matters. Furthermore, there was an appreciable though decreasing percentage of non-Belgian whites in the Congo. Nevertheless, as regards the contribution of capital, the Congo was and remained an essentially Belgian affair. The small amount of foreign capital resulted from strategic considerations that essentially dated back to the Leopoldian era. The Belgian authorities were always very reticent when foreign investors or businessmen attempted to invest in the Congo, or when immigrants knocked on its doors. This was a question of avoiding contact between the Congolese populations and other foreign countries or neighbouring colonies as much as possible. The

---

[24] M.-R. Thielemans, ed., *Albert Ier. Carnets et correspondance de guerre 1914–1918* (Brussels, 1991), pp. 60, 66, 252 (king's conversation with the American Colonel House).

Belgian authorities thought that unrest in the adjacent colonies would threaten law and order in the Congo.[25]

Finally, this mistrust was laden with consequences: The Congo essentially developed in seclusion. As a leading Belgian diplomat, Fernand Vanlangenhove, somewhat anxiously observed in 1954, "Up until now, the colony has lived in isolation but, given the development of education among the native masses as well as the growing influence of movements over them, it seems that there will be difficult times ahead in the near future", a prediction that was ominously accurate.[26]

The Belgian authorities therefore decided to refute any accusations made against them and to dissipate any doubts about their colonial activities raised abroad. Without any external aid or interference, they wanted to make the Congo a model colony that was better managed than any other, where there was no skimping on investments and where the indigenous populations were well-treated. In the end, official Belgium was convinced that it had fulfilled that commitment. The exemplary success of its economic development and social progress in the 1950s not only earned praise from abroad, but also dazzled the very authors of this 'colonial miracle'. Clearly, since Belgium took 'such good care' of the native Congolese, they would have no desire for independence – at least according to official views. In 1952, Wigny, the former minister of colonies, indicated the "objective of our national policy: an education that will be administered with such wisdom, generosity and intuition that the Congolese will not want to leave us".[27] In the face of attacks against the Congo from abroad, there was no need to fear the reactions of the colony's inhabitants, because "our natives are far wiser than is believed. They identify with the Belgian cause. We tell them that our attitude is driven by the concern to defend our sovereignty, *their* sovereignty, the sovereignty of *their* country".[28]

The assessment of exemplary behaviour not only blurred the reality concerning the natives who "were happier in the Congo than anywhere else". In the upper echelons of Belgian society, this tirelessly repeated and deeply internalised view even modified self-perception.[29] The success of the colonisation of the Congo became a matter of national pride and honour. As Louis Franck, the second minister of colonies, lyrically exclaimed: "[F]rom a small nation in Europe, we have become a great power in Africa. Thanks to the Congo, we have found a place for ourselves among the restricted number of populations with vast interests and fine ambitions outside Europe, in territories whose expanse and future are immense".[30] In 1946, Pierre Orts, a former Belgian diplomat

---

[25] AGR, MCM, 8 January 1954, pp. 16–8; 9 September 1955, pp. 23–4; 6 May 1955, p. 15.
[26] AA, AE-2, n° 1801ter (3283), "Note", by L. Smolderen, 31 August 1954.
[27] AMAE, AF-I-17 (1948–1953), "Voyage aux États-Unis (...)", by P. Wigny, 1952, p. 4.
[28] AMAE, AF-I-1, DG-P – Colonial Section (1953–1955), "Opinion de Monsieur Louwers", 27 April 1953.
[29] AMAE, AF-I-17 (1940–1947), letter to De Vleeschauwer, minister of colonies, 29 September 1943.
[30] L. Franck, "Que représente le Congo pour la Belgique?", in F. Passelecq, ed., *L'essor économique belge. L'expansion coloniale* (Brussels, 1931), p. 537.

who later turned to business, pointed out that Belgium had rid itself of its old inferiority complex thanks to the Congo, the loss of which "would lead to the nation's moral collapse".[31] This idea persisted among some people until the dawn of decolonisation, reaching a climax, as shown in this passage from a letter from King Baudouin to Prime Minister Eyskens on 4 September 1959: "If – God forbid – we were to lose the incomparable inheritance bequeathed to us by the genius of King Leopold II and which, up until now, has been our pride, Belgium would suffer incalculable moral and material harm, and those responsible for this abandonment would risk unanimous disapproval".[32] These assertions show how deeply Belgian elites had internalised their identification with the Congo.

Who Led the Belgian Congo on the International Scene? Internal Tensions and Centrifugal Tendencies[33]

The Congo's special position on the international scene explains certain constants of Belgian colonial policy. One final structural matter requires investigation. It follows from a seemingly simple question that, nevertheless, had major implications: Who was looking after the colony's foreign policy? The Colonial Charter provides a clear and unambiguous answer: "The kingdom's Minister of Foreign Affairs has Belgium's relations with foreign powers regarding the colony within his remit" (Article 28). This measure was a reaction to the Leopoldian past. The Congo had to be prevented, once and for all, from endangering Belgium's interests. Furthermore, the whole world had to know that the colony was firmly secured to its new motherland. In reality, the external management of the Congo led to two sorts of problems: on the one hand, to tensions between the minister of foreign affairs and the minister of colonies; on the other hand, to frictions between Belgium and the colony. These repeated clashes somewhat weakened Belgium's external position, as certain divisions became exposed on the international scene. The diplomatic management of the Congo sometimes seemed to lack clarity and direction. In 1923, publicist Pierre Daye openly asked the question: "Does the Congo have a foreign policy?"[34]

The Belgian diplomatic service and the senior colonial civil service were not always in perfect harmony. During the 1914 war, the two ministers concerned sometimes had opposing viewpoints. After the war, the minister of colonies, Louis Franck, was in favour of a restrictive interpretation of Article 28, "in order to virtually reduce the role of Minister of Foreign Affairs to a simple

---

[31] P. Orts, "La Charte de San-Francisco, un tournant de la colonisation", *Revue coloniale belge*, 1, 16 (1 June 1945), p. 2.

[32] Quoted in C. Franck & Cl. Roosens, "Le Roi Baudouin et la politique étrangère", in C. Koninckx & P. Lefèvre, eds., *Le roi Baudouin* (Brussels, 1998), p. 158.

[33] J. Vanderlinden, "Le gouvernement du Congo belge (1908-1960): un aigle doublement bicéphale?", *Yearbook of European Administrative History*, 18 (2006), pp. 21–62.

[34] P. Daye, "Le Congo a-t-il une politique extérieure?", *Le Flambeau*, 6, 2 (28 February 1923), pp. 125–42.

mission to ratify the colony's activities".[35] After Franck's departure, the divergences seemed to even out, but they did not disappear altogether. The ministries of colonies and foreign affairs continued to clash occasionally or to 'go it alone', especially when in contact with international institutions or during trade negotiations.

Between 1940 and 1944, the rivalries between the incumbent of the colonies and the head of the Belgian diplomatic service intensified. The stake was significant: Their misunderstandings influenced Belgium's position during the Second World War.

Another recurring problem was the role and position of the governor-general of the Congo in the Belgian colonial system. Around 1922, Minister of Colonies Franck confronted a strong-minded Governor-General Maurice Lippens. Lippens wanted more powers; he could not "very well see how [the governors of the English and French colonies] could accept the continual interference of the minister in the country's administration and the influence of offices that did not depend on them".[36] During the Second World War, Governor-General Pierre Ryckmans also had restricted room in which to manoeuvre. A few fundamental issues caused all these tensions. For example, could the governor-general take initiatives concerning foreign policy? Could he maintain direct contact with the neighbouring colonies, or did he always have to go through Brussels? Added to these tensions were the autonomist tendencies of certain Belgians in the Congo who demanded more decision making powers; even a form of self-government.

For decades, these questions troubled decision makers in Brussels and Léopoldville, leading to discussions, proposals and counter-proposals. Ultimately, the trouble hinged on the crucial problem of the colony's level of external autonomy. Did the Congo have room to manoeuvre on the international scene?

Despite all the friction, official Belgium steered a steady course. It was the Belgian diplomatic service that held the Congo's reins on the global scene. It was neither up to the minister of colonies nor the local authorities to maintain special relations with the other colonies or independent nations. Once again, we see the pathological fear of foreign influence on the Congo. The Belgian colony had to be isolated from the rest of the world. The Belgian political leaders also feared the autonomist tendencies of the white colonists.[37] They still believed, at the end of 1952, that any break with the principle established by Article 28 of the Colonial Charter "would be a grave danger for the preservation of Belgian sovereignty in Africa".[38] The desire for absolute control of

---

[35] AMAE, AF-I-1 (1948–1949), "Note concernant l'application de l'article 28 de la Charte Coloniale", by O. Louwers, 13 April 1948, p. 17.
[36] Archives du Palais royal (APR), secretariat Albert I (M.L. Gérard), n° 4/21/a, GG Lippens to the king, 2 November 1922.
[37] AMAE, AF-I-26 (1948–1960), "Note", by O. Louwers, 19 December 1949, p. 3.
[38] AMAE, AF-I-1, DGS-Colonial Section (1950–1953), "Note. Mission de M. Claeys Boùùaert au Congo belge", by O. Louwers, 17 November 1952.

the Congo by Brussels – and Brussels alone – is a thread running throughout the entire history of colonial Belgium.

Belgium, the Congo and the World, From One War to Another (1908–1940)

International Tensions Prior to 1914

Belgium was faced with an enormous task when it annexed the Congo. Not only was Belgium obliged to rebuild the *internal* foundations of the Congo Free State, it also had to manage an extremely complex and even explosive *international* issue. Great Britain was openly hostile, waiting several years to officially recognise the Belgian Congo. France, which had a formidable asset, the famous pre-emptive right, observed the Belgian Congo with interest. And, despite its apparent weakness, Portugal was also problematic for the Belgians owing to its hold over the left bank of the mouth of the River Congo. Germany was a different case. At delicate moments since 1885, it had supported first the Congo Free State, then the Belgian Congo because this served its own interests in the face of the other major powers. But Germany also had its own colonial possessions in the region, particularly in Cameroon and East Africa. Hence, some Germans dreamed of a *Mittelafrika* that crossed right through the continent. Yet historian Jacques Willequet demonstrates that before 1914 "the Belgian Congo had never been the centre of attention for Berlin" and even that "the Congo had no better support than Germany".[39] Nevertheless, the Belgian political leaders regularly dealt with alarmist signs and complex situations.

On several occasions between 1909 and 1913, Great Britain, France and Germany sounded each other out on the subject of the Belgian Congo. In 1909, a border dispute in the east of the Congo forced the Belgians to confront the English and the Germans, who were getting ready to settle the question to the detriment of Belgium. After some military posturing, the issue was finally solved through negotiations (agreements of 14 May and 11 August 1910).[40] But soon afterwards, the Belgian government perceived other worrying signs. In 1911, French prime minister Joseph Caillaux expressed his opinion that it was necessary to redistribute the colonies in Africa. Inevitably, this would be to the detriment of the Belgian Congo. According to other rumours, France would agree to surrender its pre-emptive right over the Belgian colony to Germany. By "painting the possibility of acquiring the Belgian Congo in such glowing colours, the French diplomatic service offered Germany an easy concession" in order to calm the tensions that existed between these two countries in Africa, particularly in Morocco.[41] Then in 1911, the British

---

[39] J. Willequet, *Le Congo belge, op. cit.*, pp. 418–9.
[40] P. Van Zuylen, *L'échiquier, op. cit.*, p. 393–410; Wm. R. Louis, "The German-Belgian-British Kivu-Mfumbiro Conference of 1910", *Bulletin des Séances de l'ARSOM*, 7, 6 (1961), pp. 839–58.
[41] C. Brossel, "Les British Documents on the Origins of the War et le Congo belge", *Congo*, I-1 (January 1940), pp. 19–20.

minister of foreign affairs, Sir Edward Grey, spoke with Germany about possibly sharing the Belgian Congo. The following year, the British war minister, Richard Burdon (Lord Haldane), evoked the same possibility during a mission in Berlin. In 1913, as we have seen, a senior German political leader mentioned the possibility of the disappearance and the sharing out of the Belgian colonial empire to a French diplomat. And all this was happening at a time when Britain had still not officially recognised the existence of the Belgian Congo! In 1912, the Belgian minister of war informed the British military attaché in Brussels that "England [is] a possible enemy and, as such, [must] be monitored. We [can] no longer consider it as a power to which Belgium can confidently turn for help".[42] The recognition of the Congo by the British the following year, just before the start of the Great War, relaxed the atmosphere between the two countries.

The Belgian Congo and the First World War

The conflict that broke out in August 1914 profoundly changed the international situation.[43] Following the German occupation of most of Belgium, the Belgian government in exile was not only confronted with the way the war was being conducted in Europe, but also with events in the Belgian Congo. The stakes were high because even if Belgium recovered its independence "the colonial part of its national heritage remained in danger should the European war have a doubtful outcome".[44] Once again, there were fears for the colony's very survival. During various more or less secret brainstorming sessions and international negotiations, the Belgian Congo once again appeared as a possible bargaining chip during a settlement of negotiated peace.[45] For the Belgian authorities, the status of colonial power thus added a new, extremely important dimension in the conduct of the war.

On 7 August 1914, a few days after the beginning of the war in Europe, the Belgian government initially tried to keep the Conventional Congo Basin out of the conflict. It proposed that the neutrality provided for in the Berlin Act of 1885 should be respected.[46] Great Britain and France immediately rejected this proposal. "In order not to thwart the action of these powers," Belgium agreed "[to] abandon the strict rigour of the regime of neutrality" and allow the transit of Allied troops. "[The French and British governments] deliberately brought the war into the Conventional Congo Basin because they considered it to be in accordance with their interests. The German attack on the Belgian Congo, following this decision, could not have influenced

---

[42] Ibid., p. 45. See on this subject: M. E. Thomas, "Anglo-Belgian Military Relations and the Congo Question, 1911–1913", *Journal of Modern History*, 25, 2 (1953), pp. 157–65.
[43] See, in general, G. Vanthemsche, *Le Congo belge pendant la Première Guerre mondiale. Les rapports du ministre des Colonies Jules Renkin au roi Albert Ier 1914–1918* (Brussels, 2009).
[44] Kadoc, Cooreman Papers, n° 2.3.4.2, "Note sur la politique de guerre (…)", Pierre Orts (?), p. 31.
[45] M.-R. Thielemans, ed., *Albert Ier. Carnets, op. cit.*, sub verbo Congo.
[46] J. E. Helmreich, "The End of Congo Neutrality, 1914", *The Historian*, 28, 4 (1966), pp. 610–24.

it".[47] British military operations against German East Africa preceded the first German shots aimed at the eastern region of the Belgian Congo on 22 August 1914. Contrary to what was said in the Allied propaganda, Germany did not trigger the hostilities in central Africa. In exchange for Belgium's acceptance of the infringement of strict Congolese neutrality, the British and French authorities promised to endeavour to safeguard the territorial integrity of the Belgian colonial domain on 19 September 1914. The Declaration of Sainte-Adresse of 29 April 1916 confirmed and clarified this guarantee. From now on, the Allied powers acknowledged not only the territorial integrity of the Congo, but also its right to future compensation.

Belgium was truly dragged into the conflict in central Africa. The Belgian Congo played an appreciable role in the military operations in this region. The Congolese Force publique took part in the campaigns against the German troops in Cameroon, in British Rhodesia and especially in German East Africa. These battles deeply marked the imagination of Belgian patriots, confirming the image of a valiant Belgium. Hidden behind these *images d'Epinal* were numerous less well-known aspects: the enormous losses in human life among a native population severely tested by incessant requisitions in terms of porterage; the organisational problems of the armed forces; weaknesses in the running of military operations; and especially, regarding our subject, numerous frictions with the British allies. Minister of Colonies Renkin rose up against "the spirit of distrust" and the "lack of consideration for our colony" shown by the British.[48] On several occasions, the Belgian-Congolese troops did the British a good turn. But the British remained reticent about the Belgians' role; in particular, they were not especially happy about the Belgian occupation of a vast area of ex-German East Africa, a region they wanted for themselves. The Belgians, on the other hand, considered this a bargaining chip they hoped to use during future peace talks.

In fact, Belgian leaders were preparing for the post-war period well before the actual fighting ended. They were aiming at two essential goals: to put an end to the Berlin Act and to ensure Belgium's hold over the left bank of the mouth of the Congo River. Other than that, Belgium did not have any territorial ambitions in Africa. During the war, the government consulted the country's main players on this subject and they almost unanimously declared their opposition to any territorial ambition. As highlighted by Belgian diplomat Pierre Orts, talking to his British equivalent: "[I]mperialism – as we already know – has no followers here [i.e. in Belgium]. Therefore, we do not want to increase our colonial property. It is quite sufficient for our needs".[49] For the Belgian diplomatic service, territorial ambition concerning the mouth of the Congo was only a matter of a simple 'border correction'.

---

[47] AA, AE-2, n° 363, resp. "Note confidentielle pour M. Denyn", 23 August 1916 and letter from the minister of colonies to the minister of foreign affairs, 1 September 1916.
[48] AMAE, AF-I-26 (1876–1916), Renkin to the ministry of foreign affairs, 21 June 1916.
[49] AA, AE-2, n° 364, "Entretien officieux de M. Orts avec sir Ronald Graham du Foreign Office", 5 May 1917, p. 7.

The first aim of the war was to get rid of the burdensome Berlin Act legacy. In 1917, Belgium and France began discussions to attempt to do away with these "constraints that both states will be delighted to see disappear [because] Belgium would like to regain its complete freedom in Africa".[50] In Belgium itself, the 'free trade' aspect led to discussions: Some wanted to lead a protectionist policy and favour Belgian economic interests; others wanted to maintain the open door policy, even after the possible abrogation of the Berlin Act. But in any case, it was necessary to wait until the end of the war for this issue to be truly dealt with. Thus, during the Paris peace talks in 1919, the victors also examined the fate of the Berlin Act. The United States was opposed to its complete abrogation and wanted to maintain a certain 'internationalisation' of Africa. In 1919, the Allied forces finally signed a new agreement, known as the Saint-Germain-en-Laye Convention, that considerably modified the Berlin Act of 1885. Some clauses were removed – for instance, the neutrality of the territories in the Conventional Congo Basin. Others were considerably amended or mitigated, among others, those that related to navigation on the Congo and the stipulations concerning humanitarian aspects and religions. The main clause of the new agreement related to trade. It allowed unlimited entry rights to be levied, although it maintained the principle of equality in trading terms. Therefore, any measures favouring national economic interests were forbidden. The Belgian diplomatic service was more or less content with the modifications obtained. It relieved Belgium from certain political constraints to which its colony was subjected. As one of the Belgian negotiators specified: "[W]e have done everything in our power to obtain the abolition of the international constraints that were burdening our colony. We succeeded in part; the unwavering opposition of the United States did not allow us to obtain more".[51]

Belgium had arrived at an essential element: The new agreement brought the Congo closer to 'common law'. Consequently, it "got rid of a source of confusion from which our colony was suffering, since it tended to lead us to believe that the Belgian Congo had been placed under a very special regime, at the end of which foreign powers would have some sort of right to control and monitor our administration".[52] During the following decades, the Saint-Germain-en-Laye Convention remained an essential reference point in Belgium's international colonial positioning. From a trade point of view, the Congo remained open to the whole world.

The second aim of the war was the rectification of the Bas-Congo border. This problem had been a concern for Belgian leaders for a long time. Owing to its strange territorial constitution and geographic anomalies, the Congo could easily enough be strangled by some malicious foreign power. Indeed, owing to

---

[50] AA, AE-II, n° 293 (2901), "Conversations relatives à la révision de l'Acte de Berlin", p. 2.
[51] AA, AE-2, n° 1801 (3283), E. de Gaiffier to Paul Hymans, minister of foreign affairs, 21 May 1920.
[52] AMAE, AF-I-1 (1920–1921), Minister of Foreign Affairs Hymans to Belgian ambassador Baron Moncheur, 6 May 1920, pp. 9–10.

The Congo and Belgium's External Position

the diplomatic vagaries of 1884 and 1885, the Belgians did not have control over the two banks of the mouth of the River Congo. Portugal, then the holder of the left bank, did not pose a real threat. But a redistribution of the colonies could lead to the eviction of this 'weak' coloniser and allow another power to take over in this region. In such a case, the Belgian Congo would be at its mercy, because this new neighbour could cut off all access to the sea. One of Belgium's essential war aims was therefore to loosen this stranglehold. Belgium hoped to take advantage of the territories it occupied in East Africa. These could serve as a bargaining chip. In exchange for the transfer of these territories to the British, the British could exert pressure on the Portuguese, who would be persuaded to hand over the left bank of the Congo and to accept, as compensation, territorial expansion elsewhere. These audacious calculations came to nothing, in particular because Portugal refused to modify its colonial borders despite the recurrent – yet unproductive – attempts of Belgian diplomats to persuade Lisbon to change its mind.

After the war, Belgium risked coming back completely empty-handed from the peace conference in Paris. The major powers, in their deliberations on the fate of the African colonies seized from defeated Germany, managed to completely 'forget' Belgium's wishes. Belgian diplomats had to vigorously intervene to obtain even a modest territorial compensation *in extremis* in favour of Belgium.[53] In May 1919, the British and Belgian negotiators, Lord Milner and Pierre Orts, finally reached an agreement. The small territories of Ruanda and Urundi, which formerly belonged to Germany, were handed over to Belgium in the form of 'mandates' entrusted to it by the recently created League of Nations.[54] It was the United States that actually prevented France and Great Britain from sharing out the former German colonies as they would have liked to do – with no constraint upon their sovereignty. The international regulation of the colonial system, very modestly inaugurated by the Berlin Act of 1885, took on a whole new dimension. The system of mandates meant that the mandatory powers had to rationalise their management of their territories in the face of global public opinion, represented by the League of Nations. The special regime to which Ruanda and Urundi were subjected prevented these territories from being purely and simply annexed to the Belgian Congo. From then on, the Belgian colonial empire would be composed of two distinct parts, the vast colony of the Congo and the small mandates of Ruanda and Urundi, even though Belgian authorities tried to bring these two entities closer together on the administrative level. The movement towards the 'internationalisation' of the colonies further increased after the Second World War – to the great displeasure of the Belgian colonisers, as we shall soon see.

---

[53] S. Marks, *Innocent Abroad: Belgium at the Paris Peace Conference of 1919* (Chapel Hill, 1981), pp. 317–21.
[54] I. Vijgen, *Tussen mandaat en kolonie. Rwanda, Burundi en het Belgische bestuur in opdracht van de Volkenbond (1916–1932)* (Louvain, 2005); Wm. R. Louis, *Great Britain and Germany's Lost Colonies 1914–1919* (Oxford, 1967).

Continuing Distrust and Threats during the Inter-War Period

For the time being, though, the Belgian Congo seemed to have overcome a dangerous hurdle at the beginning of the 1920s: It had survived the turbulence of the world conflict. The scepticism of certain Belgian leaders gave way to a genuine colonial consensus; national capital, which flowed into the Congo, ensured its economic development. The colony thus asserted its *Belgian* character. With regard to international relations, the situation seemed to have stabilised. When addressing itself to other colonial powers, Brussels presented the Belgian Congo as a factor of stability. Meanwhile, in Europe, Belgium played the role of a buffer state between the major powers. According to the Belgian authorities, the Congo fulfilled a similar role in Africa, since it "form[ed], in the most harmonious way, the uniting force between the great colonising nations. It is clear that its disappearance would cause many troubles".[55] For the big powers, it was better to have little Belgium as a neighbour in Africa than as another ambitious power. At the same time, the Belgian Congo itself would gain from having as many European neighbours as possible. This is why, in 1919, the Belgian diplomatic service would have preferred the ex-German East Africa not to go to Great Britain, but to another country instead, such as Italy.[56]

In relation to London, some tensions remained. Bad memories lingered: the attitude of the English in relation to the Congo Free State, the delayed recognition of the Belgian Congo, the friction and disagreements during the war. Furthermore, the Belgians also feared so-called South African imperialism, that is, the hegemonic will of the British dominion of South Africa in the central and southern regions of Africa. Later, the Belgian authorities would also be wary of the tendency towards autonomy and the regrouping of a 'white' Africa. For a long time, these same authorities had also been afraid of English attempts to penetrate the Katanga Province, which had become an essential element of the Belgian colonial system. In short, Brussels remained extremely vigilant in relation to any action that would reinforce the British 'encirclement' of the Congo.

Belgium maintained far more cordial relations with France in regard to colonial matters, despite the existence of several sticking points. One of these concerned the construction of the railway line from Brazzaville to Pointe Noire by the French Republic, which competed with the Belgian railway line from Léopoldville to Matadi. Belgium also endeavoured to reinforce its ties with Portugal. The smaller colonial nations had to stick together, because they could "feel all sorts of suspicions and envies burgeoning around [them]".[57] This tendency was reinforced by the intensification of Belgian economic links with Angola and Portugal (railways, diamonds, banks, etc.). Portugal and its west African colony continued to occupy an important place on Belgium's

---

[55] AMAE, AF-I-1 (1920-1921), Minister of Foreign Affairs Hymans to ambassador Baron Moncheur, 06 May 1920, p. 13.
[56] AMAE, AF-I-1 (1922), "Note pour M. le Ministre", by O. Louwers, 24 January 1922, p. 6.
[57] AMAE, AF-I-1 (1931-1935), Hymans, minister of foreign affairs, to Everts, Belgian ambassador in Berlin, 5 February 1931.

international horizon. At first sight, Italy seemed farther away from the Congolese scene, but the Belgian authorities were nevertheless concerned about the human and economic forays of the Italians into the Congo. They endeavoured to contain this movement, especially through the foundation, in 1928, of the chartered company Comité national du Kivu, which promoted the settlement of Belgians in this eastern region of the Congo.

Despite this apparent stabilisation of the Congo's international position, the fate of the colony continued to concern Belgian political circles. These worries would determine Belgium's international position for almost two decades. The critics of the Leopoldian past, of Belgium's so-called inability to manage an immense colony, resurfaced from time to time on the international scene. Although of no great importance, they nevertheless troubled the Belgian authorities. They maintained a climate of suspicion and conferred a sense that Belgium's colonial status was temporary and somehow not to be taken seriously.

Another worrying subject that resurfaced at regular intervals was the question of the 'internationalisation' of the colonies. During the First World War, the British Labour Party declared itself in favour of this option. Belgian Socialist Vandervelde fought against this idea, which earned him the recognition of King Albert. Throughout the 1920s and 1930s, the idea reappeared in progressive circles. Each time, the Belgian colonial and diplomatic leaders opposed it. The League of Nations's system of mandates was also badly perceived in Belgium, because it too resulted from a growing emphasis on the internationalisation of colonialism. Brussels, for instance, noted with displeasure that "the colonial states are [increasingly] monitored" concerning the delicate issue of forced labour.[58] Finally, during the 1930s, there was regular talk of 'Eurafrica'. Thanks to its close links with Africa, so the story went, Europe had a wonderful future ahead. This idea implied that all the European nations, even those that had no colonies, would have access to Africa's immense riches. The idea of a sort of European 'condominium' in Africa was taking shape.

This was the sticking point for the Belgian authorities. For them, these attempts were simply a means to seize the colonies from those European powers that actually possessed them. The small nations, endowed with an outsized colonial empire would, of course, have to pay the price for the operation. In their opinion, this manoeuvre was directly in line with the key problem of 1920 and 1930: Germany's colonial claims. In 1918 and 1919, Germany lost all its colonies, which were redistributed in the form of mandates. But under the Weimar Republic, and again under the Third Reich, there was a movement that demanded the reinstatement of Germany as a colonial power. Official Belgium anxiously followed these developments. Once again, the Belgian colonial domain, now increased with the addition of Ruanda-Urundi, seemed to be coveted and threatened. In Belgium, the hatred of the 1914 aggressor lived on.

---

[58] AMAE, AF-I-1 (1929–1930), "Note pour M. le Ministre", by O. Louwers, 26 November 1929, p. 3.

The more or less secret talks that took place before the war were reinterpreted in light of the events of 1914 through 1918. From then on, Germany was presented as the ogre that "had already set its heart on our colony well before the war".[59] This was an inaccurate or at least simplistic vision, as we have just seen. On the other hand, there is no doubt that in the 1920s, Belgian diplomats posted abroad picked up signals that aroused concerns in Brussels. In a humiliated and vengeful Germany, certain newspapers or groups, along with a number of more or less significant figures, demanded that their country be once again endowed with colonies. At times, their eyes fell more or less explicitly on the Congo and/or Ruanda-Urundi. On a number of occasions, the Belgian authorities bared their teeth: for instance, in 1928, Belgium let it be known that it would not allow "itself to be stripped of its colonial empire, and for this reason, it was obliged to use arms to defend its possessions".[60]

The issue took a more dangerous turn in the second half of the 1930s. Despite the fact that Hitler did not consider the colonial issue as essential, it continued to trouble minds and assumed a new international dimension when the British began their colonial appeasement policy. London thought that redistributing the colonies would satisfy the Nazi appetites. Diplomatic talks were conducted at the highest level. The Belgian Congo and the Portuguese colonies had to pay the price for the operation. According to historian Carl Pansaerts, "Britain was willing to surrender parts of the Belgian Congo and Portuguese Angola in order to buy-off Hitler's goodwill with regard to Central and East Europe". Berlin was, in fact, more honest towards Belgium and Portugal than London since the Germans let it be known that they were not really interested in such an agreement, whereas the British "more than once pulled its two oldest allies' legs by stating that their African colonies were not being discussed".[61] There was, however, a troubling detail. The British secretary of state to the colonies, Ormsby-Gore, confirmed that King Leopold III had told him that Belgium "might be prepared to make some contributions in West Africa".[62] Might this be a symptom of the king's personal colonial policy on the eve of the Second World War?[63]

In any case, in the face of these dealings, the Belgian government remained inflexible. There was no question of touching the Belgian colonial empire. Faced, however, with the claims of the colonial have-nots, the Belgian authorities did

---

[59] O. Louwers, *Le Congo belge et le pangermanisme colonial* (Paris, 1918), p. 1.
[60] Letter from Hymans, minister of foreign affairs, to the Belgian ambassadors, 20 July 1928, quoted in O. Louwers, *Le problème colonial du point de vue international* (Brussels, 1936), pp. 124-5.
[61] C. S. Pansaerts, "Anglo-German Conversations on Colonial Appeasement, and the Involvement of the Belgian Congo (October 1937-March 1938)", *Cahiers du Centre de Recherches et d'Études historiques de la Seconde Guerre mondiale*, 16 (1994), pp. 40, 68-9.
[62] W. R. Louis, "Colonial Appeasement, 1936-1938", *Revue belge de Philologie et d'Histoire*, 49, 4 (1971), pp. 1187-8.
[63] See also the talks between H. Schacht and King Leopold III in 1937, as mentioned in APR, secretariat of Leopold III (Capelle), XV A/7, n° 178, note "Quelques réflexions au sujet des déclarations de M. Schacht".

formulate a response. It was based on the regime of the Saint-Germain-en-Laye Convention. If the conventional 'open door' regime could be extended to *all* the African colonies, it would no longer be necessary to claim one's own space to find markets and raw materials. Since trade and business would become free *everywhere* in Africa, as they already were in the Belgian Congo, it would be pointless to redistribute the colonies. The complexity of this position became clear. Belgium proposed to 'internationalise' the colonies, an option it usually rejected. This somewhat contradictory attitude allowed for the protection of Belgian *political* sovereignty in the Congo. And, at the same time, Belgian businessmen would have the chance to trade and invest in a much broader space. Protectionist colonial powers would no longer isolate their African domains from the global economic trends. Needless to say, this Belgian suggestion came up against the hostility of the other colonial powers. This was how things stood when the Second World War broke out.

Belgium, the Congo and the World, from the Second World War to Independence (1940–1960)

The Belgian Congo, by no Means Insignificant during the Second World War

At the end of the 1930s, Belgium attempted to remain outside the impending global conflict but, despite its policy of independence, the country was once again dragged into war on 10 May 1940. After eighteen days of fighting, the Belgian army surrendered. This time, the country was completely occupied. At the end of May 1940, overcome by Germany's lightening attack, the Belgian government found itself in the depths of France. In addition to the military defeat, there was a major political crisis. King Leopold III and the ministers disagreed on the attitude they should adopt towards the Nazi victory. The king considered the German victory definitive and felt that fighting should therefore cease. He did not want to side with Great Britain and France, two countries he did not consider as allies. The government, though, wanted to continue the war alongside the French and the British. According to the constitution, the king of the Belgians could not take any personal political initiatives, that is any not covered by at least one member of the government. King Leopold II had continuously violated this rule: The entire Congolese venture was based on his maverick attitude. In 1940, Leopold III also contravened this constitutional rule. He refused to follow the policy recommended by his ministers, thus leading to the Royal Question that would divide Belgium for more than a decade. Strangely, neither the king nor the government ever envisaged the possibility of the monarch leaving occupied Belgium to go to the Congo, at that point the only free part of the Belgian territory. Yet this option would have enabled the king to distance himself from Germany without clearly siding with France and Britain. In fact, the king's choice to stay in Belgium was inspired by his plans to construct an authoritarian political regime in Belgium, under the aegis of a victorious Germany, with himself at its centre.

The colonial empires in general played an important role in the conduct of the Second World War. The main colonial powers lost important parts of their possessions, particularly in Asia. In sub-Saharan Africa, the British had managed to maintain their empire quasi intact, with the exception of Somaliland, temporarily occupied by the Italians. In the French territories, the problem was of a different nature. A crucial question was whether these colonies would side with the collaborationist Vichy regime or with the free French under General de Gaulle. In August through November 1940, only French Equatorial Africa chose to support de Gaulle. At the end of 1942, Vichy lost the rest of its colonies in Africa, including the Maghreb. The British and French African colonies were of great importance for different reasons: economic strength (due to strategic raw materials), legitimacy, wartime psychology, diplomatic weight, military capacity and strategic position.[64] In this game, the Belgian Congo also played a far from negligible role, not only for the Belgian authorities themselves, but for the other belligerents.

The Congolese problem by far exceeded the position of Belgium because, for all the warring nations, the Belgian colony was far more important than in 1914. Thanks to Belgian investments, it had become one of the main producers of raw materials worldwide. Before and throughout the war, the Congo therefore remained an important element on the international scene. At the end of 1938, the British Foreign Office refused to guarantee the preservation of Belgian sovereignty in the Congo.[65] On the eve of the conflict, King Leopold III probed Great Britain on the subject of a renewal of the Sainte-Adresse Declaration of 1916, but obtained only an evasive response from London.[66] On 10 May 1940, the very day hostilities began between Germany and Belgium, Belgian authorities approached Great Britain and France to obtain a declaration guaranteeing the neutrality of the Congo and the respect of its territorial integrity during a future peace settlement. London refused to grant this guarantee, since the presence of the Belgian colony at its side was considered too important. Paris was initially inclined to comply with Belgium's request, but finally decided to react in the same way.[67] At the beginning of the war, the British left no doubt as to their intentions: They were not going to allow the Congo to fall into German hands.[68]

[64] K. Jeffery, "The Second World War", in J. M. Brown & Wm. R. Louis, eds., *The Oxford History of the British Empire. Vol. 4, op. cit.*, pp. 306–28; M. Thomas, *The French Empire at War 1940–45* (Manchester, 1998).
[65] C. Koninckx, *Koning Leopold III, diplomaat voor de vrede* (Sint-Niklaas, 1987), p. 74.
[66] AMAE, AF-I-1 (1953), "Le Congo belge et les grandes puissances", by O. Louwers, June 1954, p. 18; R. Keyes, *Outrageous Fortune: The Tragedy of Leopold III of the Belgians 1901–1941* (London, 1984), pp. 136–43.
[67] NA, Colonial Office (CO), n° 323/1791/15, J. G. Ward (of the Foreign Office) to the undersecretary of state of colonies, 28 May 1940.
[68] "Archives britanniques concernant l'histoire de Belgique en 1940", *Courrier hebdomadaire du CRISP*, 526–527 (1971), p. 5 and sq. (declaration of Lord Halifax, secretary of state to the Foreign Office); J. Gérard-Libois & J. Gotovitch, *L'An 40, la Belgique occupée* (Brussels, 1970), p. 254.

France also had a certain interest in the Belgian Congo. Even before the start of the hostilities, and again when the Belgian army, led by the king, surrendered on 28 May 1940, the French prime minister, Paul Reynaud, outraged by the king's 'betrayal', declared that he reserved the right to use the Belgian Congo as a 'bargaining chip'.[69] Shortly before the collapse of the Third Republic, France even envisaged sending troops to occupy Léopoldville.[70] Germany was also concerned about the Belgian colony; before and during the war, the Third Reich continued to play with the idea of a great German *Mittelafrika*, to which the ex-Belgian Congo would belong.[71] During the summer of 1940, the director of the Dutch aviation company KLM, Albert Plesman, submitted a settlement plan, based on a British pre-war plan, to Reichsmarschall Hermann Goering; a plan that included Africa and the Belgian Congo.[72] Even Vichy France, speculating on a possible dismemberment of Belgium, thought of establishing a Franco-German entity in Africa, notably at the cost of the Belgian colonial domain.[73]

During this period of war, all the international players were quite clearly interested in the fate of the Belgian Congo one way or another. Would it fall into the hands of the Allies or into those of the Axis powers? The answer was far from clear.

The Congo, an Essential Element of Belgian Policy in 1940

Cut off from their homeland, and physically and morally exhausted, the Belgian ministers were in despair by June 1940, when France surrendered. Those who wanted to abandon the fight thought of returning to Belgium and accepting German occupation. But then, a specific factor turned out to be decisive. On 18 June 1940, the government issued a law decree (*arrêté-loi*), a decision fraught with consequences. The minister of colonies, Albert De Vleeschauwer, was given full legislative and executive power to manage the Congo as administrator-general of the colony. The decree also stated that if or when the minister was unable to fulfil his office, that power would be passed to the governor-general.

What was the rationale for this decision? The ministers wanted to prevent the colony from becoming an 'estate without a master' if the government should disappear or De Vleeschauwer lose his status as minister. This decision,

---

[69] P. Reynaud, *Au cœur de la mêlée 1930–1945* (Paris, 1951), p. 664; C. Koninckx, *Koning Leopold III, op. cit.*, p. 149.

[70] AMAE, AF-I-1 (1953), "Le Congo belge et les grandes puissances", by O. Louwers, June 1954, p. 18 and J.-L. Vellut, "L'ombre ...", art. cit., p. 82.

[71] C. Metzger, *L'empire colonial français dans la stratégie du 3ᵉ Reich (1936–1945)* (Bern, 2002), pp. 233, 237, 529.

[72] AMAE, AF-I-26 (1948–1960), E. Graeffe (Belgian ambassador in The Hague) to Spaak, minister of foreign affairs, 21 June and 7 July 1949. The relevant file is now kept in the Dutch National Archives in The Hague (2.05.80, file 2117). I thank Marc Dierikx of the Huygens Institute for Netherlands History, who generously passed this information on to me.

[73] J.-L. Vellut, "L'ombre...", art. cit., p. 82.

however, did not imply that the colony should continue the armed struggle alongside the British – according to the Belgian ministers the Congo had to remain neutral. Indeed, the Belgian government sought to defend the Congo against ... possible British encroachment![74]

Since economic and political aspects were intertwined in this affair, it is also necessary to observe the behaviour of the big companies during these crucial days in June 1940. The business leaders of the Congolese private companies, which were part of Belgium's Société générale, withdrew to the French city of Bordeaux. They contested the need for this exceptional measure that would endow the minister of colonies with special powers. Among other things, they feared legal objections. Objections were certainly raised by the circles surrounding King Leopold in occupied Belgium, as we shall soon see. When De Vleeschauwer, newly endowed with his powers as administrator-general of the colony, met these businessmen, he urged them to transfer the decision making centres of their companies to Portugal, Great Britain, Canada or the United States. They refused, intending to return to Belgium as quickly as possible.[75] Furthermore, an internal note of the Société générale confirms their idea that "as soon as we return to Belgium, we must endeavour to ensure the links with the colony, in agreement with the occupying forces. This need will be especially felt if the war lasts".[76] Some business leaders even told the minister that acting otherwise "would not be loyal towards Germany".[77]

The leaders of the Société générale were not the only ones to think along these lines. In occupied Belgium, King Leopold III pursued his personal strategy, despite being officially a prisoner. For him, the fight was over and there was therefore no question of the Congo siding with the British. The Congo was a sizeable stake, because the neutrality of the Belgian colony – or any connection with the Axis forces – would allow Germany access to this gigantic reservoir of natural riches. In occupied Belgium, some were already thinking of an agreement with the Nazi authorities concerning the Congo. In their opinion, Belgium risked losing its colony if the Congo were to rise up against the Germans who, at that time, seemed certain of complete victory. On the other hand, if Belgium and the Congo were to side with the occupying forces, there could well be Belgian territorial claims to the detriment of France and Great Britain!

In Brussels, the occupying forces set up a Kolonial Politisches Büro that sought to establish links with the services of the ministry of colonies that had

---

[74] J. Velaers & H. Van Goethem, *Leopold III. De Koning, het land, de oorlog* (Tielt, 1994), p. 365; J. Stengers, *Léopold III et le gouvernement* (Gembloux, 1980), p. 95.

[75] AGR, Société générale de Belgique – 3rd fund (SGB-3), n° 35, "Procès-verbaux du Comité colonial de Bordeaux. PV n° 12 – Réunion du 21 juin 1940"; R. Brion & J.-L. Moreau, *La Société générale de Belgique 1822-1997* (Antwerp, 1998), pp. 339-40.

[76] AGR, SGB-3, n° 32, "Rapport concernant les opérations du Comité SG en France mai-juin-juillet 1940".

[77] Kadoc, De Vleeschauwer Papers, n° 342, De Vleeschauwer to Félicien Cattier (of the SGB-group), 26 September 1940.

remained in Belgium.[78] Perhaps it was someone from this office who contacted an official at the Union minière to say that Germany was especially interested in Katanga: The big mining company could remain, but German influence over it would have to be increased.[79]

It is quite clear that influential Belgian political and economic circles were not disposed to engage the Congo in resistance against the Nazis. In other words, the Belgian Congo faced the same dilemma as the French colonies: Which camp would it choose? Ultimately, a number of crucial economic and political decisions pushed the colony into the British camp. First of all, the Belgian merchant fleet was placed under British control, possibly thanks to the influence of Félicien Cattier, a leading personality of the Générale group who was also president of the Compagnie maritime belge.[80] Moreover, on 25 June 1940, the management of the London office of the Banque du Congo belge signed an agreement with the British authorities.[81] This agreement stipulated that "the London office will accept no instructions from any office of the Banque du Congo belge in continental France or in territory occupied by or under the control of the enemy".[82] The London branch of the bank made no secret of its intention to abandon neutrality in the Belgian Congo and to side with the English. This crucial decision constituted the first step towards the integration of the Belgian Congo into the British war effort.

Great Britain paid particular attention to the Belgian Congo. After the capitulation of King Leopold III and the Belgian army on 28 May 1940, the fate of the Belgian colony seemed highly uncertain. This uncertainty increased a few weeks later when the Belgian government fell into complete disarray following the military and political collapse of France. Would the authorities in Léopoldville acknowledge the legitimacy of Administrator-General De Vleeschauwer? Was there a risk that they would fall into the camp of Germany and the king? In such a case, the British would not only lose a precious source of raw materials, essential for the running of the war, but the Congolese troops would also threaten the neighbouring, poorly defended British colonies. The governors of these colonies informed London of their concerns. The very day of the Belgian surrender, a crisis meeting was held in London, the subject of which was the Belgian Congo. The Admiralty suggested the possible military occupation of crucial points in the Belgian colony, while other British authorities remained sceptical, since the troops required for this action were sadly

---

[78] CEGES (Centre d'Études Guerres et Sociétés contemporaines), Brussels, Van Hecke Papers, microfilm 73, "PV van de ondervraging van den Heer Van Hecke", 14 February 1946, pp. 2–3.
[79] AGR, Louwers Papers, n° 374, "Note sur le programme de négociation coloniale pour le moment du règlement de la guerre", 16 August 1940 (author most probably Louwers).
[80] G. Devos & G. Elewaut, *CMB 100: A Century of Commitment to Shipping* (Tielt, 1995), pp. 124–7.
[81] This private bank, member of the Générale group, was also the emission bank of the Belgian Congo.
[82] Fortis Historical Centre, Brussels, "Mémorial" file, note "Banque du Congo belge, Londres – Période de 1940 à 1944", p. 4.

lacking. Britain therefore turned towards another solution: If the anti-German Belgian authority were to collapse, it would be absolutely necessary to encourage an 'independent' Congo.[83]

Britain would, in the end, not have to resort to the extreme solution of an independent Congo because several events occurred in Belgian political circles that prevented total capitulation to the Germans. This is when the tribulations of Minister of Colonies De Vleeschauwer, invested with his powers as administrator-general of the colony, would become decisive. At the end of June 1940, he was still not ready to commit the Congo to Great Britain.[84] He was in Lisbon at the time and intended to withdraw to either the Congo or the United States. At that moment, the Belgian ambassador in London, Cartier de Marchienne, warned De Vleeschauwer that there was a strong possibility that the British government would recognise a group of left-wing Belgian politicians who had fled to London.[85] De Vleeschauwer, wanting to avoid this possibility, changed his mind. He arrived in London on 4 July 1940, not only as a Belgian minister in office, but also and especially as the administrator-general of the colony. He met the British authorities, including Churchill himself, and offered them the Congo's economic aid.[86] He also instructed active Belgian companies abroad not to obey instructions from managing bodies situated in occupied Belgium.[87] It should nevertheless be noted that this offer concerned the *economic* war effort. At that time, it was not yet a question, in his eyes, of involving the Congo in the *armed* fight against the Axis forces.

Conscious of the importance of the Congo, the British acknowledged and treated De Vleeschauwer as a representative of the legitimate Belgian government. However, they also pressed him to persuade at least some of his colleagues to join him. By October 1940, three had established themselves in London to continue the fight against Germany: Minister of Finance Camille Gutt, Prime Minister Hubert Pierlot and Minister of Foreign Affairs Paul-Henri Spaak. Still, the British remained very cautious. They envisaged the possibility

---

[83] National Archives, London (NA), Foreign Office (FO), n° 371/24282, Trenchard to Halifax (British minister of foreign affairs), 8 July 1940; Halifax to Trenchard, 11 July 1940; the South African minister of foreign affairs to the high commissioner in London, 3 July 1940; the governor of Uganda to the secretary of state of the colonies, 5 July 1940; notes "Draft statement" and "Present position"; NA, Colonial Office (CO), n° 323/1791/15, "Position of the Belgian Congo", minutes of an inter-departmental meeting, 28 May 1940.

[84] H. Van Goethem, ed., *August De Schryver. Oorlogsdagboeken 1940–1942* (Tielt, 1998), p. 455 (note 291).

[85] Kadoc, De Vleeschauwer Papers, n° 285, Cartier de Marchienne to De Vleeschauwer, 26 June 1940. Some Belgian businessmen, present in Lisbon, had also advised him to turn to the British in order to save the Belgian interests. First the Liberal MP and future minister of colonies Robert Godding (NA, FO, n° 371/24282, R. Godding to Genon, 26 June 1940), and also Max Horn, influential businessman and long-time advisor of Belgian colonial authorities in economic matters (J.-F. Crombois, *Camille Gutt 1940–1945* [Gerpinnes, 1999], p. 100).

[86] Kadoc, De Vleeschauwer Papers, n° 342.

[87] J. Vanderlinden, *Pierre Ryckmans 1891–1959: coloniser dans l'honneur* (Brussels, 1994), p. 437.

that the power of the Belgian government could disappear. In the meantime, on 11 July, Colonel Mackenzie had left for the Congo at the head of a shadow mission composed of a number of soldiers. One of the aims of this nebulous, controversial and somewhat inglorious mission (in case Belgium completely capitulated and there was no longer a Belgian representative government) was to "establish, then support any national committee in the Congo that was established there".[88] Another, more successful, mission in August 1940 was entrusted to Lord Hailey. Its official objective was to facilitate the organisation of the production and supply of raw materials essential to Great Britain. However, the instructions to Hailey's mission also included a secret political chapter that was unknown even to the Belgians: Keep the Congo on the side of the British, in case the Belgian authorities should fail.

Afterwards, a senior civil servant from the Foreign Office summarised the situation as follows: "At one point, we thought we might have to give up the Belgian government and go for a 'Free Congo'". In the end, the Hailey mission did not have to implement this project; it was entirely and successfully devoted to the organisation of the economic war effort.[89]

If the British authorities thought they could – as a last resort – count on a 'free' and allied Congo, it was thanks to the co-operative attitude of the governor-general, Pierre Ryckmans, who also played a decisive role in the fate of the Belgian Congo during the war.[90] From the beginning of the conflict, the Congo faced a complex situation. First, it was particularly difficult to know exactly what was happening in Europe. Furthermore, Belgian colonial society was overrun with various movements. Neutralist and royalist elements rubbed shoulders with those people or groups who wanted to pursue the fight with the English. Initially, big companies such as the Union minière in the Haut-Katanga region were lukewarm towards the idea of making a war effort alongside the British. Business leaders preferred the Congo to remain neutral and possibly tried to influence Ryckmans to opt for this solution.[91] The staff of the Force publique recommended declaring neutrality and even independence for the Congo, all under the authority of the governor-general.[92] But the governor-general refused to take a defeatist stance and would not give way to these pressures. Despite his commitment to the dynasty and the king himself, Ryckmans opted to pursue the war against the Germans.[93] At the beginning of June, the British consul-general relayed this essential piece of news to London: The local

---

[88] NA, FO, n° 371/24282, telegram from the War Office, 8 July 1940; n° 371/26347, E. J. Joint, British consul general in Léopoldville, to the FO, 27 June 1941.
[89] NA, Cabinet Papers (CAB), n° 21/1006, FO to Lord Hailey, 14 August 1940 and FO to E. J. Joint, 16 August 1940; FO, n° 371/30794, Roger Makins (FO) to C. Hope Gills, British consul general in Léopoldville, 16 February 1942.
[90] J. Vanderlinden, *Pierre Ryckmans, op. cit.*, passim.
[91] R. Brion & J.-L. Moreau, *De la mine à Mars. La genèse d'Umicore* (Tielt, 2006), p. 215.
[92] J. Vanderlinden, *Pierre Ryckmans, op. cit.*, pp. 429–30, 437–8.
[93] NA, FO, n° 371/24282, E. J. Joint to the FO, 5 June 1940.

authorities in the Belgian Congo supported the British war effort and therefore, the "Belgian Congo should be regarded as allied territory".[94]

First Ryckmans's attitude, then De Vleeschauwer's, placed the Congo firmly into the British camp. These developments were, not surprisingly, badly received by the German authorities. In a meeting between the leaders of the Association des Intérêts coloniaux belges, they threatened the big Belgian colonial companies with sanctions.[95] Meanwhile, the Leopoldist circles in Brussels were also opposed to the Congo's commitment to the fight against the Nazis. In a conversation with the *Militärbefehlshaber*, General Alexander von Falkenhausen, Leopold III expressed his discontent with the governor-general's position.[96] According to the king, the Congo had to remain neutral. A very delicate aspect of the problem concerned the possible *military* engagement of the Congo in the fight against the Axis forces. So far, the Belgian authorities in London had shown that they were ready to mobilise the Belgian colony for the United Kingdom's *economic* war effort. However, the potential provision of Congolese *troops* to the British was to have more serious consequences. These troops would fight against Italy, because the latter had major territorial ambitions in Africa. Using its own African possessions as bases, Italy hoped to conquer the neighbouring British colonies, including Egypt. But, surprisingly enough, there was no official war between Belgium and Italy, despite the fact that Rome's German ally was occupying the country! King Leopold III had close family ties with Italy's leading circles, his sister being married to crown prince Umberto.

The king and the politico-administrative circles that gravitated around him endeavoured to prevent the Congo from engaging its military and economic potential to fight alongside Great Britain. In August 1940, Octave Louwers, an influential senior civil servant in colonial matters who was part of the Leopoldist circles, wrote two notes underlining the dangers inherent in Congolese support of the British, particularly in a war that set them against the Italians. Primarily, such support would give the Italians a rationale for attacking and invading the Congo. "The consequences may be fearsome because if the Germans are victorious and peace must be negotiated (…) we can rest assured that the Congo will be taken from us".[97]

To prevent the entry of the Congo into the British camp, the Leopoldist circles put pressure on Belgian diplomatic representatives, stressing the need to maintain the Congo's neutrality. In September 1940, the king's secretary, Count Robert Capelle, sent instructions to the Belgian diplomat in the Swiss town of Bern, who then passed them on to the other Belgian diplomatic posts, that the Belgian

---

[94] NA, CO, n° 323/1791/15, telegram from the Colonial Office, 12 June 1940; NA, FO, n° 371/26328, "First year of the war. Summary of events in Léopoldville/Brazzaville", by E. J. Joint; 7 January 1941.

[95] *Livre Blanc 1936–1946. Volume 1. Mémoire* (Brussels, s.d.), p. 285; *Recueil de documents établi par le Secrétariat du Roi* (S.l., s.d.), pp. 388–90.

[96] J. Velaers & H. Van Goethem, *Leopold III, op. cit.*, p. 503.

[97] APR, Cabinet of Leopold III, file VI (Colonie 1940–1943), "Note", 14 August 1940 and "Note", 24 August 1940.

colony had to remain outside the conflict between the Germans and the British – a conflict in which the Belgians were no longer involved.[98] In October 1940, Leopold III and his entourage even envisaged sending an emissary to Léopoldville in order to explain the royal point of view to the Congolese authorities. An evasive response from Hitler, from whom Leopold had requested the authorisation to act, finally prevented this plan from going ahead.[99] Initially, the Belgian government in exile in London (and Ryckmans in the Congo) actually refused to declare war on Italy and to thus engage the colony in military operations. But many Belgians in the Congo did not understand why they could not fight the Italians, the allies of the Germans who were occupying Belgium! Tensions rose in the colony, eventually leading to an attempted (and aborted) military putsch. Finally, on 19 November 1940, after Italian airmen had bombarded the United Kingdom from Belgian territory, the Belgian government in London acknowledged a state of war between Belgium and Italy. Soon, the Congolese colonial troops were launched into military operations in Africa against the Italians. The Congo's commitment to the British and free French was finally complete.

During these dramatic weeks, the fate of the official government had been hanging from a thread. It is quite possible that without the Congo and the unique combination of personal, political and economic factors involved, *legitimate* Belgian governmental power would not have been maintained during the war.[100] Although some Belgian politicians were in London as of June 1940 and wanted to continue the fight against the German occupying forces, they were not invested with constitutional legitimacy. The *colonial* dimension of Belgium, and especially the particular turn it took, finally led the legal government to pursue the war effort in London. Thus, a rupture of Belgium's *institutional continuity* was avoided during the Second World War. The status of colonial power in Belgium therefore had a crucial impact on the country's internal life. It prevented an upheaval, a rupture in the legal functioning of the national institutions. And it also led to the survival of the *Belgian* Congo itself. Without the decree of 18 June, and without the action of De Vleeschauwer, Ryckmans and a handful of businessmen, Belgian sovereignty in Africa would probably have come to an end in 1940 or at least would have been suspended for many years. The British government would have supported the creation of a free Congo. But in the end, the presence of the Belgian colony, alongside the Allied forces and led by the legitimate Belgian government, negated all these eventualities. The Congo was and remained Belgian.

The Belgian Congo during the Second World War: Internal and External Tensions

Belgian activity in the Second World War was essentially due to the Congo. Though the Force publique participated in the Allied campaign in northeast

---

[98] A. De Jonghe, *Hitler en het politieke lot van België* (Antwerp, 1972), pp. 233–5.
[99] J. Gérard-Libois & J. Gotovitch, *Léopold III. De l'an 40 à l'effacement* (Brussels, 1991), pp. 70–1.
[100] J. Stengers, *Léopold III, op. cit.*, pp. 91–118.

Africa, defeating the Italians in Ethiopia, notably with the victory at Saio in July 1941, the colony's impact was not crucial to actual military operations. The Congo's essential role was as a supplier of strategic raw materials. If the Belgian ministers present in London carried some weight and enjoyed some sort of credibility in the face of the Allied authorities, it was precisely thanks to the Congo. They were perfectly conscious of this: "The Congo enjoys a great prestige here [i.e. in the United States] and is our greatest asset".[101]

The patriotic memory, shaped by Allied propaganda, presents an idealised image of the collaboration between the Allied forces, the Belgian government and the Congo during the war. But this co-operation, though very real, should not overshadow the various frictions that existed between all these parties, as well as the tensions that ran through each of them. There were conflicts between the Allied countries; between the Belgian ministers themselves; between those ministers and the Congolese authorities; between the Belgian political and business worlds; and finally, between the pro-Allied colonial authorities and the oppositional movements in the colony. All these forces (except, perhaps, for the last one) were, of course, fighting a common enemy, and the various frictions did not assume the same importance. But, despite all the details, it was far from the perfect harmony that the propaganda evokes.

In the second half of 1940, the British mission led by Lord Hailey was present in the Congo to stimulate and direct production towards Britain's war needs.[102] This mission led to the Belgian colony being "placed under informal guardianship" by Great Britain.[103] The British and Belgian authorities then concluded a series of agreements (in particular, that of 21 January 1941) that integrated Congolese currency and trade into the British economic zone.[104] In 1942, Great Britain, the Belgian government in London and a new belligerent, the United States, negotiated a tripartite agreement that was to determine the Congo's participation in the Allied economic war effort. This agreement was never signed by the Belgian authorities, but was nevertheless applied de facto. This strange situation highlights the tension between the Belgian government and its Anglo-Saxon partners. Belgium continued to deeply distrust any foreign interference in *its* colony. It wanted to keep absolute control over this lever that was vital to its sovereignty. Furthermore, the Congo had to serve the country's economic restoration after the war. In fact, the government wanted to "introduce a clause that would give Belgium back its control of the colony's products after the liberation [and] this is what prevented the formal signing of

---

[101] AMAE, AF-I-17 (1940–1947), De Vleeschauwer to the government in London 6 June 1942.
[102] J.-F. Crombois, *Camille Gutt, op. cit.*, pp. 221–327; B. Fetter, "Changing War Aims: Central Africa's Role, 1940–41, as seen from Léopoldville", *African Affairs*, 87, 348 (July 1988), pp. 377–92.
[103] J.-L. Vellut, "La stratégie africaine des grandes puissances, de la drôle de guerre au coup gaulliste à Brazzaville", in *De Gaulle, la Belgique et la France Libre* (Brussels, 1991), p. 62.
[104] J.-Cl. Willame, "Le Congo dans la guerre: la coopération économique belgo-alliée de 1940 à 1944", in *Le Congo belge durant la Seconde Guerre mondiale. Recueil d'études* (Brussels, 1983), pp. 213–52.

the agreement" which the Belgian authorities respected in practice.[105] Another cause of irritation for the Belgian authorities was the presence and action of official British and American agents in the Congo. They behaved "as though they were at home", an intolerable attitude in the eyes of the Belgian authorities.[106] Another factor further complicated the situation: disagreements between the Americans and British themselves. The Americans had their specific objectives in mind and wanted to strengthen their post-war position.

In fact, this misunderstanding between Belgium and the Allies masked another one. Within the government itself, exiled in London, Minister of Colonies De Vleeschauwer was particularly sensitive with regard to his authority. He would not put up with any attacks on Belgian prerogatives in the Congo. His intransigent attitude not only irritated Belgium's U.S. and British allies, it also clashed with the more conciliatory position of the other members of the Belgian government, in particular Spaak, the minister of foreign affairs. Besides differences in character or personal sensitivities, the recurring problem of how the Congo would be represented on the international scene was raised once more. As we saw earlier, the ministers of colonies and foreign affairs often differed with regard to the colony's external policy. In the end, De Vleeschauwer was completely isolated, discredited and exhausted. These dissensions affected Belgium's position in relation to the Allies. Unfavourable impressions and misunderstandings built up. The United States and Great Britain even wondered whether Belgium really wanted to support the war effort.[107] The Belgian ministers were well aware of the problem, even if they clearly rejected the accusation that they were 'sabotaging' the war effort.

The Belgian government's worries did not stop there. Within the Congo itself, neutralist or Leopoldist movements continued to stir. Some considered that the government had 'sold' the Congo to the Americans and the English, an opinion that, unsurprisingly, was also expressed in occupied Belgium. In the colony, the Belgian government in London and the colonial authorities were openly criticised, particularly by a senior ecclesiastical figure, Mgr. de Hemptinne, vicar apostolic of Katanga.[108] The pro-Allies Congolese authorities endeavoured to control these discordant voices, which could play into the enemy's hands.[109]

Furthermore, the Belgian government in London had to face yet another problem: the movement towards autonomy within the colony itself. Once again, the authorities back 'home' were confronted with the old demon, reinvigorated by a whole series of factors: the uncomfortable position of the government in

---

[105] AMAE, AF-I-1 (1943–1945), "Note pour M. le Ministre des Colonies", by A. Moeller, 20 June 1945, p. 1.
[106] AMAE, AF-I-17 (1940–1947), De Vleeschauwer to Spaak, 24 March 1942.
[107] AMAE, AF-I-26 (1928–1947), L. Oliphant, British ambassador, to Spaak, 13 July 1943.
[108] APR, Cabinet Leopold III, file VI (Colonie 1940–1943), "Mémoire (…)", by J.-F. de Hemptinne, 15 December 1943; G. Feltz, "Mgr. de Hemptinne pendant la Seconde Guerre mondiale", in *Le Congo durant la Seconde Guerre, op. cit.*, pp. 419–37.
[109] AGR, MCM, 20 January 1944, p. 13.

exile; its internal divisions; the difficulties of communication with the colony and the resulting misunderstandings; the strengthened self-awareness and self-confidence of the Belgian colonists in the Congo; their desire to settle the affairs of a colony that was further than ever from Europe; and, finally, Ryckmans himself, a governor-general with a strong personality. The minister of colonies and governor-general often collided. From Léopoldville's point of view, it was very difficult to conduct affairs owing to the lack of decision making powers. Ryckmans deplored the "deep divergences between the government and myself on nature of the Governor-General's mission".[110] But from the government's point of view, these 'divergences' threatened Belgian's sovereignty in the Congo. Little by little, the Congo was creating links that no longer passed through London and which, after the liberation, risked no longer passing through Brussels either. The Belgian government therefore wanted to put an end to the Congo's autonomist tendencies. The United States, in particular, exercised a hitherto unknown interest in the Belgian colony, especially in terms of trade – a completely new factor that pervaded the post-war period. The governor-general's powers were at the centre of the problem. The decree of 18 June 1940 had granted the minister of colonies, or, if necessary, the governor-general, extraordinary powers. Ryckmans made use of the wide-ranging possibilities that were offered to him until the cabinet meeting of April 1942 abrogated the decree.[111] When, in 1944, the governor-general requested the reinstatement of his powers, De Vleeschauwer refused. He believed that this would render the minister of colonies superfluous. This intransigence was not shared by his colleagues.[112]

The final source of problems and friction for the Belgian government was the Congolese business world. Directors of big companies tended to follow their own policies. The business tycoons of the Société générale, in particular, identified the Congo's well-being with their companies' profitability. Among other things, tension arose regarding the export companies' (exaggerated) prices for supplies for the Allied forces. In the eyes of the authorities, the private sector made copious profits in the wartime economy.[113] The lack of co-ordination between the Belgian political authorities and the world of business did nothing to improve Belgium's public image among the Allies, who deplored flaws in control and co-ordination among the Belgian authorities, citing a 'profiteering' attitude in certain private Congolese companies and a lack of involvement in the war effort. As for the private sector and the white population in the Congo, they too had complaints about the authorities and other countries: an already top-heavy tax system; the lack of consideration for their intense productive efforts that wore out both infrastructure and manpower; the lack of deliveries of finished products from the Allies that led to all sorts of shortages; and the

[110] AA, Pétillon Papers, n° 19, GG's report to the government, n° 17, of 8 December 1941 and n° 32 of 30 March 1942; J. Vanderlinden, *Pierre Ryckmans, op. cit.*, pp. 421–600.
[111] AGR, MCM, 29 April 1942.
[112] AGR, MCM, 22 May 1944, p. 144; 25 May 1944, p. 152.
[113] AMAE, AF-I-1 (1939–1942), "L'intérêt politique du Congo (...)", by J. Jennen, economic advisor to the ministry of the colonies, 14 November 1942, p. 8.

The Congo and Belgium's External Position

overzealous control of the civil service. Edgar Sengier, the head of the Union minière, living in New York, fiercely denied that his firm "made enormous profits". How could it, in the face of such heavy taxes and amortisements?[114]

The full extent of the complexity and importance of Belgian-Congolese relations between 1940 and 1944 appears in two crucial cases. The first is the financing of the Belgian authorities. In order to survive and manage expenses, the Belgian government in London asked for advances from the Banque du Congo belge.[115] The sale of raw materials was an important source of foreign currency for the colony. Since it was very difficult to purchase manufactured goods abroad, the Congo accumulated enormous financial reserves. Part of these available funds were used to finance the Belgian government in London. In other words, the resistant homeland survived thanks to loans from the colony. Belgium therefore accumulated a significant war debt in the Congo. After the war, the colony's 'unfailing solidarity' towards its endangered motherland would be celebrated, not to mention receiving the motherland's eternal gratitude. Once again, this official rhetoric erased a far more complex reality. In fact, the Banque du Congo belge had reluctantly offered its full collaboration for the financing of the Belgian government in London. In May 1942, the minister of finance, Camille Gutt, fulminated in the middle of a cabinet meeting:

Since the beginning, the colony has lent us the sums necessary to cover our management. But, every time, these sums have been more difficult to obtain, and a short while ago, we were told that after this semester, the Congo could no longer supply us. I therefore asked – because I knew that the Congo (…) was overflowing with riches – M. De Vleeschauwer to provide me with a statement. (…) He promised to send it to me, but I have not received it. I had to insist, and finally he explained the reason for his hesitation : (…) the *Banque du Congo belge* did not like the *Banque nationale* knowing its business. (…) This year, the colony exports (…) will total 90 or 100 million dollars (…). It would be astonishing if it could not find £8½ [million] out of this sum for Belgium. (…) I am asking the colony for a constant and trusting collaboration [and that] it provides me with a complete, true, sincere statement every month".[116]

Gutt was keen to discuss Belgium taking over the colony's military expenses, but "the Congo would have to give its agreement beforehand with a view to a more effective collaboration with Belgium".[117] This long quotation reveals various rivalries, exacerbated by the difficult circumstances of the war: the frictions between the Belgians in the Congo and the Belgians in Great Britain; between the various key figures who constituted this circle in London; and between the authorities and the private sector.

---

[114] Quoted in J. Gotovitch, ed., *Documents diplomatiques belges 1941–1960. Vol. 1. Le gouvernement de Londres 1941–1944* (Brussels, 1998), p. 127; R. Brion & J.-L. Moreau, *De la mine*, op. cit., pp. 218–20.

[115] H. Van der Wee & M. Verbreyt, *De Nationale Bank van België 1939–1971. Boekdeel 1. Oorlog en monetaire politiek* (Brussels, 2005), pp. 384–5.

[116] AGR, MCM, 7 May 1942, p. 8, 9, 14, 16–17.

[117] AGR, MCM, 30 June 1942.

The second critical issue, this time including foreign protagonists, was uranium, of which the Congo was the main producer. Thanks to its control over the Congolese uranium deposits, Belgium had a valuable lever in its relations with powerful countries, especially during the Second World War when the atom bomb was being developed. When the American officials leading the famous Manhattan Project went in search of uranium, they came into contact with Edgar Sengier, a senior director of the Union minière du Haut-Katanga, who was in New York. Sengier told them that large quantities of uranium were already being stocked in the United States. These stocks would serve to make the bombs dropped on Hiroshima and Nagasaki. Belgium, the United States and Great Britain engaged in long and complex negotiations regarding this eminently strategic raw material.[118]

The first agreements were made directly between the Union minière and the American authorities. The Belgian authorities were only informed of the deal later, when Sengier encountered difficulties in his negotiations with the Americans. Furthermore, he hesitated to conclude commitments of such importance *alone*. Hence the difficulty surrounding the talks conducted between the British, Belgian and American authorities in 1944. "Traditionally treated as an unequal partner, if partner at all, Belgium now played for full equality".[119]

Faithful to their traditional line, the Belgians were opposed to the idea that foreign powers, even Allies, should control the uranium reserves. During these negotiations, the minister of colonies was particularly intransigent, but not all the Belgian ministers were in complete agreement. Throughout these talks, the private sector continued to play a special role within the framework of a sort of parallel diplomatic service. Hence, the familiar *leitmotifs* echoed in the uranium issue. Finally, the secret tripartite agreement was concluded in September 1944. Belgium agreed to sell Congolese uranium at a fixed price only to the two other signatory countries. It also accepted an infringement of its sovereignty by agreeing not to develop any civil nuclear activity without the consent of the United States. In return, the United States would provide technical and scientific aid for the development of this new sector, whose importance looked to be enormous. It was due to this secured source of supply in uranium that the United States was able to construct its nuclear arsenal.

This was an exceptionial situation: For once, Belgium and the Belgian Congo had front row seats during the global confrontation between the major powers, in this case, the Cold War. When Belgian political life returned to normal in 1945, the agreement, the content of which was not revealed for military security reasons, was the subject of internal controversies. Hadn't the Belgian government 'sold off' the Congo's riches? What was the exact nature

---

[118] P. Buch & J. Vanderlinden, *L'uranium, la Belgique et les Puissances* (Brussels, 1995); J. E. Helmreich, *Gathering Rare Ores: The Diplomacy of Uranium Acquisition, 1943–1954* (Princeton, 1986), as well as other articles by this author on the subject; R. Brion & J.-L. Moreau, *De la mine, op. cit.*, pp. 226–52.

[119] J. E. Helmreich, *United States Relations with Belgium and the Congo, 1940–1960* (Newark, 1998), p. 52.

of its commitment in relation to the Americans and the British? The Belgian Communists, in particular, criticised the attitude of the national authorities, who, in their opinion, behaved like the 'lackeys of U.S. imperialism'. Much more important than this quite predictable criticism were the frustrations of the Belgian authorities themselves. The rewards promised by the United States were late in coming. The United States continued to remain aloof and treat the Belgians with distrust. The Belgians were also unhappy with the price of the deliveries, which raised new discussions between the partners. Finally, a new agreement was concluded in 1951. A uranium export tax, paid by the buyers, was established. This special income was to be used by Belgium to finance its own future civil nuclear industry. Ex-Governor-General Ryckmans, one of the main Belgian protagonists in this affair, endeavoured, in vain, to obtain a financial contribution from the Americans for the development of the Congo. By the end of the 1950s, the Shinkolobwe mines, from which the precious ore was extracted, were practically exhausted. Other sources of uranium replaced Belgian-Congolese uranium. Over some fifteen years, Congo's uranium reserves had played a brief but critical role on the global scene. "As for the Congo", confirmed historians Buch and Vanderlinden, "it was probably the only one to lose out" because the special income resulting from this particular underground resource passed it by.[120] On the other hand, the tax of 1951 allowed Belgium to lay the foundations of a civil nuclear industry. It remains, however, uncertain whether Belgium had benefitted from a major advantage compared with the other European nations who, despite not possessing this natual resource, did not in any way lag behind in the development of nuclear activities.

Various Suspicions after the Second World War

Imperceptibly, the uranium affair led Belgium into the next period, the span between the end of the Second World War and the Congo's independence. Indeed, the consequences of this major conflict, and in particular the emergence of the United States as a superpower, were to shape the course of events that confronted the Belgian colonisers between 1945 and 1960. On an international level, the final act of Belgian colonisation began with new concerns. Once again, the Belgian Congo seemed to be threatened, but the nature of the danger had changed. It was no longer the ambitions of Germany, Great Britain or France that were a worry. The Belgians endeavoured to keep the Congo outside of the various political and economic initiatives that aimed to construct a unified Europe.[121] In the negotiations leading up to the Treaty of Rome in 1957,

---

[120] P. Buch & J. Vanderlinden, *L'uranium, op. cit.*, p. 150.

[121] E. Deschamps, "La Belgique et l'association des pays et territoires d'outre-mer (PTOM) au Marché commun (1955-1957)", in M. Dumoulin, e.a., eds., *La Belgique, les petits États et la construction européenne* (Brussels-Bern, 2003), pp. 119-45; Idem, "L'Eurafrique à l'épreuve des faits: la Belgique, la France et les projets de barrages hydroélectriques en Afrique (1954-1958)", in M.-Th. Bitsch & G. Bossuat, eds., *L'Europe unie et l'Afrique. De l'idée d'Eurafrique à la Convention de Lomé I* (Brussels, 2005), pp. 165-84; Idem, "Le projet de communauté politique européenne et la question coloniale. Étude du cas belge (1952-1954)", *Annales*

the French had successfully insisted that the colonies be associated with the European Economic Community.[122] The Belgians had supported these French demands owing to a "general identification with French interests, rather than as a specific commitment to the inclusion of the colonies in the EEC schemes", as historian Louis Sicking explained.[123] Indeed, the Congo was subjected to an 'open door' regime. Above all, the possible loss of political control of its colony frightened the Belgians.[124] But some Belgians also feared that the opening up of new economic opportunities in the neighbouring European countries might attract Belgian investments away from the Congo.[125] All these elements explain why, in 1959, the Belgian diplomatic service still considered it necessary to "be wary of too great a Europeanisation (...). Belgium's efforts in the Congo must be envisaged from a national angle, although this angle must be sufficiently open to allow the collaboration of Europe. What must be avoided (...) is the absorption of the Belgian effort into a Eurafrica complex which, for the moment, is destined to be dominated by extreme points of view".[126]

The Belgian authorities also remained highly vigilant in relation to the 'Communist peril'. Attention was focused on the activities of Moscow and its satellites in black Africa. However, the real influence of Communism remained extremely weak in the Congo. Neither the Belgian Communist Party, nor the Eastern Bloc nations managed to make significant inroads. The rivalry with the communist bloc, and more particularly, the resulting threat of military conflict, made the Congo all the more precious in the eyes of the Belgian authorities. As noted in a document of the Ministerial Defence Committee in 1953: "If NATO forces were unable to stand up to a Russian attack, our only asset from a national point of view would be the colony".[127] At the beginning of the 1950s, plans were made for the evacuation of the government and its administrative services to the Congo, which would thus become a veritable national stronghold in case of Soviet occupation.[128] Hence, the Belgian Congo played a role in the defence strategy of the West within the framework of the Cold War. This explains the Belgian army's increased interest in establishing a firmer foothold in the Congo, in particular through the construction of the Kamina base (in Katanga) and the Kitona base (in Bas-Congo) as of 1948 and 1949. Belgian

---

d'Études européennes de l'UCL (1998-1999), pp. 55-95; Idem, "L'Afrique belge et le projet de Communauté politique européenne (1952-1954)", in E. Remacle & P. Winand, eds., *America, Europe, Africa 1945-1973* (Brussels-Bern, 2009), pp. 307-23.

[122] L. Sicking, "A Colonial Echo: France and the Colonial Dimension of the European Economic Community", *French Colonial History*, 5 (2004), p. 207-28.

[123] Ibid., p. 213.

[124] AGR, MCM, 15 March 1957, p. 8.

[125] E. Deschamps, "L'Afrique belge (...)", art. cit., pp. 318-9.

[126] AMAE, AF-I-1 (1959), "Réunion de contact Belext – Minicoru – Inforcongo tenue le 23 avril 1959", p. 4.

[127] B. Cleys, *Andries Dequae. De zelfgenoegzaamheid van een koloniaal bestuur (1950-1954)* (Louvain, 2002) unpublished master's thesis in history, KUL, ch. 1 (available on www.ethesis.net).

[128] J. Temmerman, "Le Congo, réduit national belge", in *Congo 1955-1960, op. cit.*, pp. 413-22.

metropolitan troops were stationed there beginning in 1953. However, these measures caused some frictions between the Belgian Ministry of Defence, on the one hand, and the colonial administration and the Force publique, on the other. At the end of the 1950s, the Belgian authorities felt the need for coordination between the metropolitan and colonial defence forces.[129]

Ultimately, for Brussels, the main threat that hung over the Belgian Congo was not Western Europe or the Eastern Bloc. As strange as it may seem, it came from the other side of the Atlantic. The Belgian leaders distrusted the United States of America. In addition to the United States' traditionally anticolonialist attitude, there were factors particular to that period. To appeal to young independent nations and/or to outdo the Soviet Union, the American diplomatic service favoured decolonisation. Furthermore, American economic interests coveted the rich colonial domains. They were suspected of wanting to break down the imperial barriers in order to be able to invest massively or divert trade currents to their own advantage.

During the war, the Belgian authorities picked up on a number of dangerous signals. In American official circles, some spoke of revising the political status of Africa. In particular, Belgian sovereignty in the Congo was called into question. In 1943, Foreign Minister Spaak even feared that the Congo might be placed under international trusteeship once the war was over.[130] Ultimately, these fears turned out to be unfounded, but a certain uneasiness remained. Throughout the 1940s and 1950s, the Belgian colonisation of the Congo aroused interest in the United States. There were certainly laudatory assessments – which the Belgians noted with open satisfaction. But the praise was accompanied by more critical notes. Protestant missionaries complained about discrimination against them. Furthermore, the negative image created during the era of Leopold II had not completely disappeared. Those who willingly admitted that things had changed since that period of darkness and that the Congolese natives were well treated on a material level nevertheless stressed that the Belgian authorities had completely neglected the cultural and political development of the indigenous populations. "In short, they reproach us – the expression comes from a coloured American student – for 'reducing the natives to their digestive system'. There is no doubt: we take care of the material well-being of the blacks. (…) But our efforts in the spiritual and especially intellectual domain are less sincere. (…) 'They [the Belgians] seek to force-feed their citizens with material benefits in order to dull their desire for independence'", was the diagnosis reported by the Belgian ambassador in Washington.[131]

For the Belgian authorities, this attitude showed that the United States understood nothing of colonial reality. In Belgium's opinion, granting political rights to the local population and the creation of a black intellectual elite cut

---

[129] AGR, MCM, 25 January 1957, pp. 1–2.
[130] R. Brion & J.-L. Moreau, *De la mine, op. cit.*, p. 222.
[131] AMAE, AF-I-17 (1948–1953), "Les tendances anticolonialistes aux États-Unis", 8 October 1953, pp. 9–10.

off from the masses would be extremely dangerous. But the Belgians wanted to show that they were perfectly capable of leading the Congo out of underdevelopment. The launch of an ambitious 'Ten-year plan for the economic and social development of the Belgian Congo' (1949-59) was situated within this context.[132] The economic modernisation of the colony was therefore a means of dismissing a political independence considered too premature and dangerous, both for the Congo itself and for Belgium.

Between 1945 and 1960, a certain distance continued to overshadow the relations between Belgium and the United States. Faithful to their tradition, the Belgians wanted to exclude any foreign influence in the Congo, including American businessmen, diplomats and politicians. The Americans, on their part, hesitated on which attitude to adopt in relation to the Belgian colony. On the one hand, they did not want to clash with Belgium, their Western ally.[133] On the other hand, certain American leaders observed with some concern the Belgians' slow progress in leading the Congo down the path towards political independence. Finally, the distance between Washington and Léopoldville remained significant. In general, the United States adopted a low-profile stance in the Congo and did not set itself up as an adversary to Belgian colonisation in Africa.[134]

Colonial Belgium against the UN
In the second half of the 1940s, the Belgians were concerned with another threat from over the Atlantic: the United Nations.[135] Set up by the Charter of San Francisco in 1945, this new world organisation replaced the League of Nations. From the beginning, the atmosphere was very hostile towards colonial powers. The young independent nations and the Eastern Bloc countries attacked colonialism. The United States neither followed suit nor thwarted them, either through conviction, calculation or even weakness – such was the view of the Belgian political leaders. Great Britain, France and Belgium were therefore constantly on the defensive. They had to account for their management of the 'trust territories', the former mandates of the League of Nations. And far more serious than that: The new institution also wanted to intervene in the *colonies themselves*, to the great displeasure of the Belgians. Article 73 of the Charter stipulates that the colonial powers "recognize the principle that the

---

[132] G. Vanthemsche, *Genèse et portée du 'Plan décennal' du Congo belge (1949-1959)* (Brussels, 1994).

[133] CEGES, J. Delvaux de Fenffe Papers, n° AA/669/22b, Belgian embassy in the United States, to J. Delvaux de Fenffe, director general of the Policy of the Ministry of Foreign Affairs, 28 July 1954.

[134] J. E. Helmreich, "US Foreign Policy and the Belgian Congo in the 1950s", *The Historian*, 58 (1998), pp. 315-28; Idem, *United States Relations, op. cit.*; G. Th. Mollin, *Die USA und der Kolonialismus. Amerika als Partner und Nachfolger der belgischen Macht in Afrika 1939-1965* (Berlin, 1996); J. Kent, "United States Reactions to Empire, Colonialism, and Cold War in Black Africa, 1949-57", *Journal of Imperial and Commonwealth History*, 33, 2 (May 2005), pp. 195-220.

[135] J. Vanderlinden, ed., *Documents diplomatiques belges 1941-1960. Tome VIII – Territoires d'Outre-mer* (Brussels, 2004), pp. 289-513.

interests of the inhabitants of these territories are paramount" to their colonies. Among other things, they had to provide information to the United Nations concerning their management of these territories. In 1946, the General Assembly created a temporary ad hoc committee responsible for examining this information. Its existence was extended several times and in 1952 it adopted the title of Information Committee. The Belgian saw this committee as extremely dangerous. They feared that the adversaries of colonisation would take advantage of it to extract political information in order to criticise the internal management of the colonies and even recommend changes. In short, the door was wide open to the internationalisation so feared by the colonies. All manner of interference would undermine and finally destroy the colonial empires. At the end of the 1940s and throughout the 1950s, the UN threat to Belgium's sovereignty of the Congo aroused lively reactions in certain Belgian official circles. Some even envisaged leaving the UN. Pierre Wigny, president of the Christian-Democrat party's colonial commission, put it in these terms: "If they will not listen to us, then we must envisage our withdrawal [from the UN]. But this time, we shall leave the UN, not because we refuse its policy, but because others are sidestepping it".[136] Belgium felt trapped by "a system of near guardianship which is a real danger for our sovereignty over the Congo".[137]

Such was the pessimistic diagnosis of the Belgian authorities in the second half of the 1940s. How should they react? First of all, Belgian colonisation had to be 'faultless', a true model. As we have seen, this consideration influenced internal colonial policy. The economic development and social progress of the Belgian Congo were part of this defensive strategy. Belgium also recommended bringing the colonial powers closer together. Belgium was not in the same situation as the Netherlands, which, after the loss of Indonesia in 1949, only retained its South American and Caribian possessions and Western New Guinea (until 1962). Priority access did not pass via Lisbon either, because Portugal only held a marginal place on the international political scene. In order to face anti-colonialist attacks, Belgium therefore endeavoured to form a joint front with London and Paris. These three colonial powers did indeed draw closer together. Bilateral and tripartite conferences took place; inter-colonial co-operation agreements were concluded.[138] There was, however, never really a complete understanding between them. The Belgians often defended and even adopted a tougher stance than the British or the French. Their attitude towards the Information Committee is one example. Brussels was radically opposed to it, while London and Paris were more moderate. Initially, the Belgians – unwillingly – agreed to participate in its work, but finally, in 1953, they decided, after many hesitations and internal differences, to shut the door on the committee.

[136] AGR, Louwers Papers, n° 267, "Attitude à prendre par la Belgique à l'ONU au sujet du Congo belge", by P. Wigny, 13 November 1952.
[137] AA, AE-2, n° 1801ter (3283), "Attitude de la Belgique à l'ONU en matière coloniale", p. 5.
[138] J. Kent, *The Internationalisation of Colonialism: Britain, France, and Black Africa 1939-1956* (Oxford, 1992).

Brussels also launched an ideological counter-attack. At the beginning of the 1950s, two senior Belgian United Nations representatives, diplomat Fernand Vanlangenhove and ex-Governor-General Ryckmans, developed an argument known as the 'Belgian position' (*thèse belge*). Its reasoning was as follows: The colonial territories were not alone in governing indigenous populations. Countries such as Brazil or India were also confronted with the 'native' problem. More often than not, the fate of these populations was less enviable than those of the Congolese natives. So why was the focus only on the colonial powers? *All* the countries concerned were supposed to be subject to inquiries and criticism. Was it right that some UN members were put under the watchful eye of the international community while others escaped it? According to Belgium, either the practices of the Information Committee had to be generalised, or they had to come to an end. The United Nations' Charter could not be applied selectively. The 'Belgian position' met with polite interest from Great Britain and especially France, but in the end, Belgium was alone in defending it. The British diplomatic service made it known that it would not publicly support Belgium's reasoning; however, it still encouraged Brussels to publicise this analysis. When the Belgian position got a positive or understanding reaction from such or such a foreign diplomat, the Belgian leaders rejoiced, believing that their argument was beginning to bear fruit. It was readily affirmed in the beginning that the unwavering attitude of Belgium concerning its colonial rights earned it the respect of other countries. But in the end, the exact opposite occurred. During the 1950s, Belgium was seen as the diehard defender of old-style colonialism and suffered increasing diplomatic isolation.

A number of Belgians believed that the official attitude of their country was leading to a dead end and that it was time to change direction. Raymond Scheyven, the future minister of the Belgian Congo, was very familiar with the diplomatic circles through his senior position as Belgian representative in various UN authorities. In 1957, he considered that "the presentation of the Belgian position to the UN has brought us a great deal of hostility".[139] But to no avail. On the eve of Congolese independence, the Belgian authorities were still focusing on what, in their opinion, was the main threat hanging over Belgian colonisation, that is, other foreign countries. Blinded by their own preconceptions, they reacted with surprise when the final blow was struck by an actor they believed had only a minor role: the Congolese population itself. In 1960, Congolese independence threw Belgium and its former colony onto the centre of the international stage.

Conclusion

If we measure the importance of a country by the number of neighbours it has, the Congo must surely be one of the most important nations on the planet. Apart from China, Russia, Brazil (veritable continent-like countries) and Sudan, no

---

[139] AA, AE-2, n° 1801ter (3283), R. Scheyven to F. Vanlangenhove, 6 March 1957, p. 4.

other political entity in the world shares so many borders with other nations: no less than nine. Of course, the importance of a nation is not measured from this perspective. But this simple fact reminds us of one of the Congo's essential particularities: Owing to its configuration, it forms a veritable hub in the continent where it is situated (much like Belgium itself in Europe). The Congo is one of the main pieces in the African puzzle. Its great natural and mining riches add a crucial dimension to its purely spatial and demographic significance.

The contrast between the vast Congo and the modest European country that colonised it was one of the threads running through the history of Belgian colonialism. The Congo drove the national pride of the motherland. Belgium found itself at the head of an empire that stood out on the globe. It is true that without the intra-European rivalries in the Congo River basin, the Belgians would never have established themselves in central Africa. The Congo owes its present land mass to the sovereign of a small European country, Leopold II, a megalomaniac dreamer and a merciless businessman who *personally* succeeded in worming his way into the workings of the colonial powers. If Belgium finally managed to join the highly restricted colonisers' club, it is because of fortuitous and fleeting circumstances, and not because of a well-planned project that was pursued *as a nation*. Did Belgium therefore become a colonialist "in a fit of absence of mind"? Let us not push this paradox too far. As soon as the Leopoldian enterprise had taken root, certain political and economic forces in Belgium did indeed put a lot of effort into the colonial project. They wanted to give it a real national foundation that exceeded the person of the king himself.

Despite any internal doubts, official Belgium had well and truly *wanted* to accept the Leopoldian legacy, a legacy that endowed it with an international status it did not enjoy before. Thanks to its colonial possessions, Belgium played a role in international politics; it frequented the world's political elite, so to speak. Owing to its domination over the Congo, it had been thrust into the front row during some great moments of contemporary history, such as the Second World War and the Cold War. But this participation was not completely positive. Before 1908, the adventurist policy of Leopold II in the Congo put Belgian neutrality in danger. After the annexation of the Congo, the vagaries of the colonial policy influenced Belgium's relations with other countries; the precise inventory of these influences has yet to be drawn up. And there is another question that deserves to be re-examined in the light of the Congo: Did the status of colonial power diminish the advantages from which Belgium benefitted (and continues to benefit from) as a 'small power' without geopolitical interests of its own and without any real strategic weight?[140] Did the Congo dent the reputation and means of action Belgium enjoyed as an honest broker?

One thing is certain: Belgium's hold over the Congo was not always looked upon kindly. Belgium was indeed confronted with continuous doubts concerning its political sovereignty in Africa. Other countries often called into

---

[140] J.E. Helmreich, *Belgium and Europe: A Study in Small Power Diplomacy* (The Hague-Paris, 1976).

question Belgium's ability as a coloniser, both from a moral and material point of view. Apart from the continuing questions concerning the horrors of the rubber business, Belgium's true ability to colonise this vast territory was a recurring issue. On several occasions, in particular before the two World Wars, the Congo was the subject of negotiations between the major powers that excluded the Belgians, thus reinforcing the idea that their colony was coveted and threatened. Belgium therefore wanted to prove, beyond doubt, the solidity and quality of its colonial venture. It endeavoured to distance foreign influences, insofar as it was possible. Persuaded of the exceptional nature of its colonial action, it ultimately isolated itself from the global forum. When it came to the Congo, the Belgians did not always do justice to their reputation as ardent partisans of internationalisation. Belgium willingly said yes to a united Europe, to NATO and to the United Nations – except when its own colonial interests were at stake. As 'diehard colonialists', the Belgians were very poorly thought of by numerous international players after 1945. By the time it was faced with the serious problems of the Congo's decolonisation in 1960, Belgium found itself completely alone.

4

The Congo and the Belgian Economy

The colonisation of the Congo not only disrupted the local economy, it also affected that of the metropole. But how and to what extent? These questions have been asked ever since colonialism came into being. In the nineteenth century, the answers were generally optimistic and simplistic. According to Leopoldian propaganda, the Congo would bring incredible wealth to Belgium: "This new market, which we owe entirely to the wisdom and foresight of the King, may, for many years to come, prove a fertile ground for entrepreneurship for our country; a sure source of wealth from which all ranks of the nation, be they merchants, employees or capitalists, will be able to draw almost endlessly".[1] For decades, the official discourse would continue to emphasise the benefits the colony brought to the economy of the metropole. Quite often, this was as far as the representation and perception of the complex colonial relationship went. But this was by no means a typically Belgian attitude; it was universal.

A less schematic approach involved comparing the costs and benefits of colonial policy. Again, this is not typical of Belgium. During the colonial period, attempts were made to draw up balance sheets for imperialism in other countries as well.[2] One question has captivated many contemporary historians, especially in Great Britain: "Was [the Empire] worth it?"[3] At the time of the Congo's annexation, many Belgians asked how much the colony would cost them. Opponents argued that taking over the Congo would be detrimental to the taxpayer. Numerous authors subsequently tried to demonstrate that the balance of the colonisation of the Congo was positive.[4] Eventually, in 1957, historian Jean Stengers published a book titled *Combien le Congo a-t-il coûté*

---

[1] M. De Ramaix, *La question sociale en Belgique et le Congo* (Brussels, 1891), p. VII.
[2] G. Clark, *The Balance Sheets of Imperialism* (New York, 1936).
[3] A. R. Dilley, "The Economics of Empire", in S. Stockwell, ed., *The British Empire: Themes and Perspectives, op. cit.*, pp. 101-29 (quotation on p. 121); B. Etemad, *De l'utilité des empires. Colonisation et prospérité de l'Europe (XVIe – XXe siècles)* (Paris, 2005), pp. 12-3.
[4] F. Baudhuin, *La Belgique après le centenaire* (Leuven, 1931), pp. 213-72.

*à la Belgique?*⁵ In this work, he asserted that previous attempts to calculate the cost of the Congo's colonisation had been too limited in scope or erroneous. He also pointed out that different aspects of the calculation, such as public versus private finances, were commonly confused. His analysis showed that Belgium's *public* spending on the colony had, in fact, been very limited. The Congo had cost the Belgian taxpayer hardly anything at all.

On the other hand, Stengers leaves his readers in the dark about that other aspect of the overall balance sheet: private finances. Was the Congo really a blessing for Belgian capitalism and for the country as a whole? There can be no doubt that the Congo provided ample business opportunities. Some Belgian investors and entrepreneurs certainly amassed fortunes there. But the question is particularly tricky. How can one determine, for example, the sums wasted in ill-fated Congolese adventures? Or the losses incurred by Belgian investors in colonial bonds? And how can one properly assess the (direct and indirect) consequences for companies not involved exclusively in trade with the Congo? How might the Belgian economy have developed had it not focused so intensely on its colony? Would Belgium perhaps have become even wealthier without this colonial input? After all, an economy that is geared unilaterally to colonial trade may be more vulnerable, or at least less dynamic, than a genuinely open economy. We shall limit ourselves to a general survey of the colonial impact on Belgium's economy, without having the ambition to answer all these questions.

It is rather remarkable that no recent scientific publications explore the mark that the Congo left on the Belgian economy.⁶ In this chapter, we will consider the legacy of the Congo Free State and then examine the economic relationship between Belgium and the Congo, starting with one of the most striking aspects: trade. Subsequently we will broaden the analysis to financial flows. In order to gain insight into these 'external' aspects, we need to consider the fundamental choices that shaped the economic ties between the two entities. Finally, we will discuss the impact of the Congo on Belgium's internal economic structures.

Brief Outline of Belgium's Economic History

Economic development in the area that would become Belgium was quite remarkable even before the country's creation in 1830.⁷ Belgium was, in fact, the first country on the continent to follow Britain's industrial example. Modern technology was introduced in such crucial sectors as textiles, coal mining and metallurgy. New capitalist enterprises blossomed, especially in Wallonia, the French-speaking part of the country. Industrial production soared. By 1890,

---

⁵ J. Stengers, *Combien le Congo a-t-il coûté à la Belgique?* (Brussels, 1957).
⁶ M. Van De Velde, *Économie belge et Congo belge* (Antwerp, 1936).
⁷ R. Leboutte, J. Puissant & D. Scuto, *Un siècle d'histoire industrielle. Belgique, Luxembourg, Pays-Bas. Industrialisation et sociétés 1873–1973* (Paris, 1998).

Belgium was the world's largest producer of cast iron, outstripping Germany and Britain. In Flanders, the city of Ghent was a centre of modern industry, mainly thanks to its many textile factories.

Because the home markets were so limited, international trade was of vital importance for this teeming Belgian industry. The export of manufactured goods and coal to neighbouring countries was crucial from the beginning of industrialisation. Belgium's contribution in total European exports grew from 2.98 per cent in 1830 to 8.36 per cent in 1890.[8] Imports were also very important; large quantities of cheap food came from abroad, for example from Argentina. This was an essential element in the maintenance of Belgium's comparatively low wage levels. From the middle of the nineteenth century onwards, Belgium's trade policy was very liberal. Particular interest groups sometimes advocated protectionist measures but, except for a few specific cases, the Belgian authorities never adopted a protectionist policy, not even during heavy crisis periods such as the 1880s and 1890s and the 1930s. During the *belle époque*, Belgian capitalists turned to the wider world, investing heavily in metal and coal mining industries (for example, in Russia) or in transport. The port of Antwerp was Belgium's main window on the world and it grew in importance, especially during the second half of the nineteenth century. Around 1840, Antwerp ranked only twelfth to eighteenth in the list of the world's most important ports. By the beginning of the 1880s, it had climbed to fourth position.[9] Paradoxically, however, imports and exports were handled mostly by foreign ships, since the Belgian commercial fleet was quite modest. In short, Belgium was, and still is, a small, open economy. It had achieved spectacular foreign trade and investment performances well before the Congo was added to the economic mix.

Another particular feature that distinguished Belgium from other European countries was the early and preponderant role of banks in industry. A few powerful financial institutions, especially the Société générale de Belgique, not only granted investment credit to the industrial firms, but also became important shareholders. By the end of the nineteenth and the beginning of the twentieth century, these banks had managed to dominate large sections of the Belgian economy.[10] In 1931, for instance, the Société générale controlled twenty-five to thirty per cent of coal mining; thirty per cent of the chemical industries; about half of the iron and steel works; forty per cent of artificial silk production; forty per cent of the glass industry and so forth. Given the role of this sector in Belgian colonial history, it is worthwhile taking a closer look at the non-ferrous industries. Long before the Congo Free State was created, Belgium already played an important role in these particular markets. In 1869, for instance,

---

[8] P. Bairoch, "La Belgique dans le commerce international 1830–1990", in P. Klep & E. Van Cauwenberghe, eds., *Entrepreneurship and the Transformation of the Economy (10th–20th Centuries): Essays in Honour of Herman Van der Wee* (Leuven, 1994), p. 630.
[9] P. Bairoch, "La Belgique", art. cit., pp. 648–9.
[10] G. Vanthemsche, "State, Banks and Industry in Belgium and the Netherlands, 1919–1939", in H. James, H. Lindgren & A. Teichova, eds., *The Role of Banks in the Interwar Economy* (Cambridge, 1991), pp. 105–6.

Belgium's share of world zinc production amounted to thirty-seven per cent. In this sector too, the Générale had gained supremacy, controlling sixty to seventy-five per cent of zinc production in 1931, and 100 per cent of copper production. But the mixed banks did not control all of the Belgian industrial sectors. The textile factories remained largely autonomous.

By the middle of the twentieth century, Belgium's industrial and commercial performance had become somewhat less impressive. Even before the First World War, Belgium's share in total European exports had fallen from 8.36 per cent in 1890 to 6.65 per cent in 1913. At the end of the nineteenth century, new sectors such as the chemical and electrical industries were established, but between the two World Wars, Belgium was no longer at the cutting edge of innovation in these sectors. Most Belgian industries continued to do what they did in the past. After the Second World War, the Belgian economy was lagging behind those of its neighbouring countries.[11] However, in the late 1950s and the 1960s, foreign multi-national corporations considerably boosted Belgian economic performance. Their investments were concentrated in the northern part of the country, which led to a spectacular shift in Belgium's economic centre of gravity. The old Walloon industries were on the wane, while many new enterprises were created in Flanders. This rapid transformation of Belgium's regional economic structure stirred up the strife between the linguistic communities and accelerated the transition from a unitary to a federal state. The mighty holding companies created in 1934 and 1935, when the Belgian authorities abolished mixed banking, still played a decisive role in the Belgian economy. But in the 1950s trade unions and progressive forces, particularly in Wallonia, held those holding companies responsible for Belgium's lack of economic dynamism.[12]

Some questions about what would happen when the colonial empire was introduced into this general picture are inevitable. Did the rather unexpected intrusion of the Congo change the international orientation of the Belgian economy? Was the structure of the Belgian economy affected by the colony? What role did the powerful mixed banks and holding companies play in the colonial economy? And, finally, was Belgium's traditional free trade attitude influenced by the existence of the colony?

The Economic Legacy of the Congo Free State

The Congo and Non-Discrimination in Trade
As we have seen, the Congo Free State bequeathed an important diplomatic heritage to Belgium after 1908. The same was true in the field of economics. Indeed, the diplomatic and economic aspects of colonisation were closely connected. This connection was forged with Leopold's very first initiatives in the Congo Basin. Circumstances were such that his original commercial

---

[11] I. Cassiers, Ph. de Villé & P. Solar, "Economic Growth in Post-war Belgium", in N. Crafts & G. Toniolo, eds., *Economic Growth in Europe Since 1945* (Cambridge, 1996), pp. 173–209.
[12] A. Mommen, *The Belgian Economy in the Twentieth Century* (London, 1994).

ambitions quickly became a political matter. In trying to establish his Congo Free State, Leopold played the free trade card, pledging that no commercial privileges would be granted within his territory. It was a ploy designed chiefly to gain the support of Great Britain, a staunch proponent of free trade. The Act of the Berlin Conference (1885) expressly prohibited any form of protectionism. It guaranteed freedom of navigation on the Congo and banned the levying of import duties within the Conventional Congo Basin. Exports, by contrast, were freely taxable.

The reality in the Congo Free State was, however, quite different. The king's domanial policy was the loophole in the free trade clause. In fact, trade in the Congo was anything but free as the government and a few private concessionary companies more or less monopolised all profitable activities. This state of affairs saved the Congo Free State from bankruptcy, but it was in breach of the spirit of the Berlin Act and consequently prompted criticism both in Belgium and abroad. Even before 1895, when the financial manna began to drop from heaven, Leopold II tried to fill the state coffers in another way. He wanted to lift the ban on import duties imposed by the Berlin Act. At the anti-slavery conference held in Brussels in 1890, the signatory powers accepted this proposal. Henceforth the Congo Free State was entitled to levy import duties of up to ten per cent. The first customs tariff came into force in 1892. Still, any import duty regime had to respect the principle of non-discrimination. In other words, all countries were to be treated equally. Trade favouritism and protectionism remained unacceptable.

The Belgian Congo that superseded the Congo Free State was subject to the agreements made at Berlin and Brussels. In 1919, these rules were amended under the terms of the Saint-Germain-en-Laye Convention, which abolished the import duty ceiling of ten per cent for the entire Congo Basin. Henceforth, the Congo was free to pursue its own customs policy, as long as it adhered to one fundamental rule: It should in no way discriminate against any of the countries that signed the Convention. In practice Belgium would interpret the principle more broadly and treat all countries in a non-discriminatory way.

Belgian and Foreign Capital in the Construction of the Congo Free State

A second economic legacy of the Free State to the Belgian Congo concerned the structure and nationality of the business community in the colony.[13] Belgium embarked on its colonial adventure rather unprepared. The business community in Brussels was not exactly lining up to become involved, as overseas territories played a marginal role in Belgium's economic activities.[14] When Leopold

---

[13] J.-L. Vellut, "Réseaux transnationaux dans l'économie politique du Congo léopoldien, c. 1885–1910", in L. Martaing & B. Reinwald, eds., *Afrikanische Beziehungen, Netzwerke und Räume* (München, 2001), pp. 131–46; R. J. Lemoine, "Finances et colonisation. La concentration des entreprises dans la mise en valeur du Congo belge", *Annales d'Histoire économique et sociale*, 6, 29 (30 September 1934), pp. 433–49.

[14] G. Kurgan-van Hentenryk, "Les milieux d'affaires belges et l'outre-mer vers 1885", in *Le centenaire de l'ÉIC. Recueil d'études* (Brussels, 1988), pp. 461–5.

II founded his colonial enterprise, Belgian investors had shown no interest whatsoever. Foreign businesses, such as the Dutch company Nieuwe Afrikaanse Handels Vennootschap, dominated commercial activities in the Congo estuary. Britain was also actively engaged in trade throughout this region. Just a few months after the establishment of the Congo Free State, a British consortium of financial heavyweights put forward a plan for the construction of a railway line.[15] It was then that Leopold, wanting to prevent a strong foreign hold on his Congo, asked his collaborator, the officer Albert Thys, to gauge the interest of Belgian business circles. Stanley, who had helped Leopold to build the Congo Free State, remarked bitterly that "every day the king is closing the Congo to the English and seems resolved to make it more and more Belgian".[16] Thys had to expend some effort to find financiers for the establishment, in 1886, of the first Belgian private enterprise to do business in the Congo, the Compagnie du Congo pour le Commerce et l'Industrie (CCCI).[17] After the establishment of the CCCI, a core of 'Congolese' companies emerged in Belgium. But around 1892, the relationship between Leopold and those in Thys's circle began to sour as Thys grew increasingly unhappy with the king's economic policy. The companies that had been established under Leopold's direct or indirect initiative found themselves paralysed by the monarch's obstinate approach. They began to press for economic freedom and a takeover of the Congo by Belgium. Despite attempts at mediation and reconciliation, the relationship between the Thys group and the court remained strained.

However, Leopold II went full steam ahead. From the start of his African adventure, the king had maintained contacts with both Belgian and foreign financiers. He was looking for loans and therefore conceived fake financial constructions in which these financiers would serve as puppets while Leopold pulled all the strings. One of the persons involved in such dealings was Alexandre de Browne de Tiège, a prominent member of Antwerp's financial circles. Banker Léon Lambert was another influential figure whose support was instrumental to the success of Leopold's initiatives in the Congo. In 1892, when the king had outlined his domanial policy, and after it had become apparent that wild rubber was a profitable line of trade, two companies were established: the Société anversoise du Commerce du Congo, with Browne de Tiège as its principal stakeholder, and the Anglo-Belgian India Rubber Company (ABIR), with its input of foreign capital. The Congo Free State (and hence Leopold) also held substantial stakes in both companies. The concessions they obtained would generate enormous profits from 1896 onwards. In the wake of this success, numerous other Belgian enterprises were established for the purpose of developing the trade in Congolese produce. Between 1886 and 1896, just thirteen 'Congolese' companies had been founded in Belgium. Five more

---

[15] R. Anstey, *Britain and the Congo in the Nineteenth Century* (Oxford, 1962), pp. 21–36, 186–209.
[16] Cited in R. Anstey, *Britain and the Congo, op. cit.*, p. 207.
[17] *La colonisation belge au Congo et l'initiative privée* (Brussels, 1912), p. 14.

firms were established in 1897, sixteen in the year after that, and no fewer than twenty-eight in 1899.[18] Many of these companies were shady undertakings of a purely speculative nature.

Of an altogether different calibre were the companies established in the early years of the twentieth century. These were solid undertakings the activities of which went beyond trade in the Congo's natural resources such as rubber and ivory, and which tried to exploit the colony's riches in a more sustainable way. Moreover, Leopold II strove for 'an equilibrium in influences', including within the world of finance. According to a note written by Octave Louwers, an astute observer of colonial matters, the Thys group was regarded as "the group that put up the strongest resistance against the King's policy. To Leopold II, this was sufficient reason not to enhance the influence of this group and not to involve it more closely in his projects".[19] The king called instead on other Belgian financial groups, who were no longer ignoring the lure of the Congo, albeit after receiving firm financial guarantees. In 1902, Belgian businessman Edouard Empain set up the Compagnie des Chemins de Fer du Congo supérieur aux Grands Lacs africains (CFL). The CFL immediately obtained substantial land concessions as well as guaranteed minimum interest from the Congo Free State. Irrespective of the state of the economy, its shareholders could look forward to an annual dividend of four per cent. In time, the Empain group would gain a firmer foothold in the Congo. In 1900, the Compagnie du Katanga (of the Thys group) and the Congo Free State set up the Comité spécial du Katanga (CSK), in which they held respectively one-third and two-thirds of the shares. CSK would exploit and manage the immense mineral wealth of the region. In 1906, the king succeeded in convincing the country's leading bank, the Société générale de Belgique (SGB), to become involved in the Congo, despite their previous reticence towards Leopold's initiatives.[20] Together with CSK, the SGB established the Union minière du Haut-Katanga (UMHK), a company that would come to play an extraordinary role in the exploitation of the colony. The SGB also participated in the Compagnie du Chemin de Fer du Bas-Congo au Katanga (BCK) and in the Société internationale forestière et minière du Congo (Forminière). Foreign capital was likewise attracted. The British company Tanganyika Concessions Ltd, led by Robert Williams, co-founded UMHK, while the American group Ryan-Guggenheim took a stake in Forminière. The Banque de l'Union parisienne, in which the SGB was a shareholder, participated in BCK. By the eve of Congo's annexation to Belgium, the main players in the Belgian economy were all firmly committed in the colony. This commitment would have far-reaching consequences for the economic structures of both the Congo and Belgium.

---

[18] A. Poskin, *Bilans congolais. Étude sur la valeur commerciale du Congo par rapport à la Belgique* (Brussels, 1900), pp. 66–75.
[19] AGR, Louwers Papers, n° 363, "Note", s.d., written by Louwers.
[20] G. Kurgan-van Hentenryk, "La Société générale 1850–1934", in *La Générale de Banque 1822–1997* (Brussels, 1997), pp. 167–9.

On the basis of this analysis of the initial phase in the colonial economy of the Congo, we may draw a number of conclusions.[21] First, foreign and transnational 'Belgian' capital played an important role in the development of the colony, though its impact would later be underestimated in nationalistically biased analyses. Second, the private Belgian colonial players appeared on the scene only gradually and rather belatedly. They only became truly involved on the eve of the disappearance of the Congo Free State. Third, the development of the Congo led to other initiatives, including many undertaken elsewhere in the world. Groups that became active in the Congo also developed an interest in other regions of Africa and indeed in other continents as well. For example, investors such as ABIR, who made good money trading Congolese rubber, would later invest in Malaysian rubber plantations.

Commercial and Financial Contacts Between Belgium and the Congo

The Congo's Significance to Belgian Foreign Trade

Our analysis of the economic relationship between Belgium and the Congo will start with a look at the most obvious data, namely those concerning trade flows. We begin with the position Congo occupied in Belgium's foreign trade (see also Table 2 in the Appendix).[22]

Certain aspects immediately catch the eye. For one thing, trade between Belgium and the Congo is characterised by alternating periods of strong growth and stagnation, or even decline. Taking 1913 as our base year (index 100; amounts in gold francs for 1914), it emerges that Belgian imports from the colony increased sharply right up to the early twentieth century. Between 1906 and the start of the Great War, this growth dwindled. The war itself and the subsequent reconstruction coincided with a further decline in imports from the Congo. Expressed in constant currency, imports in 1923 were less than half what they had been in 1913. Then there was a sharp recovery. In the 1927-9 period, the value of imports quadrupled. Over the next decade, with its deep economic crisis, trade once again slumped. It would be the end of the 1930s before it had recovered to its 1929 level. The Second World War was followed by another era of growth. In 1956, imports were fourteen times greater than they had been in 1913 and four times greater than in 1939. Colonial imports from the Congo contributed significantly to the reconstruction of Belgium after the Second World War. The Belgian economy was able to readily import

---

[21] See J.-L. Vellut, "Réseaux ...", art. cit., passim.

[22] For the sake of accuracy, we immediately draw attention to a problem that we shall discuss further in due course, namely the questionability of trade statistics by geographical distribution. The references to countries of origin and destination are not always entirely accurate. After all, goods destined for (or originating in) a particular country might easily have reached their final destination via a transit port, while the statistics mention these intermediate ports as either the 'final destination' or the 'place of origin'. However, no 'corrected' data regarding the origins and destinations of goods are available.

The Congo and the Belgian Economy 151

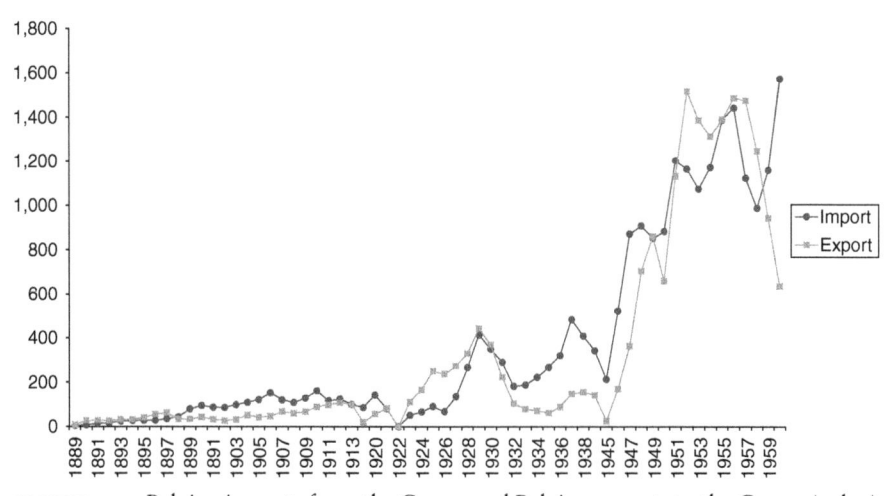

FIGURE 4.1. Belgian imports from the Congo and Belgian exports to the Congo (value), index 1913=100.

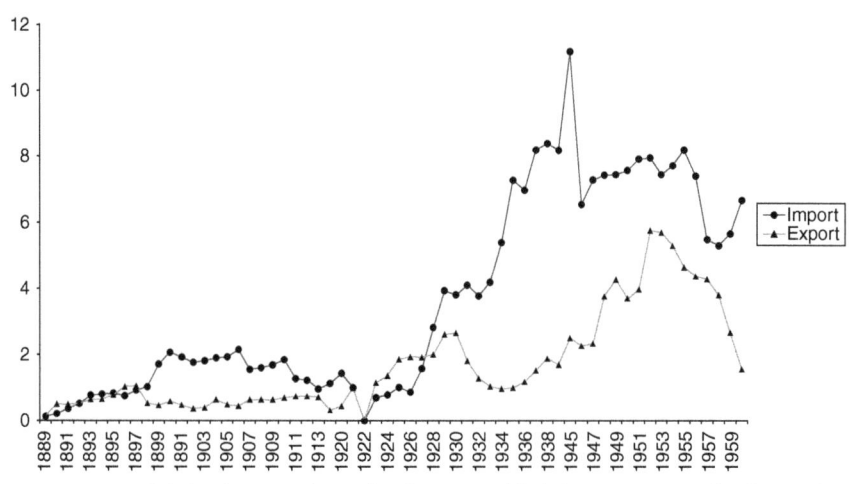

FIGURE 4.2. Belgian imports from the Congo and Belgian exports to the Congo in percentage of total Belgian imports and exports.

raw materials without needing to spend foreign currency, thanks to the parity between Belgian and Congolese francs.

A similar, though not identical, pattern is discernible in *exports* of Belgian goods to the Congo. Before the Great War, exports grew significantly slower than imports. A first leap occurred between 1910 and 1914. After the war, Belgium made a greater effort to develop its colony, as is apparent from exports of equipment for transport and mining infrastructure. These exports easily surpassed imports of raw materials from the Congo. However, during the crisis of the 1930s, exports declined far more sharply than imports did. After the Second World War, as trade between Belgium and its colony picked up again, exports received an additional boost. By 1952, the value of exports was fifteen times greater than before the Great War and ten times greater than in 1939.

Trade between Belgium and the Congo should also be seen in the wider context of Belgium's total foreign trade. Prior to 1885, no goods were imported from the Congo to Belgium; in 1892, imports from the Congo represented a modest 0.5 per cent of total imports, but by 1900 this proportion had grown to two per cent. In the course of the subsequent three decades, the relative weight of imports from the Congo declined again, so that by 1923 the colony represented just 0.7 per cent of overall imports. However, colonial imports suddenly began to accelerate from 1927, peaking in 1938 at a proportion of 8.3 per cent. This figure would subsequently be surpassed just once, in 1945, when imports from the Congo accounted for eleven per cent of total imports. From 1946 onwards, the proportion fluctuated around seven per cent, only to decline again in the final years before the Congo's independence (1956–60) to between five and six per cent.

Matters were slightly different in relation to exports. The Congo's share in Belgium's total exports evolved differently. In 1890–1913, it varied between 0.5 and one per cent. After the war, this share increased to around two per cent, a level that was maintained for over a decade. However, the crisis of the 1930s hit hard, slashing exports to the Congo by half. After the Second World War, export trade to the colony picked up fast, accounting for between four and five per cent of Belgium's total exports. Another observation is that the share of exports to the Congo in total Belgian exports is lower than the share of imports from the Congo in total Belgian imports. In other words, the Congo was always less important to Belgian producers who were looking for outlets than to those seeking to import raw materials.

In the meantime, and on the basis of the previously cited figures, we must conclude that the Congo occupied a rather marginal position in Belgium's total foreign trade. For years on end, the colony accounted for a meagre one to two per cent of imports and exports. Nonetheless, there are two important exceptions to be observed. First, for a ten-year period (1948–58), exports to the Congo rose to between four and five per cent; second, and more significant still, imports from the Congo amounted to between four and eight per cent of overall Belgian imports for a period spanning more than three decades (1929–60).

Trade with the Congo can be assessed in comparison to Belgium's relations with other trading partners. In 1905, trade flows between Belgium and Chile were comparable to those with the Congo Free State (forty-eight million Belgian francs in imports from and nine million in exports to Chile, as compared to respectively fifty-nine and eleven million for the Congo). In 1913, Russia was a much more important trading partner than the Congo. In that year, Belgium imported five times more from Russia than from the Congo and it exported three times more to Russia than to the Congo. For many years, trade with Argentina similarly outperformed that with the Congo. In 1913,

Belgian imports from the Congo amounted to just fifteen per cent of imports from Argentina; twelve years later, in 1925, the proportion was only twelve per cent. The corresponding figures for exports were twenty-nine per cent and sixty-two per cent. Not until the 1940s did the Congo overtake Argentina in the ranking of Belgium's trading partners. For a number of years, however, the colony performed as well or better than some European countries. In 1955, imports from and exports to the Congo were worth respectively 11.6 and 6.4 billion Belgian francs, which is more than the corresponding figures for Italy (2.1 billion and 3.0 billion) and almost the same as those for the UK (12.0 billion and 8.9 billion). In the ranking of trading partners for 1936–8, the Congo occupied sixth place insofar as imports were concerned and eleventh place among the export countries. By 1953, the colony had moved to sixth place in both rankings.

Another interesting question is to what extent did trade between Belgium and the Congo diverge from the pattern observed in other colonial empires? The answer to this question is complicated by the fact that the major powers such as Great Britain and France also had colonies in other parts of the world, especially in Asia. This is why the following table lists both the figures relating to the sub-Saharan African colonies and the trade within the entire empires.[23]

From the end of the nineteenth century to the middle of the twentieth century, all the colonial powers developed stronger commercial links with their respective empires. It is well known that from the commercial point of view, both Great Britain and France increasingly confined themselves within imperial boundaries, owing to the policy of 'imperial preference'. The same evolution can be observed in the sub-Saharan colonies. Belgium was no exception in this general trend: As was the case for the other imperial powers, the share of the colony in total metropolitan trade increased markedly. But three observations make the Belgian case stand out. First, as we shall see, unlike the other colonial powers, the Belgian authorities did not embrace an overt protectionist policy. The increasing commercial importance of the Congo for Belgium was due to other factors. Second, it is quite clear that Belgium had far weaker commercial links with its empire than the other imperial powers.[24] This, of course, applies to the *total* British and French colonial empires, but also to their respective sub-Saharan colonies. The share of trade with their African territories was larger for Britain and France – and even for the far more modest coloniser, Portugal – than it was for Belgium. But there was one exception: During the inter-war period, the share of imports from the Congo in total Belgian imports was greater than the share of imports from sub-Saharan colonies in total British imports.

---

[23] Trade between non-African Portuguese colonies and Portugal was negligible; this is why the figures relating to the former are not mentioned here.

[24] The Netherlands is not listed in this table because it had no African colony. Nevertheless, the Dutch empire also represented a large part of metropolitan export and import before the inter-war period (e.g. 21% of export and 17.5% of import in 1911–13) – a part that nevertheless steeply diminished before the Second World War (8.9% of export and 9.3% of import in 1936–38). B. Etemad, *De l'utilité, op. cit.*, p. 267.

TABLE 4.1. *Share (in %) of the Total Empire (dominions included) (= EMP) and of the sub-Saharan African Colonies (= SA) in the Exports and the Imports of Great Britain, France, Portugal and Belgium (1879–81 to 1945–51)*

	GB/SA Export	GB/SA Import	GB/EMP Export	GB/EMP Import	F/SA Export	F/SA Import	F/EMP Export	F/EMP Import	P/SA Export	P/SA Import	B/SA Export	B/SA Import
1879–81	0.5	0.3	33.0	22.2	0.5	0.8	6.2	4.8	3.1	2.0	–	–
1911–13	1.9	0.5	36.0	20.4	1.6	1.8	14.0	10.7	13.9	3.2	0.7	1.2
1927–29	3.2	2.3	39.8	22.8	2.6	2.9	17.5	12.6	11.6	7.4	2.2	2.9
1936–38	4.4	3.3	43.6	35.6	4.6	6.5	29.0	26.4	11.4	10.5	1.6	8.1
1945–51	7.2	8.0	49.7	42.6	8.9	9.4	34.4	25.2	25.4	12.8	4.5	7.3

Nota bene: For Portugal and Belgium 1956–8 instead of 1945–51.
B. Etemad, *De l'utilité des empires*, op. cit., pp. 177, 211, 239, 288; H. d'Almeida-Topor & M. Lakroum, *L'Europe et l'Afrique. Un siècle d'échanges économiques* (Paris, 1994), p. 83.

Indeed, we shall see that imports from the Congo, particularly of copper, grew in importance before and after the Second World War, making this mineral a crucial factor in the relationship between colony and metropole.

Despite the relatively modest share of the Congo in Belgium's *total* foreign trade, the colony was very important to *specific sectors of industry*. From 1895, the lion's share of imports consisted of rubber and ivory, with Belgium generally serving as a transit country. Gradually, though, the relative weight of these two commodities declined as imports of other raw materials, including minerals and agricultural produce, grew. But while the trade flow between the Congo and Belgium clearly became more diversified, nine commodities still accounted for ninety per cent of overall trade: copper, tin, gold, cobalt and zinc in mining; cotton, palm oil, palm nuts and coffee in agriculture.

During the inter-war years, Belgian industry imported increasing amounts of raw materials from the Congo, as the evolution of the colony's share in the total value of imported raw materials shows: 1909: 3.14 per cent; 1913: 1.57 per cent; 1920: 2.77 per cent; 1929: 6.98 per cent and 1935: 10.1 per cent. Again, a number of commodities clearly dominated. In 1935, no less than eighty-seven per cent of Belgium's copper imports originated in the Congo (compared to just eighteen per cent in 1913). By 1935, the colony accounted for even higher proportions of imports of other raw materials, such as tin (ninety-nine per cent), cobalt (ninety-seven per cent) and palm nuts (ninety-four per cent, as compared to just fourteen per cent in 1913).[25] Between 1953 and 1958, copper alone represented forty-one per cent of total Congolese exports to Belgium. Similarly, export trade to the Congo was dominated by a limited number of articles, mainly iron and steel products (metal constructions, vehicles, machines, locomotives, etc.), which between 1925 and 1939 accounted, on average, for forty-nine per cent of Belgian export value to the Congo.[26] In 1929, metal construction accounted for 10.5 per cent of Belgian exports to the Congo. In sum, the growing importance of the colony to Belgium's foreign trade between 1920 and 1950 was attributable mainly to a limited number of sectors: non-ferrous metals for imports and metal construction and metallurgical products for exports.

Belgium's Significance to the Congo's Foreign Trade

Let us now consider the relationship from the Congo's perspective: What was the significance of Belgium to the colony's foreign trade? Trade flows between full-blown capitalist nations and countries belonging to what would come to be known as the 'Third World' are typically asymmetrical. Developing countries usually have a marginal significance to the overall foreign trade of industrialised nations, whereas the industrialised nations often account for most of the foreign trade of the developing countries. A similar relationship is observed between Belgium and the Congo. Official statistics for the colony's foreign

---

[25] M. Van De Velde, *Économie belge, op. cit.*, pp. 73–5.
[26] "La collaboration de l'industrie belge à l'équipement des entreprises congolaises", *Revue coloniale belge*, 1, 11 (15 March 1946), p. 7.

trade indicate that Belgium was dominant in the Congolese import and export trade (see Table 3 in the Appendix). Before 1914, Belgium accounted for between sixty-four and seventy-four per cent of the Congo's imports, while ninety per cent of its exports were destined for Belgium.[27] After the First World War, these shares declined somewhat. In the inter-war period, between forty and fifty-six per cent of the Congo's imports originated in Belgium. Belgium accounted for a similar share in the Congo's exports during the 1920s, but then the proportion increased again during the 1930s to over eighty per cent. Trade relations between Belgium and the Congo were obviously suspended during the Second World War, when countries such as the United States and South Africa became the Congo's main trading partners. After the war, Belgium quickly regained its prominent position in the Congo's foreign trade. Between 1947 and 1960, Belgium supplied between thirty and thirty-eight per cent of the Congo's imports, while between forty-five and fifty-eight per cent of Congolese exports were destined for Belgium. The post-war reconstruction of Belgium proceeded quite smoothly thanks to Belgium's access to the Congo's raw materials without the need to spend foreign currency. As we shall see, the currency parity between the Belgian and the Congolese franc was instrumental in this regard.[28]

Once again, the question arises of how Belgium compares with other colonial powers. In this instance, however, there is no unequivocal answer, as a distinction needs to be made not only between the various overseas territories of the European nations, but also between different eras. In general terms, after 1945, France's share in the foreign trade of its sub-Saharan colonies was greater than Belgium's share in the Congo's import and export trade. The post-war French empire showed a tendency to retreat into itself. However, before the Second World War and in the British Empire, the situation was much more complex.[29] Still, on the whole, the Congo was open to imports from countries other than Belgium. After all, the exceptional international status of the Congo (under the terms of the Berlin Act and subsequently the Saint-Germain-en-Laye Convention) ruled out any protectionism. Nonetheless, the openness of the Congo's foreign trade was less apparent in its exports. In the 1930s, between seventy-five and eighty-five per cent of goods shipped out of the colony were destined for Belgium. After the war, this proportion gradually dropped to between fifty-eight per cent in 1950 and forty-five per cent in 1958. In comparison with many other colonies in sub-Saharan Africa,

---

[27] Some goods were nonetheless shipped directly abroad. We shall return to Belgium's role as a 'transit hub' later.

[28] Example of vegetable oils: see AGR, MCM, 27 January 1947, p. 97.

[29] J. Forbes Munro, *Britain in Tropical Africa 1880–1960* (London, 1984), p. 22; H. d'Almeida-Topor & M. Lakroum, *L'Europe, op. cit.*, pp. 105–6. In comparison with the Congo and Belgium, the volume of trade between the Netherlands and its colony Indonesia was modest during the inter-war period. H. Baudet & M. Fennema et al., *Het Nederlands belang bij Indië* (Utrecht, 1983), p. 35.

especially the French territories, the Congo was less dependent on trade with its colonial ruler.

Real Trade Flows, Current Transactions and Balance of Payments
Thus far, we have based our analysis on the most obvious information source, namely foreign trade statistics. However, these sources tell us nothing about the final destination of the goods concerned.[30] After all, many of the goods imported from the Congo to Belgium were subsequently processed or refined and exported to other countries. Conversely, goods shipped from Belgium to the Congo may have originated in a third country, even though the foreign trade statistics show them to have come from Belgium. In other words, the previously cited figures exaggerate the role that Belgium played in the foreign trade of its African colony, while they underestimate the role of other trading partners. This qualification further underlines the relatively marginal significance of the colony to Belgium's foreign trade.

Is it possible to arrive at more accurate figures? In the inter-war period, the Belgian and Congolese authorities tried to analyse the various trade flows more thoroughly. Unfortunately, they got no further than some tentative indications. A study from around 1934, for example, shows that Belgium's share in Congolese imports amounted to no more than twenty per cent in 1930 and sixteen per cent in 1933, while the official statistics mention respectively fifty-one and forty-three per cent.[31] Many goods shipped from Belgium to the Congo had actually originated elsewhere. It is also estimated that, of the fifteen thousand five hundred tonnes of copper shipped from the Congo to Belgium in 1923, no less than nine thousand tonnes were re-exported.[32] Half of the non-mineral products that arrived in Belgium in 1938 were not processed there but shipped onwards to other countries.[33] In that same year, sixty-one per cent of the copper and ninety-one per cent of the tin to arrive in Belgium from the Congo were

---

[30] We also ignore the fact that, from 1922 onwards, the statistics concern not just Belgium, but the Belgian-Luxembourg Economic Union (BLEU). Luxembourg's trade with the Congo is estimated at 0.3 billion out of a total of 6.9 billion in 1956 (R. de Falleur, "Le Congo et l'activité économique de la Belgique", *Cahiers économiques de Bruxelles*, 8 [October 1960], p. 580). Moreover, the foreign trade statistics of the Congo also include figures for Ruanda-Urundi. Some circumspection is called for in relation to the values mentioned in the Congo's export statistics (see infra). Economist Gaston Vandewalle has previously published a corrected overview, but this relates to the Congo's *overall* trade, without a division by country (in other words, it does not provide an overview of imports from and exports to Belgium): G. Vandewalle, *De conjuncturele evolutie in Kongo en Ruanda-Urundi van 1920 tot 1939 en van 1949 tot 1958* (Ghent, 1966), appendix 2 (pp. 238–62).

[31] "Rapport sur les travaux de la Commission d'Interpénétration économique de la Belgique, du Congo belge et du Ruanda-Urundi", *Congo* (April 1935), p. 39.

[32] AGR, Louwers Papers, n° 269, "Note de M. Louwers sur trois questions d'ordre colonial", 6 March 1925 (on the data for 1923).

[33] AA, AE-II, n° 299 (2902), "Les relations commerciales de la Belgique et du Congo", December 1943, p. 13.

re-exported after refining.[34] In the early 1950s, the Central Bank of the Belgian Congo published statistics detailing the final destination of Congo's exports. They show that, in 1949, 1950, 1951 and 1952, Belgium accounted not for respectively fifty-five, fifty-eight, fifty-seven and fifty-seven per cent of the Congo's exports (as claimed in the official statistics), but for only thirty-three, thirty-eight, forty-three and thirty-five per cent. The United States emerged as a much more important trading partner than suggested by the official figures. In 1951, approximately twenty per cent of Congolese exports were sold to U.S. buyers, as opposed to thirteen per cent according to the statistics.[35]

We shall leave to others the unenviable task of correcting the statistics on foreign trade between the Congo and Belgium. Nonetheless, this disparity invites us to expand our analysis to include financial flows and to consider a broader geographical context. This approach immediately reveals an important aspect of the economic relationship between Belgium and its colony: If a country imports more than it exports, it has a negative trade balance. This would appear to have been the case for Belgium and the Congo judging by the trade statistics. With the exception of the first half of the 1920s, when the Congo's infrastructure had yet to be developed, Belgium consistently purchased more in the Congo than it sold to the colony. On these grounds, one would be inclined to conclude that Belgium had a negative trade balance with the Congo. However, the corrected figures produced by the central banks of the Congo and Belgium at the end of the 1940s paint quite a different picture. As pointed out earlier in these figures, goods that were eventually shipped onwards to other countries are not attributed to Belgium, which makes a substantial difference. The value of 'genuine' Belgian imports was lower. Hence, the undistorted trade balance for 1949–56 recorded a cumulative *surplus* of two billion Belgian francs.

Moreover, the cash flow associated with the buying and selling of goods represents just a part of the broader transfers. Together they constitute *current transactions*, which include the cost of transport and insurance, as well as diverse financial transfers such as dividends on investments, private donations, the payment of colonial pensions and so forth (see Table 3a and 3b in the Appendix). Belgium was, after all, an important distribution hub or intermediate station for raw materials from the Congo destined for factories or end users in other countries. Obviously, Belgian insurers and forwarders also profited, and the general infrastructure in Belgium likewise benefitted from this activity. In 1957, the Congo faced increased freight and insurance costs while, globally, freightage costs had actually dropped and volume had stagnated. According to an analysis by the Belgian Ministry of Economic Affairs, this rather unusual situation was attributable to "the rigidity of the rates, occasioned by

---

[34] E. Van der Straeten, "Le commerce extérieur", in *Congrès colonial national. V^e session, nr. 20* (Brussels, 1940), p. 9.
[35] *La situation économique au Congo belge en 1950* (Brussels, 1951), p. 97; Idem ... *en 1951* (Brussels, 1952), p. 160.

monopolies".[36] The Belgian transport firms were, in other words, charging the Congo excessively high rates for its services. This was due, for instance, to the protected status of the Compagnie maritime belge and its subsidiary the Agence maritime internationale, which charged higher rates.[37]

To the previously listed payments one should add the aforementioned cash flows, specifically income on investments (such as dividends) that found their way to other countries and to Belgium in particular. These outflows were more substantial than the net private capital inflow into the colony (see Tables 3a and 3b, col. 3 and 7 in the Appendix). Ultimately, then, the balance of current transactions between Belgium and the Congo shows a substantial *surplus* to the benefit of the colonial ruler. Conversely, the Congo's balance of current transactions in respect to Belgium exhibits a structural deficit. Between 1948 and 1956, the cumulative deficit added up to over fifty-two billion Belgian francs.[38] This is indicative of the significance of the colony to Belgium's *global* economic position. In comparison with other countries, the Congo recorded a surplus, as it sold more in the international marketplace than it purchased. Between 1949 and 1956, total exports amounted to 192 billion francs as compared to imports worth 128 billion francs, representing a surplus of sixty-four billion francs. This money was used to cover the deficit on the balance of current transactions with Belgium. A note originating within the Société générale summarised this situation as follows: "One could in fact say that the economy of the Congo spent half of the surpluses realised through its trade with countries outside the Belgium-Luxembourg Economic Union on deficits in its trade with the latter".[39] In other words, the colony was a net contributor to the equilibrium in Belgium's foreign accounts. In the words of a Belgian economist writing at the end of the 1950s: "The Congo thus contributes substantially to reducing Belgium's dollar deficit and it is thanks to its surplus in the dollar zone and in the [European Payment Union] zone that the Congo is able to make good its deficits with the Belgian-Luxembourg Economic Union".[40] The role that the Congo played in balancing Belgium's foreign accounts corresponds fairly well to what has been observed in other colonial empires. British India and the Dutch Indies, for instance, played similar roles in the global positions of Great Britain and the Netherlands.[41]

The balance of current transactions is just part of a more encompassing notion, namely the balance of payments, which also takes into account long-

[36] Ministry of Economic Affairs, *L'économie belge en 1957* (Brussels, 1958), pp. 430–1.
[37] Kadoc, Dequae Papers, n° 614, "Note à M. le DG Craen", by F. Blondiau, Director, 12 February 1954, pp. 8–9.
[38] "De handels- en financiële betrekkingen tussen België en zijn overzeese gebieden" *Tijdschrift voor Documentatie en Voorlichting van de Nationale Bank van België*, 33 (February 1958), vol. 1, n° 2, p. 88. There are no comparable data for the preceding years.
[39] AGR, Finoutremer, n° 2052, "Le déséquilibre de la balance des paiements entre le Congo belge et la Belgique", note by BCK, 7 September 1955, p. 3.
[40] R. De Schutter, *Le financement interne au Congo belge* (Paris, 1957), p. 13.
[41] P. J. Cain, "Economics and Empire: The Metropolitan Context", in A. Porter, ed., *The Oxford History of the British Empire. Vol. 3. The Nineteenth Century* (Oxford, 1999), p. 50; B. Etemad, *De l'utilité, op. cit.*, pp. 165 and 264–5.

term capital flow.[42] Tables 3a and 3b show that these capital flows varied from period to period and that, moreover, the private and public funds evolved differently.[43] The Congo experienced two important periods of capital inflow. During the second half of the 1920s and again in the 1950s, investments peaked, and Belgium's colony surpassed the other colonised territories in this respect. In the inter-war period, the Congo accounted for 11.7 per cent of all the capital invested in Africa, which was substantially more than the overseas territories of either France or Portugal (4.2 and 5.4 per cent respectively).[44] After the Second World War, vast quantities of capital flowed into the Congo. By 1953, per capita investments in the Congo amounted to twenty-five dollars, compared to nineteen dollars in the French colonies, fifteen dollars in the British and only three and a half dollars in the Portuguese.[45] A substantial proportion of these investments resulted from an increase in self-financing by Congolese enterprises after the war. The capital imports have to be weighed against amounts leaving the country, once again primarily for Belgium.[46] From 1932, more capital was exported from the Congo than was imported into the colony (see column 7 of Table 3a). During the 1950s, the balance of incoming and outgoing *private capital* was positive in some years and negative in others. The inflow of public funds, on the other hand, remained positive throughout this period, and sometimes emphatically so (see columns 9 and 12 of Table 3b). On the eve of independence in 1959, the overall capital balance of the Congo turned negative, as large amounts of capital were withdrawn.

The Flow of Public Capital

It is important that we should consider the scope of public and private funding. In order to gain insight into the former, we need to go back in time.[47] The Congo Free State received financial assistance from Belgium via various channels. It could count on state loans, but also on the private funds of the king and financial aid from the Belgian state in the shape of loans it was never required to repay. There were also costs associated with the deployment of Belgian officers in Leopold's various projects and so forth. In all, the Belgian state spent some forty million gold francs in the Congo between the start of Leopold's colonial adventure and 1908. Conversely, Belgium earned sixty-six million gold francs from its colony, mainly thanks to the real property that Leopold II relinquished and the works he had privately funded. Clearly, then, the Congo Free State was

---

[42] J.-L. Vellut, "Le Zaïre à la périphérie du capitalisme: quelques perspectives historiques", *Enquêtes et Documents d'Histoire africaine*, 1 (1975), pp. 114–51.
[43] G. Vandewalle, *De conjuncturele evolutie, op. cit.*, pp. 77 and 155. Post-1945 figures from *Bulletin de la Banque centrale du Congo belge et du Ruanda-Urundi (BCCBRU)*.
[44] S. H. Frankel, *Capital Investment in Africa: Its Course and Effects* (Oxford, 1938), p. 203.
[45] AGR, Finoutremer, n° 2052, "Le déséquilibre (…)", note cited earlier.
[46] To avoid any misunderstandings, it should be pointed out that income from investments (such as dividends and profit shares) that was channelled abroad (Belgium included) is recorded under current transactions. Definition in *BBCCBRU*, 1, 4 (October 1952), p. 110.
[47] J. Stengers, *Combien le Congo, op. cit.*, passim.

ultimately profitable to Belgium. Nonetheless, during the public and political debate on a possible takeover of the territory by the Belgian state, fears were expressed that the Congo might become a financial quagmire for the national treasury. Obviously the lack of transparency in the king's financial dealings had helped create these fears. In order to avoid any catastrophic financial haemorrhage, the Colonial Charter separated the Belgian and the Congolese treasuries. The underlying principle was quite clear: Belgium would not be pouring money into the Congo. The Belgian taxpayer would only be required to pay the (modest) cost of operating the Ministry of Colonies in Belgium itself. All other costs associated with the colonisation would be borne by the Congo.

Things did not, however, always turn out that way in practice. In the early 1920s, when a modernisation of the Congo's infrastructure was necessary, Belgium provided the required and theoretically repayable credit, but the loan was never repaid. During the slump of the 1930s, the Congo's economy and budget came under such pressure that the colony's very existence came under threat. Although the Belgian state faced some serious budgetary problems of its own between 1933 and 1940, it came to the aid of the almost bankrupt Congolese colony with substantial subsidies (see column 4 of Table 3a). In 1934, Belgium established the so-called Colonial Lottery, the proceeds of which were intended for the ailing Congolese economy, in a scheme that would continue after the Second World War. Subsequently renamed the National Lottery, it is today one of the few institutions, outside the scientific realm, that owes its existence to Belgium's former colony.

During the Second World War, the Congo helped Belgium in its struggle against Germany. Not only did the colony lend money to the exiled Belgian government in London, it also provided military assistance to the Allies.[48] The Belgian government began to question whether the Congo should have to pay for these so-called sovereignty expenses. Surely the colony would have to be compensated. After the conflict, Belgium did acknowledge its war debt to the Congo. This would lead indirectly to Belgium's financing of the Fund for Indigenous Well-Being (Fonds du Bien-Être indigène).[49] This institution was established in 1947 for the purpose of launching social projects in the Congo, as was the Institute for Scientific Research in Central Africa (IRSAC).

After subtracting the various budgetary 'benefits' associated with the colony, Belgium's total public spending on the Congo from the 1880s to the 1950s is estimated to have amounted to seven billion current Belgian francs of 1957, the equivalent of 209 million gold francs. By way of comparison, this represented

---

[48] In total, these loans amounted to seven billion francs. Two point nine billion was paid back by the Belgian state from 1944 onwards; the balance was transmuted into certificates owned by the Bank of Belgian Congo and subsequently by the Central Bank of the Congo (for an amount of four billion francs in 1956). These certificates could be presented to Belgium for payment whenever the Congo found itself in financial trouble. This essentially meant that the Congo would, for years, be granting 'credit' to Belgium. F. Baudhuin, *Histoire économique de la Belgique 1945–1956* (Brussels, 1958), pp. 31–2.

[49] J. Stengers, *Combien, op. cit.*, pp. 116, 140.

"less than one-tenth of the Belgian State's annual expenditure; pensions spending alone amounted to 12.5 billion francs [in 1956], which was almost twice as much as the Congo had cost over a period of seventy years. Clearly no other colony had cost so little, with the possible exception of Indonesia to the Dutch during a number of years", as Jean Stengers concluded after meticulous research.[50]

Just a fraction of the public funds that Belgium transferred to the Congo were genuine gifts. In other words, Belgium's colonial policy towards the Congo was never particularly generous, as was noted both at home and abroad. This had already engendered fierce criticism from a fervent colonialist in 1912, who argued that the Congo needed a lot of money and that Belgium should therefore assist its African territory financially: "A mother should help her child take its first steps. (…) The colony ought to have found a mother, but in fact she has turned out to be no more than a stepmother!"[51]

The familial metaphor, quite common in colonial rhetoric, was sometimes reversed. Minister of Colonies De Vleeschauwer, for example, asserted in 1939 that, as parents have the duty to care for their children, so the Belgians cared for theirs, namely the Congolese, as the support that the colony had received since 1933 demonstrated. Conversely, he noted that "parents may expect their children to contribute as much as possible to maintaining the household. (…) This duty becomes all the more compelling if the parents are in dire financial straits".[52]

The stinginess of the Belgian authorities towards the colony was undoubtedly due in part to the precarious state of Belgium's treasury. A telling example in this respect is the fact that Belgium only reluctantly came to acknowledge its war debt to the Congo. The minister of finance and his colleague in charge of colonies disagreed entirely on this matter. The former noted "that [the metropole] could hardly bear an increase in its public debt, while the Congo came out of the war richer".[53] Hence 'poor' Belgium would be unable to offer assistance to its rich colony. It was a message that received very little sympathy abroad, where it was seen as a further blemish on Belgium's colonial policy.[54]

More and more Belgian politicians and people in the administration felt that the country should change its policy towards the Congo and offer financial support. In 1936, Governor-General Pierre Ryckmans had already criticised Belgium's all too modest assistance to the Congo.[55] Ten years later, he denounced the country's hesitance in acknowledging its war debt to the colony.[56] In 1958,

[50] Ibid., pp. 350-1.
[51] Lt. Gen. Baron Donny, "Les relations du Congo belge avec sa mère patrie", *Bulletin de la Société belge d'Études coloniales*, 11 (November 1912), pp. 12 and 21.
[52] A. De Vleeschauwer, *Belgique-Congo. Conférence à la SBEE, le 20 novembre 1939* (S.i., 1939), p. 8.
[53] AGR, MCM, 6 June 1947, p. 7 (and numerous earlier discussions within the Cabinet).
[54] AA, AE-II, n° 1801ter (3283), R. Scheyven to F. Vanlangenhove, 6 March 1957.
[55] AA, AE-II, n° 1802bis (3283), "Situation économique du Congo. (…) Discours prononcé par M. Ryckmans", 26 October 1936, p. 142.
[56] P. Ryckmans, *Étapes et jalons* (Brussels, 1946), p. 215.

The Congo and the Belgian Economy 163

former Governor-General Léo Pétillon, who was now a government minister, pleaded to his colleagues for financial assistance to the Congo, but to no avail.[57] All warnings and requests were ignored: After the Second World War, Belgium offered no assistance to the Congo whatsoever, apart from redeeming its war debt to the colony. Even the ambitious Ten-Year Plan for 1949–59, designed to enhance the economic and social development of the colony, was not financed by Belgium. The Congo was required to borrow these funds. It was not until the eve of the Congo's independence that Belgium's national budget provided for financial assistance to the colony: half a billion francs in 1959 and 2.7 billion the following year.

This rather lengthy digression on the financial relationship between Belgium and the Congo offers three important insights. First, it reveals Belgium's lack of generosity towards its colony. Second, it outlines the context in which Belgium's 'development assistance' materialised, a topic which will be considered further in Chapter 5. Third, it provides a better understanding of the significance of the public capital flows, which provided the starting point for the whole discussion. Indeed, it emerges that the public funds that were transferred to the Congo were primarily loans, which the colonial treasury took out in order to cover its own financial needs. Between the two World Wars, the colony's public debt had increased substantially, from sixty-five million francs in 1925 to 374 million francs in 1936.[58] Subsequently, the exceptional circumstances that presented themselves during the Second World War allowed the Congo to reduce its outstanding debt. In the prosperous years after the war, the Congo even entrusted the metropolitan treasury with some of its financial reserves. But in the second half of the 1950s, this situation was reversed. Expenses rose while revenues lagged behind. The reports by the De Voghel Commission, established by the Belgian government to look into the financial predicament of the Congo, sounded the alarm.[59] Beginning in 1960, the Congo's revenues would amount to twelve to thirteen billion francs, while expenses were expected to reach between twenty and twenty-one billion francs. The Belgian Cabinet admitted that the colony's budgetary deficit was structural and fundamental.[60] The financial relationship between metropole and colony changed drastically: "[F]ormerly the [Belgian] Treasury drew some of its resources from the Congo, while now it is the other way round".[61] Belgium had to give some financial

---

[57] AMAÉF (Nantes), Consulat général de France à Léopoldville (1934–59), n° 5, R. Bousquet (French ambassador in Brussels) to French Ministry of Foreign Affairs, 7 November 1958. See also L. Pétillon, *Récit. Congo 1929–1958* (Brussels, 1985), p. 475; AGR, MCM, 22 September 1958, pp. 1–4.
[58] G. Heenen, "Les finances du Congo belge", in *Histoire des finances publiques en Belgique* (Brussels, 1955), vol. 3, p. 322.
[59] Franz De Voghel, vice governor of the National Bank, chaired this commission. Its reports can be found in, among other places, Kadoc, De Schryver Papers, n° 11.3.33.1, reports of 6 August and 9 October 1959. The second has also been published in J. Marres & I. Vermast, *Le Congo assassiné* (Brussels, 1974), pp. 86–136.
[60] AGR, MCM, 25 July 1959, p. 6.
[61] AGR, MCM, 6 December 1957, p. 7.

assistance to its colony. In the meantime, the colony's debt reached new peaks in the 1950s, primarily as a consequence of expenses incurred in the context of the Ten-Year Plan. The considerable inflow of capital to the Congo during the final decade of the colonial era ultimately contributed to the deterioration of the colony's public finances, though it was not the main cause. The repayment of public debt took six per cent out of the Congolese budget in 1950, but this proportion would increase threefold to eighteen per cent by 1958.[62] Some critics argued that the miserable financial situation of the Congo provided the real motivation for Belgium to relinquish its colony. However, there are no concrete indications that this was a contributory factor to the hasty decolonisation. We will return to this issue in Chapter 5.

So, throughout its history, the colony was required to borrow. Questions surround the terms on which it borrowed and whether there was any hidden agenda. As far as access to the financial markets is concerned, the interests of Belgium's treasury did not always coincide with those of the colony. Moreover, there are indications that the Belgian government repeatedly put the Congolese treasury on the spot, as the following examples demonstrate. When the colony sought a loan in 1922, Belgium made it borrow abroad at a worse rate than it could have obtained in Belgium. And in 1924, the Belgian government opposed the idea that the Congo might introduce treasury bonds on the Belgian market, as these would compete with Belgian loans. Ten years later, with Belgium in full financial crisis, the colony was coerced, despite its strong resistance, into joining the Belgian treasury in a substantial foreign loan, known as the Mendelssohn Loan. Later in the year, as the Belgian franc was devalued, the colony suffered substantial exchange rate losses, while the gains from a revaluation of gold flowed exclusively to the Belgian treasury. The colony protested vehemently against this gross injustice, but would never recuperate any of its money. In 1956, the ministers in charge of colonies and finance disagreed over attempts by the former to float loans on the American money market, as the latter felt this might have a detrimental impact on the Belgian treasury.[63] In 1957, businessman and future Christian-Democrat minister of the Belgian Congo Raymond Scheyven lamented that Belgium was causing the Congo "unacceptable difficulties through its loans policy on the Belgian market".[64] In the same year, the Belgian minister of finance admitted that the previous government had used the product of a loan for the Congo to cover its own metropolitan expenses.[65] And one final example: In 1959, Governor-General Hendrik

---

[62] M. Zimmer, "Les finances coloniales jusqu'en 1960 et leurs conséquences", in M. Frank, ed., *Histoire des finances publiques en Belgique. Tome IV-2. La période 1950–1980* (Brussels, 1988), p. 952.

[63] R. Brion & J.-L. Moreau, *La Banque nationale de Belgique 1939–1971. Vol. 2. La politique monétaire belge dans une Europe en reconstruction (1944–1958)* (Brussels, 2005), pp. 469–70.

[64] AGR, MCM, 13 November 1922, pp. 8–9 and 1 December 1924, pp. 10–11; J. Stengers, *Combien, op. cit.*, pp. 294–301; AA, AE-II, n° 1801ter (3283), note "Relations financières entre la Belgique et le Congo", March 1957.

[65] AGR, MCM, 6 December 1957, p. 7.

Cornelis denounced "the lack of foresight of the Belgian governments which have not allowed the Congo, particularly in 1956 and 1957, to contract loans on the international markets".[66] When it came to financial matters, Belgium tended to sacrifice the best interest of its colony to further its own cause.

The Private Capital Flows

Let us now consider the position of Belgium in overall private capital investment in the Congo and, conversely, the Congo's position in Belgium's private foreign investments. The nature of the Leopoldian era determined the provenance of the capital invested in the Congo. From the establishment of the Congo Free State, foreign (mostly British) investors were lining up to provide capital. Leopold maintained ambivalent and even contradictory relations with every player in this colonial poker game, including Belgian politicians and foreign powers, as well as private investors. His approach was inspired by the overriding ambition to create a profitable colony with an ensured Belgian presence. Foreign investors were attracted at certain moments but repelled at other times, depending on the financial and/or strategic needs of the moment.[67] At the same time, the spectre of an exclusive or at least dominant presence of foreign capital in the Congo was used to persuade some of the big players in the Belgian economy to invest in the colony.

This tactic explains the particular position of foreign capital in the Congo Free State towards the end of its existence: Foreign capital was definitely present, but to a limited degree. The real control rested with the authorities and/or private Belgian groups. Between 1885 and 1908, no less than eighty-six per cent of the invested capital was Belgian, compared to just fourteen per cent foreign, mainly British and American.[68] Throughout the colonial era, Belgian capital would retain the upper hand. According to an official study estimating capital investment in the Belgian Congo, some 46.5 per cent of investments made in the Congo between 1887 and 1953 were of Belgian origin and 49.2 per cent of Congolese origin. As has been pointed out, self-financing by Congolese enterprises was very important, especially after the Second World War. Just 4.3 per cent of the capital invested in the Congo was foreign capital.[69] Nonetheless, the

---

[66] AGR, MCM, 13 November 1959, p. 4.
[67] Some notable examples: U.S. capitalists Ryan and Guggenheim, when the Forminière and the American Congo Company were created in 1906; the Banque de l'Union parisienne when the Compagnie du Chemin de Fer du Bas-Congo au Katanga (BCK) was created also in 1906 and British group Tanganyika Concessions Limited (with Robert Williams) when the Union minière du Haut-Katanga was founded the same year. See F. Buelens, *Congo 1885–1960. Een financieel-economische geschiedenis* (Berchem, 2007), passim.
[68] AGR, Finoutremer, n° 511, "Montant du capital-actions et des emprunts (...), de 1858 [sic] au 1er janvier 1909", note of the CCCI, 3 March 1944.
[69] Ministry of the Colonies, *Les investissements au Congo belge* (Brussels, 1955), pp. 24–5; "Essai d'estimation du capital investi au Congo belge", *BBCCBRU*, 4, 8 (August 1955), pp. 289–305; F. Haex & D. Van den Bulcke, *Belgische multinationale ondernemingen* (Diepenbeek, 1979), p. 153; Ministry of the Belgian Congo and of Ruanda-Urundi, *Statistiques des mouvements de capitaux au Congo belge et au Ruanda-Urundi de 1887 à 1956* (Brussels, 1958), pp. 201–9.

study adds that the contribution of foreign capital is underestimated, as part of the Congo's self-financing stems from companies also holding foreign capital. Perhaps a 1959 estimate by the National Bank of Belgium comes closer to the truth. It puts the proportion of Belgian capital in total foreign investment in the Congo at around seventy-five per cent.[70]

After its takeover of the Congo Free State, Belgium wished to safeguard the national character of the colony. Apart from the cultural, political and religious aspects, this policy also had an economic dimension. The Belgian government was wary of foreign capital and discouraged foreign investments. However, this did not prevent a number of important foreign companies from gaining a foothold in the Congo. For example, after having been rebuffed by the British colonial authorities, who had refused the creation of plantations in Nigeria and Sierra Leone, the UK multi-national Lever Brothers signed a convention with the Belgian authorities in 1911. This led to the creation of the Huileries du Congo belge, which exploited large plantations in the colony.[71] But a year later, in 1912, Minister of Colonies Jules Renkin drew his colleagues' attention to the "genuine danger" of a capital increase at Union minière. Measures had to be taken in order to prevent the strengthening of foreign interests in the company.[72] Many other examples can be given of the Belgian authorities' distrust of non-Belgian investors or traders during the inter-war period.[73] This isolationist attitude persisted after the Second World War. In 1955, the Congo made great efforts to boost its economic development, but the fear persisted that "a massive injection of foreign, mainly American, capital would create a genuine political risk. (...) As the Americans (...) would subsequently settle in the region [of the Lower Congo] in large numbers, it would not be long before their influence surpassed that of the Belgian State".[74] In the same year, the government reaffirmed its intention to take any measures necessary to limit the amount of foreign capital in Congolese enterprises to a maximum of forty-nine per cent.[75]

The Belgian authorities not only discouraged potential foreign investors, they encouraged Belgian investors to look towards the colony. During diplomatic talks with France in 1923, the Belgian representatives asserted unashamedly that "the policy of the Belgian government is geared towards encouraging

---

[70] "De handels- en financiële betrekkingen tussen België en zijn overzeese gebieden", *Tijdschrift voor Documentatie en Voorlichting van de Nationale Bank van België*, 33, vol. 1, 2 (February 1958), p. 99.

[71] M. Havinden & D. Meredith, *Colonialism and Development: Britain and its Tropical Colonies 1850–1960* (London, 1996), pp. 113 and 158.

[72] AGR, de Broqueville Papers, n° 347, note "Augmentation de capital de la société UMHK".

[73] AMAE, AF-I-17 (1884–1925), O. Louwers to the minister of foreign affairs, 14 February 1921; Belgian ambassador Cartier de Marchienne to Count de Ramaix (of the Ministry of Foreign Affairs), 27 February 1925; AMAE, AF-I-1 (1939–42), "Note", from O. Louwers, 28 June 1939.

[74] AMAE, AF-I-1 (1955–6), note "La Commission nationale pour le Développement économique du Congo belge", O. Louwers, 9 May 1955, p. 8.

[75] AGR, MCM, 6 May 1955, p. 8.

TABLE 4.2. *Belgian Capital Exports in the Form of Foreign Direct Investments (FDI) 1879–1939 (in millions of current Belgian francs, annual averages)*

	1879–90	1891–1900	1901–10	1914–20	1921–30	1931–9
Europe (- Russia)	12.8	36.4	35.7	35.2	298.1	26.5
Russia	3.2	60.9	6.6	15.3	–	–
Belgian Congo	1.4	11.9	13.3	72.5	786.8	58.8
North America	1.4	0.5	5.9	0.6	2.8	–1.0
South America	7.3	12.3	29.5	18.4	151.7	–10.0
Other	0.5	7.4	28.3	10.7	119.2	–1.4
Total	26.7	129.6	119.4	152.6	1358.8	70.8

W. Peeters, "Foreign Direct Investment within a reconstructed Balance of Payments: Preliminary Results for Belgium, 1879–1939", in V. Bovykin, et al., eds., *Public Debt, Public Finance, Money and Balance of Payments in Debtor Countries, 1890–1932/1933: IEHC Congress in Seville* (Seville, 1998), pp. 101–25 (table 6). There are no comparable data for the years 1945–60. Foreign direct investments do not relate to other financial flows, such as the purchase of foreign treasury bonds

Belgian financiers to focus their efforts on the development of this colony".[76] It is hard to gain accurate insight into how this approach worked. There can, though, be no doubt whatsoever that those Belgian private investors were indeed beginning to focus more closely on the Congo, as meticulous research by historian Wim Peeters has shown (see Table 4.2).

From the 1880s onwards, Belgian investors became more interested in foreign business opportunities. Companies holding Belgian capital were established in Latin America, the Far East, the Middle East and Russia. In some cases, including that of China, Leopold II had a hand in encouraging Belgian investors to go foreign.[77] In other instances, the international expansion occurred spontaneously, without royal intervention. Prior to the First World War, the interest of Belgian entrepreneurs focused mainly on Russia. Between 1891 and 1900, the czar's empire alone attracted almost half of Belgium's foreign direct investment (FDI). Between 1900 and 1910, the Belgian Congo accounted for 9.1 per cent of FDI. Following closely in the wake of this money were people. In 1898, 1,060 Belgian nationals lived in the Congo, compared to 2,253 Belgian expats in Russia.[78] After the huge losses suffered in Russia due to the Bolshevik Revolution, the capital flow was directed along other channels. In the 1920s, some sixty per cent of FDI went to the colony. As the amount of exported capital grew year after year, a capital stock was created. In 1913, the Congo represented 7.3 per cent of Belgium's FDI stock. By 1939, this share had increased to 29.8 per cent. At the outbreak of the First World War, forty-seven out of 267

---

[76] AMAE, AF-I-1 (1923-4), "Séance tenue le 16 février 1923 (...)".
[77] G. Kurgan-van Hentenryk, *Léopold II et les groupes financiers belges en Chine (1895–1914)* (Brussels, 1972).
[78] W. Peeters & J. Wilson, *L'industrie belge dans la Russie des tsars* (Liège, 1999), p. 57.

Belgian enterprises with FDI had been operating in the Congo, as compared to 129 companies out of 211 on the eve of the Second World War.[79]

Although they did not lose sight of the rest of the world, Belgian private investors were clearly concentrating on the Congo. By the 1950s, the colony accounted for approximately half of all Belgian private capital invested abroad.[80] In 1951, a similar proportion of Belgium's income from foreign investments originated in its African colony (2.5 billion out of a total of 5.4 billion).[81] An interesting anecdote in this respect is that, not long after the First World War, Jean Jadot, governor of the Société générale, turned down an opportunity offered by U.S. businessman Daniel Guggenheim to acquire a stake in a Chilean copper mine that would become one of the largest in the world. The Belgian motivated his decision as follows: "I must not forget that I have accepted an important responsibility for the development of the Congo. All financial resources of the Société générale must be deployed to that end".[82]

By concentrating so intensely on the Congo, Belgian investors missed investment opportunities elsewhere in the world. Still, there can be no doubt that some Belgian economic activities abroad benefitted from or were facilitated or made possible by activities in the Congo. In other words, despite the crucial importance of the colony to Belgium's foreign investments, the ties between Belgium and the Congo were by no means unilateral or exclusive. They generated business opportunities around the globe.[83]

Economic Policy Choices in Belgian-Congolese Relations

Trade and Customs Policy

Foreign trade data are determined by political choices. Public decision making in commercial issues was a delicate matter. On the one hand, Belgian politicians were partisans of free trade; on the other, they also wanted to safeguard and enhance existing ties between Belgium and the Congo. Moreover, this subtle exercise was determined by international agreements, especially the Act of the Berlin Conference and the Brussels Declaration of 1890. Under the terms of those agreements, import duties could not exceed ten per cent and preferential treatment in trade was out of the question. In other words, Belgium was unable to grant itself privileges in its trade with the Congo. However, that is not to say

---

[79] W. Peeters, "Belgische ondernemers in het buitenland, 1879-1939. Innovatief expansionisme of economisch escapisme", unpublished text presented at a colloquium of Tilburg University, 1998, p. 4.

[80] Ch. Didier, *Les relations commerciales entre le Congo belge et la Belgique* (Liège, 1959), unpublished master's thesis in economic sciences, Liège University, p. 29.

[81] Central Council for the Economy, *De interpenetratie der Belgische en Kongolese economieën* (Brussels, 1954), part 2, pp. 79-80.

[82] Cited in R. Brion & J.-L. Moreau, *La Société générale de Belgique 1822-1997* (Antwerp, 1998), p. 327; also, R. Brion & J.-L. Moreau, *De la mine à Mars. La genèse d'Umicore* (Tielt, 2006), p. 82.

[83] See J.-L. Vellut, "Réseaux ...", art. cit., pp. 141-6; G. Kurgan-van Hentenryk, *Léopold II*, op. cit., pp. 838-9 and 842.

that the Belgian government *accepted* these stipulations reluctantly. Matters were more complicated than that. Belgium was itself a champion of free trade. The country's economy was strongly export-oriented and depended largely on its access to neighbouring foreign markets. This obviously affected Belgium's position towards the Congo and colonial trade.

Still, the Belgian authorities were certainly keen to free themselves from the restrictions imposed by the Berlin Act. This gave rise to an important question during the First World War. If Belgium were able to govern its colony in whatever way it saw fit, what would its colonial trade policy be? The Belgian government consulted the country's top business leaders on the matter. Some, including industrialist and steel magnate Gaston Barbanson, argued in favour of protectionism.[84] Others (the majority) tended towards a *voluntary* free trade policy. Minister of Colonies Renkin put it as follows in 1917: "It is indeed in the interest of the development of our colony that it should remain a territory where free trade reigns.... I even wonder whether, ideally, this regime of free trade ought not to be expanded to other territories in Africa".[85]

Peace talks after the war resulted in the Saint-Germain-en-Laye Convention (1919). The principle of non-discrimination was retained, but henceforth the colonial powers in the Conventional Congo Basin enjoyed the freedom to set import duty rates. So while the prohibition on the preferential treatment of goods from Belgium or the restriction of other foreign imports remained intact, the Belgian authorities were now free to set customs duties. In other words, this was not an 'open door regime', without import and export duties. Theoretically, the colony could be protected by high customs tariffs, on the condition that they were applied universally and were not aimed against any country in particular.

So how did Belgium and its colony respond to this new situation? For one thing, the metropole opened its own borders fully to Congolese products. The law of 8 May 1924 abolished import duties on products from the colony, instead of regarding them as domestic goods.[86] As the Congo's exports did not necessarily enjoy the same benefits in other countries, commercial traffic from the Congo to Belgium grew. Belgium allowed the Congo to set its own customs duties, within the terms of the Saint-Germain-en-Laye Convention. The question remains, of course, to what extent the Belgian colonial authorities made use of this freedom. Let us consider some figures (see Table 4.3).[87]

Customs duties constituted a substantial proportion – between thirty-one and forty-two per cent – of the Congo's revenues (sum total of lines 1 and 2)

---

[84] AA, AE-II, n° 363, "Avis de M. Barbanson. Réponse au questionnaire", s.d. [1917].

[85] AA, AE-II, n° 363, draft letter from the minister of colonies to the minister of foreign affairs, May 1917.

[86] *Pasinomie*, 1924, p. 609 (art. 12); also the Royal Decree of 23 October 1924 (*Pasinomie*, 1924, p. 614).

[87] H. Leclercq, "Un mode de mobilisation des ressources: le système fiscal. Le cas du Congo pendant la période coloniale", *Cahiers économiques et sociaux*, 3, 2 (June 1965), pp. 131–2; L. Ndibu, *Le régime douanier congolais. Sa fondation, ses bases juridiques et son évolution de 1885 à 1965* (Leuven, 1967), unpublished master's thesis in economic sciences, University of Louvain.

TABLE 4.3. *Share of Customs Duties on Imports and Exports in Total Tax Revenues of the Congo and in the Total Value of Imports and Exports (in %)*

	1920	1925	1930	1932	1935	1940	1945	1950	1955	1958
1	4.6	4.9	4.5	3.3	12.5	34.2	32.1	25.2	20.7	16.9
2	26.4	29.2	13.2	13.6	14.8	8.5	7.5	17.3	15.7	14.3
3	1.1	2.0	1.5	?	4.4	11.6	12.9	9.4	9.6	7.9
4	8.5	8.7	5.4	?	12.0	8.6	7.1	8.9	8.8	10.4

1: export duties in percentage of total tax revenues
2: import duties in percentage of total tax revenues
3: export duties in percentage of total export value
4: import duties in percentage of total import value

except during the crisis of the 1930s, when it initially dropped to between sixteen and seventeen per cent. The colony's income consisted largely of duties levied on international commodity flows. Hence, the colonial customs policy was inspired primarily by fiscal considerations. Nonetheless, other interests also came into play. The contrast between duties levied on imports and exports was quite striking. Between 1920 and 1935, export duties were insignificant in comparison to the total exported value. Moreover, they constituted only a fraction of total tax revenue. Governor-General Ryckmans explained the logic behind this policy: "Most export duties were abolished or cut after the annexation of the Congo to Belgium. The government took this measure because it was concerned with stimulating local production and helping exporters of Congolese goods to withstand foreign competition on the international markets".[88] Beginning in 1935, the government took a different approach, primarily in order to compensate for the devaluation of the Congolese franc.[89] Import duties were lowered and export duties increased. Henceforth, export duties constituted a larger proportion of total export value and thus substantially boosted the colony's public revenues.

So, during the inter-war years, import duties contributed much more substantially to the colony's revenues. The new customs duty, which came into force in 1923, "was, it must be said, set with a considerable increase in revenue in mind, but also out of a concern not to jeopardise the competitive position of the colony".[90] The colonial authorities did not want to cut off the Congo from the global trade flow. Therefore, import duties were kept relatively low, as shown in line 4 in the table. Still, there were more specific considerations to take into account. For some goods (such as equipment) import duties were low, while for

[88] AMAE, AF-I-1 (1929–30), "Notes pour servir à la rédaction d'un aperçu de la politique douanière coloniale de la Belgique (période 1920–1930)", p. 3.
[89] The colonial authorities wanted to compensate for the price increases of imported goods and correct for the monetary gains on exports. P. Ryckmans, "Les conséquences de la dévaluation et du renversement de la politique douanière au Congo", *Congo* (1937), pp. 438–46.
[90] AMAE, AF-I-1 (1929–30), "Notes pour servir...", p. 2.

others they were high. Duties were high for ordinary consumption goods that 'Congolese' industry, often established with Belgian capital, was able to produce itself. Hence, some Belgian products were affected as much by Congolese customs duties as competing products from other countries. The purpose of these high levies was to provide support for and protection to local manufacturing industries. As a result, Belgian capital found its way to 'Congolese' companies producing consumer goods. As we shall see, this unusual evolution would stir debate back in Belgium.

Monetary Policy: The Linkage of the Belgian and the Congolese Francs
When Belgium annexed the Congo, it chose to safely separate its own finances from those of its colony.[91] Hence, the Congo was given a separate monetary system. Under an agreement with the colonial authorities, the Bank of the Belgian Congo, founded in 1909 as a private financial institution, acquired the privilege of issuing the 'Congolese franc' (CF). Theoretically, this currency was independent from the Belgian franc (BF). In practice, however, the two currencies were firmly linked. This is less obvious than would initially appear. In French Indochina, the piaster led an existence entirely detached from the French franc.[92] The Indian rupee was also an independent currency not always pegged to Britain's pound sterling.[93] The leaders of the Belgian colonial empire made a different choice. The value of the Congolese franc was equated to that of the Belgian franc (1 CF = 1 BF). Thus, the fortunes of Belgium's monetary unit would inevitably impact the colony's currency. During the First World War, the value of the Belgian franc dropped below that of the colonial currency in the international exchange markets. The reason was clear: The Congolese economy was doing well, while that of Belgium was suffering under wartime occupation. In 1919, sterling was worth CF 25.40, compared to BF 31. Still, the Belgian government decided in that same year to link the Congolese franc to the Belgian franc. This measure represented a de facto devaluation of the Congolese franc. A contemporary financial analyst summarised this situation as follows: "Hence, united with the Belgian franc in exchange rate and differing from it only in form and currency symbol, the Congolese franc follows its

---

[91] For the period after 1944, see W. Pluym & O. Boehme, *De Nationale Bank van België 1939–1971. Boekdeel 3. Van de golden sixties tot de val van Bretton Woods* (Brussels, 2005), pp. 373–8; O. Boehme, "Monetary Affairs in the Heart of Africa: The National Bank of Belgium and Finance in Congo, 1945–1974", *Journal of European Economic History*, 36, 1 (2007), pp. 13–45; H. Leclercq, "Du Congo au Zaïre. Un siècle d'histoire monétaire", in *La France et l'outre-mer. Un siècle de relations monétaires et financières* (Paris, 1998), pp. 577–97; "Exposé historique du Franc congolais dans ses rapports avec le Franc belge", *BBCCBRU*, 6, 11 (November 1957), pp. 437–54; E. Mambu, *A Modern History of Financial Systems of Congo 1885–1985*, unpublished Ph.D. thesis from the University of Greenwich, 2003.

[92] P. Brocheux & D. Hémery, *Indochine. La colonisation ambiguë 1858–1954* (Paris, 1994), pp. 129–31.

[93] D. K. Fieldhouse, "The Metropolitan Economics", in J. M. Brown & Wm. R. Louis, eds., *The Oxford History of the British Empire. Vol. 4*, art. cit., pp. 93–4.

metropolitan senior for better and for worse".[94] And indeed, worse was yet to come. The Belgian currency was devaluated in 1926 and once again in 1935. On both occasions, the Congolese franc was dragged along. During the Second World War, the Congolese economy was integrated into the British Empire, so that the Congolese franc became part of the sterling zone. It experienced yet another devaluation, whereby its parity with the Belgian franc was broken. After the war, the linkage between the two currencies was restored and when the BF was devalued once more in 1949, the CF again followed suit.

The Belgian government was adamant: The linkage and parity between the Belgian and the Congolese franc were to be maintained at all costs. The presumed motivations are complex, with political, practical and psychological considerations all coming into play. To the outside world, the parity between the Belgian and the Congolese franc signified the unity of the Belgian colonial empire. Conversely, a separate monetary policy in the colony may have compromised the '*belgitude*' of the Congo, which was a veritable dogma in Belgium's colonial policy. A Belgian monetary zone, alongside other currency zones such as those of the dollar and sterling, was a source of national pride. However, the parity of the two currencies was no doubt also motivated by purely economic considerations, as it was conducive to smooth commercial and financial transactions between Belgium and the Congo. Buying and selling, or transferring capital in CF/BF held no exchange risks whatsoever and it greatly simplified accounting procedures. For example, the balance sheets of colonial enterprises were often expressed in 'francs' without specification whether these francs were Belgian or Congolese. Ending the parity of exchange between the two currencies would have caused considerable practical problems. The system stimulated trade flows from Belgium to the Congo and vice versa. And it was a way of countering or sidestepping the stipulations in the Saint-Germain-en-Laye Convention that prohibited discriminatory practices in trade.[95]

To these rather obvious considerations we might add another. The currency parity between BF and CF resulted in successive devaluations of the Congolese currency, which were unnecessary given the economic state of the country. What is more, the CF was potentially a strong currency, stronger perhaps than the BF during this particular period. The Congo's foreign trade balance exhibited a healthy surplus. Congolese products were selling well, so the CF was in demand, irrespective of the BF. Technically speaking, there was no reason for the Congolese franc to devalue whenever its Belgian counterpart did. Of course, the situation could have turned around. The CF might have grown weaker, for example if global demand for the Congo's raw materials were to collapse.

[94] M.-L. Gérard, "Note sommaire sur le change dans ses rapports avec le budget de la Colonie", in *La politique financière du Congo belge. Rapport au Comité permanent du Congrès colonial* (Brussels, 1925), p. 84.

[95] "In fact, for the metropole, the identity of parities is one of the most efficient means to realise the interpenetration of both economies and to assure its preponderance without hindering, in the colony, the export from foreign countries": "Aperçu sur l'évolution de l'organisation monétaire et bancaire au Congo belge", *Bulletin d'Information et de Documentation de la BNB*, 27, vol. 1, 6 (June 1952), p. 318.

However, there were no indications of any such evolution in the 1920s or in the 1940s and early 50s. So the close link between the Congolese and the Belgian franc was not necessarily to the benefit of the Congo or to Congolese society as a whole. Under the circumstances, it was rather more beneficial to the BF, with the CF serving almost as a crutch for the limping Belgian currency. On the eve of the 1926 devaluation of the Belgian franc, the following was noted at the second Belgian Colonial Congress: "The economic activities of the colony are an important factor, which day after day works harder to the advantage of the Belgian exchange rate. Unlinking the two currencies would arguably be to the detriment of the Belgian franc".[96]

Devaluation stimulates exports, as products become cheaper in foreign markets. Conversely, imports become more expensive, as commodity prices in the national currency increase. So how did this work in the case of the Congo and Belgium? By maintaining the link between the two currencies, the Belgian authorities were able to prevent the value of a floating CF from increasing relative to the BF. The immediate impact of this artificial devaluation of the CF was that exports of raw materials from the Congo boomed, to the benefit of the large mining and agricultural export companies. The successive devaluations of the CF, on the other hand, eroded the purchasing power of the Congolese franc and drove up the cost of living in the Congo.

These consequences were immediately apparent after the government's decision in 1919 to set a one-to-one exchange rate between the Congolese franc and the Belgian franc, rather than BF 1.15 or 1.20 to CF 1 as the actual market rate suggested. The ensuing controversy, rather exceptionally, reverberated through parliament. Former Minister of Colonies Renkin openly criticised the decision by his successor, Louis Franck: "The Congolese enterprises were outraged that they had to pay the Bank of Congo BF 120 for CF 100. They pressurised the administration into re-establishing parity between the Congolese and the Belgian currencies. The administration was wrong to give in". The new minister denied the accusation: "No-one put pressure on the government". He argued that unlinking the Belgian and the Congolese francs would have created a barrier between Belgium and its colony. His reasoning went as follows:

One would have allowed the value of the BF to drop to 60 or 50 cents; in the Congo, it would have been worth about 50% of the value of the pound, and what would the consequence of that have been? Anyone exporting 100,000 francs to the Congo would, upon arrival in Boma, retain no more than 50,000 francs. Do you really believe this approach would have encouraged people to set up new businesses? Quite the contrary: the foreigners, whose currency would be on a par with that of the Congo, would have gained an advantage and it would be easy for them to trade with the colony. So had I artificially maintained the barrier between the BF and the CF, I would in effect have supported foreign commerce to the detriment of Belgian trade. (...) I would have damaged relationships between Belgium and the Congo; I would have harmed rather than served Belgian interests.[97]

---

[96] *IIe Congrès colonial belge. Bruxelles, 6 et 7 février 1926* (Brussels, 1926), p. 268.
[97] *Annales parlementaires de la Chambre des Représentants*, 1920–1921, 15 December 1920, pp. 179 and 200.

In an interview in 1925, Franck looked back with satisfaction on his earlier decision, without which "foreign influences in the colony would have been overwhelming".[98] Because of this decision, a great deal of Belgian capital had been directed towards the Congo.

There was another side to the coin though. The decision had a negative impact on the social situation in the Congo, as prices rose and consumers' purchasing power decreased. Civil servants in the colony protested against their deteriorating social position and called for strikes. The local people suffered under the devaluation to the extent that they used money and purchased imported goods. According to Max Horn, an expert on colonial finances, if there had been no devaluation of the CF, "the Colonial Treasury would have had at its disposal considerable reserves that could have been used for social and other expenditures".[99] For decades, the linkage of the Belgian and the Congolese franc would remain controversial. During the National Colonial Congress of 1925, calls were heard for the currencies to be unlinked. More than a decade after his dispute with Franck, Renkin, who was now prime minister, stuck to his previous analysis: "The big mistake was giving up the independence of the CF vis-à-vis the BF. Some companies that borrowed in gold francs benefitted, as they were able to repay in paper money; but on the colony as a whole, this devaluation had an impact that can be felt to this day".[100] In 1940, the Congolese franc was devalued once more, for political reasons rather than out of economic necessity.[101]

During the war, however, prominent businesspeople in the Congo were keen to avoid a repeat of "fatal errors for the Congolese economy". They therefore requested the government to ensure that, after the war, the Congolese franc "would, not automatically and without benefit to the Congolese economy, lose its purchasing power through parity with the Belgian franc".[102] Their request was not met. Shortly after liberation the government restored the exchange parity. Belgium wanted to restrict the Congo's monetary autonomy as much as it could, while the colonial authorities strove for precisely the opposite.[103] The stronger the ties were between the two currencies, the stronger the position of Belgium in the international economic arena. A memo by economist Léon H. Dupriez is quite elucidating in this respect. It dates from 1940, but the analysis has relevance to the entire post-war period: "The positive trade balance of the Congo may be employed to help the metropole, but only if the Congolese franc remains fully linked to the Belgian franc.... The whole will thus benefit

---

[98] Fortis Historical Centre, Brussels, Cattier Papers, n° 2045, note on monetary policy, 1 June 1944, pp. 3–4.
[99] *La politique financière du Congo belge. Rapport ... op. cit.*, p. 146.
[100] AGR, MCM, 6 November 1931.
[101] V. Janssens, *Le Franc belge. Un siècle et demi d'histoire monétaire* (Brussels, 1976), pp. 294–9; H. Van der Wee & M. Verbreyt, *De Nationale Bank van België 1939–1971. Boekdeel 1. Oorlog en monetaire politiek* (Brussels, 2005), pp. 104–5, 385.
[102] *La Dernière Heure*, 18 June 1946, in AMAE, AF-I-1 (1946–7).
[103] W. Pluym & O. Boehme, *De Nationale Bank..., op. cit.*, pp. 375–8.

from the Congolese surpluses".[104] Another memo, drawn up in Belgian financial circles in 1944, is even more enlightening: "The overriding concern in colonial monetary policy is not to create the greatest possible wealth for the colony but rather to contribute to the prosperity of Belgium, which will in turn benefit that of the colony. Congo is Belgian territory. This fact should not be overlooked".[105] Hence, the two currencies would remain linked up to the proclamation of independence in 1960. Did the colony benefit from this situation? An internal memo from 1959 intended for the Belgian government recognised that the Congo "is in fact an integral part of the Belgian currency zone, and experiences some of its drawbacks but not all of its benefits". According to that memo, the existing monetary system had therefore to be changed.[106]

It is clear that the monetary policy had a profound yet diffuse impact on Belgian-Congolese relations. It influenced the internal state of affairs in both the Congo and the metropole. The successive devaluations of the CF had a detrimental impact on the purchasing power of all inhabitants of the Congo, whether natives or colonials, but they also contributed to the development of an industry for consumer goods in the colony. After all, local production diminished the need for imports, which had become more expensive in consequence of the devaluation. The monetary policy also stimulated exports of raw materials to Belgium. Economist Charles Lefort put in clearly in 1954: "Because of Belgium's desire to get the maximum out of its colony, the distinction [between BF and CF] has been blurred to the extent that it has become merely formal".[107]

The Problem of the 'Economic Entanglement' of Belgium and the Congo

Both the statistical data and the political facts cited would seem to indicate that the commodities flow from the Congo towards Belgium was more important than that in the other direction. Indeed, Belgian exports to the colony were confronted with the non-discriminatory policy imposed under the terms of the Saint-Germain-en-Laye Convention, which prohibited preferential treatment of imports from the metropole. In Belgium, these arrangements not always met with applause. It was felt that other colonial powers adhered to the Convention far less strictly.[108] The Belgians bore the entire administrative burden of their colony without benefitting commercially. Foreigners, it seemed, were taking advantage of the Belgians' infrastructure. They were reaping the rewards while Belgium was doing all the hard work. In 1923, a headline in the financial newspaper *L'Echo de la Bourse* asked: "When will we stop being mugs?"[109] The

[104] Cited in H. Van der Wee & M. Verbreyt, *De Nationale Bank, op. cit.*, pp. 45, 586.
[105] Fortis Historical Centre, Brussels, Cattier Papers, n° 2045, note on monetary policy, 23 June 1944, p. 5.
[106] Kadoc, A. De Schryver Papers, n° 11.3.33.2, "Relations monétaires Belgique-Congo", 23 September 1959.
[107] Ch. Lefort, "Essai sur la zone monétaire belge", *Revue économique*, 4 (July 1954), p. 588.
[108] It should be recalled that the Conventional Congo Basin extended well beyond the Belgian Congo.
[109] AA, AE-II, n° 293 (2901), *L'Echo de la Bourse* (13 June 1923).

response was that the Belgian authorities ought to demand that "the others abide by the letter of a treaty that [Belgium] respects meticulously".[110] But was the Convention the only obstacle to the growth of exports from Belgium to the Congo? Certainly not: The issue was much broader.

Publications regarding trade relations between Belgium and the Congo are rife with disconcerting observations. Belgian entrepreneurs were said to show too little interest in the Congo: "Our traders and our industrialists are not making the necessary effort to either produce or sell products that the Belgian Congo consumes".[111] Frans Janssen, a director with the Colonial Office (the trade service of the Ministry of Colonies), was well placed to analyse the problems facing Belgian exports to the Congo.[112] He observed "a real apathy" among many Belgian entrepreneurs as far as the colony was concerned. According to him, many businesses suffered from "the distrust that the colonial still inspires in Belgium".[113] In 1925, he wrote: "Our producers are ignoring their own benefits. The Congolese markets do not interest them".[114] Twelve years on, it was still felt that "the Belgian industrialists [were] defaulting".[115] To many Belgian industrialists, the Congo presented too limited an outlet and they were "not prepared to bear the cost of adapting tools to the production of goods suitable for the colony".[116]

In the Congo itself, traders and consumers were not always satisfied with the products imported from Belgium. They were often more expensive than imports from elsewhere, and their inadequate packaging and unsuitability for the tropics were also criticised: "The dissatisfaction of Katangan traders with the attitude of the Belgian suppliers is one of the principal reasons why preference is given to foreign alternatives. The Congolese market is undervalued by suppliers from the metropole, who are unfamiliar with it and think that anything will do for this backwater and its inhabitants".[117]

The government conducted an incessant campaign to arouse interest in the colony among Belgian investors. The private sector likewise tried to promote exports of finished products. The Association pour le Perfectionnement du Matériel colonial, which was established in 1910 and whose membership

---

[110] *L'Essor colonial et maritime* (16 April 1931) (in AA, AE-II, n° 299 [2902]).
[111] AMAE, AF-I-26 (1928–47), "Note pour M. le Ministre", by O. Louwers, 15 May 1928, p. 5.
[112] That is the department at the Ministry of the Colonies entrusted with promoting colonial trade.
[113] "Le commerce d'exportation vers la colonie. Une conférence de M. Janssen, à la Chambre de Commerce de Bruxelles", *L'Echo de la Bourse*, 3 May 1936 (in AA, Governor-General Papers, [GG Papers], n° 20.474).
[114] F. Janssen, *La réclame commerciale et le placement des produits belges au Congo* (Brussels, 1925), p. 4.
[115] AA, GG Papers, n° 20.474, "Commission coloniale économique permanente. PV de la 6ᵉ séance", 22 March 1937.
[116] AMAE, AF-I-1 (1923–24), "Note pour M. de Ramaix", by O. Louwers, 9 February 1923, p. 4.
[117] AA, GG Papers, n° 19.227, F. Heenen (director of Eastafship, in Beira, Mozambique) to the governor-general in the Congo, 7 January 1936.

would grow to 685 members within two decades, had as its objectives the standardisation of capital goods exported to the colony and the desire to enhance and facilitate their delivery. It focused primarily on goods for the metal industry. "Unfortunately," noted the association after a period during which Belgian exports to the colony had actually boomed, "we cannot but observe and regret that many entrepreneurs and merchants remain deaf to our calls and show too little interest in our work".[118]

During the crisis of the 1930s, the problem took on an additional dimension. Belgian exports, not only to the Congo (see Table 2 in the Appendix), but also to most other markets, were in freefall. In the colony, Belgian products were meeting with greater competition from an expanding local processing industry. Moreover, dumping practices by foreign companies were a growing source of concern. Japanese products in particular were flooding the Congolese market. In the second half of the 1930s, Japan became the second largest importer to the Congo (and the largest to Ruanda-Urundi). In 1937, two-thirds (in value) and three-quarters (in volume) of the Congo's textile imports came from Japan. "Just a few years ago, most of the cotton cloth used in the Congo came from our country" lamented the Belgian textile producers bitterly.[119] Belgian exports had indeed suffered heavily under competition from these Japanese imports. But even the Congolese textile producers felt threatened by this 'yellow danger'.[120]

A number of questions imposed themselves. Was it time for policy measures that would boost trade between Belgium and the Congo? Might the Congo prove the salvation of the ailing Belgian economy? Certainly more and more people were thinking along those lines. In 1934, the Belgian government established the Commission d'Interpénétration économique de la Belgique, du Congo belge et du Ruanda-Urundi. Comprised of colonial civil servants and prominent figures from the economic arena, the commission's purpose was to consider ways of enhancing trade between the metropole and its colony: "We must achieve that Belgium sells more Belgian products in the Congo. Thus, Belgium must enrich the Congo in order that the Congo will in turn enrich Belgium".[121] Would Belgium follow the example of France and Britain and retreat into its colonial empire? It was always an underlying concern of the Belgian authorities that they might lose their grip on the Congo as a result of intensifying foreign economic relations. In return for their massive sales to the Congo, the Japanese promised to buy more Congolese products. The director of the Colonial Office did not take this possibility lightly: If exports to Japan

---

[118] *Association pour le Perfectionnement du Matériel colonial. Congrès de 1930* (Brussels, 1930), p. 24.
[119] AMAE, AF-I-1 (1939–42), Association générale Textile belge to the minister of colonies, 5 January 1939.
[120] AA, AE-II, n° 299 (2902), the Utexléo company to the GG in the Congo, 13 December 1943.
[121] "Rapport sur les travaux de la Commission d'Interpénétration (...)", art. cit., p. 3.

were to grow, "Belgium would increasingly lose control over the Congo and then the problem would become frightening".[122]

After having considered the various products that were imported and exported, the Commission d'Interpénétration concluded that the economies of the Congo and Belgium should cooperate more closely. The commission recommended measures to substitute tropical produce from the colony for imports from elsewhere. Significantly, it added that, in order to attain this goal, Belgium should not change its customs regime. Earlier, Belgium had taken a number of measures to boost imports from the Congo, such as import duties on coffee (1932), sugar, cacao and fruits from elsewhere. Such interventions would, though, remain exceptional. Belgium's government and industry were worried about the prospect of price increases in the domestic market. Moreover, if Belgium were to have closed its borders to produce from other countries, it would have been hit by counter-measures that might have damaged its industry even more seriously.

However, Belgian exports to the colony were a different matter. The Commission d'Interpénétration deplored "the remarkable inadequacy of the Belgian share in Congolese imports". Some commission members openly criticised the Saint-Germain-en-Laye Convention, pointing out that "industrialists [had] expressed surprise at not being offered a preferential regime when importing into the Congo". The commission's final report was less radical, but it still proposed a number of measures for enhancing Belgian exports without violating the Convention. Even before the creation of the commission, the ministry of colonies had been considering 'ways around' the non-discrimination articles.[123]

Yet the Belgian government refused to resort to overt or covert protectionism. Its official position was still that the open door policy was beneficial to the Congo. It was seen to enhance the colony's development and to reduce the cost of living for its inhabitants. More important still, the Saint-Germain-en-Laye Convention had a political significance, for it was "in some ways a guarantee against the appetites of the Great Powers".[124] As mentioned before, because all countries were allowed to trade with the Congo, the larger colonial powers were denied an important argument for demanding a redistribution of the colonies whereby Belgium might lose its overseas territory. Belgian diplomats actually worked towards an expansion of the Convention to all of Africa. The Belgian authorities assumed that this strategy would not only safeguard Belgium's sovereignty over the Congo, but also open up new markets to Belgian business: "It is better for Belgium to hold a small share in trade in large parts of the world under a generalised system of economic freedom and equality than

---

[122] AA, OC, n° 411, director of the Colonial Office to the administrator-general of the colonies, around 1936-7.

[123] AA, AE-II, n° 306-309 (2903), note "La Convention de Saint-Germain-en-Laye et la politique commerciale", 17 November 1933.

[124] AA, AE-II, n° 299 (2902), note (probably) by Halewyck de Heusch, 28 November 1943.

to have a large share in trade with the Congo thanks to protectionist measures that the abolition of the terms of the Convention of Saint-Germain-en-Laye would have allowed us".[125] So the Belgian authorities refused to artificially boost Belgian exports to the Congo. Imports from the colony were deemed more important. The Belgian customs law of 1924, the Congolese customs policy and the monetary policy all contributed to the growing flow of raw materials, the only trade of genuine concern to the large Belgian companies. Hence, the recommendations of the Commission d'Interpénétration about the enhancement of imports from the Congo were followed more meticulously than those about exports to the colony.[126] After reading the commission reports and conversations with commission members, an anonymous colonist said: "I got the impression that the commission was more concerned with increasing Belgian imports of colonial goods than with stimulating Belgian exports to the Congo. When I asked for an explanation of this position, I was told that Belgian industrialists are not interested in the Congo".[127] These words seem to sum it up pretty well.

After the Second World War, the notion of the Belgian-Congolese entanglement persisted, albeit in a different context.[128] The recession had, after all, made way for a strong expansion. Belgium took the decision to modernise the Congo. Large sums of private capital were invested in the colony. The purchasing power of the Congolese population began to rise and an increasing number of Belgian nationals began settling in the colony. Conditions were right for a resumption of Belgian export trade to the Congo – as long as one could stay ahead of foreign competition. The observations from before the war appeared not to be entirely out of date, judging by the report of the Commissioner's Office for the Ten-Year Plan, which was actually devoted to mutual economic dependency between Belgium and the Congo. Foreign competition was most apparent in the field of consumer goods. Belgium "would appear not to have made the necessary efforts to adapt its industry to this kind of production or to gain a firm foothold in the Congolese market". Reference is made to the high price of many Belgian products, and to the "lack of method" among Belgian producers, "who come and go on the Congolese market as they see fit, and who consider it as a second-hand market that is only of interest to them when trade to the traditional markets slackens".[129] In the course of the 1950s, a number of Belgian employers' organisations tried to increase their influence in the

---

[125] AMAE, AF-I-1 (1943-45), "La Conférence de San Francisco et la question coloniale", from O. Louwers, 15 March 1945, p. 17.

[126] AA, AE-II, GG Papers, n° 20.474, "Rapport sur les conclusions des travaux de la Commission (...)", s.d.

[127] J. B., "L'interpénétration économique Belgique-Congo", *L'Avenir colonial belge* (21 June 1935), p. 1 (in AA, GG Papers, n° 20.474).

[128] In 1951, a permanent commission was set up to coordinate the Belgian and the Congolese economies (the installation followed in September 1952).

[129] Commissariat au Plan décennal, *Interpénétration économique de la Belgique et du Congo belge* (Léopoldville, 1953), pp. 6, 9, 12, 16, 18.

Congo. They set up missions and established permanent offices in the colony. The federation of the chemical industry, for example, asserted that "the Belgian exporters should abandon their ostrich policy of merely frequenting purchasing offices in Belgium while foreigners are more active in the Congo itself".[130] The Federation of Belgian Industries (Fédération des Industries belges), the national and multi-sector employers' organisation, in turn organised prospecting missions to the Congo.[131] Equally notable are the initiatives of the metal industry, driven primarily by the influential association Fabrimetal. The Congo would actually become this industry's primary export market.[132]

Indeed, the strong growth of Belgian exports to the Congo between 1947 and 1957 was mostly attributable to the metal industry. Between 1947 and 1950, equipment and production goods accounted for seventy-eight per cent (in value) of Congolese imports from Belgium, while consumer goods represented just twenty-two per cent. In that same period, the metropole supplied forty-eight per cent of all production goods imported by the Congo. Of all consumer goods imported into the Congo, only twenty per cent came from Belgium.[133] Still, Belgian exports to the Congo declined drastically during the final three years of the colonial era.

The Congo and Belgium's Economic Fabric

How did the economic relationship between Belgium and the Congo impact Belgium's economic structures?[134] The sector-related aspects depended on the general structure of the Belgian economy, which in turn bore the mark of the Congo Free State.

The Relative Weight of the Major Colonial Corporate Groups
When it came to initial investments in the Congo, Belgian capital needed encouragement from Leopoldian circles. The exceptional circumstances under which the Belgian economy became economically involved in the Congo explain the huge role that certain private companies came to play in the colony. While independent small and medium-sized companies of Belgian (or Greek, Portuguese or any other) origin also descended on the Congo and helped define its social fabric, from a macroeconomic perspective they had hardly any impact at all. It was a handful of large corporations that represented Belgium's economic interests in the Congo. The first Belgian companies in the Congo were established

---

[130] *Rapport de la mission de l'industrie chimique au Congo belge et au Ruanda-Urundi. Juillet 1955* (S.l.n.d.), p. 11.
[131] See "Rapport de la mission de la FIB au Congo belge et au Ruanda-Urundi, 26 avril – 19 mai 1957", *Bulletin de la FIB*, 12, 31 (10 December 1957), pp. 2179–208; R. Pulinckx, "Les échanges belgo-congolais", *Industrie. Revue de la FIB*, 3, 5 (May 1949), pp. 336–9.
[132] *Fabrimetal*, 325 (15 September 1952), p. 731.
[133] Ch. Didier, *Les relations commerciales, op. cit.*, pp. 129–30.
[134] Two descriptive studies from that period: G. Hostelet, "L'importance du Congo belge dans l'économie de la Belgique", *Bulletin de la Société royale de Géographie d'Anvers*, 62 (1948), 1–2, pp. 68–92 and M. A. G. Van Meerhaeghe, "De economische betekenis van Kongo voor België", *Tijdschrift voor de Belgische Handel*, 69, 10 (October 1955), pp. 15–24.

from scratch. Initially small, they would eventually grow more influential, particularly in the early twentieth century when the large Belgian financial groups began to follow in their footsteps. Nineteen hundred and six was a pivotal year in this respect, as this was when the Société générale de Belgique (SGB) entered the fray.[135] The consequences were momentous for both the colony and Belgium. A number of powerful mixed banks, not least the SGB, held important parcels of shares in various sectors of Belgium's economy, including the coal, metal, glass and electricity industries. Consequently, these financial groups had a significant impact on the national economy. In the latter years of the Congo Free State, colonial activity was grafted onto this internal Belgian power structure. This graft worked surprisingly well, exceeding all expectations.

The impact of these mixed banks/holdings in the Congo can hardly be overemphasised. These financial groups controlled most large companies in the colony.[136] According to an estimate from 1934, some 6.4 billion of the 8.3 billion Belgian francs invested in the Congo were in the hands of four large groups: the SGB, Empain, Bank of Brussels and Cominière. The SGB alone accounted for 5.4 billion. In other words, Belgian financial commitments in the Congo were highly concentrated and depended entirely on a limited number of central command posts. Various holdings and sub-holdings, such as the Compagnie du Katanga and the CCCI, controlled a wide range of Congolese enterprises and operated in all economic sectors (transport, finance, agriculture, mining, energy production, real estate, etc.).

In Belgium, the concentration of capital meant that there were few independent links with the colony. Outside the playing field defined and controlled by the mixed banks/holdings, few *large* Belgian enterprises maintained strong ties with the Congo. This explains why decision makers in the metropole were not particularly interested in Belgian exports to the colony. One of the exceptions was the textile industry, which remained beyond the sphere of influence of the mixed banks/holdings. Consequently, when the textile industry experienced problems in its export trade, as we have just seen, it was unable to influence trade policy. At the other end of the spectrum was the Belgian metal industry, deeply embedded in companies controlled by the banks/holdings. This sector strongly influenced the export policy in the Congo, where it equipped companies and supplied materials for the development of a transport infrastructure.

The activities that the financial groups developed in the Congo also had an influence on the metropolitan economic structure and activities. First, it was under the influence of the colony that the degree of financial concentration in Belgium increased.[137] The first colonial enterprises (the Thys group[138]) sought a rapprochement with the SGB and would eventually merge with it. The Banque

---

[135] R. Brion & J.-L. Moreau, *La Société générale, op. cit.*

[136] L. Delmotte, *De Belgische koloniale holdings* (Leuven, 1946); F. Buelens, *Congo 1885–1960, op. cit.*

[137] R. J. Lemoine, "Finances et colonisation", art. cit. and "La concentration des entreprises en Belgique ", *Revue économique internationale* (June 1929).

[138] This was the first group of colonial enterprises founded in Belgium, essentially by the king's collaborator, Albert Thys (see Chapter 2).

d'Outremer, established by the Thys group in 1899, had a considerable colonial shareholding. In 1928, it was taken over by the SGB, which thus became the prime economic player in the Congo.[139] In 1924, the country's second bank, the Banque de Bruxelles, rearranged its colonial shares, integrating them into a new company called Crédit général du Congo.[140]

Second, the Congolese adventure resulted in closer ties between government and the business community. As we have seen, the Congolese and Belgian authorities played a decisive role in the establishment of large colonial enterprises. Belgian investors only became interested in the colony after the colonial government started participating and/or agreed to provide financial assistance. As a result, the public and the private sectors became entangled. This typically Congolese approach also left its mark in Belgium. The entanglement of government and private capital had consequences for both partners. The colonial authorities held substantial shares in innumerable colonial enterprises. This portfolio would come to play an instrumental role in relations between Belgium and the independent Congo from 1960 onwards. However, the public sector entrusted the management of these enterprises to experts from the private sector, thus providing a powerful means of leverage. The influence of the mixed banks and holdings increased accordingly. More than ever before, they were now the government's privileged partners.

Third, events in the Congo obviously had an impact on the internal structure of the financial groups. Colonial activities were added to the range of industries within which the banks and holdings had, for varying lengths of time, been operating. Consequently, the organisational charts of those companies, and the SGB in particular, became a lot more complex. Connections emerged between the different branches as, for example, activities in the Congo influenced the transport and metal industries. This point is essential for a proper understanding of how the colony influenced Belgium's economic sectors. The relative importance of the colonial activities in the share portfolios held by the holdings and mixed banks grew. The example of the SGB speaks for itself. In 1911, the colonial stocks accounted for 3.7 per cent of the total market value of the company's share portfolio; by 1929, after the merger with the Banque d'Outremer, this proportion had risen to 13.7 per cent, only to grow further to a huge 43.7 per cent by 1952. By the eve of independence, the proportion of colonial holdings had fallen to 24.1 per cent.[141]

Colonial Business: Stock Market Activities and Profits
The question of the profitability of colonial investments is a major theme in international historical research. Once again, British historians have taken the lead. According to Davis and Huttenback, investments in the empire were more

---

[139] G. Kurgan-van Hentenryk, "La Société générale ...", *op. cit.*, pp. 239–44.
[140] J. M. Moitroux et al., *Une banque dans l'histoire. De la Banque de Bruxelles (...) à la BBL* (Brussels, 1995), pp. 70–1.
[141] R. Brion & J.-L. Moreau, *La Société générale*, pp. 273, 390.

profitable than investments at home before the mid-1880s, but this was not at all the case in the period before the First World War. Other historians, however, have questioned their method and conclusions.[142] Reviewing all the evidence, Andrew Thompson concludes that "[It] is hard (...) to make a convincing case for the superiority of colonial over either domestic or foreign investment".[143] Examining the French case, Jacques Marseille observes, conversely, that colonial enterprises offered "very decent" profits during the inter-war period.[144] Pierre van der Eng's careful analysis of the benefits generated by the Dutch empire in Asia provides yet another conclusion: "The returns on the actual amounts of foreign capital invested in Indonesia were not extraordinarily high".[145] How does the Belgian evidence fit into this complex picture?

During the colonial period, several Belgian observers and actors tried to evaluate the profitability of colonial investments. Unfortunately, but quite understandably, these attempts were not free of economic and political bias. Clearly, public opinion was divided over the issue of colonial interests. Business circles and conservative commentators tended to minimise the profitability of private investments in the Congo, while official sources and progressive analysts tended to make the opposite claim. One such study compared the sales value of Congolese enterprises in the period 1913–39.[146] Mining, which in 1939 accounted for seventy-one per cent of the market value of Congolese enterprises, was found to have a yield that was "exceptionally high in such turbulent times. It was primarily thanks to mining shares that Congolese corporations were able to count on such a satisfactory yield". The results of industrial corporations (which were established in the colony more recently) appear to have been "satisfactory, especially relative to the yield of comparable Belgian industries".[147] At the other end of the spectrum, we find the plantation industry, which recorded a negative yield.

Another study, dating from 1946, measures the profitability (defined as the ratio of profits or losses on the capital) of all Congolese enterprises from their establishment up to 1938. This study mentions a very good profitability for mining (+17.1 per cent) and banks (+16.6 per cent) and less favourable but still

---

[142] L. E. Davis & R. A. Huttenback, *Mammon and the Pursuit of Empire: The Political Economy of British Imperialism, 1860–1912* (Cambridge, 1986); A. R. Dilley, "The Economics of Empire", art. cit., pp. 117–8.

[143] A. S. Thompson, *The Empire Strikes Back? The Impact of Imperialism on Britain from the Mid-Nineteenth Century* (Harlow-London, 2005), pp. 162–4 (citation p. 164).

[144] J. Marseille, *Empire colonial et capitalisme français* (Paris, 1984), p. 113.

[145] P. van der Eng, *Economic Benefits from Colonial Assets: The Case of the Netherlands and Indonesia 1870–1958* (Groningen, 1998), p. 23 (http://ideas.repec.org/p/dgr/rugggd/199839.html).

[146] G. Van de Velde, *Le rendement des placements (1865–1939)* (Leuven, 1944). The author of this study compares the evolution of the market price of different kinds of investment (including corporate stocks, such as colonial shares) between two given dates. So the term used in this book's title ('rendement') does not correspond with the traditional sense of that word in French, 'return on investment'.

[147] G. Van de Velde, *Le rendement*, op. cit., pp. 400, 458 and 460.

positive results for industrial enterprises (+3.7 per cent), with negative figures for plantations (-13.9 per cent), agricultural enterprises (-21.5 per cent), real estate firms (-8.2 per cent) and trading companies (-5.7 per cent). Analysing these figures in 1946, economist Fernand Baudhuin drew a rather negative conclusion: "Congo has not yielded as huge a profit as is often imagined. Its profitability has been modest, especially for a young country. In reality, the profitability of enterprises and investments has been considerably lower than is generally assumed".[148] Robert Godding, a businessman who would himself become minister of colonies in 1945, asked the then minister of colonies to draw up an overview of the capital invested in the Congo and the profits and losses made between 1885 and 1939. It emerged that the 1.9 billion gold francs invested generated 660 million francs, an average yield of 2.85 per cent per annum, "which is not excessive by anyone's standards" according to the minister, who called the results "rather disappointing".[149]

Other studies disagree. Governor-General Pierre Ryckmans, who was not particularly popular among business circles, claimed that, in a thirteen-year period (1927-39), the Belgian Congolese enterprises made a net profit of 7.8 billion on a fully paid capital of 7.2 billion: "They paid 835 million in taxes, or less than 12% of the total. During that same period, the Congo paid 5.3 billion in dividends to Belgian shareholders".[150] The Central Bank of the Belgian Congo regularly scrutinised the balances of the Congolese enterprises.[151] According to these studies, the profitability of the Congolese companies is "significantly higher than that of companies in Belgium or abroad" and may be characterised as "exceptionally high". Between 1951 and 1956, the ratio between dividends and assets fluctuated between 4.4 per cent and 5.3 per cent in Belgium, compared to between 11.6 per cent and 13.1 per cent in the Congo.[152] The Belgian Ministry of Economic Affairs used to publish similar statistics, which became widely disseminated after their inclusion in a book by communist journalists Pierre Joye and Rosine Lewin. These data showed that the profitability of investments in the Congo was far greater than that of investments in Belgium (see Table 4.4).[153]

These figures were disputed in business circles. According to the leadership of the SGB, some qualification was called for, as the results varied strongly from sector to sector. "The average profitability is highly dependent on the

---

[148] Preface by Baudhuin in H. de Villenfagne de Loën, *Études sur les problèmes coloniaux* (Brussels, 1946), pp. 5–6; M. Van de Putte, *Le Congo belge et la politique de conjoncture* (Brussels, 1946), p. 50 sq.: net profits and losses in per cent of capital paid from 1927 to 1939: 32.3 / 18.6 / 16.6 / 12.2 / 3.7 / -0.5 / -5.0 / -1.7 / -2.8 / 6.9 / 12.5 / 16.0 / 11.4.

[149] R. Godding, "Aspects de la politique économique et sociale du Congo belge", *Bulletin de la Société royale de Géographie d'Anvers*, 61, 1 (1946-7), p. 34.

[150] P. Ryckmans, *Étapes et jalons, op. cit.*, p. 216.

[151] This public institution was established in 1951-2 to supersede the Bank of the Belgian Congo as an issuing institution.

[152] *BBCCBRU*, 7, 1 (January 1958), pp. 14–5.

[153] Ministry of Economic Affairs, *L'économie belge en 1957, op. cit.*, pp. 316–7; P. Joye & R. Lewin, *Les trusts au Congo* (Brussels, 1961), p. 57.

TABLE 4.4. *Net Profits as a Ratio of Capital and Reserves*

Year	In Belgium	In the Congo
Average for 1936–39	7.00 %	10.10 %
Average for 1947–50	6.88 %	15.07 %
Average for 1951–54	8.20 %	21.48 %
1955	8.19 %	18.47 %
1956	9.40 %	20.16 %
1957	9.49 %	21.00 %
1958	7.85 %	15.10 %

wealth of just a few companies, most specifically mining corporations such as UMHK and Minière du BCK. If these companies are left out of the equation, the difference in profitability and payment of dividend between Belgian and Congolese companies is significantly smaller". Business circles also noted that the profitability of Belgian companies was much lower than that of British and American corporations. Therefore, the profit ratios of the Congolese enterprises were not 'excessive', but comparable to those recorded in other countries.[154] It was further pointed out that part of the profits of these large corporations flowed to the government, as it was a major stakeholder.

Obviously, profitability varied from sector to sector; some, including the most important of all, namely the mining industry, would appear to have generated substantial profits that were probably higher than those recorded in Belgium. This holds in particular for large companies such as UMHK. Economist André Huybrechts confirms this conclusion in a 1970 study. However, after finding that the profitability of the domestic Congolese transport industry was generally modest, he asserts that "the other industries ... recorded a variable but generally very good profitability (up to twenty-six per cent in 1951) that exceeded that of companies in Belgium".[155]

A recent contribution by economist Frans Buelens has closed the debate once and for all. After a thorough analysis of the performance of colonial shares on the stock exchange, he came to the conclusion that, overall, colonial companies fared much better than their Belgian counterparts. According to him, "the Congolese economy was a goldmine for the Belgian investors".[156] The yields of the Congolese mining companies were especially impressive. They ranked amongst the world's best financial performers.

[154] Both quotations are from the same source: AGR, Finoutremer, n° 2052, "PV nr. 769 du Comité intérieur colonial de la SGB du 3 juillet 1958", pp. 3-4. A similar opinion came from 1946 in *Revue coloniale belge*, the mouthpiece of private investors (1 September and 1 November 1946, pp. 146 and 277).

[155] A. Huybrechts, *Transports et structures de développement au Congo* (Paris-The Hague, 1970), p. 127.

[156] F. Buelens, *Congo 1885–1960, op. cit.*, p. 581–604 (quotation p. 599); F. Buelens & S. Marysse, "Returns on Investment during the Colonial Era: The Case of the Belgian Congo", *Economic History Review*, 62, S1 (2009), pp. 135–66.

The breakthrough of colonial businesses into Belgium's economy was of course also felt on the stock market. The period from 1896 to 1898 saw the establishment of numerous Congolese companies. This sudden input by the colony generated a speculative wave on the bourse, leading to the crisis of Congolese securities in 1900 and 1901.[157] Many undertakings went bankrupt and even 'serious' companies experienced great difficulties. But the slide did not prevent Congolese stocks from continuing to occupy a prominent place on the Belgian stock exchange in the years and decades to come. This was not unlike the development in Great Britain, where colonial shares played an increasing role on the stock exchange, either as 'safe' investments, or as speculative items.[158] In the early 1950s, they accounted for between ten per cent and seventeen and a half per cent of trade and twenty per cent to thirty-five per cent of the value on the Brussels bourse.[159] The colony was unquestionably important to the Belgian stock market. However, the question arises whether colonial stocks were also popular beyond capitalist circles, among the general public. Estimations, primarily by contemporaries, suggest they were.[160] Shares in the leading colonial enterprises, such as UMHK or the Kilo Moto gold mines, were seen to offer a safe and lucrative investment opportunity. Nonetheless, such colonial shares were not impervious to irrational value fluctuations, in both the positive and the negative sense. Towards the end of the 1920s, speculative fever pushed the colonial shares up to dizzying heights, followed by a crash in subsequent years. A top business leader testified: "Capitalists who had, without giving it much thought, bought 'Katangas' for 170,000 francs were now selling for 12,000 without good explanation. Shares in *Union minière* dropped from 13,000 to 1,200 francs".[161] In 1935, the managers of the SGB reiterated that mining shares were overvalued.[162]

The Impact of the Congo on the Various Sectors of the Belgian Economy
We can now briefly examine how the Congo affected the different sectors of the Belgian economy. The basic outlines of this impact become apparent in a brief reiteration of previously made observations: The Congo and Belgium were connected by a substantial flow of raw materials, especially minerals and a number of agricultural products; the metropole redistributed many of these goods, be it directly or in a processed form; a number of powerful holding companies, closely linked with the government, stamped their mark on colonial

---

[157] B. S. Chlepner, *La marché financier belge depuis cent ans* (Brussels, 1930), pp. 83, 91.
[158] A. S. Thompson, *The Empire, op. cit.*, pp. 163–5.
[159] "L'évolution du marché des valeurs coloniales", *BBCCBRU*, 3, 6 (April 1954), pp. 153–4; "L'évolution du marché des valeurs coloniales en 1954–1955", *BBCCBRU*, 4, 6–7 (June-July 1955), p. 259.
[160] For example H. de Villenfagne de Loën, *Études sur les problèmes coloniaux, op. cit.*, p. 15.
[161] E. Van der Straeten, "Les sociétés coloniales dans la vie économique et sociale du Congo", *[Bulletin mensuel de la] Société royale des Ingénieurs et Industriels*, 5 (1937), p. 453.
[162] AGR, Finoutremer, n° 798, "PV n° 279 du Comité intérieur colonial de la SGB", 24 October 1935, p. 2.

economic activities; Belgian exports to the Congo, which were less substantial than imports, consisted primarily of metal production goods and the Congo was never a mass market for Belgium's consumer goods industry. The principal sectors of industry affected by the colonial trade were international transportation (port operations, maritime business and air transport), the diamond industry and the non-ferrous metal industry. The name of the SGB, a company that succeeded in just a matter of years in developing a conglomerate of colonial subsidiaries, crops up regularly in this context.

The port of Antwerp is undoubtedly the first Belgian player to have felt the impact of the budding economic ties between the Congo and Belgium. Just a few years after the foundation of the Congo Free State, the Belgian seaport became the leading global market for ivory. Trade expanded from 46,500 kg in 1889 (compared to 301,000 kg in London) to 336,000 kg in 1900 (320,000 kg in London). Antwerp also became a prime cobalt hub, with ninety per cent of global production originating in the Congo. The rubber trade likewise boomed: In 1889, Antwerp handled 4,600 kg of rubber, compared to 5.8 million kg by 1901. (This was, however, still not as much as either Liverpool or Hamburg.)[163] As years went by, rubber would decline in relative importance to Antwerp, partly because of reduced extraction and partly because other colonial goods were increasingly shipped around the world via the Belgian port. After all, many of the goods imported from the Congo were intended for other destinations. Antwerp's role as a global transit hub for Congolese goods generated additional business for Belgian trading firms. For the time being, we lack sufficiently accurate data to properly assess the impact of the colony on this branch of Belgium's economic activity. Still, the Congo's share in Belgian port traffic should not be overestimated (see Table 4.5).[164]

Of the total tonnage arriving at or departing from Belgian ports (of which Antwerp is obviously the biggest), just a small fraction is connected with the colony. Not until the 1930s would the threshold exceed one per cent. If we consider goods arriving in the port of Antwerp, we see that, in 1934, the Congo accounted for 2.23 per cent in terms of tonnage and 6.10 per cent in terms of value. The export percentages are even lower: 0.71 per cent in terms of tonnage and 2.10 per cent in terms of value.[165] Clearly, the port of Antwerp continued to be strongly oriented towards global maritime traffic, with the colony occupying a modest, even a marginal, position.

However, these kinds of statistics offer no more than a partial insight into the relationship between the port city and the Congo. For his first economic projects, Leopold II relied fully on the Antwerp business community, whose presence would continue to be felt after the Leopoldian era had come to a close. Numerous important 'Congolese' undertakings were headquartered in

---

[163] M. Van de Velde, *Économie belge, op. cit.*, pp. 160–72.
[164] *Annuaire statistique de la Belgique et du Congo belge* (Brussels, 1895–1939). There are no statistics beyond that year.
[165] M. Van de Velde, *Économie belge, op. cit.*, p. 173.

TABLE 4.5. *The Congo's Share (in %) in Belgian Port Activity (1895–1939)*

Year	Arriving vessels: Number	Arriving vessels: Tonnage	Departing vessels: Number	Departing vessels: Tonnage
1895	0.17	0.37	0.18	0.43
1905	0.19	0.41	0.20	0.42
1920	0.23	0.66	0.22	0.58
1925	0.26	0.58	0.34	0.70
1930	0.44	1.00	0.49	1.12
1935	0.30	0.74	0.32	0.74
1939	0.70	1.77	0.71	1.79

Antwerp. The Antwerp Chamber of Commerce, the lobby group of the local commercial and industrial firms, was an early supporter of Leopold's Congolese adventure.[166] More so than any other Belgian city, Antwerp epitomised the link between Belgium and its colony. Before the age of commercial aviation, most Belgians travelled to the colony on the so-called Congo boats, which sailed from Antwerp. Every departure and arrival attracted crowds of relatives and friends to the quays along the river Scheldt.

However, at the proclamation of the Congo Free State, Belgium's merchant fleet was not particularly well developed.[167] Originally, therefore, people and equipment were shipped to the colony on foreign ships, sometimes sailing from foreign ports. This situation was quite illustrative of the artificial nature of the ties between Belgium and the Congo. In 1886, the Compagnie gantoise de Navigation was established, probably at the insistence of Leopold II. It was supposed to operate a service between Antwerp and Boma, but was closed down the following year. In 1888, the king signed a deal with British shipping companies specialising in services to East Africa for the inclusion of Antwerp and Banana on their routes. However, Leopold and Belgian entrepreneurs didn't give up their dream of a Belgian company connecting Antwerp with the Congo. Eventually, in 1895, two shipping companies were founded: the Compagnie belge maritime du Congo (CBMC) and the Société maritime du Congo (SMC). The investment capital was partly Belgian and the vessels would sail under the Belgian flag, but in fact the companies in question were subsidiaries of large British and German shipping companies. SMC stopped running in 1901, while CBMC was thoroughly restructured in 1911. The British firm that had previously held almost all the shares sold most of its holdings. The Banque d'Outremer acquired sixty per cent while the rest remained in the hands of British and German shipping companies. The early twentieth century was an era of transition for the Belgian maritime sector. Between 1916 and 1920, various other shipping companies were founded. These would eventually merge in

---

[166] G. Devos & I. Van Damme, *In de ban van Mercurius. Twee eeuwen Kamer van Koophandel en Nijverheid van Antwerpen-Waasland 1802–2002* (Tielt, 2002), pp. 130–2.
[167] G. Devos & G. Elewaut, *CMB 100: A Century of Commitment to Shipping* (Tielt, 1995).

the course of 1929 and 1930 to form the Compagnie maritime belge (CMB). This company, belonging to the SGB group, would become the most important player in the Belgian maritime transport market.

Unlike its precursor, CMB served destinations other than the Congo. Nonetheless, the colony accounted for about two-thirds of its activities.[168] Except between 1931 and 1935, CMB proved to be a profitable venture, with traffic to the Congo the main source of revenue. Agreements with other shipping companies protected CMB against the vicissitudes of competition. Deals with Congolese companies and the colonial authorities guaranteed stable and advantageous conditions. The connection between Belgium and the Congo (and vice versa) that was used by all passengers and goods was, therefore, a protected domain. Thanks to the Congo, Belgium gained a modest foothold in the global shipping market, an area where it had previously not played a prominent role. Moreover, the activities of CMB had a trickle-down effect on other industries of the national economy. Most of CMB's vessels, for example, were constructed at Belgian shipyards. CMB also took the lead in related business activities, such as ship repair and shipping agencies, further enhancing the prestige and importance of the company. Thus, the impact of CMB extended far beyond its own workforce of approximately 3,000 Belgians and 900 Congolese in 1960.

To an extent, similar developments occurred in aviation.[169] After the First World War, the rise of air transport opened up possibilities. The business community immediately understood the significance of this new mode of transportation. In 1919, with assistance from other financial institutions, the Banque d'Outremer established the Société nationale pour l'Étude des Transports aériens (SNETA). SNETA focused primarily on the possibility of commercial aviation in Europe, though it also looked at the Congo. Thanks to moral and financial support from King Albert I, the first commercial air connection to the colony was launched in 1920-1. After numerous disappointments and endless negotiations, SNETA, the Belgian state and the Congo reached agreement on the creation of a new national airline company called Société anonyme belge d'Exploitation de la Navigation aérienne, or Sabena (1923). It was founded according to the system of 'mixed' Congolese companies. The Belgian and Congolese governments were the majority stakeholders, with management in the hands of representatives working for private investors. Public authorities would provide the required funds to allow the company to function properly. Sabena operated flights in Europe, but also contributed to the development of air transport in the Congo, where the company succeeded in just a few years in developing an efficient and comprehensive network of services. The first flight from Brussels to Léopoldville, by pilot Edmond Thieffry in 1925,

---

[168] AGR, SGB-3, n° 166, "Rappel des activités maritimes – et de la CMB en particulier – avant les événements", p. 1.
[169] G. Vanthemsche, *La Sabena et l'aviation commerciale belge 1923–2001. Des origines au crash* (Brussels, 2001).

was primarily of symbolic significance. It would take another ten years before regular commercial flights became available between Belgium and the Congo. After the Second World War, the route quickly gained in stature, becoming the jewel in the company's crown.

Sabena held a monopoly on regularly scheduled flights between Belgium and the Congo and within the colony. This privileged and protected status proved to be quite lucrative. Services to and within the Congo were a good source of revenue and soon became the mainstay of the company's operations. However, they were not sufficient to cover losses incurred on other connections. Sabena would return profits only in 1944-7, 1951-2 and 1955-7. Every other year it operated in the red, surviving by the grace of public funding. The company continued to be partly privately and partly publicly owned, though its actual management was in the hands of the private shareholders.

Over the years, the Société générale de Belgique gained influence, particularly after the Second World War when Gilbert Périer was appointed director. The close ties between the various sectors is also apparent from the fact that André de Spirlet, the managing director of CMB from 1947 to 1973, was also the principal representative of the private shareholders on the Sabena board; he was also responsible for the transport section of the SGB. After the Second World War, Sabena gained control over the small airline company Sobelair, which primarily operated charter flights to the Congo. With a workforce of ten thousand, Sabena was one of Belgium's biggest employers.

Antwerp and the Congo were also connected through the diamond industry.[170] Diamonds were first extracted in the Congo, in Tshikapa (Kasai), in 1907. During the inter-war period, the Congo became the world's number one producer of industrial diamonds, thanks to the activities of large concerns such as Forminière and Société minière du Bécéka. In 1948, the capital of Forminière was primarily in the hands of the Congolese government (fifty-five per cent), the U.S. Ryan-Guggenheim group (twenty-five per cent) and the SGB (four per cent). Despite the SGB's minor shareholding, its representatives ruled the roost. Shortly before the outbreak of the First World War, Congolese diamonds started arriving in Antwerp, which had already established itself as an important diamond centre. After the war, Forminière began to sell gems directly from Antwerp without passing through London, previously the heart of the global trade in raw diamonds. This was seen as a threat to the international monopoly and the cartel (De Beers and the London Syndicate) that controlled the production of and global trade in raw diamonds. In 1926, a deal was struck with Forminière and other Congolese producers. It came at a time when the market had been shaken by overproduction and price declines, leading to bankruptcies and unemployment, particularly in Antwerp. The partners were keen to avoid chaos in the global production and sales network for

---

[170] E. Laureys, *Meesters van het diamant. De Belgische diamantsector tijdens het nazibewind* (Tielt, 2006); O. De Bruyn, *Histoires de diamants: la Société minière du Bécéka au Congo* (Brussels, 2006).

diamonds. The Belgian colonial firms agreed to sell exclusively to the London Syndicate, which in turn pledged to give priority to supplying Antwerp – even with diamonds from elsewhere than the Congo. In sum, the Belgian Congolese companies adapted to the existing system and further enhanced the regulation of the global diamond trade.

The Antwerp diamond industry, which had existed before the colonisation of the Congo, benefitted from the system of regulation and protection. It expanded from four thousand employees in 1932 to twelve thousand by 1936 to between twenty-three thousand and twenty-five thousand by 1940. At this point, Antwerp was outperforming the other European diamond centres, including Amsterdam. When Antwerp's position was seriously threatened by the Nazi occupation, swift action by the industry and the authorities, backed by De Beers and the London trading partners, averted the danger. After the Second World War, Antwerp regained its status as one of the world's leading centres for the processing and trading of diamonds. Obviously this dominant position was due largely to the weight of the Belgian Congolese concerns involved.

Other raw materials from the Congo, such as non-ferrous metals, were also of great importance to Belgian industry.[171] Since the early nineteenth century, Belgium had had a non-ferrous metal industry centred particularly on zinc production in the province of Liège. However, 100 years later, the local mining areas were becoming exhausted and increasingly large quantities of raw materials had to be imported. This went hand in hand with a relocation of the non-ferrous industry to Antwerp at a time when there was no question yet of imports from the Congo. The breakthrough came in the inter-war years, as the colony rose to prominence and came to account for the lion's share of global tin, copper, cobalt and uranium production. The largest part went to Belgium. This flow of trade injected new dynamism into existing companies and formed the basis for the establishment of new factories. In 1917, the SGB acquired a majority stake in the Compagnie industrielle Union, a modest company that had, since its foundation in 1908, operated a number of plants in the Campines (a region in the north of Belgium near Antwerp). Under the impulse of the SGB, Compagnie industrielle Union had been processing Congolese ores since 1911. A substantial recapitalisation in 1919 coincided with the renaming of the firm as the Société générale métallurgique de Hoboken (SGMH).[172] SGMH would soon rise to prominence in the SGB's industrial empire as its rapidly developing plants in Antwerp and in the Campines began to process ores such as tin, copper and uranium.

Through a complex strategy of mergers and participation in new companies, the non-ferrous activities of the SGB expanded and included the development of the Compagnie des Métaux d'Overpelt-Lommel, Corphalie (zinc) and

---

[171] Conseil professionnel du Métal, *Avis sur l'évolution des rapports entre les industries congolaise et belge de l'étain, du zinc et du cuivre* (S.l.n.d. [1958]).

[172] *Société générale métallurgique de Hoboken 1908–1958* (Brussels, 1957).

the Société générale des Minerais (for the commercialisation of the products). By now, Belgium's industry was almost entirely dependent upon the Congo for its supply of raw materials (in 1951, ninety per cent of all cobalt and tin and seventy per cent of all copper). After processing in Belgium, the ores were re-exported. At the same time, the colony was increasingly processing its own raw materials, especially after the Second World War. This explains why, by independence, the Congo's share in the supply of certain Belgian factories had declined. In 1951, some thirty-four per cent of concentrated zinc ore came from the Congo, compared to just thirteen per cent by 1957. This trend was reinforced by the fact that, in 1951, the SGB established a company in Canada that processed ores from elsewhere.[173] This conglomerate of enterprises and activities in the non-ferrous metal industry had some impact on the Belgian economy. The employment figures speak for themselves. In 1930, the non-ferrous industry employed 10,783 people; by 1967 the workforce had grown to 19,416. Belgium's involvement in the production, processing and commercialisation of Congolese ores meant it now occupied a significant place in the global market. The Belgian Congolese enterprises were part of international cartels specialising in copper, tin or cobalt, and had become important players in the industry. By 1956, Belgium's non-ferrous metal industry was second only to that of the United States. That same year, Belgium also topped the global rankings in terms of exports.[174] Between the wars, the country saw a remarkable breakthrough in its radium industry. The first batch of uranium ore arrived in Belgium in December 1921; barely half a year later there was an operational radium plant at Olen and it would not be long before Belgium's radium industry had developed to global proportions. By 1927, Belgium was already producing 180 grammes of radium out of a world production of 506 grammes.[175] After the Second World War, uranium from the Congo constituted the basis for Belgium's nuclear power programme.

The mark of colonialism was less evident in other areas of economic activity in Belgium, and certainly in other industrial sectors. The relationship between the colony and a particular activity in the national economic fabric was determined by either the export flows or the supply of raw materials. Towards the end of the 1920s and in the early 1950s, the only companies to export substantial amounts to the Congo were metal construction firms. In 1953, the colony accounted for 8.7 per cent of the total value of Belgian metal exports. In the sub-sectors 'machines and electro-technical materials' and 'transport materials' the share increased to respectively 18.9 and 20.9 per cent. By contrast, the value of Belgian textile exports (1953) to the Congo amounted to just 1.8 per cent of the total. The chemical industry performed little better, with 3.3 per cent.

---

[173] G. Kurgan-van Hentenryk & J. Laureyssens, *Un siècle d'investissements belges au Canada* (Brussels, 1986).
[174] R. Evalenko, *Régime économique de la Belgique* (Brussels, 1968), p. 418.
[175] A. Adams, *Het ontstaan en de ontwikkeling van de radiumindustrie in België* (Ghent, 1988), unpublished master's thesis in history, University of Ghent, pp. 49, 90, 225.

The non-ferrous metal industry is an atypical example of how Belgian enterprises were supplied with Congolese raw materials.[176] If one considers only those import flows for which the Congo was a supplier alongside other countries, one notices that the colony accounted for forty per cent of the total value of raw materials. However, an analysis per product reveals considerable variation. For ores in general, the proportion was fifty percent, but the proportion declined to an average of twenty percent for agricultural produce. Within the latter group, there is again quite a bit of variation. Belgium imported ninety-six per cent of its palm oil from the Congo, ninety-seven per cent of its palm nuts, and forty-one per cent of its rubber, but just twelve per cent of its coffee and eleven per cent of its cacao. Likewise, just fifteen per cent of Belgium's cotton imports were supplied by the Congo; colonial producers, it seems, were barely finding their way in to the substantial Belgian textile industry.[177]

The Congo, the Holdings and Belgium's Economy

One last and fundamental question remains: How did the colonial experience affect the overall dynamics of the Belgian economy? This question has been asked by other colonial powers and is still widely debated by British historians. D. K. Fieldhouse, for instance, asked if "... the existence of relatively soft sterling markets for British manufactures [had] a debilitating effect on British industry, enabling static firms and products to survive?" He leaned towards a positive answer: In his eyes, the evidence "suggests that these two decades of featherbedding [have] blunted the edge of British industry".[178] In Andrew Thompson's opinion, on the other hand, "[T]he Empire did not 'featherbed' British industry, and (...) the colonies were not life-rafts into which British manufacturers could effortlessly escape when faced by intensifying international competition".[179] In his work *Empire colonial et capitalisme français*, the late Jacques Marseille also asked whether, in the long run, the colonies were or were not profitable to France. His answer was that the French colonial empire in fact became "a burden insofar as it contributed to slowing down the modernisation of France's production apparatus".[180] Is it possible to observe a similar phenomenon in Belgium?

The 'featherbedding' scenario proposed in the British and the French cases does not seem to be applicable to Belgium because national industries could not hide behind colonial walls. When exporting to the Congo, Belgian enterprises were confronted with international competition, just as they were in other part of the world, even if some mechanisms, such as monetary regulation or institutional settings, clearly held some advantages for them. The main Belgian industry exporting to the Congo, namely metal construction, was far

---

[176] F. Baudhuin, "L'approvisionnement du pays en minerais", *Bulletin d'Information et de Documentation de la Banque nationale de Belgique*, 14, vol. 1, 5 (May 1939), pp. 384–91.
[177] Central Council for the Economy, *De interpenetratie, op. cit.*, part 1, p. 22.
[178] D. K. Fieldhouse, "The Metropolitan Economics of Empire", *op. cit.*, p. 109.
[179] A. S. Thompson, *The Empire, op. cit.*, p. 170.
[180] J. Marseille, *Empire colonial, op. cit.*, p. 367.

from being a backward sector. On the contrary, according to international standards, it was a highly competitive and state-of-the-art business. Furthermore, the development of sectors such as the diamond industry, non-ferrous metallurgy and transit economic activities, due to the Congo, illustrates a point made by P. J. Marshall regarding the effect of colonialism on the British economy: "British economic relations with its empire tended to reflect trends already established in the British economy and to strengthen certain of them".[181] This observation also applies to one of the main impacts of the Congo on the Belgian economy: the strengthening of the grip of the mixed banks/holding companies on the national economy.

Indeed, the Congo came to occupy an important place in the policies of the mixed banks and subsequently the holdings. As we saw, some colonial subsidiaries recorded impressive profits. These Congolese enterprises and their metropolitan parent companies were an important thread in Belgium's economic fabric. This leads to the following hypothesis: Thanks to their colonial activities, these mixed banks and holding companies acquired additional weight in Belgian society. The question then arises whether this was a positive evolution for the national economy as a whole or not. The performance of particular Belgian industries was not directly weakened by the existence of colonial markets. However, through the holding companies' investment strategy, which was strongly influenced and strengthened by the Congo, we may be confronted with a specific Belgian variant of the 'imperial curse' on national economic dynamism. Initially in the 1930s, and subsequently during the 1950s, the progressive fringe of Belgian public opinion cast a watchful eye on the holdings. According to these critics, the people involved were more interested in consolidating their own position than in promoting any genuine renewal. This, critics claimed, resulted in a degree of immobility. Recent research tends to agree with this analysis. On the one hand, colonial activities contributed to a certain degree of economic diversification and modernisation through the development of the non-ferrous metal industry, the spearhead radium industry, the airline business and so forth. But on the other, they may have 'confined' Belgium's economic forces to a highly profitable, but traditional framework that was insufficiently exposed to renewal. According to historian Wim Peeters, Belgium's foreign direct investments (particularly in the Congo) did not lead to economic innovation. On the contrary, they rather stifled it: "The closed context of the colonial economy with a strict policy of vertical integration (raw materials for the metropole) and, on the other hand, the absence of international competition, kept the institutional framework in place. The absence of internal and external competition prevented any innovation and confirmed the colony's place in a system that had probably already become obsolete prior to the Second World War".[182] Another historian, Michelangelo Van Meerten, suggests that

---

[181] P. J. Marshall, "Imperial Britain", in P. J. Marshall, ed., *The Cambridge Illustrated History of the British Empire* (Cambridge, 1996), p. 328.
[182] W. Peeters, "Belgische ondernemers (...)", art. cit., p. 13.

the independence of the Congo had a psychological impact. According to Van Meerten, the end of easy and guaranteed profits in the colony convinced certain economic players to concentrate more on Belgium and its position within the European Economic Community.[183] Might Belgian investors indeed have neglected other avenues towards innovation and diversification, attracted as they were to the opportunities offered by the Congo? Might the Belgian holding companies have strengthened themselves and subsequently have become more rigid due to their colonial assets? The answers to these questions are of course essential for a proper understanding of the *structural* impact that the Congo had on the Belgian economy. Far more research is needed in order to answer these questions and to fully understand the investment strategies of the holding companies in relation to the Belgian, colonial and global settings.

Conclusion: The Overall Impact of the Congo on Belgium's Economy

Until the late 1950s, it was impossible to assess the overall significance of the colony in relation to Belgium's economy. At the time of the Congo's independence, however, economists began to show greater interest in the question. National accounts were drawn up, meaning there was no longer any need for guesswork. A study from 1960 considered the hypothetical effect of a "complete breakdown in economic relations" between Belgium and the Congo.[184] Its conclusions contrasted strongly with the sometimes disastrous predictions by others.

Figures for 1956 show that, directly or indirectly, exports of goods and services to the colony provided jobs to approximately seventy-five thousand people, or 2.1 per cent of the working population. If one adds to the trade relations the return on colonial investments, then the Congo, in that same year, accounted for 3.3 per cent of GNP, 3.6 per cent of the state's tax revenue and the same share in Belgium's National Income (3.3 per cent of wages and salaries, 1.1 per cent of the income of individual companies and rental income, 14.5 per cent of dividends, interests, bonuses and profits that capital companies transferred to the reserves). The 1960 study concludes that a rift would, in the short term, affect at least twenty-five thousand employees in Belgium, excluding the thirty thousand active Belgians in the Congo who would return to Belgium. It estimates the economic fallout of a hypothetical total breakdown in relations with the Congo at 2.4 per cent of GNP.[185]

---

[183] M. Van Meerten, *Capital Formation in Belgium 1900–1995* (Brussels-Leuven, 2003), p. 312.

[184] R. de Falleur, "Le Congo et l'activité économique de la Belgique", *Cahiers économiques de Bruxelles*, 8 (October 1960), pp. 569–640.

[185] Several evaluations were made at the time. The De Voghel commission (mentioned earlier) considered three hypotheses (minimal, moderate and maximal effects). These correspond with a decline in GDP by respectively 0.25 per cent, 3.65 per cent and 6.02 per cent (the extreme case is considered unlikely). Kadoc, De Schryver Papers, n° 11.3.33.1, "Deuxième rapport de la Commission pour l'Étude des Problèmes financiers du Congo", 9 October 1959, pp. 44–6. SGB also made an evaluation: "Incidence d'une rupture complète des relations économiques

However, the author also asserts that "it seems the Belgian economy's growth rhythm would not be affected in the longer term [hence] the possibility of a total rift with the Congo would not be a catastrophe for the Belgian economy". One specific aspect is underlined: A complete rift "would wipe out the traditional surplus on the balance of payments on current accounts" – a surplus that was entirely due to the economic relationships between Belgium and its former colony. Similarly in 1970, economist Fernand Baudhuin asserted that the Congo "played but a secondary role" in Belgium's economy.[186] This conclusion makes an analysis of post-colonial relations between Belgium and the Congo all the more interesting. Did the 'total rift' that some feared back in 1960 actually materialise? Or was it rather 'business as usual', despite the dramatic events witnessed in the young republic? Some tentative answers will be provided in the next chapter.

In the meantime, let us return once more to the colonial era. The economic ties between Belgium and the Congo stamped a characteristic colonial mark on Belgium's economy. As far as imports were concerned, the Congo was open to global trade. Belgian exporters were not operating in a protected market and had to compete with foreign rivals as well as local producers; success was by no means guaranteed. This was, of course, in stark contrast to, for instance, the French experience, where the colonial empire sheltered some industries. Nor did Belgium introduce the equivalent of the British 'imperial preference' in the 1930s.[187] With the exception of metal construction, the Congo was of marginal significance to Belgian industries. The Congo had no exclusive partners when it came to export trade either, though a substantial proportion of its raw materials was shipped to Belgium. The customs policies of Belgium and the Congo, combined with the currency parity between the Belgian and the Congolese franc, stimulated exports of Congolese raw materials to Belgium, which clearly imported more than needed to satisfy domestic demand. To a degree, Belgium served as an international distribution centre for raw or semi-processed materials from the Congo. The ties between the Congo and Belgium also compensated for the imbalance in Belgium's foreign trade accounts – in this respect, Belgium's colonial experience resembles that of the other imperial systems. In this sense, the metropole undoubtedly benefitted from its status as a colonial power.

The latter aspect should, however, be seen in a broader context. Belgium's ties with the colony clearly had other invisible yet indisputable benefits. Without

---

entre la Belgique et le Congo", 1960 (report kept at the Contemporary History Department of the Royal Museum for Central Africa in Tervuren, III/CK 676).

[186] F. Baudhuin, *Histoire économique de la Belgique 1957–1968* (Brussels, 1970), p. 228.

[187] J. Marseille, "The Phases of French Colonial Imperialism" in A. N. Porter & R. F. Holland, eds., *Money, Finance, and Empire, 1790–1960* (London, 1985), p. 134–5; B. Porter, *The Lion's Share: A Short History of British Imperialism 1850–1983* (London-New York, 1984), p. 269; B. R. Tomlinson, "The British Economy and the Empire, 1900–1939", in C. Wrigley, ed., *A Companion to Early Twentieth Century Britain* (Oxford, 2003), p. 203; J. Frémeaux, *Les empires coloniaux, op. cit.*, pp. 123–4.

any hesitation whatsoever, Belgium gave precedence to its own interests over those of the colony in more ways than one. Belgium's monetary policy was designed primarily to protect its own national currency, even if that meant imposing a series of devaluations on the Congolese economy by dragging along the Congolese franc. The same holds for loans, where the Belgian treasury looked after its own interests to the detriment of the Congo's public finances. The manner in which the Belgian authorities designed and handled their 'privileged relationship' with the Congo (for example in the field of transport networks and management of trade) resulted in lower revenues or greater costs for the colony. However, while these effects are quite clear to see, it is extremely difficult, if not impossible, to quantify them with any great accuracy.

This brings us to another aspect of how Belgium benefitted from its colony. Clearly, the creation of the Congo was not inspired by diplomatic, religious or humanitarian motives. The conceptions and actions of the man who set the whole undertaking in motion – Leopold II – leave little room for doubt in this respect: He wanted to make money and amass a fortune. Of course, he claimed that his actions were intended to enhance Belgium's prosperity and grandeur – and he certainly believed his own propaganda. He also invoked a 'civilising mission', but this was really no more than a thin veil to disguise his material objectives. The private enterprises that, encouraged by the king, invested in the Congo obviously stayed there because they were making a profit, not because of any abstract notion of 'developing' the Congolese economy. Initially, these enterprises were not concerned at all with alleviating social needs; there was no question of providing housing, hospitals and schools. Such concerns grew later, as a result of productivity requirements. We have explained how, in some sectors, especially mining, profits in the Congo were most probably much higher than in Belgium. Since these profits were (mostly) generated through Belgian capital invested in the Congo, part of the profits flowed back to Belgium – from where they would, subsequently, be reinvested in the colony. Still, these capital flows were not always in balance. In the 1930s and the 1950s, the colony usually saw a greater outflow (particularly of private capital, in the shape of dividends or bonuses) than inflow. Most of this outflowing capital was returned to the country where it had originated: Belgium.

So was Belgian capitalism indebted to the colonial activities in the Congo? Did the country owe its wealth and affluence to its colony? Certainly the colonial propaganda spread this notion, but in fact the colonial contribution – however important – was only part of a much wider dynamics that was driven (and continues to be driven) by other sources, most notably by domestic demand which had benefitted from an increased purchasing power since the end of the nineteenth century and, crucially, by the growing markets in neighbouring countries. To complete the picture of the macroeconomic relationship between Belgium and the Congo, we should remember that Belgium was notably stingy towards the Congo when it came to public funding. The Belgian taxpayer contributed hardly anything at all to the country's 'civilising project'. The Congo raised most of the required resources itself, in the form of taxes from Congolese residents, tax revenues from companies and other economic actors, customs duties and the like.

Matters become more concrete as the focus shifts to the microeconomic level and the consequences of colonialism on the internal economic structure of Belgium. In 1969, René Sterkendries, an executive with the SGB, authored a note titled "*Le Congo. Réflexions d'un Belge*".[188] It contains the following passage:

At the time [the 1950s], the story went that Belgium's economic wellbeing and wealth depended on the exploitation of the Congo. Well, [relations with that territory] contributed between 4 and 5% to our national income. Events confirm this analysis: the Belgian economy in its totality experienced hardly any backlash at all from the deteriorating relationship between the two countries, as the growth following the gradual opening of the Common Market provided a counterweight. That is not to say that Belgian savings were not hit hard, or that no families were ruined, or that cornered industries were not forced into a painful conversion.

These lines refer to the post-colonial developments analysed in the next chapter. As we shall see, Sterkendries was right in stating that the economic impact of the Congo's independence on Belgium remained rather modest for the most part. What makes the quote rather extraordinary, though, is that this *post factum* qualification of the Congo's significance to Belgium came from an author associated with the SGB. After all, as has been demonstrated in the preceding paragraphs, this mighty holding was omnipresent, not only in the Congo, but also in Belgium itself. Indeed, most of the companies that experienced a significant impact from the colony – be it in the shape of their foundation or reorientation, or through a substantial boost of their activity – actually belonged to the SGB's sphere of influence.

There are plenty of examples: the foundation of CMB (maritime transport) and Sabena (aviation), the unprecedented boom in diamond processing and trading in Antwerp (under the impulse of Forminière), the rise of the non-ferrous metal industry (grouped around Métallurgie Hoboken) and so forth. In each of these instances, the mighty SGB played its part, often with support from the authorities. The more or less discreet presence of the Belgian state is, for that matter, not the only infringement of the 'rules' of the free market, for, in one way or another, these initiatives invariably took place under the protection of anti-competitive practices such as monopolies, agreements, cartels and so forth.

It would be an exaggeration to restrict the Congo's impact on the Belgian economy to the SGB. Independently from this holding, various trading companies helped maintain the flow of goods and services between Belgium and its colony, and they contributed to Belgium's role as a global transit hub for raw materials from the Congo. The port of Antwerp benefitted substantially

---

[188] AGR, SGB-3, n° 631, "Le Congo. Réflexions d'un Belge. Projet" (text for a speech to an American audience), 15 July 1969, by René Sterkendries, advisor to SGB.

from that goods flow. Other financial groups also invested in the Congo and the returns on those activities enhanced their financial leverage so that they were able to take further initiatives in the Congo, in Belgium or elsewhere. Many companies were either supplied by the Congo or sold their products there. However, these various aspects of the economic relationship between the Congo and Belgium cannot compete quantitatively or qualitatively with the conglomerate around the SGB that profoundly and durably changed the shape of Belgium's economy. These companies were instrumental, and their close contacts with the public authorities further enhanced their impact. Further research is needed in order to accurately assess how the colonial activities affected the internal structure of the Belgian holdings as well as their relative weight within the Belgian economy and, more generally, the position of Belgium in the world. Did the Congo enhance the position of the holdings within the Belgian economy? If so, was it beneficial or detrimental to the national economy? Or neither? For the time being, these questions remain unanswered. We can only assume that the holding companies were indeed fortified by the colonial experience, and we can formulate the hypothesis that this evolution contributed to a certain lack of dynamism in the Belgian economy. But far more research is needed here.

The considerable investments made by the Belgian private sector in the Congo certainly had an effect: They made it possible to enhance and safeguard the *Belgian* nature of the colony, a concept central to Belgium's colonial policy. In the Congo itself, these investments created a wealth that undoubtedly exceeded the expectations of the founders. However, they also resulted in a fundamental reorientation of the Belgian economy in relation to the rest of the world. After all, the driving forces behind Belgium's economy retreated to some extent into bilateral business relations with the colony. The question arises of whether, in the long term, this enhanced the dynamic nature of the national economy or not. Where the historian reaches his limitations, the reader can use his imagination and indulge in some speculation regarding the question of how Belgian capitalism might have evolved had its resources not been diverted so massively to the Congo.

5

Belgium and the Independent Congo

Belgium has played an important role in the history of the independent Congo, but the reverse is not necessarily true. This is quite natural: The mark of the colonial power on the colonised territory lasts longer than that of the colony on its metropole. In fact, this phenomenon was common to all the former colonial empires during the second half of the twentieth century; it is one of the symptoms of the fundamental asymmetry that characterises the relationship between the 'centre' and the 'periphery'.

So what does the post-1960 Congo signify to Belgians? First and foremost, it is a source of personal emotions and perceptions that are the spice of daily life. For the ex-colonials who returned home there are memories of bygone days, sometimes drenched in nostalgia, sometimes in bitterness. In most Belgian minds the Congo lives on as an amalgam of vague, distorted, fading images of a faraway land. But however important these aspects of post-colonial social and cultural history may be, we shall leave them aside in the present chapter. Instead, the focus of our analysis will be on the Congo's significance in Belgium's political and economic arenas.

Strictly speaking, the Congo no longer falls within the realm of Belgian internal affairs. Various institutions, parties, pressure groups, public figures and the news media hold strong opinions about the former colony, which remain a source of occasional discord. But as far as the nation of Belgium is concerned, the Congo is a foreign policy issue and an important aspect of diplomacy. The contrast between now and the 1960s, when the Congo occupied a central role in Belgium's foreign policy, is clear. There has been a comparable evolution in the economic sphere, one that started earlier and manifested itself more emphatically than that of the political and diplomatic spheres. Business relations between the two countries were maintained for some time after the transition to independence, before deteriorating irreversibly. Similarly, Belgium's substantial level of investment in the Congo dwindled, save for some rare exceptions. By the end of the twentieth century, the former colony's economic significance to Belgium had become quite marginal.

We might compare the situation to a protracted and painful divorce (while keeping in mind that the 'marriage' was enforced on one of the partners). Certainly the paths of the two countries have diverged quite strongly since 1960, and it is fair to say the fate of the one has been rather more enviable than that of the other. Contrary to some pessimistic predictions, Belgium emerged from a precipitous and dramatic decolonisation in remarkably good shape. Although the 1960s heralded the decline of Wallonia's industry and witnessed some difficult transformations in certain sectors – and some painful confrontations between the country's different linguistic communities – Belgium's economy as a whole was booming and spending power increased spectacularly. The loss of its colony in no way cast a shadow over the country's golden sixties. In the two decades that ensued Belgium would, of course, suffer under a huge economic crisis, with rampant unemployment and massive budgetary shortfalls. However, this is nothing compared to what the Congo has gone through since its independence. The fledgling nation has been beset by almost every imaginable scourge: civil war and massacres, dictatorship and repression, foreign invasions, disease and malnutrition.

Looking at certain pre-1960 documents, one is struck by predictions that *did* come true. They were made by the diehards of the Belgian colonial corps, who stubbornly went against the current of the times. In 1954, at the Ministry of Foreign Affairs, it was argued that the political emancipation of the 'natives' should not proceed too quickly: "The greatest catastrophe that could possibly befall the Congo would be a premature autonomy that it cannot handle. There is no native authority that is capable of running the country. It would signify a return to chaos".[1] Elsewhere we read that "'[S]elf-determination' (…) often leads to misery and exploitation of the masses by a small group of agitators".[2] Chaos, misery, exploitation of the masses: These notions summarise quite well the terrible fate of the Congo's population since its independence. The vast majority of the Congolese experienced no improvement in their quality of life after independence; quite the contrary in fact. The infrastructures for education, health and the economy in which the Belgians had taken such pride were destroyed much more quickly than they had been constructed. The question therefore arises whether there was a causal relationship between the decolonisation of the Congo and the country's sudden demise. Does this sad observation *a posteriori* in any way justify colonisation or prove that decolonisation was a mistake, as some argue? Above all, does it absolve Belgium of all responsibility for the situation?

Most likely not. In their arguments, the authors of the aforementioned predictions unwittingly touched upon a fundamental flaw in Belgium's colonial

---

[1] AMAE, AF-I-1 (1953–1954), note titled "Question coloniale", by G. Grojean, 19 February 1954.

[2] AMAE, AF-I-1 (DGS-Section coloniale), 1950–1953, "Note pour M. le Ministre", from L. Smolderen, 14 September 1954.

policy, a policy that, for decades, was based on two principles: the rejection of the formation of a native elite and the protection of the Congo against foreign influences. One might legitimately suggest that Belgium actually contributed to the origins and unfolding of the Congo's post-colonial tragedies. This delicate suggestion once again highlights the importance of studying Belgium's foreign policy vis-à-vis the post-colonial Congo. Before we turn our attention to that particular issue, however, we must first provide a brief synopsis of the Congo's history in the three decades after 30 June 1960.

The Congo after 1960: On a Slippery Slope Towards Catastrophe

The Congolese Crisis and the Impossible Stabilisation (1960–1965)
On 5 July 1960, just a few days after the declaration of independence, the Congolese army staged a mutiny.[3] This triggered a chain reaction that seriously compromised the future of the young nation. Aggression towards Belgian expatriates caused widespread panic and prompted a vigorous response from the Belgian government that, on 10 July, sent troops to the Congo, uninvited by the Congolese authorities. This military operation led to a break in diplomatic relations between the two countries and ultimately required an intervention by the United Nations (Security Council Resolution n° 143 of 14 July). Henceforth, the issue of the Congo would secure a place in the international political agenda. The Congo's appeal to the UN was in part inspired by another crucial event. On 11 July, the province of Katanga had declared its independence from the Congo, in a move that threatened the country's unity.[4] The separation was the work of local politicians, specifically the circles of 'President' Moïse Tshombe, but it was also supported by Belgian authorities and industry, including the influential Union minière du Haut-Katanga. The Katangan independence drive also gained support from white extremists in South Africa. Then, on 8 August, the 'diamond province' of Kasai declared its independence from the Congo as État autonome du Sud-Kasaï. In 1961, it actually became the Royaume fédéré du Sud-Kasaï, headed by the *mulopwe*, or king, Albert Kalonji Ditunga.

---

[3] I. Ndaywel è Nziem, *Histoire générale du Congo, op. cit.*, part 7; J. Vanderlinden, ed., *Du Congo au Zaïre 1960–1980* (Brussels, s.d. [1981]). The series *Congo 1959* (Brussels, 1960) to *Congo 1967* (Brussels, 1968) (one volume per year) is an essential information source on this period, as is the series *Courrier africain du CRISP (CA)*, Brussels, 1960–8, followed by *Cahiers du CEDAF*, Brussels, 1971–92 and by *Cahiers africains*, Brussels, 1992-. Various U.S. authors have made substantial contributions to the historiography of the independent Congo, including C. Young, *Introduction à la politique congolaise* (Brussels, 1968), and C. Young & Th. Turner, *The Rise and Decline of the Zairian State* (Madison, 1985); D. J. Gould, *Bureaucratic Corruption and Underdevelopment in the Third World: The Case of Zaire* (New York, 1980); Th. M. Callaghy, *The State-Society Struggle: Zaire in Comparative Perspective* (New York, 1984); M. G. Schatzberg, *The Dialectics of Oppression in Zaire* (Bloomington, 1988). See also Zana Aziza Etambala, *Het Zaïre van Mobutu* (Leuven, 1996).
[4] J. Gérard-Libois, *Sécession au Katanga* (Brussels, 1963).

The Congo was, thus, embroiled in a struggle between the major international powers.[5] The United States wanted to keep the former Belgian colony within its sphere of influence. Therefore, Washington did not favour the 'Katangan solution'. It reeked of neo-colonialism, which made it counterproductive in the eyes of the Americans and could, in their view, contribute to the spread of communism on the African continent.[6] However, the presence of a UN peacekeeping force provided some stability. It not only kept the Katangan secession in check, but helped maintain it, all the while simultaneously putting pressure on the lawful Congolese government of Patrice Lumumba, who was increasingly seen as a threat to Western interests. Next, there followed a series of interventions designed to keep the Congo in the Western camp: the replacement of Lumumba by President Kasavubu (5 September); the coup by Colonel Mobutu, who temporarily suspended the legislative institutions (14 September) and replaced them with an extraordinary body known as the Board of Commissioners-General; and the house arrest of Lumumba (10 October), followed by his arrest and extradition to Katanga, where he was assassinated on 17 January 1961.

After the disposal of Lumumba, peace was restored only gradually and not without difficulty. Beginning in December 1960, the authorities in Léopoldville, who themselves lacked constitutional legitimacy, had to contend with a pro-Lumumba government in Stanleyville in the east of the country, which claimed to be the only mandated authority in the Congo. So by early 1961, the Congo had no fewer than four different governments. In March, a number of these antagonists started negotiations, but the talks proceeded chaotically, with numerous unexpected twists. A first step towards normalisation of the situation was taken in August. The pro-Lumumba authorities joined ranks with a new, legitimate, parliament-backed government under the leadership of former trade unionist Cyrille Adoula. A further step towards restoration of Congolese unity was taken in October 1962, when the secession of Kasai was resolved. The biggest problem in 1961 and 1962 was the persistence of the Katangan leaders and their foreign supporters, particularly the Belgians. After military intervention by the United Nations, the Katangan secession eventually came to an end in January 1963 with the installation of a government of unity that enjoyed parliament's confidence. The Congo seemed to be back on the road towards stability.

Unfortunately, the return to peace would prove short-lived. In early 1964 civil strife broke out in Kwilu and in east Congo. The central authorities soon lost their grip on large parts of the national territory. In July 1964, the former

---

[5] L. De Witte, *De rol van de Verenigde Naties, de regering-Eyskens en het koningshuis in de omverwerping van Lumumba en de opkomst van Mobutu* (Leuven, 1996); D. N. Gibbs, *The Political Economy of Third World Intervention: Mines, Money, and U.S. Policy in the Congo Crisis* (Chicago, 1991); J. Kent, *America, the UN and Decolonisation: Cold War Conflict in the Congo* (London-New York, 2010).

[6] R. Yakemtchouk, *Les relations entre les États-Unis et le Zaïre* (Brussels, 1986).

'president' of Katanga, Moïse Tshombe, formed a new Congolese government. Some Belgian politicians and businessmen regarded Tshombe, who had just returned from exile, as the man who could resolve the Congo's internal difficulties. With military and logistical support from Belgium and the United States, the authorities in Léopoldville succeeded in regaining control of the situation. It was in this context that a Belgian military operation was launched in November 1964 to free Westerners from the hands of insurgents in Stanleyville and Paulis. After the rebellion, the political situation in Léopoldville remained volatile. The struggle for power continued as the country headed for a confrontation between Tshombe and Kasavubu. Then, in late 1965, the situation took a new, decisive, political twist when the commander in chief of the Congolese National Army, General Joseph-Désiré Mobutu, seized power.

Mobutu in Power (1965–1997)

This was not the first coup that Mobutu had orchestrated. Previously, in September 1960, he had intervened to *temporarily* sideline the 'bickering and incompetent' political elite. The new coup of 1965, again supposed to be temporary, was actually the start of Mobutu's thirty-two-year stint at the helm of the country. As such, it was a pivotal moment in the history of the young Congolese republic. The exceptional duration and apparent stability of Mobutu's reign hid a gradual decay of the state and a systematic neglect of the economy that resulted in deteriorating living conditions. Mobutu's regime was, in fact, the main instigator of these pernicious developments.

There is no denying that, for almost three decades, the Congo enjoyed peace (with the exception of short episodes of trouble which will be mentioned later), and seemed to be developing a regular economic and social fabric. However, from a political perspective, it had experienced a complete reversal. After a transitional period, Mobutu abolished all existing institutions, outlawed all political movements and established a single party known as the Mouvement populaire de la Révolution (MPR). Autonomous social organisations, such as trade unions and youth movements, were likewise replaced with state-controlled surrogates. All other centres of power (the church, universities, media) were effectively silenced. Free elections were unheard of in the Second Republic over which Mobutu, now at the centre of a genuine personality cult, reigned with an iron fist. The Congo became a police state with a sprawling network of secret agents. Many political adversaries of the regime were physically eliminated.

Mobutu also used ideology as a weapon. To legitimise his position with the Congolese and in foreign public opinion, particularly in Africa and the Third World, Mobutu launched his 'authenticity policy'. Under the new clothing rules, for example, the traditional European suit was banned. European-sounding names of persons and places were scrapped and replaced with 'authentic' African names. Supposedly 'genuine' African symbols increasingly came to permeate every area of daily life. Finally, in 1971, the Congo was renamed Zaire.

These changes coincided with the rise of a veritable kleptocracy; quite literally a regime of thieves.[7] Corruption and incompetence had been widespread before Mobutu's era, but now they assumed previously unseen proportions. The president, his family and relatives and the 'barons of the regime' (along with their cronies) established a system of theft on the grandest scale. The levers of power gave them access to the nation's economic riches, which were promptly and shamelessly plundered. A handful of senior civil servants were thus able to amass enormous fortunes, much of which would be transferred to foreign accounts or invested in foreign real estate.[8] During the 1970s, Mobutu was one of the richest men in the world. This theft of the nation's profits was a serious detriment to public services and the country's infrastructure. The production apparatus sank even deeper into disrepair after the Congolese government expropriated numerous private companies. This catastrophic economic policy led to the accumulation of massive foreign debt, runaway inflation and continuous devaluations of the national currency. For the people of the Congo, it was the start of a long period of misery.[9]

History shows that many dictatorships survive despite poor economic performance, and Mobutu's Congo was no exception. Still, one wonders about the mechanisms that kept in place a regime whose abuses were widely known. The regime undoubtedly owed its survival in part to internal factors such as brutal repression and a tight grip on civil society. Active and peaceful domestic opposition could not succeed in turning Congolese policy around. Armed opposition, for its part, was restricted mainly to a number of flashpoints in the east of the country, such as Laurent-Désiré Kabila's ineffective guerrilla war. The Congolese opposition in exile, primarily in Belgium, made a lot of noise, but it was weak and divided and had been infiltrated by Mobutu's secret police.

These factors do not, however, explain everything. Mobutu's regime could, after all, not have survived unaided. Its economic and financial predicaments were so great that they could not have been resolved without international assistance. That assistance was repeatedly forthcoming. In 1977 and 1978, the regime faltered in the face of military operations launched from neighbouring countries, the so-called Shaba Wars. The United States, Morocco, Belgium and France offered Mobutu military and logistical support, thereby keeping him in power. In other words, Mobutu partly owed his prolonged period in power to the approval of the West.

Mobutu, who was born in 1930, had worked during the era of Belgian rule first as a sergeant with the Force publique and subsequently as a journalist and

---

[7] J.-C. Willame, *L'automne d'un despotisme. Pouvoir, argent et obéissance dans le Zaïre des années quatre-vingt* (Paris, 1992); C. Braeckman, *Le dinosaure. Le Zaïre de Mobutu* (Paris, 1992).

[8] "Zaïre. Rapport sur sa crédibilité financière internationale", by Erwin Blumenthal, 20.04.1982, p. 26, published in full in *Info Zaïre. Bimestriel du Comité Zaïre*, 36 (October 1982).

[9] J. Maton & H.-B. Solignac Lecomte, *Congo 1965–1999. Les espoirs déçus du 'Brésil africain'* (Geneva, 2001) (online http://www.oecd.org/dev/publication/tp1a.htm. http://www.oecd.org/dataoecd/57/41/1909637.pdf).

as an informer to Belgium's State Security Service, the Sûreté de l'État.[10] The young Mobutu also maintained contacts with the American CIA, specifically with Lawrence Devlin, the CIA station chief in the Congo. Devlin, according to the American ambassador to the Congo, was "as close personally to Mobutu as any non-Congolese I know of".[11] In 1959–60, Mobutu befriended Lumumba, who appointed him chief of staff of the Congolese National Army. However, Mobutu promptly disposed of his benefactor – only to extol him post mortem once his own dictatorship had been established. Mobutu's shady past explains why Washington trusted him. The White House saw him as an ally and a staunch defender of Western interests. In the eyes of the Western powers, Mobutu was like a dam holding back the tide of communism in Africa. Businesspeople and politicians counted on his power to make things work. Western leaders saw him as a man who, despite personal shortcomings and excesses, could guarantee the unity of the Congo. The choice was simple: Mobutu or chaos. In the 1970s, Europe and the United States would fail to acknowledge the ultimate reality of this choice: first Mobutu *and* chaos but, eventually, only chaos.

Still, we should not underestimate the complexity of the situation. The Congolese president was not just a puppet on the string of the foreign powers. He was often unpredictable and would sometimes adopt positions or take measures that were contrary to the best interests of the West or, perhaps more accurately, those of individual Western nations. A master tactician, Mobutu succeeded perfectly in playing Belgium, France, the United States, Russia, one against the other. He understood the art of manipulation and pleasing, and was fully aware of the power of image and word, as Belgian diplomats would repeatedly discover to their shame and regret. But Mobutu's personal interests always came first: He was determined to stay in power and to enrich himself, two aspects of his regime that were inextricably linked. Consequently, Mobutu frequently caused irritation, anger or despondency abroad. Ultimately, however, his political 'life insurance' managed to save him: his tight grip on one of the most important countries in central Africa, and his close links with the West.

Twice, then, an exceptional personality had stepped forward in an extraordinary international setting to stamp his indelible mark on the history of the Congo. Towards the end of the nineteenth century, in the midst of the scramble for Africa, it had been Leopold II; a century later, at the height of the Cold War, it was Mobutu. However, with the fall of the Berlin Wall and the implosion of the Eastern Bloc at the end of the 1980s, Mobutu became cornered. Cunning, he chose for a flight forward, calling in April 1990 for a change of course, announcing the end of his single-party MPR and proclaiming a new era of multi-party politics. A National Sovereign Conference was convened to oversee

---

[10] J. Chomé, *L'ascension de Mobutu* (Brussels, 1974); S. Kelly, *America's Tyrant: The CIA and Mobutu of Zaire* (Washington, 1993), p. 10.
[11] S. Kelly, *America's Tyrant*, op. cit., p. 11; M. G. Schatzberg, *Mobutu or Chaos? The United States and Zaire, 1960–1990* (Lanham, 1991), especially pp. 85–6; L. Devlin, *Chief of Station, Congo: A Memoir of 1960–1967* (New York, 2007).

the transition to this new form of government, dubbed a 'Third Republic'. This heralded the final phase of Mobutu's regime, which by now had gone bankrupt and become internationally isolated. The endless palavering and devious manoeuvres that took place in subsequent years merely served to extend time for a president diagnosed with prostate cancer and desperate to hang on to power. As he fell, he dragged his country along into the abyss of ruin.

The coup de grace followed in 1997. Remember that in 1994, Rwanda, the Congo's small eastern neighbour, had been rocked by violent regime change and genocide, resulting in the destabilisation of the entire Great Lakes region. The new leaders in Kigali soon began to interfere with the Congo's internal affairs, crossing into its territory in pursuit of soldiers and supporters of the ousted regime whom they wanted to eliminate. In order to attain their goal, the Rwandan leaders offered support to the Congolese rebels of Laurent-Désiré Kabila, who had been slowly withering away in east Congo.[12] With the help of these troops, Kabila was eventually able to deliver the death blow to the ailing regime of Mobutu. Now terminally ill, Mobutu fled Kinshasa in May 1997 and died just a few months later, on 7 August, in the Moroccan capital of Rabat. Under the new regime, the Congo rapidly slid into chaos once again, fighting civil war and foreign invasions – but these more recent developments fall outside the scope of this book.

The Independent Congo and Belgian Foreign Policy

Belgium's Attempts to Mould the Congo (1960–1965/1967)

Back in 1970, the late Jules Gérard-Libois, a pre-eminent expert on the Congo, distinguished two periods in Belgium's policy towards the Congo.[13] Between 1960 and 1966, Belgium felt it could mould its ex-colony into the desired shape. Belgium believed it "had a POLITICAL role to play in the Congo and that all that the former colony stood for could only be safeguarded if one could ensure by sometimes risky POLITICAL means that an acceptable Congolese regime be put in place". Gérard-Libois goes on to argue that, after 1966, "the Congo was politically a different country, where Belgium as such was not involved; though relationships might be disrupted if the considerable interests of Belgium or the individuals looking after them were to come under fire".[14] This analysis remains valid more than three decades on, despite subsequent revelations regarding the pre-1970 era. Still, at least one further phase needs to be added, namely the gradual reduction of major Belgian interests until virtually nothing remained.

---

[12] On these developments, see F. Reyntjens, *The Great African War: Congo and Regional Geopolitics, 1996–2006* (Cambridge, 2009).

[13] G. de Villers, *De Mobutu à Mobutu. Trente ans de relations Belgique-Zaïre* (Brussels, 1995); O. Lanotte, C. Roosens & C. Clément, eds., *La Belgique et l'Afrique centrale de 1960 à nos jours* (Brussels, 2000).

[14] J. Gérard-Libois, "Avant le voyage royal. Dix ans de relations Belgique-Congo", *Courrier hebdomadaire du CRISP (CH-CRISP)*, 483 (1970), pp. 2–3.

In 1959–60, the consensus among Belgian decision makers was that it was up to Belgium to mould the Congo into the desired shape. They initially considered the option of granting the Congo a 'limited' independence. This semi-autonomous status would allow Belgium to retain power of decision in a number of privileged key areas. Events, however, quickly refuted this line of thought. The Congolese negotiators refused to accept such restrictions and demanded full independence. During the roundtable talks of early 1960, the chief Socialist negotiator, Henri Rolin, expressed it quite aptly: Belgium was handing over to the Congolese "all the keys" to their country. But the Belgians would decide which doors remain locked. They wanted to install intermediaries so that behind each Congolese leader or civil servant there would be a Belgian advisor to help determine when, where and how a particular key should be used. The Development Cooperation Department, established for this very purpose, would play a crucial role in Belgium's Technical Assistance Programme.

Without foreign aid, the Congo would not have been a viable independent state. That was the sobering legacy of Belgium's colonial policy. On the eve of the Congo's independence, there were just a handful of university graduates in the colony. Few Congolese ever got the opportunity to study abroad, and the first Congolese university was opened only in 1954. Even then, in the latter days of its colonial empire, Belgium made sure that no faculty of law would be established in the Congo, and it was not until 1961 that the first engineers and physicians graduated.[15] In the months leading up to independence, some efforts were made to place Africans in mid-level executive positions, both in government and in the private sector. However, this hastily implemented and belated measure did not allow the country to regain the ground lost over the previous decades.

Following the crisis of July 1960, the dream of a peaceful, gradual and Belgian-backed transition to an independent Congo faded. Two weeks after the declaration of independence, diplomatic relations between the two countries were severed. Still, this was not the end of Belgium's presence in its former colony. Quite the contrary. In fact, Belgium's stake became more diversified and more deeply embedded and, in the light of the tragic events that ensued, quite high-profile. The mutiny in a number of units of the Congolese army set the whole process in motion. Some of the mutineers abused Belgian expatriates, prompting panic among the white community, many of whom wanted to flee. Towards the end of 1959, there were approximately one hundred and twelve thousand Westerners living in the Congo, including some eighty-nine thousand Belgians. As the mutiny broke out, the aircraft of the national carrier, Sabena, were commandeered to organise an airlift from the Congo to Belgium. What followed was a mass exodus. Between 9 and 28 July, Sabena evacuated around twenty-five thousand people. Others fled via alternative routes, with many crossing the Congo River to Brazzaville, the capital of the former French

---

[15] P. Bouvier, "Le rôle des enseignements universitaire et supérieur dans le processus de la décolonisation congolaise", in *Congo 1955–1960. Recueil d'études* (Brussels, 1992), pp. 81–93.

colony. The total number of departures is estimated at thirty-eight thousand. Beginning on 16 July, the Belgian government installed an "Information commission on violations of persons committed in the Republic of the Congo". It was comprised of magistrates and supported by a team of social assistants, nurses and so forth. Its report, which remains unpublished, is based on testimonies by almost all of the sixteen thousand adults who returned to Belgium in those turbulent days.[16]

The work of the commission offers accurate insight into the extent of the abuse suffered by the Belgians. According to the report, there was no evidence of systematic killings. In all, several dozen Belgians lost their lives, including twenty or so in Katanga, the province where most of the violence occurred. Reference is made to insults and humiliations. Some Belgians were beaten, forced to partially or completely undress, imprisoned, made to dance barefoot, spat at, doused with water or otherwise denigrated. The most harrowing incident substantiated in the report is sexual violence.[17] It is assumed that several hundred cases of rape occurred across the Congo. A number of atrocities (including mutilations) were reported, but the commission was unable to confirm them. The commission was also unable to quantify the material losses suffered by the individuals who had left the Congo in such haste, quite often never to return.

Some may feel that this enumeration fails to capture the sense of trauma suffered by the former colonials and their Belgian relatives and friends during these dramatic events. Others may argue that the plight of the Belgians in the Congo in July 1960 has attracted too much attention. After all, the local population likewise fell victim to murder, torture, rape and theft, and on a much larger scale. It is therefore worthwhile repeating here that this book focuses deliberately on Belgium and the Belgian perspective on events.

The crisis in the Congo reverberated throughout Belgian society and shocked public opinion. The government's decision to send in troops was, therefore, met neither with hostility nor rejection; on the contrary, it was largely applauded, except by the Belgian Communist Party, which openly opposed the move. While military action generally met with approval, some Belgians nevertheless took to the streets to protest against 'politics', which they held responsible for the global Congo debacle. In one famous press photo, a young demonstrator is seen holding a placard with the not so subtle slogan "*Livrés aux sauvages par des incapables.*"[18] ("Delivered to savages by incompetents"). But

---

[16] Ceges, AA/1819, "Rapports de la Commission d'Information sur les atteintes à la personne commises dans la République du Congo depuis le 30 juin 1960", 35, 33, ? and 93 p., dated 4 August, 16 August, 15 September and 22 October 1960 (the third report is missing, but the final report summarises the previous ones). These reports consist first and foremost of an enumeration of individual facts. Excerpts are provided in W. J. Ganshof van der Meersch, *Fin de la souveraineté belge au Congo* (Brussels, 1963), pp. 434-53.

[17] P. Monaville, "La crise congolaise de juillet 1960 et le sexe de la décolonisation", *Sextant. Revue du Groupe interdisciplinaire d'Études sur les Femmes et le Genre*, 25 (2008), pp. 87-102.

[18] P. Verlinden, *Weg uit Congo. Het drama van de kolonialen* (Leuven, 2002), p. 177.

this movement was short-lived and did not have a lasting influence on Belgian political life.

Belgian troops sprang into action on 10 July 1960, entering the Congolese theatre simultaneously in Matadi, Luluaburg, Élisabethville, Léopoldville and elsewhere. Belgium's military intervention elicited varied responses, then and now. Some called it a strictly humanitarian action designed to save lives, while others denounced it as pure neo-colonial aggression. Did the Belgian government lose its cool? Was its response proportionate? Did other considerations come into play?[19] Certainly the fact that the objective of the initial military operations was the economically strategic port of Matadi, where there were hardly any Belgian residents, would seem to suggest so. While the military intervention most probably saved some lives, it probably also provoked attacks on white residents in areas that had previously remained calm or where peace had already been restored.[20] The entire event suggests that the Belgian government took insufficient account of the Congolese authorities who had made an effort to end the mutiny and appease the situation. This Belgian attitude – characterised by a combination of disdain and scepticism towards the Congolese leaders – would continue to define relations between the two countries for years after the fateful events of 1960.

The military operation had, additionally, the effect of isolating Belgium internationally. After all, sending of troops coincided with support for the Katangan secession, a policy choice inspired by obvious motives and with equally obvious political consequences. The centrifugal, if not openly autonomist, forces in the wealthy province were not new.[21] They had lain dormant since long before independence and were now incited into action by Belgians in Katanga and white rulers in African countries tainted by apartheid. In the months before independence, the call for secession was picked up by the principal nationalist movement in the region, known as Conakat. Moïse Tshombe, who had the ear and trust of many whites in central Africa, led this party. In early July 1960, as the Congo descended into turmoil, these forces joined ranks and took the decision to separate Katanga from the Congo. They could, moreover, count on strong backing in Brussels, including from certain ministers, the royal court and Union minière du Haut-Katanga, the main business entity in the region.

Without the technical, administrative, intellectual, military and financial support of the Belgians, Katanga's 'independence' would never have materialised. The taxes and levies paid by UMHK, which used to constitute a third of all revenues of the former colony and thus also of the new state, henceforth flowed to the Katangan treasury, inevitably causing a financial headache in Léopoldville. The Belgians set up an administration and worked out a judicial system. A Belgian Technical Mission (Mistebel) initially led by Harold

---

[19] P. Demunter, 1960. L'agression belge au Congo (Paris, 2010).
[20] L.-F. Vanderstraeten, De la Force publique à l'Armée nationale congolaise. Histoire d'une mutinerie juillet 1960 (Brussels-Gembloux, 1985).
[21] R. Yakemtchouk, Aux origines du séparatisme katangais (Brussels, 1988), passim.

d'Aspremont Lynden, deputy chef de cabinet to Prime Minister Eyskens (and future minister of African affairs), made sure the improvised Katangan government received the necessary assistance. Matters were taken so far that a Banque nationale du Katanga and a national airline called Air Katanga were established with help from, respectively, the Belgian National Bank and Sabena.[22] The Katangan armed forces also received foreign assistance: Mercenaries were recruited in Belgium.[23]

But some qualification is required. It should be pointed out that Belgian opinion on these momentous events diverged. Some found it a risky undertaking, and even among the proponents of the Katangan secession there was no unanimity. The hardliners dreamt of a central and southern Africa under white rule, possibly fronted by a black puppet regime. Others saw Katanga as a haven of peace and order, a region where the dream of a transition to a post-colonial state where former colonials would continue to be welcome and play a decisive role might become a reality. Many Belgian leaders saw this stability as an intermediate step in the reconstruction of the Congo, pending the elimination of the Congolese politicians who were presently 'ravaging' Léopoldville.

In other words, the scenario of a *reconstruction à la katangaise* implied the elimination of Lumumba and all of his supporters. The strategy also required that close contacts be maintained with political circles in Léopoldville. Neither Belgium nor any other country ever officially recognised Katanga as an independent state.[24] In January 1961, despite the rift in diplomatic relations between the Congo and Belgium, the Congolese government allowed the Belgian Technical Assistance programme to set up shop in Léopoldville. It operated as best it could. Many Congolese politicians did, in fact, surround themselves with Belgian advisors.

These were certainly testing times for Belgian diplomats. On 14 July 1960, at the request of the Congolese government, the UN Security Council adopted a resolution calling on Belgium to withdraw its troops from the sovereign state of the Congo. This was followed by another resolution on 22 July. The pullout eventually began on 28 July, but it would take until 31 August before all the Belgian soldiers had left the country. Meanwhile, support to Katanga continued. On 21 February 1961, the United Nations once again called for an end to all military or paramilitary involvement in the Congo by Belgium or any other country and a withdrawal of all foreign advisors. The UN took a very negative view of Belgium's Technical Assistance strategy, which it considered as interference in Congo's internal affairs. In the corridors of the UN, Belgian delegates

---

[22] W. Pluym & O. Boehme, *De Nationale Bank van België 1939–1971. Boekdeel 3. Van de golden sixties tot de val van Bretton Woods* (Brussels, 2005), pp. 409–29; O. Boehme, "The Involvement of the Belgian Central Bank in the Katanga Secession, 1960–1963", *African Economic History*, 33 (2005), pp. 1–29.

[23] R. Pasteger, *Le visage des affreux. Les mercenaires au Katanga (1960–1964)* (Brussels, 2005).

[24] J. Stengers, "La reconnaissance *de jure* de l'indépendance katangaise", *Cahiers d'Histoire du Temps présent*, 11, (March 2003), pp. 177–91.

were treated as pariahs.[25] The Belgians, for their part, were convinced that their actions had been legitimate, and they continued to make the point that it was only thanks to Belgium's assistance that the Congo had not descended into total chaos. They could not understand the international ostracism that had been imposed on them since July 1960 and even more so since the assassination of Lumumba in January 1961. In several Eastern European and Third World countries, demonstrations took place against Belgium's allegedly neo-colonial policy, and in some places, Belgian embassies came under attack.[26] Whereas the criticism from the communist and non-aligned countries was to be expected, the Belgian leaders were dumbfounded by the – at best – lukewarm support from the United States and other NATO allies. In 1960–1, Belgium felt misunderstood and completely isolated in the global political arena. However, according to historian Alan James, Great Britain more or less supported Belgium on the diplomatic scene. London thought that Belgian intervention had prevented worse scenarios (particularly communist expansion). The British also had interests to defend in the Congo, "a material tie supplementing the emotional bonds of 'natural' sympathy which Britain felt for Belgium". But the Belgians were also sometimes "a bit of an embarrassment", and support for Belgian policy could not be taken too far, or it might jeopardise global British interests.[27] As a result, Belgium was left feeling somewhat abandoned.

Still, the international community's position should not really have come as a surprise. Belgium had after all, from the start of its colonial adventure, tried to go it alone. Colonial authorities had always isolated the Congo from foreign interference. Some Belgian politicians were quite aware that their country's isolation was due to its colonial policy. In May 1960, Minister Scheyven confided the following to the French ambassador: "Belgium, which always wanted to colonise the Congo alone, now also stands alone in the face of decolonisation".[28] After the eruption of the Congolese crisis, Belgium would pay the price for its isolationist attitude. In September 1960, NATO Secretary-General Paul-Henri Spaak asserted the following: "Belgium was wrong not to have discussed its colonial policy with its NATO allies prior to 30 June. Today it regrets their position. However, had it consulted properly with its allies about its African policy, matters might have been quite different. But the Belgian government chose instead to go it alone in the Congo".[29]

A few months later, Spaak himself came to play a leading role in relations between Belgium and the Congo.[30] In April 1961, the Eyskens government,

---

[25] Kadoc, Van Bilsen Papers, no. 6.4.1/1, Comhaire (from New York) to Van Bilsen, 11 August 1960.
[26] F. Cogels, *Souvenirs d'un diplomate*, Brussels, 1983, pp. 213–6.
[27] A. James, *Britain and the Congo Crisis, 1960–63* (London-Houndmills, 1996), pp. 40–1.
[28] AMAÉF (Nantes), fonds Consulat général à Léopoldville, n° 2, Raymond Bousquet, French ambassador in Brussels to MAÉF, 18 May 1960.
[29] Fondation P.-H. Spaak, Bruxelles, Spaak Papers, n° 6231, "Entretien de Monsieur P.-H. Spaak avec Monsieur P. Wigny, le mercredi 14 septembre 1960", pp. 1–2.
[30] M. Dumoulin, *Spaak* (Brussels, 1999), pp. 592–621.

which had weathered the Congolese storms, was succeeded by a coalition of Christian-Democrats and Socialists, in which Spaak served as minister of foreign affairs. It was agreed that, henceforth, African policy would be a matter of foreign affairs rather than internal affairs, in order to end the ambivalence in Belgium's policy towards the Congo. This new Congo policy had three priorities: the stabilisation of the situation in the former colony; the normalisation of relations between Belgium and the Congo; and an end to Belgium's international isolation.

The stabilisation of the situation was complicated and delicate, as it implied a resolution of the Katangan issue. Spaak wanted the Congo's unity to be restored, which meant siding with the governments in Léopoldville and the United States.[31] However, he did not wish to impose a solution and therefore argued for a negotiated settlement with the secessionists and against the use of force. But he ran into stubborn resistance from the Katangan leaders and the management of certain large corporations, particularly UMHK, who were firmly committed to the independence of the mining province.[32] Obviously these businessmen were concerned about their quite profitable installations in Katanga and felt that a negative attitude might prompt the Katangan government to destroy the mining infrastructure. Spaak shared their concerns, but, on the other hand, he and some prominent figures in Belgium's economy (particularly within the SGB) were very aware that Union minière's pro-Katangan position was a threat to economic interests elsewhere in the Congo.[33] A succession of negotiations, diplomatic contacts and military action by UN forces brought no solution. In fact, the UN operations were met with indignation in Belgium, as they also affected the lives of Belgians in Africa. Ultimately, in January 1963, the intervention by the UN brought to an end the Katangan secession. UMHK breathed a big sigh of relief as, thanks to Tshombe's intervention, its installations had remained unharmed.[34] But did the Belgian company subsequently show its gratitude to its Katangan saviour? That question remains open to debate. However, it would certainly seem that, in the months and years that followed, the company and the Katangan leader continued to maintain a close relationship.

Although the Katangan episode had come to an end, the consequences of the situation that Belgium had created would continue to weigh heavily on the Congo. First, there was the shadow of Tshombe, who had sought exile in Europe. How would he behave in years to come? Would he continue to promote separatism? Second, the Katangan gendarmerie, which had effectively served as the troops of the rebellious province, had not been disarmed and had been allowed to flee to neighbouring countries. Some had even been recruited

---

[31] Thorough analysis of the attitude of the United States regarding the Katangan secession in J. Kent, *America, op. cit.*
[32] R. Brion & J.-L. Moreau, *De la mine à Mars. La genèse d'Umicore* (Tielt, 2006), pp. 310–25.
[33] D. N. Gibbs, *The Political Economy, op. cit.*, p. 134.
[34] AGR, Finoutremer, n° 2061, PV n° 870 of Comité Intérieur Africain (CIA), 28 February 1963.

into the Congolese army. Hence, they posed a continuous threat to the leaders in Léopoldville. Third, Union minière had clearly demonstrated its might. Mobutu would take these three crucially important elements on board when he eventually seized power.

The normalisation envisaged by Spaak would lead to the restoration of diplomatic relations on 27 December 1961. In April 1962, Charles de Kerchove de Denterghem resumed his role as Belgium's ambassador to the Congo in Léopoldville. According to the French ambassador in Léopoldville, Belgium was a loyal supporter of the government of Cyrille Adoula.[35] Nonetheless, neither Belgium nor the United States put great faith in the authority and power of the new Congolese leadership, whose prime minister they described rather belittlingly as "the best man available". The Belgian authorities were astonished by the dire state of the Congo's political and administrative apparatus, as well as the poor quality of its political elite. As the French ambassador to Belgium put it:

[The Belgian diplomat Robert Rothschild,] who had witnessed the collapse and demise of Chiang Kai-Shek's regime in China, thought he had seen the very worst of chaos, incoherence, messiness, incompetence, negligence and corruption. Well, according to him, the Congolese have pushed the boundaries of disorder to an extreme, both in public and in private management.[36]

After a visit to the Congo, where he met the country's political leaders, the vice governor of the Société générale de Belgique, Jules Dubois-Pelerin, summarised his impressions to his colleagues behind closed doors: "Everything is black and yet very colourful, always picturesque, and occasionally peculiar, if not laughable. Notwithstanding the respect one must inherently show for authority, it is sometimes impossible to suppress a smile or even outright laughter, which can in turn have dire consequences".[37] The few archives that have been opened to research confirm unequivocally that corruption was rife among the Congo's political elite.[38] There can be no doubt whatsoever that the administration of the fledgling state was a catastrophe and that political leadership skills were

---

[35] AMAÉF (Nantes), Ambassade de France à Kinshasa, n° 14, Final mission report by French ambassador in the Congo, 3 August 1963, pp. 18-19.
[36] AMAÉF (Paris), série Europe 1961-1970, sous-série Belgique, n° 160, Henry Spitzmuller, French ambassador to Belgium to the MAÉF, 26 October 1964.
[37] AGR, SGB-3, n° 167, handwritten memo (*confidentielle*) from J. Dubois-Pelerin, 14-15 February 1964, pp. 22-3.
[38] See AGR, SGB-3, n° 167, M. Van Weyembergh (vice chair of the board of UMHK) to A. de Spirlet, 20 August 1968 ("Bomboko's request to SGM to provide him with land in Kinshasa is stupefying"); Ibid., "Entretiens avec Mr. Nendaka, ministre des Finances de la RDC", by J. Feyerick, 29 May 1969 (Nendaka requests a boat and caravans and refers to "his money"); AMAÉF (Paris), série Europe 1961-1970, sous-série Belgique, n° 173, H. Spitzmuller, French ambassador in Brussels to the MAÉF, 10 February 1965: Adoula "is in the hands of the Italian consortium ENI"; he has moreover been "bribed" by the U.S. embassy (D. N. Gibbs, *The Political Economy, op. cit.*, p. 128) and so forth. The first two quotes date from the early Mobutu era, but they obviously also apply to the preceding years.

lacking. But is that so surprising considering how unprepared the Congo had been to make a transition to independence? The lack of training given to African leaders and the hasty departure of many Belgian civil servants in July 1960 obviously contributed to the demise of the Congo's administration.

The chaos was such that the Belgian decision makers adopted an attitude towards their Congolese colleagues that, in euphemistic terms, may be described as critical. The Congolese were deeply offended, a psychological factor that would come to play a defining role in the relationship between the two countries. The necessity of respect for the Congo and its people would re-emerge in Mobutu's rhetoric. The president and his entourage used this argument effectively to heighten the tension between Belgium and the Congo and to blow hot and cold towards the former colonial ruler. Jef Van Bilsen, the chef de cabinet (for development co-operation) of Foreign Minister Harmel, warned his boss that "the failure of [Belgium's] Congo policy is in part due to the caste spirit of some and to the persistent disdain of people in your entourage for the leaders in Kinshasa".[39]

To the Americans and Belgians, the weakness of the central government in Léopoldville was a further reason to strengthen the Congolese National Army. To this end, military co-operation between Belgium and the Congo was enhanced. From early 1964, as uprisings grew in Kwilu and east Congo, it actually became a priority. The Western powers suspected that the insurrections were communist inspired since one of the leaders, Pierre Mulele, was known to have undergone training in the People's Republic of China. The Adoula government seemed unable to get the situation under control. It tried to strike a secret deal with Belgium, whereby Belgium could, at the request of the Congolese, send in troops. The idea was backed by the United States, who saw it as a way of keeping the Congo in the Western camp. Belgium would act as a kind of military subcontractor in a strategy designed to stem the tide of communism in Africa. However, Spaak was unwilling to go down this road. He was worried that Belgium might be dragged along in an endless string of military operations, effectively making central Africa into a Belgian version of Indochina or Algeria.[40]

The Belgian government was, moreover, fed up with the lack of decision making and leadership qualities within the Congolese leadership and it considered (once again) the option of regime change.[41] Hence, the Belgian diplomatic service established contacts not only with Tshombe, but also with the rebels.[42] Belgium's preferred option was, after all, the installation of an

[39] Kadoc, Van Bilsen Papers, n° 6.13.1/3, Van Bilsen to Harmel, 7 February 1968.
[40] AGR, MCM, 12 December 1963, p. 4 (the Belgian ministers had the impression that "everything drifts apart in the Congo"; Spaak was no longer able to establish human or political contact with Adoula); NA, FO, n° 371/176656, British embassy to FO, 11 June 1964 and 8 August 1964. See also M. Dumoulin, *Spaak, op. cit.*, p. 607.
[41] NA, FO, n° 371/176656, British embassy to FO, 11 June 1964.
[42] R. Rothschild, *Un phénix nommé Europe. Mémoires 1945–1995* (Brussels, 1997), p. 291; M. Dumoulin, *Spaak, op. cit.*, p. 607–8; NA, FO, n° 371/167266, British embassy to FO, 29 November 1963.

enlarged Congolese government, as a sign of 'national reconciliation'. Under such a scheme, all forces in the Congo would have to work together to safeguard and enhance the unity of the country. Spaak was able to convince the Adoula government that this was the way to go.[43] This eventually led to the appointment of Tshombe, the former rebel leader, as the new prime minister of the Congo in July 1964. However, this was not at all what Spaak had had in mind. He was surprised and worried by the evolution, as he distrusted Tshombe, who, according to American diplomatic circles, had nonetheless received active support from a number of large Belgian corporations, including UMHK.[44] After Tshombe's accession to power, Belgium was confronted with a delicate choice. On the one hand, it could give unconditional (military) support to the Congolese government. This option might drag Belgium into a large-scale international conflict, with progressive African countries and even Russia backing the rebels. On the other hand, Belgium could withdraw all support to Tshombe. This option would almost certainly lead to the downfall of the central Congolese government. The Congo would slip into chaos and would fall apart, some parts being taken over by its neighbours. Tshombe himself might go back to Katanga and revive the secession with the help of South Africa and Portugal. Finally, the Belgian government opted for a solution in between these two radical solutions.[45] Military aid was increased without direct Belgian involvement. Colonel Frédéric Vandewalle, a former chief of the Colonial Security Service and one of the leading figures behind Belgium's support to the Katangan secessionists, became a military advisor to the new Congolese prime minister. With assistance from white mercenaries and the regular Congolese army, he set out to recapture the rebel-held territories.[46]

In the meantime, Belgium – with American backing – had been preparing to drop soldiers into Stanleyville and Paulis (now known respectively as Kisangani and Isiro). In these two towns, rebel forces were holding several hundred foreign hostages, primarily Belgians.[47] In two air operations, on 24 and 26 November 1964, Belgian paratroopers succeeded in evacuating around 2,000 individuals, but the rebels still killed probably between 100 and 300 Westerners. This new military intervention by Belgium was met with criticism. Colonel Vandewalle, who was on his way to Stanleyville with ground forces, said about the decision to drop commandos in the city so shortly before his arrival that "a different political solution, involving less improvisation, would have had a less bloody

[43] NA, FO, n° 371/176656, Spaak to Adoula, 12 June 1964.
[44] D. N. Gibbs, *The Political Economy, op. cit.*, pp. 153–4.
[45] This was Spaak's analysis in AGR, MCM, 23 December 1964, p. 14–15.
[46] Ph. Borel, "La politique belge à l'égard du Congo pendant la période des insurrections (1963–1964)", in C. Coquery-Vidrovitch, A. Forest & H. Weis, eds., *Rébellions – révolutions au Zaïre 1963–1965* (Paris, 1987), vol. 2, pp. 7–35.
[47] AGR, MCM, 20 and 27 November 1964, pp. 1–2 and 2–10; P. Nothomb, *Dans Stanleyville* (Louvain-la-Neuve, 1993); A. Rouvez, e.a., *Disconsolate Empires: French, British and Belgian Military Involvement in Post-Colonial Sub-Saharan Africa* (Lanham, 1994), pp. 326–31.

outcome".[48] Once again, Belgium was accused of neo-colonialism by Eastern Bloc and developing countries. In the UN Security Council, Spaak argued vehemently that the one and only purpose of the intervention had been to save human lives. He succeeded in preventing a downright condemnation of the operation by the UN. The resolution that the Security Council adopted on 30 December 1964 merely called for all mercenaries to leave the Congo and for an end to all foreign intervention. In the course of 1965, the last rebel strongholds were subdued.

During the turbulent 1963–5 period, Belgian-Congolese relations were also affected by other, less spectacular but equally important factors. The consequences would be felt for a long time to come. To understand their origins, we must once again return to the era of Leopold II. This was the period when the colonial authorities joined forces with private investors to establish some of the large companies that would ultimately form the backbone of the Congo's economy. The value of the substantial shareholdings held by the colony – generally referred to as the 'Portfolio' – was estimated in 1960 at 37.3 billion francs.[49] On the eve of independence, the yield from the Portfolio represented 8.2 per cent of the Congo's regular revenue.[50] In other words, the stakes involved were very high, both financially and in terms of economic power.

After the declaration of independence, the shares in the Portfolio ought to have been transferred simply and quickly to the young Republic of the Congo. However, a number of factors prevented this from happening. In 1959–60, political and economic leaders in Belgium expressed concern at the possible consequences of such a transfer. They pointed out that the young state would become an important, if not the most important, shareholder in large corporations that hitherto had been led by groups of private investors (primarily the SGB) while the colonial authorities willingly stayed in the background. With a view to maintaining control over this important economic and financial lever, the Belgian government considered establishing a so-called development fund, in which the Congo could place its Portfolio. This fund would be managed jointly by the Congo and Belgium (with Belgium contributing to the capital). The idea, which was in keeping with the previously discussed notion of a 'limited decolonisation', was submitted to the Congo's delegates at the official Belgian-Congolese economic, financial and social conference held from 26 April to 16 May 1960. This meeting immediately became known as the economic roundtable conference, in comparison with the political roundtable conference that had taken place earlier.[51] The proposal concerning the Portfolio

---

[48] F. Vandewalle, L'Ommegang. Odyssée et reconquête de Stanleyville 1964 (Brussels, 1970).

[49] By way of comparison, the expenses on the Congo's 1959 budget sheet amounted to just 14.7 billion.

[50] M. Zimmer, "Les finances coloniales jusqu'en 1960 et leurs conséquences", in M. Frank, ed., Histoire des finances publiques en Belgique. Tome IV-2. La période 1950–1980 (Brussels, 1988), pp. 947, 954.

[51] Kadoc, De Schryver Papers, n° 11.3.33.1, "Verslag van de Commissie voor de Studie der Financiële Problemen van Kongo", 6 August 1959, p. 16 (known as the De Voghel Commission;

was, however, rejected. The Congolese delegates, ill-prepared for such technical discussions, were suspicious and refused to commit themselves. Other pressing issues, such as the colonial debt, were not resolved either, as the negotiators failed to reach agreement.

A number of crucial measures, taken unilaterally and hastily by the Belgian parliament just a few days before independence, increased the distrust of the future Congolese leaders. A law passed on 17 June 1960 allowed Belgian companies that operated under Congolese law to opt for Belgian legal status while keeping their headquarters and position in the Congo. Other measures concerned the so-called chartered companies, legal constructs dating from the Leopoldian era, to which the authorities had granted privileges. Besides the CFL (Compagnie des Chemins de Fer du Congo supérieur aux Grands Lacs africains) and the Comité national du Kivu, there was the Comité spécial du Katanga (CSK), the principal shareholder in UMHK, in which the colonial authorities held a majority stake. CSK was dissolved on 24 June 1960 under an agreement between the two shareholders, the private company Compagnie du Katanga and the Belgian Congo, confirmed by decree on 27 June 1960. All these important decisions were taken just a few days before independence. The dissolution was perceived by the Congolese as a manoeuvre to ultimately prevent the future state from acquiring a majority stake in UMHK, to which it would otherwise have been entitled.

The chaos that ensued in the newly independent Congo prevented a short-term resolution of these important economic and financial matters. When the political situation in Léopoldville had more or less stabilised, the Adoula government opened talks with Belgium to get these contentious issues (known as the *contentieux*) out of the way. The essential point was aptly summarised during a meeting of the Belgian government: "For the Congolese, the debt is a Belgian affair in which they are not concerned at all. But curiously, they also consider themselves as the natural heirs of the Congolese portfolio".[52] Difficult and prolonged negotiations eventually led to an accord on 20 March 1964.[53] Belgium agreed to recognise the Republic of the Congo as the holder of the Portfolio, but the actual transfer of the titles would only take place after the Congo had reached agreements with the various chartered companies. Regarding the Belgian Congo's outstanding debt, it was agreed that the burden would be shared between the two countries.

A unilateral decision by the Congolese authorities on 29 November 1964 jeopardised these agreements. They passed a decree that refused to recognise the Belgian decisions of May and June 1960 regarding the chartered companies

---

see Chapter 4); the second report of the commission speaks of a 'Société de Développement'. See also J. Gérard-Libois & J. Heinen, *Belgique-Congo 1960* (Brussels, 1989), p. 89; F. De Voghel, "La Table ronde économique 1960", in *Congo 1955–1960. Recueil d'études* (Brussels, 1992), pp. 229–43; K. Bultynck, *De Economische Rondetafelconferentie België-Kongo 1960* (Brussels, 1999), unpublished master's thesis in history, VUB.

[52] AGR, MCM, 2 August 1963, p. 10.
[53] AGR, MCM, 24 March 1964, pp. 1–8.

and dissolved the CSK.[54] This dissolution was detrimental to Belgium's interests, as it disregarded the rights of the private shareholder, Compagnie du Katanga. Fresh negotiations ensued, eventually leading to the accords of 6 February 1965.[55] The Congolese government ironed out its differences with both the private shareholders and the Belgian authorities. The SGB group was satisfied with the outcome of the talks, in which its leadership had played a decisive role.[56] Upon his return to Léopoldville, Tshombe triumphantly waved a briefcase representing the Portfolio, which was now entirely in Congolese hands.[57] A definitive solution was also found for the burden of debt. The Congo would assume the old *interior* colonial debt (the titles issued on the Congolese market for an amount of twenty-three billion francs), while Belgium pledged to repay the colonial debt that was covered by a state guarantee and had been issued in the foreign market (eleven billion francs). However, this did not resolve all the contentious issues, as the detailed negotiations had yet to start. Under the Mobutu regime, the matter would be brought up again and again, and previously made agreements called into question.

Belgium and Mobutu: A Prolonged Case of 'Cyclothymic' Diplomacy

The replacement of Adoula with Tshombe failed to restore stability in the Congo. On the contrary: The rivalries between the country's leaders continued. By now, Belgium was thoroughly fed up with the political twists and turns in its former colony.[58] On 24 and 25 November 1965, General Mobutu deposed President Kasavubu and the new prime minister, Evariste Kimba. Again, there were suspicions that Belgium had had a hand in these events, but Etienne Davignon, Spaak's chef de cabinet, was quick to deny this to the British ambassador, showing him correspondence suggesting that Belgium's ambassador in Léopoldville had also been taken by surprise. Davignon did, however, agree that Belgium's refusal to provide additional support to the Congo may well have strengthened the opposition against Kasavubu. He also conceded that the Belgian government was not unhappy to see Kasavubu and Prime Minister Kimba go, adding that Mobutu, while not brilliant as a general, was at least tough and relatively honest. Still, according to British diplomatic sources, the Belgian Ministry of Foreign Affairs definitely suspected that certain members of Belgium's military assistance programme had offered support to the forces

---

[54] "Le décret sur les compagnies à charte", *Études congolaises*, 8, 1 (January-February 1965), pp. 36–44.

[55] AGR, MCM, 12 February 1965, pp. 9–10.

[56] AGR, Finoutremer, n° 799, PV n° 900 of the Comité intérieur africain (CIA), 11 February 1965, pp. 3–5.

[57] J.-P. Verwilghen, "Les dissolutions successives du CSK", *Études congolaises*, 8, 3 (May-June 1965), pp. 1–55; "Le contentieux belgo-congolais", CA, 46 (30 April 1965).

[58] NA, FO, n° 371/181665, C. Ramsden, Britain's ambassador in Brussels, to FO, 8 January 1965. Spaak had a rather positive opinion of Mobutu: according to the Belgian politician, the general had shown, during the past few years, "fairly correct political reactions" (AGR, MCM, 3 December 1965, p. 11).

opposing the president.[59] On the other hand, the involvement of the CIA in Mobutu's coup now seems beyond doubt.[60]

Be that as it may, Spaak assured the new ruler in the Congo that President Kasavubu's policies in recent years had been a source of concern to Belgium. "Therefore," he said, "we can only rejoice at this turnaround and the opportunities for a revival that present themselves. The Belgian government shall do its utmost to assist you in any way you wish".[61] However, it would not be long before the relationship between Belgium and the Congo ran into troubled water again. It was a sign of things to come: For the next three decades, the relationship would be marked by a succession of incidents and crises of varying magnitudes, followed by sudden twists, reconciliations and mutual declarations of love. American political scientists Crawford Young and Thomas Turner have described the relationship between Belgium and the Congo under Mobutu in detail.[62] Their illuminating analysis, confirmed by the work of the pre-eminent Belgian expert on the Congo, Jean-Claude Willame, reads like the diagnostic history of a patient suffering from cyclothymic disorder, with its characteristic succession of euphoric and depressive episodes. However, behind the highs and lows, the overriding trend of the relationship was undeniably downwards.

In 1966, after just a few months in power, Mobutu provoked the first full-blown crisis when he nationalised Union minière du Haut-Katanga. The Belgian giant was superseded by Gécomin, later renamed Gécamines. A confrontation ensued between the SGB group and the Congolese authorities that would take several months to resolve, as we shall see. Even before his move to nationalise UMHK, Mobutu had had to deal with another problem. In July of 1966, a mutiny broke out in certain units of the Congolese army (Armée nationale congolaise, ANC). Barely a year later, Mobutu had to contend with the ANC's white mercenaries, led by Belgian Jean Schramme, who staged an uprising in east Congo with assistance from the former Katangan gendarmerie. Mobutu suspected (perhaps justifiably so) that the rebellion had been organised by the West, specifically by Belgium, in an effort to get rid of him and restore Tshombe's regime. In June 1967, Mobutu may have had a hand in the spectacular abduction of his rival, who was eventually locked up in Algeria, where he died in mysterious circumstances in 1969. These events had repercussions for the Belgian community in the Congo: In the summer of 1967, twenty-five expatriates were killed in incidents. In August of that same year, Belgium's embassy in the capital was looted by Congolese demonstrators. In sum, relations reached a new low. Belgian diplomatic circles, now under the leadership of

---

[59] NA, FO, n° 371/181665, C. Ramsden, Britain's ambassador in Brussels to FO, 26 November 1965 ; V. Dujardin, *Pierre Harmel. Biographie* (Brussels, 2004), p. 309.
[60] S. Kelly, *America's Tyrant, op. cit.*, pp. 166–70; D. N. Gibbs, *The Political Economy, op. cit.*, p. 163.
[61] Quoted in M. Dumoulin, *Spaak, op. cit.*, p. 621.
[62] C. Young & Th. Turner, *The Rise, op. cit.*, p. 394; J.-Cl. Willame, *L'automne, op. cit.*, p. 161.

Christian-Democrat Pierre Harmel, began to wonder openly whether Belgium ought not to withdraw completely from the Congo.[63]

However, for the time being, at least, there was no definitive rift. In the course of 1968 and 1969, relations were gradually restored. The reconciliation was sealed with two symbolic visits to Brussels by Mobutu (1968 and 1969). King Baudouin and Queen Fabiola returned the honour in 1970, visiting the Congo to attend festivities marking the tenth anniversary of independence. The Congolese head of state called on Belgian investors to return to his country.

So would everything return to normal? Not quite. By 1973 trouble was once again brewing. As part of his authenticity policy, Mobutu announced the so-called Zairisation (30 November 1973), followed by a 'radicalisation' (31 December 1974). Foreign companies were nationalised and taken over by friends of the regime.[64] The nationalisations obviously affected many Belgian entrepreneurs.[65] On 25 November 1975 and 17 September 1976 Mobutu announced a partial return of the so-called radicalised properties to their former expatriate owners in an attempt to mitigate the disastrous consequences the measures had had on the Congo's economy. Initially forty per cent and subsequently up to sixty per cent of the nationalised properties were given back. Furthermore, a Congolese-Belgian agreement of March 1976 provided compensation. Nonetheless, the damage to the Congolese economy was substantial and relations with Belgium had again become strained. It would take a considerable diplomatic effort by Tindemans's government to sort matters out.

As usual, the strain did not last. In 1977 and 1978, Shaba twice became the arena of war.[66] On 8 March 1977, armed troops of the Front de Libération nationale du Congo (FLNC), with quite a few former Katangan gendarmes among their ranks, crossed over into the mining province of Shaba, as Katanga was now known. The central authority was only able to survive thanks to an intervention by its Western allies in combination with Moroccan troops. The rebels withdrew in May 1977, but only until the FLNC could launch a new offensive on 13 May of the following year. This time, they captured the important mining town of Kolwezi. Here, and elsewhere in the province, Westerners were killed in never entirely resolved circumstances, though they are believed to have fallen victim to the regular Zairian army rather than to the rebel forces.[67] Nonetheless, the deaths of these foreigners provided a perfect justification (or pretext) for a new military intervention by the West. French troops, quickly followed by Belgian commandos, entered the fray on 19 May 1978, ending the threat to Mobutu's regime. Still, the Belgian government assumed a "carefully

---

[63] V. Dujardin, *Harmel, op. cit.*, pp. 308–33; Kadoc, Van Bilsen Papers, n° 6.13.1/2.
[64] Lutumba-Lu-Vilu Na Wundu, *De la zaïrianisation à la rétrocession et au dialogue Nord-Sud* (Brussels, 1976).
[65] C. Young & Th. Turner, *The Rise, op. cit.*, pp. 356–8.
[66] R. Yakemtchouk, *Les deux guerres du Shaba* (Brussels, 1988); A. Rouvez, *Disconsolate Empires, op. cit.*, pp. 331–40.
[67] I. Ndaywel, *Histoire générale, op. cit.*, p. 756; survey by J.-Cl. Willame cited in *Info Zaïre*, 5, 1 (October-November 1979), no page numbering.

attentive and reserved attitude" in the whole affair, much to the dissatisfaction of Mobutu, who would find it hard to forgive Belgium its "lack of enthusiasm" in helping him.[68]

In the decade that followed, the succession of highs and lows continued. Prime Minister Wilfried Martens's first visit to the Congo in 1981 would be remembered for his statement that he "love[d] this country, its people and its leaders".[69] The visit provided a brief respite before a series of further, more or less severe, crises. The causes (or pretexts) were very diverse. Belgium had allegedly shown a 'favourable' attitude towards the Congolese opposition present in and active from Brussels. The Congo had failed to pay off its debt; some creditors had grown impatient and were suing the state of Zaire before a Belgian court. Belgian national Ronald Van den Bogaert had been incarcerated in the Congo on accusations of maintaining subversive contacts with the Congolese opposition. The list of bones of contention goes on and on. Interspersed among these confrontations were brief periods of reconciliation, as epitomised by the visit of King Baudouin and a later visit by Belgian dignitaries to celebrate the twenty-fifth anniversary of the country's independence in 1985.

Invariably, though, the financial predicament of the country was of central importance. The Congo's foreign debt was huge, straining its relationship with the International Monetary Fund. In 1988–9, a new and especially severe crisis broke out between Belgium and the Congo, one that would only be resolved after difficult negotiations in the Moroccan capital. Under these so-called Accords of Rabat of July 1989, Belgium agreed among other things to cancel a large part of the Congo's debt.

This turned out to be the ultimate attempt to patch up the troubled relationship between Kinshasa and Brussels. The following year, in May 1990, a massacre took place at the University of Lubumbashi that was believed to have been orchestrated by Mobutu's secret service in an attempt to eliminate opponents of the regime. This incident would lead to a definitive rift. The Belgian government demanded a full explanation for the killings, but Kinshasa did not comply. Initially, diplomatic relations were not severed and attempts were made to set matters straight but, eventually, Mobutu's political credit ran out. Belgium refused to offer further support to his regime and terminated all official development co-operation with the Congo.[70]

In September 1990, as looting broke out in Kinshasa, the government in Brussels felt it had to send in troops to evacuate Belgian nationals. This operation proceeded against Mobutu's will. A similar scenario unfolded in 1993, when foreigners once again got caught up in the Congo's internal problems and needed to be evacuated. Belgium only began to reinvest in its diplomatic

---

[68] J.-Cl. Willame, "Les relations belgo-zaïroises. Réflexions sur une pratique de la politique étrangère", *Res Publica*, 22 (1980), p. 443.
[69] W. Martens, *De Memoires* (Tielt, 2006), pp. 502, 506, 512–13.
[70] Kadoc, Mark Eyskens papers, n° 74, "Conclusions de l'entretien que le Ministre des Affaires étrangères, M. Mark Eyskens, a eu avec son Collègue zaïrois, M. Bagbeni Adeito Nzengeya, à Bruxelles le 13 janvier 1992".

relations with the Congo after the fall of Mobutu in 1997 and, even more so, after the eruption of civil war the following year. In 1999, under the impulse of the new minister of foreign affairs, Louis Michel, a prominent figure of the French-speaking Liberal Party, Belgium tried to broker peace between the warring factions and called for international attention to the conflict and assistance in the divided country's reconstruction.

Characteristics and Foundations of Belgium's Policy towards Mobutu
After this brief overview of the turbulent relationship between Belgium and Mobutu's Congo, we turn our attention to the underlying structures. First we shall make a number of observations in relation to the essential characteristics of Belgium's policy vis-à-vis Mobutu's regime. Subsequently, we shall look at the actual diplomatic mechanisms involved and conclude with a discussion of the consequences of Belgian-Congolese relations for Belgium's domestic politics.

During the Mobutu era, two successive evolutions defined the relationship between Belgium and the Congo. The first coincided with a fundamental shift away from the era of 'political moulding'. Before Mobutu's rise to power, Belgium had actively interfered in the Congo's internal affairs. In the course of 1966 and 1967, it became apparent that Mobutu, who was deemed unpredictable and largely uncontrollable, often took action without waiting for instructions or approval from Brussels. In the months following his coup, he gradually consolidated his power, eliminating anyone who might pose a threat to his leadership. Hence, he created a vacuum in which he would only allow his most trusted followers to operate. Should they threaten to undermine his position, he and he alone had the power to remove them. The governments of the Congo tended to be volatile, with a characteristically quick succession of reshuffles and individuals constantly falling in and out of grace.[71] Against this backdrop, Brussels began to change its position towards the Congo. Henceforth it would not interfere in the meanderings of the Congo's politics by actively promoting or opposing one alternative over another. Belgian diplomatic efforts would henceforth focus primarily on consolidating and enhancing its relationship with the new dictator. This position was inspired among other things by the extreme sensitivity of Mobutu to any contacts between the Belgian authorities and the Congolese opposition, whether in exile or in the Congo itself. These real or assumed contacts led on more than one occasion to friction and head-on collisions between Brussels and Kinshasa.

After the era of 'political moulding' came a period when Mobutu was regarded as *untouchable*. He was the man to whom one's actions had to be adapted; the leader one always wanted to please. The transition between the two phases unfolded during the crisis years of 1966 and 1967. Minister of Foreign Affairs Harmel found himself in the eye of the storm. During a visit to the Congo in June 1966, he suffered the deep humiliation of being refused

---

[71] Between November 1965 and May 1990, there were no fewer than fifty-one cabinet reshuffles. For an overview, see I. Ndaywel, *Histoire générale, op. cit.*, pp. 693-4.

a meeting with Mobutu.[72] "The attitude of the Congo cannot be more disagreeable than it is for the moment", he told his colleagues during a cabinet meeting.[73] In response, he intended to weaken the relationship between Belgium and the political leaders of the Congo. But how far could one go in this respect? During the dramatic summer of 1967, this was the delicate question that the Foreign Affairs Department pondered. It was concluded that the ties between the two countries were too close to risk a complete rift.[74] Hence, the Belgians would continue to be present in the Congo, but slightly more reticently than had previously been the case.

So it looked very much as if Belgium was prepared to make a change in its policy towards the Congo. As we shall see, Belgium's co-operation became more geographically dispersed, as politicians stressed the need for a more balanced policy towards Africa; in other words, a policy not focused exclusively on the former colony.[75] The move prompted resentment on the part of Mobutu, who saw it as a rejection and a sign of distrust towards his leadership. Nonetheless, from the late 1960s well into the 1980s, Belgium would make it a priority to maintain good, close relations with Mobutu, even if this meant grinning and bearing it on more than one occasion.

Why this obstinacy? Clearly, the answer lies in a subtle combination of psychological, political, material and personal factors. First and foremost, one should take due account of the attitudes and the perceptions that had been formed in the past. The political generation that governed Belgium in the 1960s had personally experienced colonial rule over the Congo. To them, the Congo was important because it had been important in the past. Besides this psychological aspect, there was a diplomatic tradition that would not easily give up its familiar patterns. During the colonial era, Belgium had benefitted internationally from a 'diplomatic windfall' thanks to its presence in Africa. Socialist Henri Simonet, looking back at the years (1977–80) when he, in his capacity as minister of foreign affairs, had led Belgium's diplomatic service, formulated it in a way that might generally also have applied to his predecessors from the colonial era: "Our political contacts with Kinshasa add a dimension to our foreign policy and, as I have noted, give us a more attentive audience in Africa and in the Third World".[76] Severing all ties with Kinshasa would, in other words, reduce Belgium's international audience, which was unthinkable in the eyes of the country's political elite.

---

[72] V. Dujardin, *Harmel, op. cit.*, p. 316.

[73] AGR, MCM, 15 July 1966, p. 4.

[74] AGR, MCM, 28 July 1967, p. 14 ("The basic problem is to know whether we want to stay or to leave, in whatever form. Regarding this, one has to note that the government wants to leave, but that our Western friends invite us to stay."). See also Kadoc, Van Bilsen Papers, n° 6.13.1/2, "Sur le problème de la continuation de la coopération avec le Congo", 17 July 1967, and also numerous memos and summaries of conversations with various individuals.

[75] See for example *Het Belgisch Afrika-beleid*, Brussels, 1984, 171 p. (note on Belgium's African policy, drawn up under Foreign Minister Leo Tindemans).

[76] H. Simonet, "La politique belge vis-à-vis du Zaïre dans les années 1970", *Res Publica*, 30, 4 (1988), p. 412.

Belgium's benevolence towards Mobutu was also inspired by more practical considerations. Some politicians had personal or familial ties with the Congo, often involving business interests in companies operating in the former colony. The utility of the Congo also assumed more indirect, though equally significant, forms. Maintaining friendly relations with the Congolese president could lead to lucrative business deals, which would in turn benefit employment in the constituencies where the contracted companies were located – a factor not to be ignored by politicians preoccupied with re-election. Finally, not only was Mobutu corrupt, he corrupted others. Among those who profited from his financial gifts were Belgian journalists and media figures, as well as individuals in public office.[77]

Mobutu was able to rely on faithful supporters in the ranks of all the major political parties in Belgium. In fact, leading politicians did not even try to hide their sympathy for the Congolese strongman, whom they visited regularly and sometimes outside of the bounds of diplomatic activity. In addition to all the previously mentioned considerations, there was the realisation that the regime of Mobutu needed to be maintained so that Belgium's economic interests in the Congo would not be damaged.

So was Belgium's diplomacy geared exclusively to serving national economic interests? Surely this would be too simplistic. Politics and business have their own separate logic and do not automatically overlap. In 1964, even before Mobutu seized power, the vice governor of Société générale de Belgique, Jules Dubois-Pelerin, complained about the government's distrust of the private sector: "One senses all too easily a cruel disinterest. One feels the absence of a genuine policy".[78] It was a frustration that would not disappear under Mobutu. In 1966, André de Spirlet, another senior figure within the group, stressed "the lack of coherence in the Belgian government's policy". He, too, felt that Belgium's trade policy towards the Congo was excessively restrictive, as a result of which Belgian companies were unable to sell production goods in the former colony.[79] Many other examples show that diplomatic and economic interests did not always coincide.[80] And, sometimes, the economic interests themselves diverged. Large corporations that were part of a mighty group such as the SGB did not always have precisely the same goal as individual entrepreneurs or small investors. Clearly, politics weighed more heavily on the larger corporations than on the smaller investors.

---

[77] E. Blumenthal, "Zaïre. Rapport sur sa crédibilité financière internationale", 20 April 1982, appendix 2, question 7, published in full in *Info Zaïre. Bimestriel du Comité Zaïre*, 36 (October 1982).

[78] AGR, SGB-3, n° 167, handwritten note ("confidential") by J. Dubois-Pelerin, 14–15 February 1964, p. 43.

[79] AGR, Finoutremer, n° 799, PV n° 926 of the CIA, 8 June 1967, p. 5.

[80] AGR, SGB-3, n° 170, A. Cahen, Belgian ambassador in the Congo to F. M. De Pooter, advisor to CEDIOM, 11 October 1972, p. 5; Ibid., "Réunion du Conseil de Direction du CEDIOM du 14 septembre 1972"; Ibid., n° 897, "Compte rendu de la réunion du 16 mai 1974 du Groupe de Travail 'Syndicat de défense – Zaïre'", 21 May 1974, pp. 2–3.

Still, in the longer term, there can be little doubt that Belgian diplomacy with regard to the Congo was geared primarily towards protecting Belgian economic interests there. And yet Belgium's economic presence in central Africa noticeably declined in the 1970s and 1980s until it had all but disappeared. This evolution also explains the gradual reversal in Belgium's attitude towards Mobutu. The Congolese regime had of course been criticised by sections of Belgian public opinion for years, but now these anti-Mobutist forces, who previously had been no match for the economic lobby, were finally beginning to affect Belgium's foreign policy in the Congo. In the early 1990s, the Belgian government, under the inspiration of its Christian-Democrat foreign minister Mark Eyskens, adopted an 'ethical' stance that would lead to the ultimate rift with Mobutu. Human rights considerations were no longer secondary to Belgium's economic and strategic interests.[81] This evolution coincided with the emergence of a new generation of politicians who, unlike their predecessors, felt no personal or emotional involvement with the former colony. Mobutu's power was undeniably shrinking, and his only remaining ally was the United States.[82] This marks the start of the third phase in Belgium's policy towards the independent Congo. After the phase of 'moulding' (1960–65/66) and that of 'convivial relations' (1967–89), a 'hands-off' phase (1990–7) began. In other words, Belgium was now distancing itself from the Congolese regime.

Players and Mechanisms Involved in Belgian-Congolese Relations during the Mobutu Regime
Notwithstanding the numerous twists and turns in Belgian-Congolese relations, there are a number of recurrent patterns to be discerned. For one thing, the relationship was defined to a large extent by the personality of the Congolese head of state. While it would obviously be an oversimplification to reduce a country's foreign policy to the outlook of one single individual, there is no denying that the dictator had an immeasurable impact: He injected a peculiar mixture of emotion and calculation into the contacts between the two countries. Moreover, Mobutu remained continuously in power, while his Belgian interlocutors – whether politicians, high-ranking civil servants or leading businessmen – came and went. The Congolese leader was mercurial and did not shy away from emotional argumentation whereby diametrically opposed elements were amalgamated to suit his purpose. He was extremely sensitive to anything relating even distantly to the dignity of his person and/or country. In 1966, for example, Belgian-Congolese relations took a turn for the worse after Etienne Davignon, chef de cabinet to Minister Harmel, uttered some supposedly insulting remarks.[83] Words such as 'disdain', 'lack of gratitude', 'disrespect' and 'insults' were fixtures of Mobutu's discourse, convinced as he was

---

[81] A. Van De Voorde, *Mark Eyskens. Een biografie* (Tielt, 2003), pp. 65 and 299.
[82] Kadoc, Mark Eyskens papers, box 74, "Appel téléphonique de Herman Cohen le 4 November 1991", from A. Adam, 4 November 1991.
[83] V. Dujardin, *Harmel, op. cit.*, pp. 312–3, 325.

that Belgium 'owed' him something. In 1969, he told a deliberately chosen audience of visitors that it was thanks to him that Belgium's losing bet in 1960 had since been turned into a win; that he had in effect done Belgium a favour internationally. He slyly added that he had previously shared this very insight with the Belgian king.[84] Whenever Mobutu felt that Belgium was not expressing sufficient gratitude or, worse still, that Belgium's indebtedness to him was not recognised, crisis would loom. Conversely, his expressions of reconciliation would be emotionally charged with notions such as 'mutual respect', 'trust' or 'unbreakable ties', often generously enhanced with compliments. Some of his Belgian counterparts would get carried away; perhaps unwittingly or perhaps out of plain opportunism.

This characteristic diplomacy of emotion was invariably intertwined with other elements in Mobutu's discourse, including frequent references to history and to the colonial past in particular, which would be adapted effortlessly to any given context. In crisis situations, he liked to recall the abuses during the colonial era, the plunder his country had suffered and the manner in which Belgium had profited and continued to profit from its relationship with the Congo.[85] A particularly prominent aspect was that of the *contentieux* between Belgium and its former colony. Back in 1960, the young Mobutu had been a member of Lumumba's MNC delegation at the economic roundtable conference in Brussels, so he was familiar with the economic aspects of decolonisation. He would frequently argue that the Congolese had been disadvantaged, even 'ripped off', under the terms of the 1965 accords between Spaak and Tshombe. This allowed him to direct the disagreements between the two countries towards a topic that was close to his heart, namely that of material compensation. But as so often in Mobutu's discourse, the past proved to be a malleable concept, easily adapted to any given situation. If the order of the day was reconciliation, then he would happily emphasise its bright sides and toast to the close and friendly historical relations between the peoples of Belgium and the Congo and their common destiny. In such instances, the Belgians were described as benevolent relatives (*l'oncle belge*) rather than as exploiters and suppressors.

Rhetoric and perceptions played an important role in Congo-Belgian relations. It should not come as a surprise, then, that the media were not passive observers. They were actively involved in the diplomatic tussle. Mobutu reacted irritably whenever the Belgian press criticised him personally or wrote critically about his regime. However, these instances of supposed defamation of a head of state were not restricted to newspaper and magazine articles. In March through June 1974, a book on Mobutu by left-wing lawyer Jules Chomé caused a full-blown crisis in bilateral relations.[86] Time and again, whenever Kinshasa

[84] AGR, SGB-3, n° 167, "Entrevue Mobutu au Mont Stanley de 9h55 à 11h25", from Tihange.
[85] See for example the pseudoscientific pamphlet *Conflit belgo-zaïrois. Fondements historiques, politiques, économiques et culturels* (Paris, 1990).
[86] J. Chomé, *L'ascension, op. cit.*; AGR, MCM, 28 March 1973, pp. 2–3 and 17 January 1975, pp. 11–12; J.-F. Marinus, *L'offense aux souverains et chefs de gouvernement étrangers par la*

was unhappy with an article or editorial, the Belgian government would refer to the right of freedom of expression and the impossibility of censorship. The Belgian authorities did occasionally intervene, as in 1967, when they called for restraint on the part of the press in order not to further deteriorate the relationship with Mobutu.[87] In a recent book, journalist Walter Zinzen wrote about how, in 1978, he clashed with the directors of the Flemish public broadcaster Belgische Radio en Televisie (BRT), whom he accused of having manipulated, at the request of the Belgian government, the coverage of the Shaba crisis in order not to upset Mobutu.[88] A similar situation arose at the francophone public radio and TV station Radio Télévision belge francophone (RTBF).[89]

Naturally, Mobutu also tried to manipulate the Belgian media directly. Especially during the early days of his regime, he was able to count on support from a number of journalists, including Pierre Davister and Francis Monheim, who produced quite a few hagiographic pieces on the Congo's strongman.[90] The weekly *Spécial*, which they led from 1965 to 1979, served as Mobutu's mouthpiece in Belgium.[91] It received financial support from the Congolese president, who had 500 copies flown over to Kinshasa every week.[92] Many other Belgian journalists expressed understanding and even praise for the Congolese president, but in these instances it is harder to establish whether this benevolence was or was not remunerated. Nevertheless, it certainly seemed that any time they wished to travel to the Congo, they would get their visas instantly and could expect a hearty welcome in the country. This was in contrast to the experiences of more critical journalists, including Colette Braeckman, a senior reporter with *Le Soir*, who was actually declared persona non grata by the regime. As time went by, support for Mobutu in the Belgian media declined to the extent that, in the final years of his regime, he faced an almost unanimously hostile press. As was the case in politics, a new generation of journalists had stepped up, while those who had experienced the Belgian Congo first hand had retired. The newcomers took a less nostalgic, more critical view of events in the Congo.

Mobutu's diplomacy of emotion did not, however, exclude careful calculation on his part. His diplomatic escapades almost invariably proceeded according to the principle of action and reaction. An event in which real or artificial emotions were allowed to come into play would trigger a succession of threats and counter-threats, including the expulsions of foreigners, the withdrawal of

---

voie de la presse (Brussels, 2002), pp. 158–9, 233, 278, 327, 387, 391, 503 (also concerning other press affairs).

[87] V. Dujardin, *Harmel, op. cit.*, p. 327.
[88] W. Zinzen, *Mobutu – van mirakel tot malaise* (Antwerp, 1995), pp. 57–9.
[89] *Info Zaïre. Bimestriel du Comité Zaïre*, 4, 2 (December 1978-January 1979), p. 12.
[90] F. Monheim, *Mobutu, l'homme seul* (Brussels, 1962); Idem, *Mobutu, le point de départ* (Paris, 1985); Mobutu, *Dignité pour l'Afrique. Entretiens avec Jean-Louis Remilleux* (Paris, 1989).
[91] M. Degauque-Nayer, "Davister et Monheim, un tandem *spécial* pour la propagande mobutiste", in M. Quaghebeur, ed., *Papier blanc, encre noir, op. cit.*, vol. 2, pp. 567–90.
[92] Archives nationales congolaises (ARNACO), Kinshasa, fonds Ministère des Affaires étrangères, n° P137 – D1043, telegram from Kama-Budiaki, interim chargé d'affaires at the Congolese embassy in Brussels, to the Ministry of Foreign Affairs in Kinshasa, 1 April 1975.

ambassadors, the suspension of landing rights or other economic benefits, the annulment of contracts, the deferment of payments and so forth. More often than not, such measures would ultimately lead to insolent and opportunistic demands for compensation.

Clearly, then, Belgium and the Congo maintained a give-and-take relationship. Time and again, Mobutu would threaten to sever the ties between the two countries or, conversely, he would promise to restore them – for a price. Many such examples can be cited.[93]

There was another constant factor in the chaotic ups and downs of Belgo-Congolese relations. Mobutu invariably exploited existing rivalries in the broader international arena. He was aware that he could take advantage of the divergent interests of Western nations, playing one against the other. Immediately after his coup, on 26 November 1965, he met with the most important ambassadors assigned to Léopoldville. As the Belgian ambassador elucidated the position of his country, Mobutu, with a mixture of emotion and cunning, made it discreetly clear to the ambassador of France how attached he felt to that country. The French ambassador later revealed in diplomatic documents that "General Mobutu whispered into my ear: 'We are both republicans'. (…) He tends towards our country and attaches great importance to all things French".[94] The message did not fall upon deaf ears. France, which had already shown an interest in the Congo back in the days of Leopold II and had enjoyed a 'right of pre-emption', was keen to expand its sphere of influence in Africa. In 1963, it had declared the following intent: "It is our desire that the [former Belgian] Congo should become a member of the UAM (Union africaine et malgache); not too soon, however, for this could unbalance the UAM. In the short term, we wish to maintain good relations with Léopoldville".[95] France continued to increase its development co-operation with the Congo. The number of French expatriates in the country rose from 2,200 in 1957 to 5,000 in 1981.[96] French companies were eyeing the Congolese market. The United States, too, strengthened its presence in Mobutu's Congo, much to Belgium's annoyance.[97] According to the French ambassador in Kinshasa, the French continued to

---

[93] AGR, SGB-3, n° 170, A. Cahen, Belgium's ambassador to the Congo, to F. M. De Pooter, advisor to CEDIOM, 11 October 1972, pp. 2-4; G. Vanthemsche, *La Sabena et l'aviation commerciale belge 1923-2001. Des origines au crash* (Brussels, 2001), p. 263; Kadoc, Mark Eyskens papers, box 85, "Verslag over het onderhoud van de Heer Eerste minister en de Heer Vice-Eerste minister P. Moureaux met president Mobutu en Commissaire d'État Nguz – Dakar, 25 mei 1989", by J. Grauls; ibid., note titled "Belgisch-Zaïrese crisis", s.d. (end of June 1989), by J. Hollants van Loocke; W. Martens, *De Memoires, op. cit.*, pp. 509-12.

[94] *Documents diplomatiques français. 1965. Tome 2 (1er juillet – 31 décembre)* (Brussels-Bern, 2004), p. 651 (telegram from Kosciusko-Morizet, French ambassador in Léopoldville, to MAÉF, 26 November 1965).

[95] AMAÉF (Paris), Série Europe (1961-1970), sous-série Belgique, n° 173, "Note. Politique française au Congo (ex-belge)", 9 February 1963, p. 2.

[96] Th. Trefon, *French Policy Toward Zaïre during the Giscard d'Estaing Presidency* (Brussels, 1989).

[97] R. Yakemtchouk, *Les relations, op. cit.*, pp. 22-3; D. N. Gibbs, *The Political Economy, op. cit.*, pp. 145-94.

consider the Congo as their 'game reserve' and watched the "growing American presence closely and not without concern".[98] In sum, Belgium's dominance could no longer be taken for granted. The Congolese president realised this all too well and did not hesitate to use this shift in influence in his dealings with Belgian businessmen and politicians. During the second invasion of Shaba, he pitted the French and the Belgians against each other in order to put pressure on Belgium.

Three other aspects played a role in the relations between Belgium and the Congo: the presence of Belgian advisors, parallel diplomacy and the personalisation of conflicts. The first element has already been mentioned. During the decisive talks at the roundtable conference in Brussels, Belgian experts from various political parties assisted the Congolese delegation. After June 1960, many of these figures assumed roles in the entourages of the political leaders of the young republic, including Jef Van Bilsen, who became an advisor to President Kasavubu. This phenomenon continued well into the Mobutu era. Until the 1980s, Belgians occupied important positions in public and semi-public institutions or in large government-controlled corporations (customs, railways, water-bound transportation, quasi-autonomous public corporations and even Gécamines). In the field of military co-operation, Belgian officers monitored the (re-)organisation of and logistical support for the Congolese army and police. The Congolese experiences of these civilian and military advisors were not always easy. There were moments of disillusionment and entrapment, falls into disfavour, and sometimes highly publicised dismissals. Obviously, most of them were not able to affect Congo's orientation and foreign policy in any substantial or lasting way. But some were indeed very close to Mobutu. Commander J. Powis de Tenbossche, for example, was his military attaché and ordinance officer. When the UMHK was nationalised in 1966–7, he played a decisive part in the resolution of this crisis.[99] In the end, the presence of these Belgians around the Congolese president may have been counter-productive for Belgian interests. In 1974, the Belgian ambassador in Kinshasa, Charles Kerremans, intriguingly warned Prime Minister Leo Tindemans about "certain Belgians in Mobutu's entourage".[100]

This brings us to a second structural aspect of the relationship: the role of parallel diplomacy. In tense situations and crises, the customary channels for diplomacy (ministers, ambassadors and high-ranking civil servants) may fail. It may then be necessary to conduct delicate work behind the scenes, along more informal channels. Likewise, if one camp is divided by opposing interests, an informal approach may offer a way out of the impasse. Such mechanisms are as old as the art of diplomacy itself, but given the complexity of the

---

[98] AMAÉF (Paris), Série Europe (1961–70), sous-série Belgique, n° 162, Tanguy de Courson, French ambassador in Kinshasa, to MAÉF, 21 February 1969; E. de Crouy-Chanel, French ambassador in Brussels, to MAÉF, 1 February 1968.
[99] AGR, SGB-3, n° 167, A. de Spirlet to E. Davignon, 7 August 1967.
[100] L. Tindemans, *De memoires. Gedreven door een overtuiging* (Tielt, 2002), pp. 268 and 271.

Belgian-Congolese relationship, it is not surprising that parallel diplomacy played an unusually significant role in this instance.

Parallel diplomacy was under way shortly after the conception of the Congolese state, as would later be revealed during sessions of the Lumumba enquiry commission in the Belgian Chamber of Representatives. In 1960, with the Congo thoroughly divided and Belgium pursuing a double-faced policy towards its former colony, track-two diplomacy was a necessity.[101] Many other examples can be given for subsequent periods. For instance, Charles de Kerchove, Belgium's ambassador in Léopoldville, complained in a telegram to Minister Spaak that the chairman of the Federation of Congolese Enterprises (Fédération des Entreprises congolaises, FEC), which represented the principal Belgian companies in the former colony, behaved like a veritable 'second ambassador'.[102] Similarly, the crisis surrounding UMHK – which was after all a private company – gave rise to some 'diplomatic activity' in 1966–7, as the case was primarily resolved through direct negotiations between representatives of UMHK and the Congolese authorities. Etienne Davignon, the chef de cabinet to the minister of foreign affairs, told the British ambassador that the Belgian authorities preferred to let industry fend for itself. According to him, the large corporations had at their disposal certain methods, which the British ambassador understood to be bribery, to which the Belgian government could not possibly resort. He added that, generally speaking, they seemed to handle the Congolese more effectively than the Belgian government.[103] Clearly, Belgium's official diplomacy took a backseat to industry and relied on assistance from the SGB. Also in this very turbulent year, Mobutu called on the services of a Belgian nobleman, Prince Stéphane d'Arenberg, to pass on a spoken message to King Baudouin, thereby bypassing all official channels.[104]

The prevalence of second-track diplomacy is arguably connected with a third structural characteristic of the relationship between the two countries, namely the role of personalities. Individual strengths and weaknesses, as well as sympathies and antipathies, are a daily consideration for the Foreign Affairs Ministry, but in the context of Mobutu's 'diplomacy of emotion' they assumed an additional significance. The Congolese president maintained ambivalent affective ties with Belgium, to which he applied an unusually strong *personal* touch. During a falling out with the SGB in 1967, Mobutu refused to negotiate with some of the established figures within either the SGB itself or its mining subsidiary. Instead, he chose to talk to another executive in the Belgian company, namely André de Spirlet, whom he respected.[105] Another example: In 1969, the Congolese authorities made some very negative comments about

---

[101] *Rapport, op. cit.*, p. 602.
[102] M. Dumoulin, *Spaak, op. cit.*, p. 600.
[103] NA, FO, n° 1100/40, C. Ramsden, British ambassador in Brussels, to FO, 23 August 1966.
[104] V. Dujardin, *Harmel, op. cit.*, p. 325.
[105] AGR, SGB-3, n° 167, note titled "Congo. Mission belge. Communiqué au Gouverneur le 3 mars à 9h00": "On the presidential boat with Mobutu. Great friendship for M. de Spirlet. Antipathy for L. W. [Louis Wallef]".

Belgium embassy staff, and they expressed the wish that Alfred Cahen, a Belgian diplomat whom they appreciated and understood, would be appointed as the mission's head.[106] A few years later, Cahen was indeed made ambassador to the Congo. In 1975, Mobutu made it known that he was dissatisfied with Ambassador Kerremans, which promptly led to Kerremans being replaced by Eugène Rittweger de Moor, whom Mobutu considered a friend.[107] Belgium's ministers were also targeted in Mobutu's tactics of 'personalisation'. During the Shaba crisis, after Henri Simonet clashed with the Congolese president, Mobutu promptly indulged in persistent diplomatic ostracism of the Belgian minister. In yet another telling example of second-track diplomacy, Mobutu would only relent after mediation by his close friend, King Hassan II of Morocco.[108]

Belgian Politics and Mobutu's Congo

The Congo was a constant source of disagreement between the various Belgian political players.[109] A few examples taken from the 1970s make this clear. In 1973, the attitude towards Mobutu caused friction between Prime Minister Leburton, a staunch proponent of the Congolese regime, and his secretary of state for development cooperation, Irène Pétry, although they both belonged to the Socialist Party.[110] While it remains unproven that her disagreement with Leburton was to blame, Pétry would never again occupy a cabinet seat. In 1973, the Congo caused a second falling out between Leburton and Deputy Prime Minister Leo Tindemans, a Christian-Democrat: Leburton had arranged a meeting with Mobutu in Paris without informing his government, much to Tindemans's dismay. Later, in 1986 and again in 1988–9, the issue of the Congo's debt pitted Prime Minister Martens against his arch-rival Leo Tindemans, now in charge of foreign affairs. The conflict in Shaba also features prominently in the anthology of dissonance within the Belgian government. In 1978, Minister of Foreign Affairs Simonet expressed his outrage at statements made by Ambassador Rittweger in Kinshasa about military intervention in the copper province. Clearly Belgium's position on the Congo was far from unified. In fact, there was disagreement at the heart of government where ministers, each speaking on behalf of their own parties, expressed diametrically opposed views. It suffices to compare Leo Tindemands's memoirs on the Shaba crisis with those of Henri Simonet to understand just how divided they were on the issue at the time.[111]

---

[106] AGR, SGB-3, n° 167, "Note n° 18", from Tihange, SGB informer, 25 July 1969, p. 4.
[107] *Pan*, 17 December 1975; R. Yakemtchouk, *Les deux guerres, op. cit.*, p. 397; G. de Villers, *De Mobutu, op. cit.*, p. 82. Mobutu applied the same tactics towards the United States ambassador (S. Kelly, *America's Tyrant, op. cit.*, pp. 190, 205).
[108] G. de Villers, *De Mobutu, op. cit.*, p. 96; H. Simonet, *Je n'efface rien et je recommence* (Brussels, 1986), pp. 181–228; R. Yakemtchouk, *Les deux guerres, op. cit.*, pp. 621–32.
[109] G. de Villers, *De Mobutu, op. cit.*, pp. 52, 82, 174, 198 and so forth.
[110] *Spécial*, 5 September 1973.
[111] L. Tindemans, *De memoires, op. cit.*, pp. 337–52; H. Simonet, *Je n'efface rien, op. cit.*, pp. 181–228; see also (primarily even) the detailed analysis by R. Yakemtchouk, *Les deux guerres, op. cit.*, pp. 501–644.

The Belgian monarchy also played a significant role. King Baudouin's interest in the Congo did not appear to wane after independence.[112] In addition to visiting the Congo in 1970 and 1985, the king was a central figure in Belgium's policy towards the former colony, though his actions remained highly discreet. Initially, Baudouin took various initiatives to restore the disrupted ties between Belgium and the Congo. In 1966, he prompted Foreign Minister Harmel to pay a visit to the former colony, a trip that turned sour when the chief of Belgium's diplomatic service met with marked hostility in Léopoldville, an incident discussed previously. The following year, at the request of his government, King Baudouin sent a letter to Mobutu in an effort to control the mercenaries' crisis.[113] Commenting on a private visit by Mobutu to Brussels in 1968, a French diplomatic source asserted the following: "[It is] inspired primarily by an initiative of the Palace, not the government. The gesture of courtesy from the king to the president betrays a desire on the part of the sovereign and his entourage to seek a détente in the relationship between Belgium and the Congo".[114] With his initiative, Baudouin put an end to the reticent approach by Foreign Affairs Minister Harmel. The king expected that his gesture would help resolve any outstanding differences.

Alongside the official diplomatic channels that existed between the two countries in the 1970s, there was also direct contact between Baudouin and Mobutu. In July 1975, King Baudouin wrote a personal letter to the Congolese head of state, an initiative that, politically, came in for criticism. In the lead article of the Socialist daily *De Volksgazet*, Socialist MP Jos Van Eynde argued as follows: "One should have the king interfere as little as possible in the row between Brussels and Kinshasa. (...) The Palace has, in the past, all too often adopted positions in the formation of governments that are suggestive of the existence of ties between Belgium and Zaire other than the normal ones".[115] These words, from a prominent Socialist politician familiar with the political seraglio, raise many questions. Just a few months later, in October 1975, the Congolese state secretary for foreign affairs, Mandungu, was received in Brussels by King Baudouin and delivered a personal message from President Mobutu. Baudouin, in turn, made use of Mandungu to convey his response to the Congolese leader.[116]

The relationship between Mobutu and Baudouin eventually deteriorated, mainly because Baudouin chose increasingly to distance himself from the Congolese leader.[117] This was quite noticeable during Baudouin's trip to the

---

[112] C. Franck & Cl. Roosens, "Le Roi Baudouin et la politique étrangère", in C. Koninckx & P. Lefèvre, eds., *Le roi Baudouin* (Brussels, 1998), 159–63.

[113] V. Dujardin, *Harmel, op. cit.*, pp. 324–5.

[114] AMAÉF (Paris), Série Europe 1961–1970, sous-série Belgique, n° 162, E. de Crouy-Chanel, French ambassador in Brussels, to MAÉF, 11 June 1968.

[115] *Volksgazet*, 14 July 1975, p. 6.

[116] ARNACO (Kinshasa), dossier "Messages Ambazaïre à Minaffet Zaïre", Mandungu to the Présidence, 24 October 1975.

[117] W. Martens, *De Memoires, op. cit.*, pp. 503, 513, 515. However, Martens also notes that the king was extremely unhappy that he had not been informed about the meeting between Martens and Mobutu in Paris in July 1989 (p. 512).

Congo in 1985, when his own official speech was much more reserved than that of the Belgian government.[118] Mobutu showed a degree of bitterness over the chilly attitude of his Belgian counterpart. When criticism of Mobutu in the Belgian press became sharper and increasingly frequent, the Congolese media – obviously obeying their master's voice – responded in kind. In a tit-for-tat reflex, they threatened to make delicate revelations about the Belgian royal family.[119] While this was perhaps yet another tactical ploy by Mobutu in a seemingly endless battle of words, there may have been more to it than that. Perhaps the incident sheds some light on the complex psychology of a man whose pride was damaged and who was afraid to fall out of favour with the Belgian king. Of course, with Mobutu, it was hard to tell whether his public emotions were genuine or well-played theatrics. Be that as it may, by the late 1980s, the Belgian royal court and Mobutu were no longer on speaking terms. In 1993, Mobutu was not invited to the funeral of King Baudouin.

How did the Congo influence broader political and social forces in Belgian society? The main Belgian political parties had been actively involved in decision making regarding decolonisation. In the 1960s, the independent Congo was not a note of discord in Belgian mainstream politics. It caused no (open) confrontations and was not an issue in election campaigns. It is true that, in the aftermath of independence, some former colonials had joined forces in small organisations that tended towards the far right. They were driven by a strong sense of nostalgia, conservatism and ultra-royalist tendencies, particularly in the case of the Comité d'Action et de Défense des Belges en Afrique or CADBA.[120] In their eyes, the politicians had ruined the Congolese heritage of Leopold II to Belgium. For a while, the Congolese fiasco stirred up some anti-political sentiments, but those sentiments never developed into a full-blown political movement. Several associations of former colonials did cling to a vivid nostalgia for the good old colonial days, but they never assumed a truly political nature. They consisted of graduates of the colonial university and other persons who had lived and worked in the Congo as officers of the Force publique, civil servants or employees of colonial enterprises. Most of these organisations were and still are members of the Union royale belge pour les pays d'Outre-mer (Royal Belgian Union for Overseas Territories), consisting of thirty or so local and regional branches. Its statutes clearly stipulate that the organisation is devoid of political intent.[121] In recent years, former colonials have come to

---

[118] G. de Villers, *De Mobutu, op. cit.*, pp. 130–1.
[119] J. Bouveroux, *België uit Afrika? Rwanda, Boeroendi en Zaïre* (Antwerp, 1994), pp. 36–7. A similar attack on the palace had already been made in 1974: see G. de Villers, *De Mobutu, op. cit.*, p. 57.
[120] F. Balace, "Le tournant des années soixante", in *De l'avant à l'après-guerre. L'extrême droite en Belgique francophone* (Bruxelles, 1994), pp. 127–49.
[121] www.urome.be. Regarding the opinions of former colonials, also see F. Gillet, "Congo rêvé? Congo détruit ... Les anciens coloniaux belges aux prises avec une société en repentir: enquêtes sur la face émergée d'une mémoire", *Cahiers d'Histoire du Temps présent*, 19 (2008), pp. 79–134.

the fore again, protesting against what they regard as unjustified attacks on Belgium's former colonial policy and calling for a more balanced view of the country's colonial past.[122]

In a purely political sense, Congo's independence had no direct or profound consequences on the political landscape. But it did lead to the establishment of some pressure groups. Belgians who had suffered material damage from the economic consequences of decolonisation soon set up associations to protect their interests. The best known of these organisations is ABIA (Association belge des Intérêts en Afrique), which stood out for its radical viewpoints on political responsibilities in relation to the botched decolonisation. It was the mouthpiece of those who had been 'robbed overseas', particularly self-employed persons and SMEs whose grudges extended to the large industrial concerns.[123] Another such organisation to emerge after 1960 was known as Syndicat de Défense des Porteurs de la Dette coloniale and claimed to have a membership of forty-two thousand (out of a total of one hundred and ninety-three thousand Belgians who apparently held colonial debt certificates).[124] Towards the end of 1973, the large private enterprises in the Congo, particularly those that depended on the SGB, called on the chairman and co-founder of this syndicate, exchange broker Emile De Sagher, to set up a new group. Its purpose was to convince the government and the general public that individuals and companies who experienced losses under Mobutu's nationalisation policy should be compensated. However, the largest concerns decided to act cautiously. As leading executives of the Société générale said behind closed doors: "One should in any case make sure that the persons [who would lead the organisation] have no obvious ties with financial groups.... The support of former colonials would be highly desirable, but in view of the extreme positions generally adopted by ABIA, one must tread carefully when collaborating with this association".[125] The Syndicat de Défense des Actionnaires et des Détenteurs de Biens au Zaïre was established in 1974.

How successful were these initiatives? In 1974, De Sagher proudly announced that he had "forced the government to its knees" after negotiating full compensation. As we have seen, the Belgo-Congolese accord of 1965 provided (among other things) for the establishment of a joint fund by the two countries for the repayment of part of the outstanding public colonial debt. Moreover, a law passed on 14 April 1965 provided for partial compensation for material losses due to events in the Congo. An agreement between Belgium and the Congo on

---

[122] See: Union royale belge pour les Pays d'Outre-Mer (UROME), *La colonisation belge. Une grande aventure* (S.l., 2004).

[123] *Vérités – Waarom? Organe de l'Association des Intérêts belges en Afrique (ABIA)* [sic], 50 (January-February 1984), p. 8.

[124] See *Mémoire du Syndicat de Défense des Porteurs de la Dette coloniale belge* (Brussels, 1961) and also *Livre Noir des porteurs de la dette coloniale belge* (Brussels, 1961).

[125] AGR, SGB-3, n° 897, "Memorandum strictement confidentiel", from L. Van de Vijver to René Lamy (SGB), 18 December 1973; "Compte rendu de la réunion du 4 janvier 1974 du Groupe de Travail 'Syndicat de Défense – Zaïre'", 9 January 1974; untitled address by E. De Sagher, 22 April 1974.

28 March 1976 governed compensation to victims of the policy of 'Zairisation' over a period of some twenty years.[126] Clearly, the Belgian authorities continued to show a concern for the interests of former colonials who had lost their possessions in the Congo. Nonetheless, some former colonials – particularly the members of ABIA – found the measures inadequate and continued to criticise the government's passivity in this matter.[127]

Alongside these organisations, more progressive movements would emerge in the course of the 1960s. They would gain strength over the years and eventually succeed in influencing Belgium's policy in the Congo. These groups consisted mainly of left-wing Christians, Socialists, Communists and members of NGOs, as well as the 'Third World' movement. They monitored events in the Congo closely, observing how Mobutu flouted human rights and compromised the quality of life of the Congolese population. They were outraged at the support that the dictator continued to receive from Belgian sources. In 1975, the movement established the Zaire Committee, whose purpose was to protest against the association of Belgian politicians and businesspeople with Mobutu's Congo.[128] Eight years later, the National Centre for Development Cooperation (NCOS in Flemish) – the peak association of Flemish development NGOs – launched a campaign against Mobutu's regime and called on the Belgian political establishment to cancel its assistance to the dictator.[129] Criticism of Mobutu was increasingly voiced in the Belgian news media. In October 1991, the NCOS not only backed the Belgian military intervention in the Congo to save and evacuate Belgian expatriates, it also argued in favour of a prolonged troop presence if that would lead to a quicker fall of the regime.[130]

---

[126] Damages to the victims of 'Zairisation' would be paid in twenty annual instalments, the first ten of which were to be paid by the Congo, with Belgium pre-financing the following ten, so that the beneficiaries would be compensated after ten rather than twenty years. The Congo would then be required to repay the pre-financed instalments to the Belgian State. See Kadoc, Mark Eyskens papers, box 85, "Nota voor het Ministerieel Comité voor Buitenlands Beleid", 11 July 1989, p. 6. The Belgian-Congolese Fund (Fobelco), which has to repay part of the colonial debt, is assigned by the Belgian government to pay damages to those affected by the 'Zairisation' measures (protocol of 30 May 1997, amended on 9 February 1999): In 1998, BEF 172 million was paid (http://membres.lycos.fr/fbcbkf/fbc7.html). On the many difficulties in compensating the victims of Zairisation, see V. Delannoy & O. Willocx, *Secret d'État. Le livre noir des Belges zaïrianisés 1973–2007* (Brussels, 2007).

[127] Because the law of 1965 took account neither of 'abandoned' possessions nor of damage dating from 1964, and as it provided for only partial compensation of incurred damage. See: Kadoc, Cepess, n° 2.4.12.9, "Commission: Problèmes de décolonisation. Note introductive", 8 December 1985; *Vérités – Waarom?*, 50 (January-February 1984), p. 6.

[128] See the bimonthly publication *Info Zaïre*, 1978–86 (Royal Library: BD/33.407), and the books titled *Van Kongo Vrijstaat tot Zaïre* (Leuven, 1974); *Zaïre, ketens van koper* (Leuven, 1977); *Zaïre, le dossier de la recolonisation* (Paris-Brussels, 1978).

[129] *De Belgische samenwerking met Zaïre* (Brussels, 1989); *Beslissingsmacht: Zaïre, een voorbeeld op de pijngrens* (Brussels, 1984). Many Belgian development NGOs had their roots in the colonial era. See Jan Van de Poel, *Tussen participatie en representatie. Contextuele en structurele dimensies van de Vlaamse derde wereldbeweging, 1955-2000* (Brussels, 2011), pp. 51-85.

[130] S. Parmentier, "Belgische para's in Zaïre", *Noord-Zuid-Cahiers*, 17, 1 (March 1992), pp. 90–8.

The growing tide of criticism was also reflected on the level of party politics. Previously, Mobutu had been able to count on the goodwill of the main Belgian political factions, be they Socialist, Liberal or Christian-Democrat.[131] Invariably, economic and geostrategic considerations won the day. In fact, the Congolese president maintained excellent personal relations with many Belgian politicians, including real heavyweights such as Edmond Leburton, the francophone Socialist who led the government in 1973–4.[132] The first consistently critical voices came from the ranks of Flemish Socialist MPs. They protested against human rights violations in the Congo, the economic plunder of the country by its own political leaders and Belgium's continued support for the Congolese regime.[133] Only when the Socialists participated in government was the criticism slightly more muffled. Some members of the Flemish Socialist Party, SP, maintained good contacts with the political opposition in the Congo. This led, among other things, to the already mentioned Van den Bogaert affair in 1985–6, the umpteenth crisis between the two countries. The party and its leaders, not least its chairman Karel Van Miert, became the target of some of Mobutu's diatribes, which the president delivered with his usual sense of drama and emotion. By now, however, Mobutu's star was beginning to fade. Support for the dictator declined in the course of the 1980s. In 1990, Mobutu complained bitterly that he had "had enough of being kicked around like a football in Belgium's political backroom".[134] A definitive rift had become inevitable, as Mobutu's political credit was all but exhausted.

The Belgian Economy and the Independence of the Congo

The economic aspects of the relationship between Belgium and the Congo have been running through this analysis. In this section, we take a close look at the significance of the Congo to the economy of Belgium and, subsequently, the fate of the large Belgian enterprises in the Congo.

The Weight of the Independent Congo in Overall Belgian Economic Activity

Trade flow is an important, primary indicator of the economic ties between Belgium and the Congo.[135] Let us first consider trade in current currency

---

[131] The (small) Belgian Communist Party was very anti-Mobutu, and voices within the Flemish nationalist party Volksunie also criticised Mobutu and Belgium's continued co-operation with his regime.
[132] W. Martens, *De Memoires, op. cit.*, p. 503 also notes, by way of example, that Mobutu and the prominent Flemish Liberal politician Herman De Croo maintained close ties.
[133] For example, L. Van Velthoven, *De Belgisch-Zaïrese betrekkingen*, document of SEVI (Study and Documentation Centre Émile Vandervelde Institute), 1985.
[134] Kadoc, Mark Eyskens papers, box 117, telex from the Belgian embassy to Belgian Ministry of Foreign Affairs, 7 June 1991.
[135] As was also pointed out in Chapter 4, the data used here refer to the Belgian-Luxembourg Economic Union (BLEU).

TABLE 5.1. *The Congo's Share in Imports and Exports of the Belgian-Luxembourg Economic Union (in %)*

	Imports from the Congo	Exports to the Congo
1960	6.67	1.75
1965	3.21	1.00
1970	4.08	0.98
1975	1.44	0.55
1980	1.72	0.40
1985	0.98	0.44
1990	0.70	0.28
1994	0.51	0.10

B. Verstrepen, *De economische relaties tussen Belgiëen Zaïre (vanaf 1960)* (Brussels, 1989), unpublished master's thesis in economics, VUB, pp. 49–50; supplemented with *Bulletin Statistique*, 1990–5.

values.[136] The value of imports from the Congo amounted to thirteen billion Belgian francs in 1960. In subsequent decades, the annual figure fluctuated, with dips in 1961–4, 1971–2 and 1975, a peak of thirty-six billion in 1980 and a fall to twenty-one billion in 1994. The value of Belgian exports to the Congo evolved differently. It began at around three billion, decreased during the initial years of crisis to two billion (1961), but then grew consistently to thirteen billion by 1985. Exports remained stable for a few years, until they suddenly collapsed in the early 1990s to four billion (1994). Relative to Belgium's total export trade, however, the Congo's share declined constantly and quite spectacularly.

After independence, the Congo never accounted for a particularly large share of Belgium's import and export trade. But this had not always been the case. Among developing countries, the Congo was clearly still Belgium's main trade partner in 1960, but this would quickly change. In 1953, the Congo ranked sixth on the list of Belgium's partners for both imports and exports, but by the end of the 1960s, it was only the thirteenth most important supplier and ranked twenty-fourth among the importers of Belgian goods. In 1985, the Congo lost its status as Belgium's most important importer on the African continent to Algeria; Nigeria took over as Belgium's principal African supplier. As far as exports to all Third World countries were concerned, the Congo dropped to the tenth spot by 1980 and to the twentieth spot by 1992; in terms of imports from the same group the decline in rankings was less spectacular: second place by 1980 and fourth by 1992.[137]

---

[136] In other words: without taking into account currency devaluation.
[137] S. Marysse & P. Dupont, *L'évolution récente des relations économiques belgo-zaïroises. L'achèvement de la décolonisation* (Antwerp, 1993), p. 13 (University of Antwerp, Third World Centre, working paper 93/236); Idem, "L'évolution récente des relations économiques belgo-zaïroises. L'achèvement de la décolonisation", in G. de Villers, ed., *Belgique/Zaïre, op. cit.*, pp. 104–14.

If we compare these figures with those for the colonial period, there are a number of striking similarities. First and foremost, there is the gap between imports and exports. Belgium used to purchase a lot more in the Congo than it sold to this African country. Second, there was little change in terms of the nature of the products that Belgium and the Congo sold to each other. Before independence, there was already an imbalance in the goods that Belgium acquired in its colony, and this trend continued even more strongly in the 1970s and 1980s. Precious minerals (diamond and gold) and copper accounted for respectively twenty-nine per cent and fifty-seven per cent of the total import value from the Congo in 1987. After 1990, copper imports collapsed, so that diamonds came to represent the lion's share of legal trade. Agricultural produce disappeared almost entirely from the exports statistics after 1960. By 1970, cotton accounted for just 0.2 per cent; coffee, tea and spices for 0.8 per cent and vegetable oils for 0.5 per cent of imports from the Congo. As for Belgium's exports to the Congo, the products that had topped the list during the colonial era would continue to do so for a number of years after independence, particularly metal wares. In the early 1970s, the subsidiaries of Fabrimetal accounted for forty-five per cent of Belgian exports to the Congo. In 1960, cast iron, steel and other raw metals represented 20.4 per cent and ten years on they would still top the list. Eventually, their share began to drop (thirteen per cent in 1980, compared to 7.9 per cent in 1987). In the case of machines and electro materials, the situation was slightly different. Their share remained dominant for three decades, varying from 21.4 per cent in 1960 to 26.9 per cent in 1987 and peaking at 31.2 per cent in 1980. The share of transport material remained steady at between ten and thirteen per cent. The Belgian chemical industry saw its exports to the Congo grow from 8.9 per cent in 1960 to fourteen per cent in 1987. By way of illustrating Congo's demise, we should also mention its growing food imports. Meat and grains accounted for 3.8 per cent of Belgian exports to the Congo in 1960, as compared to 10.6 per cent in 1987.[138]

Seen from the Congo's perspective, the significance of the trade relationship was entirely different. While the Congo's share in Belgian trade dwindled, Belgium became increasingly important to the former colony. In 1958, Belgium accounted for 30.7 per cent of the value of Congolese exports, and this share would further increase to fifty-three per cent by 1970. In the following decade, it fluctuated between forty per cent and forty-nine per cent, then peaked once more at fifty-two per cent in 1981, subsequently declining to thirty-two per cent by 1986. The Congo also looked primarily to Belgium for imports. In 1964, Belgium supplied over a third (35.9 per cent) of its imports in terms of value. In subsequent years, the share fluctuated between seventeen per cent (1976) and twenty-eight per cent (1982). In other words, Belgium continued to be important to the Congo, while the Congo occupied only a peripheral position in Belgium's import and export trade. Hence, the statements by various

---

[138] B. Verstrepen, *De economische relaties, op. cit.*, pp. 57–8.

ministers about the supposed balance between the two economies appear rather insincere.

Trade, of course, is just one aspect of a much broader economic context. Economist Stefaan Marysse has analysed how the Congo gradually disappeared from Belgium's economic radar. On the basis of trade balances for 1980 and for 1992, he argues that politicians and businesspeople tended to exaggerate the impact of the Congo on Belgium's economy and employment in an attempt to justify the maintenance or enhancement of relations between the two countries.[139] Likewise in the colonial era, the significance of the Congolese economy was commonly overstated. According to his estimates, some fifty thousand jobs depended on Belgo-Congolese economic ties in 1960. Twenty years on, the figure had already dropped to eleven thousand (0.37 per cent of overall Belgian employment in Belgium), and it declined further to barely 3,000 by 1992. Another important observation concerns the balance of payments between the two countries. As we have seen, Belgium generally posted a surplus, despite a deficit on the trade balance. This was due to financial transfers to Belgium, the cost of insurance and transport and so forth. This situation persisted after independence. In the period from 1970 to 1980, the average annual surplus amounted to ten billion Belgian francs.[140] From the early 1990s, it declined sharply, to turn into a deficit of -0.4 billion by 1992. Marysse concludes that, by 1993, "the umbilical cord between the two countries had been definitively cut".[141]

Did the economic rupture between the two countries have negative effects on Belgian economic performance? Before the end of the colonial period, many politicians and businessmen asserted that Belgium's prosperity owed much to the Congo, but these assumptions always remained extremely vague. In the late 1950s economic studies showed that Congo's place in the Belgian economy was relatively small.[142] Would a complete breakdown of Belgo-Congolese relations lead to real economic hardship? Some people may have feared this, but their fears were completely unfounded. The 1960s was among Belgium's finest economic decades. Annual GDP growth rates were much higher during the 'Golden Sixties' than during the whole colonial period: 1.43 per cent in 1913–29; -0.04 per cent in 1929–38; 1.29 per cent in 1938–50; three per cent in 1950–60 – but 4.93 per cent in 1960–70.[143] Gross capital formation represented between sixteen and eighteen per cent of GNP during the years

---

[139] J. Debar & S. Marysse, *Belgisch-Zaïrese economische relaties. Het effect op de Belgische tewerkstelling* (Antwerp, 1982) (University of Antwerp, Third World Centre, working paper 82/60); S. Marysse & P. Dupont, *L'évolution récente, op. cit.* (Antwerp, 1993).

[140] This surplus covered half of the deficit in relation to other countries (AGR, SGB-3, n° 631, "Evolution économique récente du Zaïre et relations entre les économies belge et zaïroise", BNB, 11 July 1978, Chapter II).

[141] S. Marysse & P. Dupont, *L'évolution récente, op. cit.*, p. 15.

[142] See the conclusion of Chapter 4.

[143] I. Cassiers, Ph. de Villé & P. Solar, "Economic Growth in Post-war Belgium", in N. Crafts & G. Toniolo, eds., *Economic Growth in Europe Since 1945* (Cambridge, 1996), p. 175.

1954–60, but fluctuated between twenty per cent and twenty-three per cent in the 1960s.[144]

So was Belgium better off *because* it was relieved of its colony? Things may be more complicated than that. *Post hoc* does not necessarily mean *propter hoc*. The new dynamism of the Belgian economy was essentially due to heavy investments of foreign multi-national companies, mostly in Flanders; to a growing liberalisation of the Belgian economy and the demise of old production sectors such as coal production; and, most important of all, to the opening of markets following the creation of the European Economic Community.[145] In 1958, EEC countries represented 45.1 per cent of all Belgian exports and by 1968, this percentage had risen to 64.3 per cent. In the meantime, the Congo's share had fallen from 3.8 to 0.9 per cent.[146] During this period, the essential economic link between Belgium and its former colony nevertheless remained untouched. For example, the crucial link based on non-ferrous metals was only cut in the 1970s. The traditional Belgian holding companies, who were both fortified and obsessed by their activities in the Congo, may have neglected new investment opportunities in the homeland. At the end of the 1950s and during the 1960s, these new opportunities were achieved through foreign capital, which, from then on, came to play a much greater role in the Belgian economy.

In this sense, Belgium's post-colonial economic experience closely resembled that of other colonial powers. For them, decolonisation was not an economic catastrophe in any sense.[147] In the Netherlands, the slogan "*Indië verloren, rampspoed geboren*" ("Indies lost, adversity found") did not materialise after the independence of the East Indies.[148] The Dutch economy thrived, with an average annual GNP growth rate of 5.3 per cent between 1947 and 1960 (compared with 2.64 per cent between 1913 and 1921). After the loss of Indonesia, Dutch economic growth was higher than the average growth rate in Western Europe (5.17 per cent) and the United States (3.54 per cent) for the same time period.[149] France's economy also fared rather better without its colonies. Average annual GNP growth rates rose from 0.7 per cent in 1913–50, to 4.6 per cent in 1950–60 and to 5.8 per cent in the next decade.[150] In the post-colonial period, Britain alone continued to be confronted with a relative

---

[144] G. L. De Brabander, *Regionale structuur en werkgelegenheid* (Brussels, 1983), p. 42.
[145] I. Cassiers, Ph. De Villé & P. Solar, "Economic growth", art. cit., pp. 198–201.
[146] A. Mommen, *The Belgian Economy in the Twentieth Century* (London, 1994), p. 125.
[147] B. Etemad, *De l'utilité des empires. Colonisation et prospérité de l'Europe (XVIe – XXe siècles)* (Paris, 2005), p. 294.
[148] H. Wesseling, "Post-Imperial Holland", art. cit., pp. 126–8, reprinted in H. Wesseling, *Indië verloren, rampspoed geboren* (Amsterdam, 1988), pp. 285–308; J. Marseille, *Empire colonial*, op. cit., pp. 357–60.
[149] G. Vanthemsche, "Les Pays-Bas de 1940 à 1970", in D. Barjot, e.a., eds., *Industrialisation et sociétés en Europe occidentale du début des années 1880 à la fin des années 1960* (Paris, 1997), p. 424 (p. 293 for the data 1913–21).
[150] D. Barjot, "Tendance d'ensemble (1945–1970)", in D. Barjot, e.a., eds., *Industrialisation*, op. cit., p. 313.

economic decline.[151] But Andrew Thompson observes that "decolonisation did not, as anticipated, have major consequences for investment and trade. (...) We need to look elsewhere to explain the country's apparent economic 'failure' in the 1950s and 1960s".[152] This also seems applicable to Belgium's economic success in the 1960s.

Belgium's Declining Economic Presence in the Congo

After the overview of the general economic and social developments, let us next focus on some specific aspects of the gradual decline in Belgium's economic presence in the Congo. As has been explained, Congo-based companies within the SGB group had a significant impact on Belgium's economy. Therefore, we shall concentrate on the behaviour of this particular group in the years surrounding independence.

In 1959 and 1960, the private sector was caught off guard by the unstoppable momentum of decolonisation. The recently opened archives of the Société générale group do not elicit any opposition to the sudden and somewhat unexpected step towards independence. Business circles were unhappy, but felt they had to 'go with the flow'. The guidelines of the leaders of the SGB's Congolese companies asserted: "We must remain loyal and cooperate fully in the implementation of the agreements [specified in the government statement of 13 January 1959].... Our attitude must be realistic and constructive. The stakes are considerable". Apparently, then, the Belgian capitalist elite were not planning to relinquish the Congo; as far as they were concerned, it was business as usual. Still, the Congo's independence would lead to some far-reaching changes, especially in terms of a quicker 'Africanisation' of middle executive staff and a decentralisation of corporate management (as it was "towards the Congo that the nervous centre of business [would] be shifting").[153]

Not long before independence, the private sector faced a considerable problem. In late 1959 and early 1960, capital flight assumed worrying proportions. The foreign exchange reserves of the Central Bank of the Congo collapsed from 8.1 billion Congolese francs in 1959 to 3.5 billion Congolese francs in January 1960. This process was triggered by the fact that private individuals and SMEs were rushing to transfer their money to safety in Belgium. The large corporations responded differently, refraining from any unusual transactions. In fact, at the request of Minister Scheyven, who was in charge of the economic and financial affairs of the Congo, the large private companies siphoned large sums of money from Belgium to the Congo, thereby pre-empting a potential imbalance.[154]

---

[151] Average annual GNP growth rates were as follows: 2.2 per cent in 1870–1913; 1.7 per cent in 1913–50; 2.7 per cent in 1950–60; 2.8 per cent in 1960–70 (Ibid.).

[152] A. S. Thompson, *The Empire Strikes Back? The Impact of Imperialism on Britain from the Mid-Nineteenth Century* (Harlow-London, 2005), p. 178.

[153] AGR, Finoutremer, n° 2057, PV n° 778 of Comité intérieur congolais (CIC) of SGB, 5 March 1959, pp. 5–6; R. Brion & J.-L. Moreau, *La Société générale de Belgique 1822–1997* (Antwerp, 1998), pp. 400-2.

[154] AGR, Finoutremer, n° 2057, PV n° 791 of CIC, 3 December 1959; n° 2058, PV n° 795 of CIC, 3 March 1960, pp. 8–9.

Belgium and the Independent Congo

Another source of concern was the legal status of Belgian capitalist enterprises in the Congo. After World War II, there had been a kind of 'legal emigration' trend whereby numerous enterprises under Belgian law decided to operate under Congolese law, since the colony had a commercial law system of its own. This offered tax benefits and was easier from a practical business perspective.[155] In 1960, however, these companies began to have cause for concern. The future Congolese business and fiscal legislation that was to replace colonial law could very well be less favourable. Consequently, the private sector wanted to return quickly to the Belgian legal regime. The law of 17 June 1960, passed less than two weeks before the declaration of independence, made it possible for these Congo-based enterprises to become companies under Belgian law.[156] A simple decision by the companies' boards sufficed, and no approval was required from a general meeting of shareholders, as the law normally proscribes. The law also allowed companies to subsume all or part of their holdings in yet-to-be-established companies under Congolese law, without having to pay the taxes resulting from such a juridical act.[157] The purpose was clear: According to the SGB itself, the law was designed to "look after Belgian savings invested in colonial enterprises" and "to bring [them] under the protection of the State of which its principal stakeholders were citizens".[158] The Belgian government, for its part, also took a number of measures that were tailor-made for large corporations such as Comité spécial du Katanga (the main shareholder in UMHK) and designed to avoid potential trouble should the future Congolese state decide to meddle with them.

So, on the eve of independence, the Belgian corporations in the Congo were certainly not contemplating a pullout. They wanted to stay in the former colony, but preferably in a stable and safe environment. The negative image of the lawful government of Prime Minister Lumumba and the insurgence that erupted on 5 July 1960 explain in part why certain prominent figures from the private sector did not hesitate to become involved in the Katangan secession. After this province declared its independence, Louis Wallef, a top executive with Union minière, made his position quite clear in a conversation with Minister of Foreign Affairs Wigny: "The notion of a unitary state was an error on the part of the Belgian government during the Round-table conference. Fortunately, on 14 July, Katanga was saved from the government." Wigny, for

---

[155] J. Goldschmidt, "Les impôts sur les revenus au Congo comparés aux impôts belges sur les revenus", *La Revue fiscale*, 11, 2–3 (February-March 1954), p. 173; R. De Bauw, "La transformation des sociétés anonymes belges en sociétés congolaises par actions à responsabilité limitée", *Revue pratique des Sociétés civiles et commerciales*, 57, 3–4 (March-April 1958), pp. 88–92.

[156] Supplemented with the law of 20 December 1961.

[157] J. 't Kint, "La loi du 17 juin 1960 relative au statut des sociétés de droit colonial ayant leur principal établissement administratif en Belgique", *Revue pratique des Sociétés civiles et commerciales*, 59, 7–8 (July-August 1960), pp. 200–15.

[158] AGR, SGB-3, n° 170, third meeting of the restricted committee of Comité intérieur africain (CIA) of SGB, 25 March 1965; n° 166, note titled "De la constitution de filiales des sociétés demeurées belges par application de la loi du 17 juin 1960. Confidentiel", 6 November 1961, p. 1.

his part, did not share this radical viewpoint. Still, according to Wallef, the Katangan troops would advance in the spring and eventually conquer all of the Congo.[159] In the months and years that followed, UMHK would actively back the Katangan secession, believing that the company would ultimately profit. Another company from the SGB group, Société minière du Bécéka, maintained "excellent relations" with the government of the autonomous South Kasai, the diamond mining heartland. The leadership of the SGB nonetheless "insisted on immediate and full support so that [the authorities of Kasai] could deal with [the serious problems in the administration], which, if they continued, might compromise the economic recovery to which *Société minière* attaches such great significance".[160] The tragic events in the years following the transition to independence did not prevent many Belgian companies from doing profitable business in the Congo. In 1960 and 1961, UMHK operated quasi normally, extracting two hundred and eighty thousand tonnes of copper in 1958 and three hundred thousand tonnes in 1960.[161] This was followed by two hundred and ninety-three thousand tonnes extracted in 1961.[162] Other companies, such as Minière du Bécéka and Compagnie sucrière congolaise, actually produced at record levels in 1961.[163] The volumes and the value of the goods that Belgium imported from the Congo in 1960 were actually considerably higher than in the previous year, both in absolute figures and proportionally.

The Katangan secession ended in early 1963, after concerted Belgian and international efforts. As we have seen, it had not been easy to convince UMHK to give up its support for the leaders of the insurrection. However, despite the Congo's (supposedly) revived unity, the country was not out of the woods yet. In the longer term, the persistent difficulties would certainly have economic repercussions. The leadership of the SGB liked to argue that only the large corporations could maintain a semblance of normality in the Congo's political and administrative chaos. The SGB's honorary governor, Gaston Blaise, called attention to "the contrast between the continuation of activities in the private sector and the gradual collapse of all public sector structures, which [posed] a danger to private industry".[164] At the same time, the question arose whether there was any future in the region for the large Belgian corporations.

In the course of the 1960s and early 1970s, business leaders held contradictory views. In 1962, an internal SGB note offered the following analysis: "There are numerous reasons for our enterprises to pursue their efforts in the Congo, which have been unfailing since independence".[165] In 1970, despite all the difficulties of previous years, the Congo was still considered as "one of

---

[159] Rapport..., op. cit., p. 524.
[160] AGR, Finoutremer, n° 2058, PV n° 821 of CIC, 8 December 1960, pp. 1-2.
[161] AGR, Finoutremer, n° 2058, PV n° 812 of CIC, 15 September 1960, pp. 1-2; n° 2059, PV n° 842 of CIC, 9 November 1961.
[162] République du Zaïre, *Conjoncture économique*, 18 (October 1979), p. 179.
[163] AGR, Finoutremer, n° 2060, PV n° 847 of CIC, 18 January 1962, pp. 1-4.
[164] AGR, Finoutremer, n° 2061, PV n° 868 of CIA, 24 January 1963, p. 3.
[165] AGR, Finoutremer, n° 2060, PV n° 849 of CIC, 15 February 1962, p. 1.

Belgium and the Independent Congo

those African countries where private companies [were] able to undertake their activities with a reasonable chance of making a profit".[166] However, many questioned the wisdom of investing in a volatile Congo. They felt that perhaps the group ought to adopt a different business strategy. Jules Dubois-Pelerin, vice governor of the SGB, had been unequivocal in this respect in 1964: "[O]ne should not invest a further penny in this mousetrap [the Congo]. You are already running excessive risks – through no fault of your own. It would be madness to go even further".[167] Not everyone within the SGB agreed with his radical point of view, but it is striking that quite divergent analyses were made at the same time.[168]

In this uncertain and contradictory climate, the SGB began to consider a change of strategy during the second half of the 1960s. The group wanted to focus less on the Congo and broaden its horizon. In 1964, certain companies within the group had already ventured forward in this respect, but there was no common direction to their approach and sometimes they got in each other's way. This resulted in failure, as time and money were wasted. The leaders of the group watched in dismay and eventually intervened to better coordinate the various initiatives.[169] After the conflict between the Congolese authorities and UMHK in 1966-7 which will be discussed later, the group reconsidered its entire strategy in the Congo. According to the SGB leaders, there still was a profitable future ahead in the Congo for some companies. SGB governor Max Nokin felt that, in the near future, enterprises operating in Africa would not necessarily be investment companies and ought to "evolve as service enterprises".[170]

So during the 1960s, the principal Belgian investment group in the Congo was torn between two options. On the one hand, it had to maintain its presence in the country in order to protect the interests of its local companies as best it could. After all, the stakes were high: In 1969, Congolese assets still accounted for twenty per cent of the SGB's portfolio (compared to twenty-four per cent in 1959).[171] Belgolaise, one of the group's banks, continued to finance a number of businesses in the Congo. On the other hand, the group had to refrain from launching new projects. Investment in the Congo had to be scaled down and opportunities sought elsewhere in the world. The economic policy that the Congolese authorities pursued in the early 1970s led to a decisive reduction of the Belgian presence in the country's economy. Mobutu's 'Zairisation' and radicalisation in 1973-4 obviously delivered a serious blow to Belgium's

---

[166] AGR, Finoutremer, n° 799, PV n° 956 of CIA, 10 September 1970, p. 3.
[167] AGR, SGB-3, n°167, handwritten "confidential" note from J. Dubois-Pelerin, 14-15 February 1967, pp. 48-9.
[168] R. Brion & J.-L. Moreau, *La Société générale, op. cit.*, p. 405.
[169] AGR, SGB-3, n°170, PV of the restricted committee of CIA, 1964-7 (especially the third, fourth and ninth meetings of resp. 25 June 1964, 16 July 1964 and 25 March 1965).
[170] AGR, Finoutremer, n° 799, PV n° 921 of CIA, 12 January 1967, pp. 2-3.
[171] AGR, SGB-3, n° 631, note titled "Le Congo (...)", from R. Sterkendries, 15 July 1969; R. Brion & J.-L. Moreau, *La Société générale, op. cit.*, p. 390.

economic presence in the Congo and the willingness of Belgian companies to make further investments in the country.

Before we draw up the balance of Belgium's economic presence in the Congo during the 1970s and 1980s, let us first consider the transitions made in some important companies belonging to the SGB group. Compagnie maritime belge (CMB), the shipping company that had for years been associated with the Congo, swiftly changed course. While in 1960 traffic to the former colony still accounted for seventy per cent of the company's revenue, that share would decline to fifty per cent by 1966 and to barely thirty-five per cent in 1972.[172] Under a 1966 deal, the Congolese authorities committed themselves to gradually acquiring a majority stake in Compagnie maritime congolaise, a subsidiary of CMB. In 1971, the company was renamed Compagnie maritime du Zaïre, and two years later it became Compagnie maritime zaïroise. CMB lost its minority shareholding in the firm, but the two companies did agree to continue their collaboration. The connection with the Congo would remain highly profitable to the Belgian shipping company.[173]

To some extent, the airline sector evolved similarly.[174] A few days prior to the Congo's independence, Sabena amended its articles of association. The Belgian public authorities acquired a substantial part of the private shares, as investors reduced their commitment in a company that had not been profitable for many years. The SGB group retained just ten per cent of the capital; the Congolese authorities 'inherited' the shares that the colony previously controlled, twenty-five per cent of the total capital. Sabena would become a minority stakeholder in Air Congo, established in 1961 and largely owned by the Congolese state. The Belgian company initially provided technical assistance to its fledgling Congolese counterpart, but conflicts with the regime in Kinshasa would result in a rift between the two companies in 1966–7. In 1968, the Belgian state bought back the Congolese share in Sabena. As a destination, the Congo would nonetheless remain important to Sabena. Flights to Kinshasa were profitable, even if in practice a large proportion of that profit could not be transferred freely and had to remain in the Congo. The flights between the two countries also served an important symbolic and political purpose. On a number of occasions, Sabena became the pawn in a seemingly endless series of confrontations and reconciliations between Brussels and Kinshasa. In times of crisis, one of Mobutu's preferred weapons was to suspend Sabena's landing rights. Sabena, which for a long time enjoyed a quasi-monopoly on flights to the Congo, would find it difficult to strike a healthy balance in its portfolio of international connections after 1960 and consequently remained somewhat of a lame duck.

---

[172] AGR, SGB-3, n° 170, note titled "Les relations économiques et financières entre la Belgique et le Congo", 20 September 1966, p. 4; n° 631, "Examen de certains aspects des relations belgo-zaïroises", 4 February 1972, p. 4.

[173] G. Devos & G. Elewaut, *CMB 100: A Century of Commitment to Shipping* (Tielt, 1995), pp. 213, 217, 221, 225, 247.

[174] G. Vanthemsche, *La Sabena, op. cit.*, pp. 158–69; J. Naveau, *La décolonisation aéronautique du Congo* (Brussels, 2004).

The fortunes of Union minière du Haut-Katanga served to accelerate the reorientation of the SGB group in the Congo. The stakes of the conflict that erupted in 1966 between the mighty corporation and Mobutu were both material and symbolic in nature. The taxes and levies it paid represented over a third of the Congo's budget. The company was run from Brussels, while the operational headquarters were located in the Congo, a setup that was by no means unique. Control over the economic levers of the Congo was one of the *contentieux* between Belgium and its former colony. The accords reached by Spaak and Tshombe in 1965 appeared to have resolved these issues, but they would continue to preoccupy the leaders in Kinshasa in subsequent years. Making use of the option provided under the law of 17 June 1960, many companies operating under Congolese law chose to adopt Belgian status before 30 June. Most of these companies established Congolese subsidiaries to which they subsequently transferred almost all of their Congolese assets. This way, the companies had become holdings under Belgian law that, in most cases, held as their sole possession all the title deeds of property of their Congolese subsidiaries.[175] The leadership of the SGB made the following striking observation: "As the owner of all of the shares in the Congolese enterprise, the Belgian enterprise manages its subsidiary from a distance [French: *téléguider*], as it used to manage its seat in the Congo. From a Congolese viewpoint, this is abnormal, as it prevents a decolonisation of those companies".[176]

In late 1966, Mobutu precisely wished to demonstrate the Congo's economic independence. To underline his point, he chose the rather ambitious target of UMHK.[177] Skirmishes between Brussels and Léopoldville over the *contentieux* had been going on since the beginning of the year. Unlike most other Belgian colonial enterprises, which had opted to switch to Belgian legal status, UMHK did not establish a Congolese branch, despite various preparatory studies. Under the Ordinance Law of 7 June 1966, the Congolese government ordered all companies having their main plants in the Congo to locate their official headquarters there as well.[178] Lengthy negotiations between the management of UMHK and the Congolese government failed to resolve the situation. Within the Belgian company, there were two opposing views: The hardliners were against any concessions on the part of the company and wanted to push the confrontation in the hope of forcing Mobutu to his knees;

---

[175] AGR, SGB-3, n° 170, third meeting of the restricted committee of CIA, 25 March 1965.

[176] AGR, Finoutremer, n° 2060, PV n° 861 of CIA, 4 October 1962, p. 4.

[177] This period is analysed in: M. Verwilghen, "Les principaux aspects juridiques de la nationalisation de l'UMHK", *Revue belge de Droit international*, 6, 1 (1970) pp. 104–6; W. Radmann, "The Nationalization of Zaire's Copper: From Union Minière to Gécamines", *Africa Today*, 25, 4 (October-December 1978), pp. 25–47; R. Kovar, "La 'congolisation' de l'UMHK", *Annuaire français de Droit international*, 13 (1967), pp. 742–81; J. Gérard-Libois, "L'affaire de l'UMHK", *Études congolaises*, 10, 2 (March-April 1967), pp. 1–46; "L'affaire de l'UMHK", *CH-CRISP*, 350 (27 January 1967); "Le destin de l'UMHK", *CA-CRISP*, 17, 78 (May 1968); J.-J. Saquet, *De l'UMHK à la Gécamines* (Paris, 2000).

[178] Another ordinance law, from 7 June 1966 (the so-called Bakajika Law), stipulated that the Congolese state owns all land and mining concessions dating from before 30 June 1960.

the moderates took a more flexible view and sought a compromise. The hardliners won the day, but the Congolese authorities hit back hard, announcing nationalisation without compensation.[179] UMHK was to be superseded by Gécomin (Société générale congolaise de Minerais). In addition, copper exports were suspended. This marked the start of a fierce tug of war with the Belgian group. At the same time, the Congolese authorities tried to lure other foreign groups to take a stake in Gécomin. The ploy failed and the new company remained entirely state owned.[180] The memory of the Katangan secession and the support that UMHK had provided to Tshombe continued to bother Mobutu. Apparently, he told Louis Wallef, who belonged to the hardliners within UMHK, that "things were being made as hard as possible for [Wallef] because he had made things hard for the Congo by continuing to support Tshombe financially".[181]

On 17 February 1967, a deal was struck after the SGB brought a consensus figure to the negotiating table. André de Spirlet, an executive with CMB and future chairman of UMHK, first reached an agreement that guaranteed the continuation of the company's economic activities. The commercialisation of the ores extracted by Gécomin would be entrusted to Société générale des Minerais (SGM), a SGB subsidiary. SGM would also provide the necessary technical support for Gécomin to continue its mining activity. In return for this commercialisation and technical support, SGM would be entitled to very favourable financial compensations.

The technical nature of this agreement softened the blow for President Mobutu and his entourage. After all, the spectacular nationalisation measure, which had drawn the world's attention, had backfired on the Congolese leaders. Like apprentice sorcerers, they had lost control of a situation of their own making. By suspending copper exports, they cut off their own source of finance. Because the French embassy in Kinshasa maintained close contacts with Albert Ndele, governor of the Congolese National Bank, who also played an important role in negotiations with the SGB, French diplomats were well informed as to how the unfolding crisis would evolve: "Ndele, who is worried that the currency reserve may run dry, will, on behalf of the government and Gécomin, accept agreements that he knows to be leonine, for the only purpose of replenishing the treasury".[182] Minister of Foreign Affairs Justin Bomboko agreed that the contract with SGM was unfair for the Congolese, but he also felt that, "like any accord, it could be revoked".

The Belgian negotiators were wary of just this possibility and therefore demanded safeguards. They wanted Mobutu to write a letter in which he

---

[179] V. Dujardin, *Harmel, op. cit.*, p. 321; J.-J. Saquet, *De l'UMHK, op. cit.*, pp. 146, 182–3.
[180] D. N. Gibbs, *The Political Economy, op. cit.*, pp. 165–94 analyses the position of the United States in this case, specifically through the role of the businessman Maurice Tempelsman, who wanted to gain a foothold in the Congo.
[181] J.-J. Saquet, *De l'UMHK, op. cit.*, p. 207.
[182] AMAÉF (Paris), Série Europe 1961–1970, sous-série Belgique, n° 161, telegram from Touze (*chargé d'affaires* in Kinshasa) to the MAÉF, 9 February 1967, p. 2.

endorsed the deal unequivocally.[183] For that matter, the Belgian concern was quite aware that it had emerged victorious from the confrontation. In an internal document, Union minière conceded that the financial compensation under the terms of the agreement of February 1967 was "exorbitant for the execution of a simple management contract". It goes on to say the following: "If we were able to impose such a rate, this is, first of all, because we were sceptical about the longevity of the agreement and, consequently, wanted to obtain the quickest possible recuperation of our real expenses caused by the execution of the contract; and, second, because the Congolese had no other option but to accept our conditions".[184] The French ambassador noted that the authorities of Kinshasa "felt frustrated at the accord, which they were unable to avoid".[185]

In this manner, the SGB's flagship was able to cut itself loose from the Congo under a deal that was financially favourable. The new course was reflected in a name change in 1968, when UMHK became simply Union minière and immediately began to diversify its activities.[186] Under the contract between SGM and Gécomin, many of the raw materials that were processed by Belgium's non-ferrous metal industry continued to be imported from the Congo (forty per cent in 1972), but these Belgian copper transformation enterprises made serious efforts to diversify their supply channels. They had actually begun to pursue this strategy before the decolonisation, but now efforts were stepped up. In 1951, seventy per cent of Belgium's copper imports originated in the colony, but this proportion declined to sixty per cent by 1972 and to fifty-five per cent by 1980.[187] A similar pattern unfolded in imports of other raw materials.

In the beginning of the 1970s, Belgian firms still occupied a prominent position in the Congolese economy. Of all deposits in Congolese banks held by private companies, forty per cent came from enterprises entirely or predominantly constituted of Belgian capital. A similar percentage of all company benefits declared to the Congolese fiscal authorities was produced by these societies. Among these companies, the SGB accounted for the majority share of fifty-five per cent. The other four large Belgian groups (Lambert, Empain, de Launoit, Cominière) together accounted for thirty-five per cent, while the rest was in the hands of firms that did not belong to a holding company. These Belgian interests were situated primarily in the processing industry (thirty-two per cent), in mining and the metal industry (twenty-six per cent) and in agriculture (sixteen per cent). In the late 1960s and early 1970s, substantial investments were made, but these

---

[183] AMAÉF (Paris), Série Europe 1961–1970, sous-série Belgique, n° 161, telegram from Touze (chargé d'affaires in Kinshasa) to the MAÉF, 15 February 1967.

[184] AGR, SGB-3, n° 321, note titled "Indemnisation de l'UM par la RDC", by G. Assoignon, 6 March 1968.

[185] AMAÉF (Paris), Série Europe 1961–1970, sous-série Belgique, n° 160, Kosciusko-Morizet, French ambassador in Kinshasa, to the MAÉF, 8 May 1967.

[186] AGR, SGB-3, n° 313, "Communication du Président à l'assemblée générale ordinaire du 24 mai 1968", p. 3. Later still it would come to be known as Umicore.

[187] AGR, SGB-3, n° 631, note "Examen de certains aspects des relations belgo-zaïroises", 4 Feb. 1972, p. 2; J. Debar & S. Marysse, Belgisch-Zaïrese economische relaties, op. cit., p. 12.

were primarily replacement investments made with investors' own resources. A study by the University of Kinshasa dating from this period concluded as follows: "Insofar as investments in Zaire are concerned, the Belgian groups have aimed primarily at maintaining the existing apparatus. Everything suggests that they have adopted a wait-and-see approach".[188] Just prior to the 'Zairisation' drive, the principal Belgian companies still contributed a considerable share to the Congo's GNP: between eighteen per cent and nineteen per cent; or between forty per cent and forty-two per cent of the total contribution by private companies. In the final days of the colonial era, that proportion still amounted to fifty-five per cent. Between 1969 and 1975, Belgian capital on average accounted for twenty-six per cent of all foreign investment in the Congo though, again, this is lower than the corresponding percentage during the colonial period.[189]

The 'Zairisation' and radicalisation programmes whereby most foreign investments were seized by the Congolese state did not immediately terminate the already troubled relationship between the SGB and the Congo. In the second half of the 1970s and during the next decade, there would be several more confrontations. In fact, by the end of 1974, President Mobutu had already been forced to revoke some of the nationalisations. Some of the SGB-controlled companies resumed their activities, though apparently without much enthusiasm, and often out of political rather than economic considerations.[190] An agreement struck by the SGB and the Congolese authorities in 1974 not only settled the matter of compensation for UM, but also defined SGM's role in the commercialisation of the output by Gécamines (which had succeeded Gécomin in 1971). Henceforth, this would be taken care of by Sozacom, a new Congolese company that would acquire SGM's know-how and goodwill in return for payment. But the deal also covered other forms of co-operation. SGM would, for example, assist in the construction of a copper refinery in the Congo.[191] The SGB's interests in the diamond sector also diminished. Since the 1960s, the Congolese authorities had, in a series of phases, acquired a majority stake in Miba (Minière de Bakwanga, formerly known as Société minière du Bécéka).[192] From 1981, Sozacom also managed the commercialisation of diamond extraction.[193] In the early 1980s, further incidents occurred between the SGB and the Congo. In 1983, for instance, the Belgian president of Gécamines, Robert Crem, called into question the accords of 1974. He noted that the price paid to the Belgian firm Métallurgie Hoboken Overpelt for copper refinement was above the average price in the global market. He therefore insisted that the ore should be refined in the Congo itself. Mobutu also raised this issue, but it

---

[188] Baluki group, *Les investissements belges en République du Zaïre. Réalités et perspectives* (Kinshasa, 1972), pp. 29–30.
[189] G. de Villers, *De Mobutu, op. cit.*, p. 46.
[190] B. Verstrepen, *De economische relaties, op. cit.*, pp. 102–3.
[191] Ilunga Ilunkamba, "Les firmes multinationales dans l'industrie du cuivre au Zaïre: l'art de survivre", *Cahiers économiques et sociaux*, 17, 2 (June 1979), pp. 113–45 (p. 136).
[192] *Info Zaïre*, 31/1 (February 1981), p. 5.
[193] X. Mabille, e.a., *La Société générale de Belgique 1822–1997* (Brussels, 1997), p. 101.

would not be long before he reconciled with the Belgian group. In 1984, Crem resigned and was replaced as head of Gécamines by his compatriot Pierre De Merre of Union minière.[194]

Meanwhile, the SGB continued to downsize its investments in the Congo, but attempts to convert former colonial enterprises failed to meet expectations.[195] Reorganisations and mergers of companies such as CCCI and Compagnie du Katanga – both formerly powerful and prestigious societies – resulted, in 1973, in the establishment of the holding company Finoutremer (Compagnie financière européenne d'Outre-mer). By the end of the 1980s, just 18.4 per cent of its portfolio consisted in shareholdings in Congolese companies. Moreover, Finoutremer accounted for barely 4.5 per cent of the total value of the SGB's shares portfolio, so that the Congolese participation represented a very modest 0.9 per cent of the latter's holdings.[196] A page had been turned in the history of Belgian-Congolese relations. The definitive rift in relations that some had feared in 1960 had not materialised immediately. It had, rather, manifested itself over time, providing the necessary leeway for a large player such as the SGB to shift its focus to other horizons before also disappearing from the Belgian economic arena; albeit for entirely unrelated reasons.

Obviously Belgium's economic interests in the Congo went beyond the SGB. Even after the SGB's departure from the Congo, certain Belgian entrepreneurs continued to lead important companies there. This was the case of brewery group Unibra, which did, however, eventually sell its Congolese assets in 1996, two years after the death of its founder Michel Relecom. Another example is the agro-alimentary group Orgaman, led by father and son William and Jean-Claude Damseaux, which also held stakes in transport and real estate. And in the mining sector, there were the enterprises of Georges Forrest, which continue to make headlines to this day. These companies played a substantial economic and social role in the Congo and there is no question whatsoever that they also influenced public life in general and politics in particular. Still, their impact pales into insignificance next to the mark that the large Belgian corporations had left on the Congo not long before.

Belgian Development Co-Operation in the Congo

Some General Characteristics of Belgian Development Aid in the Congo
Beginning in the 1960s, Belgium's position in the world was co-determined by its development co-operation strategy, which combined humanitarian, economic and political considerations. Quite a number of Belgians lived and worked abroad under the banner of development aid. It was an evolution that had begun with the decolonisation of the Congo and would largely define Belgium's mark on the independent Congo. Some tentative calculations already

---

[194] G. de Villers, *De Mobutu, op. cit.*, p. 132; C. Braeckman, *Le dinosaure, op. cit.*, p. 232.
[195] R. Brion & J.-L. Moreau, *La Société générale, op. cit.*, pp. 454, 464.
[196] B. Verstrepen, *De economische relaties, op. cit.*, p. 102.

TABLE 5.2. *The Congo's Share in Belgium's Bilateral Assistance to Developing Countries (1960–1999)*

1960	–	1970	54.1	1980	38.4	1990	12.4
1961	82.1	1971	50.9	1981	33.5	1991	4.2
1962	66.4	1972	55.2	1982	35.3	1992	4.0
1963	85.6	1973	47.8	1983	32.0	1993	4.8
1964	80.5	1974	49.0	1984	29.3	1994	4.6
1965	82.0	1975	44.7	1985	20.6	1995	3.8
1966	72.5	1976	41.0	1986	27.9	1996	1.8
1967	65.0	1977	41.4	1987	21.4	1997	4.9
1968	67.8	1978	41.5	1988	27.1	1998	3.4
1969	54.5	1979	35.5	1989	16.7	1999	3.8

J. Brassinne, "La coopération belgo-zaïroise 1960–1985", *CH-CRISP*, 1099–1100 (1985), p. 78; supplemented by OECD – Comité d'Aide au Développement (CAD), *Examen annuel de l'aide 1971. Rapport du secrétariat et questions sur l'effort et la politique d'aide au développement de la Belgique* (Paris, 1971), tables 1 and 3 (for 1961–4), subsequently by *Répartition de l'APD par organisme de financement et de l'aide AGCD par forme de coopération* (Brussels, 1991), p. 1 and by *Verdeling van de ODA (...)* (Brussels, 1998), and finally by *La coopération belge en chiffres de 1994 à 1999* (Brussels, 2000) (for 1985–99). The figures in the various reports do not always correspond.

indicate the dominant position the Congo occupied in Belgium's development co-operation policy. It should be noted that the percentages in Table 5.2 refer to bilateral assistance rather than total assistance, which also includes Belgium's contributions to international organisations involved in development co-operation. This multi-lateral aid represents just a fraction of total aid.

The trend is clear to see. Initially, the Congo absorbed over eighty per cent of Belgium's bilateral development aid, but after Mobutu's coup this share gradually declined.[197] It decreased from two-thirds to one-third between the late 1960s and the early 1980s. Shortly before the rift between Belgium and Mobutu, the Congo's share in Belgium's total bilateral aid had declined to just over ten per cent; in the 1990s, it had all but evaporated. Despite this constant decline, until 1988–9 Belgium continued to direct its development co-operation efforts primarily at the Congo. Worldwide, only Australia assigned a larger percentage to a single recipient country; in its case, Papua New Guinea. In 1985–9, Belgium on average spent 4.5 billion francs per annum on the Congo, which was significantly more than what went to Rwanda and Burundi, formerly the Belgian suzerainty of Ruanda-Urundi, which received respectively 1.1 and 0.8 billion; followed by dozens of other countries that got substantially less.[198] Clearly, then,

---

[197] Total aid (bilateral + multi-lateral) amounted to around 0.4 per cent of GDP in 1970–90. R. Doom, *Derde Wereld Handboek. Deel 1* (Brussels, 1990), p. 166.

[198] *Concentration de l'APD accordée par la Belgique. Étude statistique* (Brussels, 1991), pp. 10 and 86–7.

Belgium's development co-operation policy towards the end of the 1980s was focused mainly on the former colonies, with other countries having to settle for the crumbs. Seen from the Congo's perspective, Belgium obviously occupied a very prominent place. In the 1960s, an average of sixty-five per cent of the *bilateral* assistance to the Congo came from Belgium.[199] Of the *global* development aid that the Congo received in 1986–8, a sizeable 38.9 per cent still originated in Belgium. France was the Congo's second biggest donor, with 15.1 per cent.[200]

First Steps in Belgium's Development Aid Programme (1959–1965)
In the 1950s, Belgium was a small colonial power that came in for severe international criticism. The country was proud of its accomplishments in the colony, but felt hurt by the constant verbal attacks from other nations. It wanted to demonstrate to the outside world that it was just as capable as any other industrialised nation of engaging in development assistance. The underlying message to the international community and to the United Nations in particular was that they should stop patronising Belgium. As a high-ranking Belgian civil servant asserted: "We, too, are pursuing a policy that resembles President Truman's famous Four-Point Program: the 'Ten-Year Plan' is after all not only an investment scheme, but also a plan for technical assistance in the coming years".[201] The assertion was slightly misleading in the sense that it failed to acknowledge that the efforts were being financed by the 'underdeveloped' region itself, not by Belgium. After all, as we have seen in Chapter 4, Belgium was far from generous towards its colony. In fact the Belgian taxpayer paid barely anything for the Congo, at least not up to the moment of independence. In this respect, 1959 was a turning point: As soon as the Congo had gained independence, it began to take advantage of the Belgian treasury's 'generosity'. In 1960–97, Belgium spent 125.8 billion francs (in current value) on development aid to the Congo. Over those three decades, the annual amounts remained relatively constant, varying from 2.2 billion (in 1968) to as much as 6.1 billion (in 1986). On average, the annual amount in assistance during that period was 3.8 billion. As the amounts in question are not adjusted for inflation, the apparent stability is deceptive. In reality, Belgium made a greater financial effort in the early years than towards the end of the period.

Shortly before the Congo's transition to independence, Belgium had – rather belatedly – come to realise that the Congo's public finance was deep in the red, and it was very doubtful that the Congolese would be capable of running their own country. Consequently, in 1959–60, the Belgian authorities tried to come up with a strategy that could effectively counter these financial and human failings while allowing Belgium to continue to play a prominent role in

---

[199] Organisation for Economic Co-operation and Development (OECD) – CAD, *Examen, op. cit.*, table 4.
[200] *Concentration, op. cit.*, illustration 55.
[201] AMAE, AF-I-1 (DGS – Section coloniale) (1953–1955), "Note. Les États-Unis et l'anticolonialisme aux Nations Unies", by Smolderen, 13 July 1953.

the independent Congo. It was in this context that Belgium's development aid programme was designed. In a memo dating from 1959, the chef de cabinet to the minister for the Congo wrote the following: "Meanwhile, in the eyes of public opinion, the Congo essentially remains dependent upon Belgium, which must consider its future. Hence, the fate of the Congo hinges first and foremost on Belgium's actions".[202] The plans that would be drawn up in the following months were very much in a grey zone where 'pronounced' development aid would in effect contribute to, and result in, limited independence. This was certainly the goal when it was suggested that a Belgo-Congolese development company ought to be established and that Belgium's grip on the Central Bank ought to be tightened in order that the colony's monetary policy could be steered.[203] The roundtable conference rejected these ideas, thereby paving the way for a far less 'obtrusive' form of aid.

At the end of March 1960, the Belgian cabinet discussed the issue of assistance to the Congo and considered the establishment of joint institutions, such as Belgo-Congolese inter-ministerial committees "charged with the design of a common development policy", as well as an institute for assistance and co-operation that might later be joined by other countries.[204] With independence imminent, there was not sufficient time to work out a detailed agreement on development co-operation. Hence, the negotiators got no further than the Friendship, Assistance and Cooperation Treaty, which was signed on 30 June 1960, the very day of independence. The treaty speaks in very general terms about the assistance that Belgium would provide in various fields. It was, however, never ratified, as just a few days later all hell broke loose.

Belgium's assistance to its former colony immediately began to develop along two tracks that were illustrative of the country's rather schizophrenic attitude towards the Congolese issue. The installation of the so-called Belgian Technical Mission (Mistebel) in Katanga was seen as a way of building from scratch this new African nation. The administration, the judiciary, the military, financial institutions and so forth were all indispensable to the proper functioning of the public authorities, and they were established and operated with active assistance from Belgium. The Katangan adventure would be short-lived: By early 1963, the secession was all but over. In the meantime, however, Brussels had not lost sight of Léopoldville, where the administration was in tatters after the exodus of Belgian civil servants. The Belgian Technical Assistance programme (Assistance technique belge or ATB) was launched and Belgium put civil servants, soldiers, magistrates and teachers at the disposal of the Congo. The United Nations requested that Belgium end this presence in the Congo,

[202] Kadoc, De Schryver Papers, n° 11.3.33.2, "Situation financière et économique. Préambule à l'entretien de M. le Ministre", around September 1959, by Willaert, Chef de cabinet to the minister for Belgian Congo.
[203] Kadoc, De Schryver Papers, n° 11.3.33.6, "Programme économique et financier pour le Congo", note from the Study Centre of the PSC-CVP, 5 October 1959.
[204] Kadoc, De Schryver Papers, n° 11.3.33.17, "Note pour le Conseil des Ministres. Politique économique de la Belgique à l'égard du Congo", 31 March 1960.

which it regarded as an instance of interference, but the Belgian and Congolese authorities ignored this call, arguing that any such withdrawal would cause a total collapse of the Congolese state.

Back in Belgium, in January 1962, the authorities established an Agency of Development Cooperation (Office de Coopération au Développement). In 1971, it was replaced by the General Administration for Development Cooperation (Administration générale de la Coopération au Développement or AGCD). AGCD was not a separate department, but part of the Ministry of Foreign Affairs. Someone within government would generally be appointed as a state secretary of development co-operation (under the auspices of Foreign Affairs), though occasionally this responsibility would be entrusted to a cabinet minister. This administrative structure would prove conducive to internal conflict, as the question arose whether and to what extent Belgium's development co-operation should serve Belgian foreign policy aspirations. In addition, there was the matter of striking an appropriate balance between development co-operation and the private sector. In other words, should development co-operation be linked with trade and investment? Or should a distance be maintained between the two? Jef Van Bilsen, who in 1955–6 had caused uproar with his call for political autonomy of the colony, was one of the advocates of a purely independent course in development co-operation.[205] He was opposed to any private sector interference that might derail the development aid process.

Belgium's development aid apparatus was constructed largely on the ruins of the former colonial administration. Most of the civil servants in the development administration had previously worked either for the ministry of colonies or for the public authorities in the colony itself. This inevitably created a good deal of continuity between the colonial structures and the post-colonial development aid programme. From the start, development co-operation was defined – some would say impeded – by this legacy. Van Bilsen, who at the government's request designed the new administration, was appointed as its first secretary-general. It was not long before he clashed head on with Robert Brasseur who, in his capacity as minister of foreign trade and technical assistance, was also responsible for development co-operation. Van Bilsen told Brasseur:

> Months ago, when you decided to set up a Department [of Development Cooperation], you intended only to appoint highly competent individuals and not to allow any party to force names upon you. (…) Since then, you have ignored my recommendations and have been exposed to irresistible pressure from three parties. Moreover, you have had to appoint colonials without being able to choose them. Oddly, this has weakened what otherwise might and should have been an exceptional team. (…) Presently no-one on my team is familiar with questions of development and underdevelopment.[206]

The operational shortcomings of the administration for development aid obviously had serious implications for the effectiveness of assistance to the

---

[205] J. Van Bilsen, *Kongo 1945 – 1965. Het einde van een kolonie* (Leuven, 1993), pp. 191–207.
[206] Kadoc, Van Bilsen Papers, n° 6.10/1, Van Bilsen to Brasseur, 15 September 1962, pp. 4–5.

Congo.[207] Between 1960 and 1965, an estimated 2,200 to 2,300 Belgian development workers were active in the Congo, in various sectors, including the administration, the judiciary, healthcare, public works, finance, communication and education (which alone accounted for over half the number). During the ATB's initial years in the Congo, improvisation and organisational inadequacy were rife. There was widespread criticism from different sides.

To begin with, the large private companies took a tough stance. The SGB insisted on "a thorough review of the methods underlying Belgium's technical assistance to the Congo". The company felt that these methods did not "tie in with existing needs".[208] Yet the business community was not opposed to the ATB in principle. On the contrary, it had been looking forward to the kind of assistance that would keep economic activity in the Congo going. Moreover, it was felt that financial assistance from the Belgian government, more specifically through the granting of a one-billion-franc loan, was entirely necessary, as this would boost Belgian exports to the Congo. However, the implementation of the deal, between 1963 and 1966, would prove an uphill struggle, much to the annoyance of the Belgian businessmen.[209] Private industry also wanted to raise awareness among the Belgian government and inform public opinion of the importance of trade with the developing world in general, and with the Congo in particular. They insisted that the national employers' association, FIB (Fédération des Industries belges), should establish a commission for development cooperation. FIB was prepared to assume the role of pressure group and mouthpiece.[210] Clearly, then, the private sector saw development aid as a tool that could be used to its own advantage.

The Belgian government, too, was entirely aware of the many problems surrounding its technical assistance to the Congo. Some development workers were performing admirably. To some extent, it was thanks to Belgium's assistance that the Congo's administration was functioning at all. However, there was clearly another side to the ATB. Many of the staff members were incompetent or morally irresponsible, and jealousies and rivalries hindered its efficiency. Many became discouraged: "By sending uneducated youngsters to the Congo to destroy everything that was achieved prior to June 1960, Belgium is squandering its own money and that of the Congo", claimed one development worker in 1962.[211] Others resigned, and it became increasingly hard to find new recruits to replace them.[212] These individual experiences were indicative of a general malaise.

[207] J. Brassinne, *L'assistance technique belge au Congo juillet 1960 – juin 1968* (Brussels, 1968), pp. 281-572. See also *CH-CRISP*, 531-532 (17 and 24 September 1971) and 1099-1100 (1985); *Études congolaises*, 3 (1962), pp. 1-11 and 9, 3 (May-June 1966), pp. 1-26.
[208] AGR, Finoutremer, n° 799, PV n° 886 of the CIA, 9 January 1964, p. 2.
[209] "L'aide financière belge au Congo: le crédit d'un milliard", *CA*, 54 (20 May 1966).
[210] AGR, Finoutremer, n° 799, PV n° 888 of the CIA, 13 December 1964, p. 3; n° 896, 8 October 1964, p. 7; n° 901, 11 March 1965, p. 6.
[211] Kadoc, Van Bilsen Papers, n° 6.10/1, P. Jacob (mining engineer) to Van Bilsen, 5 August 1962.
[212] Kadoc, Van Bilsen Papers, n° 6.10/5, A.S. Gérard to J. Van Bilsen, 29 December 1963; n° 6.13.1/2, "Note à M. le Chef de cabinet", by L. De Groote, advisor, 11 July 1967.

The overall impression was certainly that there was considerable room for improvement in Belgium's approach to development aid; in fact, most agreed it could do with a thorough overhaul. This led to new negotiations in 1963 within the Joint Belgo-Congolese Commission, which were sealed on 8 January with the signing of a new co-operation agreement between the two countries that, among other things, defined the status of the staff. Months of talks ensued concerning a more general reform of the co-operation. In 1964, Ambassador Robert Rothschild, Spaak's former chef de cabinet, put forward a plan for the establishment of a Department for Technical Assistance and the Reconstruction of the Administration, a name which in itself betrays a certain degree of ambition. The body would encompass the entire Belgian aid effort and supervise the work of all of its development workers. However, the proposal met with resistance, as the Congolese felt they would have no voice within the envisaged umbrella organisation. The prime minister of the Congo, Moïse Tshombe, rejected the idea of a 'parallel government'.

Both sides had hidden agendas. The attitudes and motivations of the Belgians and the Congolese were ambivalent to say the least. For example, while it had by now become clear that the ATB was suffering from the incompetence of some of its own staff and that Belgium was indeed willing to weed out these bad elements, the Congolese apparently wanted to protect some of the contested development workers.[213] On the other hand, it is undeniable that the ATB in many ways acted as a custodian. The Belgian development workers often seemed to order their Congolese partners around instead of offering them assistance. Towards the end of 1963, the Belgian ambassador in Léopoldville conceded to his French colleague that the Belgians "do not have the same affective and cultural ties with the Congo as the British and French can have with their former colonies". He added: "To us [Belgians], the security of our compatriots and the protection of our interests are essential. You must understand that, rightly or wrongly, my countrymen feel at home here and their presence is ubiquitous". According to the French ambassador, the attitude of the Belgians betrayed "a new guardianship, drenched in paternalism".[214]

Belgian Assistance to the Congo during the Mobutu Era

Before Mobutu seized power, Belgian diplomacy had tried to 'mould' the Congo into the desired shape. Hence, it only made sense that Belgium's technical assistance should initially also be geared to achieving that goal. After the 1965 coup, foreign policy was adapted and the interventionist reflex was suppressed.

---

[213] ARNACO (Kinshasa), Affaires étrangères, n° P107 D840, "Commission mixte de Coopération technique belgo-congolaise. 6ᵉ session. PV de la 1ᵉ séance", 9 March 1967; "Sous-commission belgo-congolaise chargée d'examiner les cas particuliers présentés par la Commission mixte. PV de la séance du 11 mars 1967".

[214] AMAÉF (Nantes), French Embassy in the Congo, n° 14, "Rapport de fin de mission (novembre 1963 - 6 février 1968)", by J. Kosciusko-Morizet, p. 36. The Belgian ambassador was Charles de Kerchove.

However, the question arises whether the development co-operation strategy was adjusted accordingly.

In 1965–7, Belgian development co-operation found itself at a crossroads. In his capacity as royal commissioner for development cooperation (1965–6), Jef Van Bilsen was charged with reforming this important policy domain. Henceforth, Belgian aid would be spread out across the developing world. The Congo became less of a focal point for Belgium, which began to interact more with other partners such as Senegal, Tunisia and countries in Latin America. In Brussels, it was felt that the ATB in Congo was ready for an overhaul. In 1966, after Van Bilsen had been appointed as chef de cabinet to the minister of foreign affairs, he described the new philosophy as follows to his Congolese partners: "We need to launch projects with clearly defined goals that must be attained within an agreed timeframe. Hitherto, Belgium's assistance has been general. We intend to review this method in order to adapt it to the new outlook".[215] Obviously the 1967 crisis had an impact on the development aid programme, and its continuation was thrown into doubt by the security situation. Both sides were on tenterhooks. To a carefully selected interlocutor Mobutu said that he was "fed up with technical assistance hanging over his head like the sword of Damocles and either being granted or denied depending on the prevailing mood, be it spontaneous or elicited, in certain Belgian circles. Rather than to allow himself to be treated in this way, he would prefer to 'suffer' for a year and to seek assistance from countries that were less fussy".[216]

In August 1968, when the crisis had subsided, new co-operation agreements were signed between Belgium and the Congo. Henceforth, any assistance would be assigned to well-defined projects. Moreover, the Joint Belgo-Congolese Commission began to take shape, and regular meetings were held to discuss existing needs and the nature of the co-operation. The number of Belgian development workers in the Congo decreased from 2,200 in 1966 to around 1,500 in the first half of the 1970s and to approximately 1,100 in the second half. In the decade after that, their presence declined further to under a thousand (850 in 1985). Belgium's assistance to the Congo focused on certain sectors. In 1977, for example, education accounted for forty-four per cent of all aid, with 8.5 per cent going to healthcare and 20.5 per cent to the economy; a further twenty per cent went to covering the country's public debt.[217] Clearly the bulk of aid went to education, which is not surprising given that between two-thirds and three-quarters of all participants were working in this sector, often at schools for Belgian children.

Belgian assistance undoubtedly achieved some noteworthy results and it kept certain vital sectors going. Many development workers clearly put their

[215] ARNACO (Kinshasa), Affaires étrangères, n° P107 D840, "ATB au Congo-Kinshasa. (…). Compte rendu de la séance du 26 octobre 1966".
[216] AGR, SGB-3, n° 167, "Memorandum concernant l'entretien du Président Mobutu avec M. De Pooter, RG/FEC le 19 août 1967", p. 8.
[217] Library of the Ministry of Foreign Affairs (LMFA), n° 2/A/2, "Rapports d'ambassade. Rapport annuel 1977 de la Mission belge de Coopération Kinshasa-Zaïre", p. 8.

hearts and souls into their jobs and carried out their assignments competently. But there is another side of this story. The annual reports drawn up by the embassy in Kinshasa frequently drew attention to certain shortcomings and to the fact that they were not being resolved. In 1973, it was noted that "many attempts have been made to rationalise co-operation, but without success". It was felt the Belgian initiatives to streamline development assistance ought to be made more selective, "in order to avoid energy being wasted".[218] The report for the subsequent year summed up criticisms of Belgium's development aid programme: excessive emphasis on assistance from white participants, with the result that the Africans were not growing sufficiently familiar with their jobs; insufficient support for economic and social development; cumbersome structures, involving slow and complicated financial and administrative procedures and so forth.[219] Ten years on, the Joint Commission still regretted "the excessively wide distribution of Belgian assistance and the ensuing lack of efficiency".[220] In 1987, it was asserted that some experts were insufficiently qualified, and that this was caused (in part) by administrative rigidity.[221] That same year, yet another plea was heard for more support for the economy (particularly agriculture) and for a concentration of effort.[222]

It would appear, then, that Belgium's aid initiatives were marred by some structural deficiencies and that they continued to co-determine the relationship with the former colony. This would lead to some highly critical studies in the 1970s. Belgian economist Baudouin Piret argued that "Belgium's public assistance to the Congo [was] a continuation of the colonial administration after the metropole's acceptance of the Congo's political independence". He also felt that it was designed primarily to protect Belgian interests.[223] The assistance was, furthermore, generating a substantial financial transfer from the Congo to Belgium, as it boosted Belgian exports to the former colony. Piret concluded his analysis as follows: "For every franc that goes to Zaire, two francs are returned to Belgium. And that is a conservative estimate. One could probably demonstrate quite easily that for each franc leaving Belgium, three are returned".[224] Henceforth, whenever relationships between the two countries took a turn for the worse, Mobutu would gratefully cite this provocative assertion. As the mutual economic ties grew looser, Belgium's relative share in assistance to the Congo declined. By the end of the 1980s, Belgian businessmen

---

[218] LMFA, n° 2/A/2, "Rapports d'ambassade. Rapport annuel 1973 de la Mission belge de Coopération Kinshasa-Zaïre", pp. 2 and 5.

[219] LMFA, Ibid., 1974, pp. 4–6.

[220] LMFA, n° 2/D/1–2, "Procès-verbal de la Grande Commission mixte belgo-zaïroise de Coopération au Développement, 18–20 July 1984", p. 19.

[221] LMFA, n° 2/A/3, "Rapport d'ambassade 1984", p. 60.

[222] LMFA, n° 2/D/1–2, "Grande Commission mixte 1987. (...) Dossier préparatoire", p. 60.

[223] B. Piret, "L'aide belge au Congo et le développement inégal du capitalisme monopoliste d'État", Contradictions, 1, 1 (January-June 1972), pp. 115–16.

[224] B. Piret, "Le sous-développement du Zaïre vu à travers la balance des paiements Belgique – Zaïre", Contradictions, 15–16 (June 1978), pp. 189–205 (quote on p. 200).

were either leaving the Congo or disregarding it. Missionary posts were no longer replenished with young clerics. Just a few hundred development workers now continued their vital activities in the former colony. Then, in 1990, as the ultimate crisis in Belgian-Congolese relations erupted, all development assistance was put on the back burner and restricted to purely humanitarian relief until the end of Mobutu's dictatorship.[225]

To conclude our overview of Belgium's assistance to the Congo, we would like to draw attention to a number of specific aspects.

First, during the post-colonial era, many Congolese obtained degrees in Belgium under a scholarship scheme. In the 1960s, about a thousand students benefited, and though the number subsequently declined, there were still 200 to 300 a year in the 1980s.[226]

Second, Belgium's development co-operation efforts were not restricted to the activities of AGCD, the official institution. Private Belgian NGOs were also active in the Congo and the Catholic Church, directly or indirectly, played an influential role in this domain, as it had since the colonial period. For a long time, the efforts of the NGOs were geared specifically to the Congo, but here, too, a change of policy was noticeable from the 1990s. In previous years, between 200 and 300 volunteers had been active in the Congo, while Belgium's nine other partner countries combined could count on only between 400 and 500. By 1997, the Congo had dropped to fourth place in the rankings, accounting for just thirty-nine aid workers from NGOs. In 1976–81, the Congo on average attracted eighteen per cent of the co-financing by NGOs (Rwanda was second at 8.9 per cent). The other beneficiary countries trailed considerably, with between one and five per cent. In 1992–7, however, the Congo accounted for just 4.7 per cent of NGO resources, ranking it only third.[227] Internally, the NGOs were highly critical of the Congo's privileged position. During the 1970s, as resistance against Mobutu's regime grew, some wondered whether such assistance to a dictatorship was warranted. But others argued that the NGOs could continue to deliver in the Congo and that they should therefore stay put. Around the mid-1980s, this became the majority view.[228] However, in the early 1990s, an open debate ensued on the effectiveness of NGO aid.[229]

Third, the countries also cooperated militarily.[230] The significance of this co-operation went a lot further than the limited presence of Belgian military

[225] P. Develtere, *De Belgische ontwikkelingssamenwerking* (Leuven, 2005), pp. 121–2.
[226] Exact figures in J. Brassinne, "La coopération (…) 1960–1985", art. cit., pp. 72–3.
[227] G. Stangherlin, "Les ONG de développement", *CH-CRISP*, 1714–1715 (2001), pp. 42, 50.
[228] R. Renard, "De Belgische niet-goevernementele ontwikkelingsorganisaties en Zaïre ", in *Wederzijds. De toekomst van de Belgisch-Zaïrese samenwerking* (Brussels, 1988), pp. 237–58 (especially pp. 247–50); R. Renard, *De rol van de NGOs in Zaïre* (Brussels, 1986).
[229] [R. Hendrickx], *Coprogram en de rel over het rapport "De Belgische NGO's in Zaïre". Witboek in opdracht van Coprogram Vlaanderen* (Brussels, 1991).
[230] "L'assistance militaire belge à la République du Congo", *CA*, 35 (15 June 1964); J. Brassinne, "Douze années de coopération technique militaire belgo-zaïroise", *Études africaines du CRISP*, 142–143 (13 October 1972); B. Colpaert, *De Belgisch-Zaïrese militaire samenwerking 1968–1987* (Brussels, 1987), unpublished master's thesis in political and social sciences, VUB.

personnel in the Congo would suggest with thirty in 1960, 420 in 1965, 180 in 1973, fifty-seven in 1977 and around 100 in the first half of the 1980s.[231] After independence, the Congo fell into chaos, and it seemed as if the country's future would depend largely on the formation of an effective Congolese army. Twice the country's military, led by Mobutu, intervened in political affairs. First from September 1960 until February 1961, when it temporarily sidelined the legal institutions, and a second time in November 1965, in a coup that marked the start of Mobutu's three decades in power. In the years between, the army had to deal with various uprisings and tried to retain unity in the country. It was, however, unprepared for this task and, without foreign assistance, was doomed to failure. Even during the one and a half years that diplomatic relations between Léopoldville and Brussels were suspended (July 1960 – December 1961), Belgian soldiers were part of the inner circle of the Congolese government. Colonel Louis Marlière, for example, was one of Mobutu's closest advisors.[232] Belgium's official military technical assistance programme (Assistance technique militaire belge or ATM) was launched in June 1963. Initially the assistance was very modest, but it soon increased in scope as rebel activity in 1964–5 posed a threat to the government in Léopoldville. As we have seen, Belgian and American military assistance, combined with the presence of white mercenaries, was crucial in defeating the rebels. The ATM, whose status was initially rather vague and ambivalent, was placed under the authority of Belgium's Ministry of Defence in February 1965, a decision that would cause tension over competences with the Foreign Affairs Ministry.[233] The ATM cost Belgium a few hundred million francs a year, which represented barely 0.3 per cent of the overall defence budget. A further agreement on military co-operation between Belgium and the Congo was signed in 1968 and amended in 1979.

Belgian military personnel played an important role in providing training and equipment to the Congolese army and assisted in the (re)construction of military law and a police force. In 1971, some eighty per cent of the Congolese military staff (from non-commissioned officers to high-ranking officers) were trained by Belgian soldiers. This form of assistance was important from a psychological point of view, as is apparent from a memo to the Belgian minister of defence dating from 1971: "[The ATM] creates an important SEMBLANCE [sic] of security, in which not only the locals and foreigners believe, but undoubtedly also the active opposition and the opposition in exile. The Congolese army would collapse within a matter of months if the Belgian and French military advisers were to suddenly vacate the scene".[234] The ATM,

[231] J.-Cl. Willame, "Landsverdediging en de militaire samenwerking", in *Wederzijds, op. cit.*, p. 108.
[232] It should be recalled here that Belgium offered substantial military assistance to the secessionist province of Katanga (training of the 'Katangan gendarmes'). Towards the end of 1960, there were around 240 Belgian military personnel in Katanga.
[233] B. Colpaert, *De Belgisch-Zaïrese ..., op. cit.*, pp. 15–6.
[234] Kadoc, P. W. Segers Papers, n° 16.25, note "Betreffende onze militaire aanwezigheid in Zaïre", (1971), p. 2.

which was also beneficial to Belgium's weapons and production goods industry, obviously felt the effects of the volatile relationship between Belgium and the Congo. Nonetheless, a source involved in the military co-operation programme would later assert that "certainly up into 1987, it was never affected by the sharp blows delivered by Mobutu or his acolytes. On the contrary, when necessary, the president used to intervene to 'take the edge off'. It is almost as if our military co-operation unfolded under his protection, as if it were a taboo, and, one might assume, the exclusive domain of the president".[235] The explanation for this exceptional situation is clear: Mobutu's power depended largely on his control of the Forces armées zaïroises (FAZ). He was, however, careful not to put all his eggs in one basket. In line with his divide and rule policy, he called on other countries, including Israel, the United States and France, to assist, equip or train his troops, especially the elite corps.

The Social Dimension of the Post-Colonial Relations Between Belgium and the Congo: the Belgians in the Congo and the Congolese in Belgium

During the colonial period, both the absolute number and the proportion of Belgians residing in the Congo were relatively modest compared to the situation in other colonies. Towards the end of 1959, there were eighty-nine thousand Belgian expatriate men, women and children in the colony. During the dramatic events of July 1960, some thirty-eight thousand left, many for good. Moreover, measures by the Belgian government facilitated the integration of former colonial officials into the Belgian public service.[236] After the decolonisation crisis, the number of Belgians in the Congo declined at a gradual rate, interspersed with more precipitate exoduses in moments of tension. Some Belgians chose to return to the Congo as soon as the situation had more or less settled down, so that by 1964, some forty-two thousand Belgian nationals remained in the former colony, less than half the number prior to independence. The large corporations provided jobs for around ten thousand employees, with twenty-five hundred working in public administration; about the same number were self-employed.[237] The Union minière crisis, the mercenary uprising of 1967 and the 'Zaïrisation' in 1973–4 further depleted the Belgian presence, so that by 1976 their number amounted to just eighteen thousand. After stabilising for a while, the Belgian population declined again to sixteen thousand five hundred in 1980. By then, there were more Belgians in South Africa (eighteen thousand) than in the Congo. The diplomatic crisis of 1990 and, even more so, the looting sprees in 1991 and 1993, both of which necessitated evacuations of Belgian

---

[235] J.-Cl. Marlair, *Les rêves des Noko. Présence militaire belge au Congo-Zaïre* (Ensival, 1993).
[236] Particularly the laws of 23 March 1960, 27 July 1961 and 3 April 1964. P. Salmon, "Les retours en Belgique induits par la décolonisation", in J.-L. Miège & C. Dubois, eds., *L'Europe retrouvée. Les migrations de la decolonisation* (Paris, 1994), pp. 191–212.
[237] AGR, SGB-3, n° 170, note on "Les relations économiques et financières entre la Belgique et le Congo", 20 September 1966, p. 15.

nationals, delivered the final blow insofar as the Belgian presence in its former colony was concerned. In 1993, there were just 2,800 Belgians in the Congo and between 1,100 and 1,200 of those were missionaries. Back in 1959, the missionary population alone had amounted to 7,500, though admittedly this figure included non-Belgian missionaries. By 1982, the number of Belgian missionaries in the Congo had dropped to 2,233. Clearly they were leaving the country less readily, and hence their proportion in the total Belgian expatriate population in the former colony rose quite notably from eight per cent in 1960 to around forty-one per cent in 1993.[238]

In total, the flow of the white population back to Belgium over the period 1945–90 was much lower in Belgium's case compared with the other European colonial powers. Some ninety thousand Belgians came back to their homeland, while this post-colonial population exodus touched no less than two hundred and seventy thousand to three hundred thousand Dutch, four hundred and eighty thousand to five hundred and eighty thousand Italians, five hundred thousand to six hundred thousand Portuguese, 1,400,000 to 1,700,000 French and three hundred and eighty thousand to five hundred thousand British.[239] In the Belgian case, the impact of the former colony on the metropole was rather marginal from a social point of view.

While the number of Belgians in the Congo steadily declined, more and more Congolese were settling in Belgium, though there was no question of a mass migration. Only about 400 to 500 Congolese lived in Belgium before the 1960s. In the run up to independence, the number of Congolese residents in Belgium rose slightly. Many of these were students who would constitute the first Congolese generation of university graduates. In the first decades after the transition to independence, the number of Congolese in Belgium quadrupled from 2,585 in 1961 to 11,828 in 1991. Their number continued to grow to 16,542 by 1995, after which it declined again to 13,572 by January 2003.[240] All in all, towards the end of the twentieth century, the Congolese community gradually grew to represent the third most important group of non-European foreigners (after the Moroccan and the Turkish communities). Still, the Congolese never represented more than a fraction of the total foreign population in Belgium: barely 1.3 per cent in 1995 (the eleventh largest foreign community in the country).[241] A certain number of Congolese came to Belgium and stayed unofficially, just like many other foreigners. It is of course very difficult to assess their exact number, since they are not registered. However, this clandestine immigration could represent some ten per cent of the registered Congolese population.[242] Many of the Congolese in Belgium have

---

[238] *Informissi. Informations pour missionnaires*, Brussels, 1970 (I, 1)-2002.

[239] B. Etemad, "Europe and Migration after Decolonisation", *Journal of European Economic History*, 27, 3 (Winter 1998), p. 465. In the case of the Dutch, this includes the so-called Eurasians.

[240] *Bevolkingsstatistieken* (Brussels, 1969–2000); *Bevolking en huishoudens* (Brussels, 2001-).

[241] A. Cornet, "Les Congolais en Belgique aux XIXe et XXe siècles", in A. Morelli, ed., *Histoire des étrangers et de l'immigration en Belgique* (Brussels, 2004), p. 378.

[242] Ibid., p. 390.

chosen to live in one particular neighbourhood near the centre of Brussels, informally called 'Matonge' in reference to a district of Kinshasa. About half of all Congolese living in Belgium reside in Brussels. The particular social composition of the Congolese population is also worth examining. In 1981, forty-one per cent, the largest group within that Congolese expatriate community, consisted of students. There was also a large group of political refugees. This is not at all surprising, as Brussels was for many years a hotbed of anti-Mobutu opposition – much to the dictator's dismay. All in all, many Congolese were not well-integrated into the regular employment market. In 1981, just 11.5 per cent were 'economically active', compared to 36.7 per cent of all immigrants.[243] Immigration from the former colony impacted very little indeed on the national employment market. Belgium did not act as a labour magnet for its former colonial subjects. Of course, this does not mean that the Congolese in Belgium remained locked in marginality. Some of them obtained Belgian nationality (3,365 in total between 1985 and 1995).[244] Some people of Congolese origin now occupy high-ranking positions in the academic world, in sports or in politics. From 2003 to 2007, Gisèle Mandaila, the state secretary for the family and the disabled in the federal government, was the first person of Congolese descent to hold a prominent position in Belgian politics.

Regarding this aspect of post-colonial relations, namely the arrival of ex-colonial subjects in the mother country, Belgium is – once again – an exception among the former colonial powers. According to Etemad's useful and careful estimates, only fifteen thousand to twenty thousand Congolese came to Belgium during the period 1945–90, while no less than two hundred and fifty thousand to two hundred and eighty thousand non-Europeans left the former Dutch colonies to settle in the Netherlands. In the case of the former Portuguese and French empires, the figures stand at seventy-five thousand to one hundred and fifty thousand and three hundred and fifty thousand to five hundred thousand respectively; whereas the migration towards Great Britain from the former empire involved no less than 1,350,000 to 1,750,000 non-Europeans.[245] It should also be underlined that Belgium never had to cope with the equivalent of the Harkis in France or the Moluccans in the Netherlands, groups of former colonial subjects who had to leave their homeland owing to their (military) collaboration with the imperial ruler.[246] In both these cases, this particular situation

---

[243] Zana Aziza Etambala, *In het land ... op. cit.*, p. 83. An analysis of migration from the Congo to Belgium in the early 1990s, in Mayoyo Bitumba Tipo-Tipo, *Migration Sud/Nord. Levier ou obstacle? Les Zaïrois en Belgique* (Brussels-Paris, 1995) (Cahiers africains, 13).

[244] A. Cornet, "Les Congolais en Belgique", art. cit., p. 378.

[245] B. Etemad, "Europe and Migration after Decolonisation", art. cit., p. 465.

[246] J. Thobie, G. Meynier, C. Coquery-Vidrovitch & Ch.-R. Ageron, *Histoire de la France coloniale 1914–1990* (Paris, 1990), pp. 547–9; T. Shepard, *The Invention of Decolonization: The Algerian War and the Remaking of France* (Ithaca, 2006); U. Bosma, *Terug uit de koloniën. Zestig jaar postkoloniale migranten en hun organisaties* (Amsterdam, 2009); H. Wesseling, "Post-Imperial Holland", art. cit., pp. 134–8.

clearly influenced the post-colonial handling of the imperial past – an aspect unknown in Belgium.

Conclusion

Phrases such as 'privileged relationship' and 'historical ties' crop up regularly in the official discourse used during state visits between Belgium and the Congo. Their precise meaning, however, depends largely on the context. Purposely or otherwise, even a seemingly neutral reference to the past, such as 'historical ties', may convey very different messages in different situations. It may carry connotations of recognition, reproach, duty or guilt, depending on who is speaking and who is listening. The expression 'privileged relationship', for its part, conceals even more diverse aspects of reality. Moreover, its meaning has shifted substantially over the years. Belgians in the early 1960s would not have used or interpreted it in the same way as we do today. Only politicians seem to use the term nowadays. In business circles, as in social or religious organisations, the notion is considered obsolete. This in itself is quite illustrative of the remarkable evolution that has taken place in the 'ties' between Belgium and the Congo.

As time passed, Belgium's presence in an independent Congo gradually declined, at varying speeds depending on the sector. Immediately after independence, civil servants fled the country in droves. To an extent, they were replaced under the Belgian Technical Assistance programme by so-called 'cooperants', but their numbers were fewer and would, for that matter, continue to decline. From about 1990, the Belgians had more or less disappeared from the Congolese scene. Still, the qualitative contribution made by these cooperants was often more substantial than their numbers would suggest. As for the Belgian missionary presence in the Congo, most stayed on after the events of 1960, but as vocations to the priesthood declined in general, so too did the number of new recruits for missionary service. In business, we must distinguish between Belgians who invested in the Congo and those who traded with the former colony. For some time, the large Belgian capital providers held on to the hope that they would be able to continue their activities in the Congo. To this end, they at least maintained the production apparatus, even if they made no significant new investments. However, from the late 1960s, Belgian investors quickly withdrew from the Congo, either voluntarily or by force. Some continued to either buy (mostly diamonds, gold and non-ferrous metals) or sell (mostly metal products) in the former colony. And initially, lucrative air and maritime transport operations were also maintained. However, this trade would gradually lose momentum, eventually grinding to a complete standstill in the 1990s.

Eventually, most Belgian businessmen and development workers left the country, while the missionaries grew older. This reduced Belgian presence was by no means reflected in a declining interest from politicians, even though their attitudes and roles did change considerably over the years. On the eve of independence, there was a clear intention to interfere in the internal affairs of the former colony and to mould the country's domestic policy, with all the inherent consequences. But after some time, it became clear to everybody, including the Belgian leaders themselves, that Belgium could not have the same ambitions as its neighbour France. After decolonisation, Paris considered its former black African colonies as a private 'backyard'. The concept of '*Françafrique*' was a basic assumption of French foreign policy; it implied toppling or establishing African leaders, establishing and running army bases in Africa, launching military operations, managing the economic and financial policy of the newly created states and so forth.[247] Clearly, Belgium did not have the military, economic and diplomatic leverage to act in such a way. From the middle of the 1960s, the ambition to mould the Congo made way for a *modus vivendi* with a dictator, for economic and/or geopolitical reasons. The military operations conducted by the Belgians after the 1960s were small-scale and temporary interventions, essentially motivated by humanitarian considerations: saving compatriots from the Congolese chaos. Their baseline was entirely different from French military interventions.[248] The policy of accommodation with the Congolese authorities largely determined Belgian diplomacy for close to three decades. But even after the economic interests had all but evaporated, the Congo remained an important factor in foreign policy. In matters relating to central Africa, Belgium – in its capacity as a former colonial ruler with what was regarded as regional expertise – would remain an authoritative voice on the international scene, at least insofar as the global heavyweights showed any interest at all in the planet's backwaters. Belgian politicians with international ambitions kept this well in mind.

The Congo's mark on Belgian society faded even more quickly than the Belgian presence in the Congo. The decolonisation and the ensuing unrest compromised Belgium's position in the international political arena for a number of years, but not in the longer term. The characteristics of the colonisation undoubtedly played a crucial role in the fact that Belgium got over the loss of its colony relatively quickly, even though the official propaganda had considered having a colony as essential to the grandeur, the wealth and even the 'moral survival' of Belgium. The most significant interfaces between the Congolese and the Belgian economies adapted almost effortlessly to the loosening of the ties between the two countries. Contrary to some gloomy predictions, there was no economic catastrophe and no massive loss of employment. In fact, quite the opposite happened, and in the 1960s, Belgium enjoyed its best economic years ever. Because the economic rupture was not sudden and because Belgium disappeared rather gradually from the Congo's economic fabric, industries that were deeply rooted in the colony had time to adjust to the transition.

---

[247] J. P. Dozon, "Une décolonisation en trompe-l'oeil", in P. Blanchard, e.a., eds., *Culture postcoloniale 1961–2006, op. cit.*, pp. 195–202.
[248] A. Rouvez, *Disconsolate Empires, op. cit.*, pp. 292, 295, 315.

Politically speaking, the transition unfolded more quickly. Unlike France, for example, Belgium was not divided over the issue of decolonisation, apart from during the momentous events in 1960–1. The country's institutions were not shaken to their foundations and neither were its social structures. Most former colonials adapted without great difficulty. The true colonial nostalgics – mostly small and independent businessmen who had lost all their possessions in the colony – were so few in number that their voices were hardly heard and it was therefore not long before those who simply wanted to turn the page of colonialism gained the upper hand. Finally, the Congolese community in Belgium was smaller than other ethnic minority groups such as Turks and Moroccans, so, again, its impact on the Belgian social fabric was limited.

General Conclusion

When the Belgian state took over the Congo in 1908, a new ministry had to be created. Strangely, it was called the ministry of colon*ies*, even though Belgium only had *one* colony and did not envisage acquiring any other overseas territories.[1] The term ministry of the colony may have sounded rather middling; the use of the plural probably struck a more imperial note, even if it did not correspond to reality. In the same vein, the Belgians proudly talked of their empire; a 'Single-Colony Empire', as historian Jean-Luc Vellut wittily put it.[2] Compared to other imperial experiences, Belgium shows many singularities. Strictly speaking, it was the *last* country in the world to officially acquire a colony. Its colonial domination started only a few years before the First World War. Of course, Belgian soldiers and officers, missionaries, businessmen and administrators had been involved in the Congo since 1885, but this kind of 'private' colonisation, by definition, had less of an impact on Belgium *as a whole* than the subsequent colonial regime characterised by full and open state involvement. Another singularity was also of great importance: Originally, colonialism was not pursued by the Belgian state as such. National authorities did not take the *initiative* to conquer overseas territory; nor did the leading political, industrial or financial circles push for colonial acquisitions. It was only after Belgium had been confronted with the Congo by a series of circumstances and coincidences that a fraction of the political world and the economic elites decided *to pursue* this opportunity.[3] In other words, in Belgium, imperialism started with a restricted social basis. In this sense, Belgium could be described

---

[1] In 1919, Ruanda and Urundi were added to the Belgian overseas domain, but they were 'mandates' and not 'colonies' in the strict sense of the word. Moreover, as we have seen in Chapter 3, they had not been Belgium's first option after the First World War. Politicians and diplomats would have preferred a border correction in the west (mouth of the Congo River), rather than the responsibility for the two small territories in the east.

[2] J.-L. Vellut, "Belgium: the Single-Colony Empire", in R. Aldrich, ed., *The Age of Empire* (London, 2007), pp. 220–37 and 309–10.

[3] In particular, an idiosyncratic, maverick king acting in a competitive international environment – the Belgian case certainly reminds us of the great importance of *contingency* in colonial history.

as a 'reluctant imperialist' – at least in the beginning, when many politicians and leading societal forces were clearly dragging their feet.[4] Once they had assumed responsibility for the Congo, however, the elite rapidly changed its mind. From that moment on, those people became convinced colonialists, right up until the very end of the 1950s. But this remarkable change of attitude could not wholly erase the rather strange beginnings of Belgian colonialism and the major side effects it was to have in the Congo as well as in Belgium.

Belgium's rather short, geographically concentrated and 'reluctant' imperial experience contrasts with the rich imperial history of other colonising powers, particularly Great Britain, France and the Netherlands. This may seem obvious, but it reminds us of the danger of rapid generalisations concerning the effects of empire on the metropole. There is no such thing as a unique colonial experience; there were many particular experiences, with different effects in each case. Britain's overseas political and economic involvement was of course a long-term phenomenon, spanning many centuries; logically, the colonial nexus could have structural, even formative influences on the metropole. Moreover, Britain ruled a whole range of contrasting regions and societies. The dominions, a complex society including India and the tropical African colonies all had different types of effects on Britain, as A. S. Thompson has convincingly shown.[5] The same can, of course, be said of France, a power that pursued intense commercial and political activities on four continents outside Europe over a period of many centuries. Likewise, the secular maritime and colonial contacts of the Dutch had a decisive impact on the economic structure and performances of their country and on the formation of the nation itself. On the other hand, Belgium belongs to the group of colonial latecomers, along with Germany and Italy. They all had relatively short colonial experiences, starting as late as the 1880s and lasting only a few decades. The German colonial nexus brutally came to an end after thirty years; the Italian empire spanned roughly sixty years; the Belgian colony existed for fifty years or so (or seventy-five if the Leopoldian period is added). Compared to the early seafarers' empires, the latecomers' colonial possessions were also much less diversified. Italy only ruled on the Mediterranean shores and in the horn of Africa; Germany's possessions were essentially located in tropical Africa (and only marginally in the Pacific). In this respect, Belgium was, again, a different case, with its 'empire' limited, as we have seen, to a single African territory. It is of course tempting to assume – *first* – that the colonial effects on the metropole were entirely different in both groups, namely the early seafarers on the one hand and the colonial latecomers on the other, and – *second* – that these effects also display some similarities *within* each group. It may be interesting to examine this hypothesis more closely, by comparing the respective national cases; a task clearly beyond the aim of this book.

---

[4] M. Ewans, "Belgium and the Colonial Experience", art. cit., p. 167.
[5] A. S. Thompson, *The Empire, op. cit.*, pp. 4, 241.

Indeed, our intention was far more modest. We have merely attempted to fill in some of the most obvious gaps in the knowledge of Belgium's colonial history – not by focusing on Belgium's actions in the Congo, but by looking at the mark of colonialism on the colonising country. In the perspective of global history, the former aspect is of course much more important than the latter. Still, the extent to which the colonisation of the Congo impacted Belgian society has barely been researched, although this angle is not only relevant to the history of the colonising country, but also to the dynamics of the colonised region.

Let us first summarise the Congo's mark on Belgium. Belgium's involvement in the colonisation of central Africa began in a very specific way. Even those scholars who are (often quite rightly) sceptical about the impact of 'great individuals' on the course of history cannot but concede that, in the case of the Congo, the personal initiatives of Leopold II went far beyond the anecdotal. His actions played an instrumental role, not only in the history of the Congo itself, but also in terms of the colony's impact on Belgium. The rather abrupt and forced manner in which the colony, as a result of the king's actions, ended up on the plates of the people of Belgium may help explain why the Congo ultimately came to occupy a rather marginal position in the country's domestic affairs, except during two pivotal moments: the takeover of the Congo Free State by Belgium and the dramatic decolonisation of 1960. Belgian public opinion was by no means enthusiastic about the takeover in 1908: The move was met with open hostility by some and with plain indifference by many others. Perhaps this explains the supposed lack of commitment to the colony on the part of the domestic Belgian population; a lack of commitment that politicians and colonials would complain about throughout the colonial era. It is up to future scholars to determine how deep-rooted the 'colonial attitude' was in Belgium. By focusing on certain aspects in our analysis of the colonial mark on Belgium, other important elements have inevitably been left largely untouched, particularly in relation to the public imagination and perception of the colonial relationship. The cultural and social aspects have also been left aside. These are lacunas we wish to emphasise rather than conceal.

Still, the colony was clearly present in the official national rhetoric, although it did not play a role in the shaping of this small nation-state, nor in its subsequent crisis in the second half of the twentieth century. The Congo, it was proudly asserted, had made Belgium greater. As far as Belgium's position in the international arena was concerned, there was certainly some truth to this claim. Thanks to the acquisition of its overseas territories, Belgium suddenly became a bigger player in the global arena than previously. However, this colonial grandeur also had its downside. Belgium, as a colonial power, repeatedly drew criticism, particularly for its isolationist policy. Belgium, often lauded for its openness and its commitment to international organisations and rapprochement, was perceived as wanting to go it alone insofar as its colony was concerned; a rather bizarre twist considering the peculiar, almost involuntary, way in which Belgium became a colonial power.

The Leopoldian origin of the Belgian presence in Africa also had an impact on the economic dimension of colonisation, in which the large financial groups and enterprises, often with close ties to government, played a strikingly dominant role. This extraordinary circumstance can help explain the economic significance of the Congo to Belgium. Certain sectors fared well in the colonial adventure and, more often than not, the Société générale de Belgique was involved in one way or another. Colonisation also meant that Belgian foreign investment was focused on the Congo rather than on other countries. Belgian foreign trade also developed along these lines, with imports from the Congo (mainly of raw materials, and non-ferrous metals in particular) always much more important than exports (mainly of metal products) to the colony. It is worth noting that the Congo was never locked up behind protectionist walls; as far as trade regulation was concerned, the Congo always remained an 'open' colony. The privileged position of Belgian interests in its colonial domain was guaranteed by other mechanisms, for example monetary policy or other non-commercial regulations. The colony therefore had an important impact on Belgium's global balance of payments, a situation quite similar to that of other colonial powers such as Great Britain and the Netherlands.

The economic and social ties between Belgium and the Congo were undoubtedly close and important, but they did not cover the whole range of Belgian society. For example, while the large financial groups played a role of great significance in the Congo, very few small Belgian entrepreneurs found their way to the colony. The Congo mainly attracted a small, highly trained and carefully selected Belgian elite; there was no question of a mass exodus of minor Belgian entrepreneurs. These observations explain the ease with which Belgium severed its ties to the independent Congo. In the early twenty-first century, the Congo plays a very minor role in Belgian society. Conversely, in the 1990s, four decades after independence, the *immediate* Belgian presence in the Congo no longer amounted to much – but that certainly does not mean that Belgium did not leave a long-lasting imprint on the new African nation.

This brings us to our final point. The very impact that colonialism had on Belgium also left a special mark on the colony *in turn*. The imperial link is never one-way, but always consists of mutual reverberations, an observation made right at the start of this book. Studying the colonial imprint on Belgium did not reveal a great deal about concrete situations in the Congolese terrain, but nevertheless exposed some constraining factors at work on the latter. As the great powers carefully watched (and coveted?) the Congo from the time of its birth, the Belgian authorities developed a defensive attitude. Their colony had to be protected, even isolated, from foreign influences. The Congo was to become a 'model colony', proving that the Belgians were capable of handling an empire all on their own. Their constant fear of losing control of the colony led to a policy that insulated the Congolese people from the outside world, prevented the formation of indigenous elites and consequently, left the colonised society wholly unprepared for independence. Modern civil society – political parties, cultural associations and social movements – was extremely weak when the inexperienced Congolese leaders took over the reins of their country. Belgian colonial policy, shaped by the early imprint of colonialism on the metropole, was certainly to blame for this. The overwhelming position of a few large (semi-)private enterprises in the colonial economy – another mark of the effects of colonialism on Belgium bouncing back on the Congolese situation – led to a disproportionate concentration of wealth; making the new nation conducive to predatory activity by the new Congolese elite. These elements significantly influenced the development of the Congo's tragedies in the final decades of the twentieth century.

Annex

TABLE 1. *The Ministers of Colonies (1908–1960)*

Name	Political Party	Dates of Beginning and Ending of Mandate	Number of Months in Office as Minister before Becoming Minister of Colonies	Number of Months in Office as Minister after or While Being Minister of Colonies
Jules RENKIN	Catholic	30.10.1908–21.11.1918	18	37
Louis FRANCK	Liberal	21.11.1918–11.03.1924	0	0
Henri CARTON de Tournai	Catholic	11.03.1924–20.05.1926	0	10
Maurice HOUTART	Catholic	20.05.1926–15.11.1926 29.12.1926–18.01.1927	0	69 (cumulating MoC with Finance Ministry)
Edouard PECHER	Liberal	16.11.1926–27.12.1926	0	0 (deceased when in office)
Henri JASPAR	Catholic	18.01.1927–19.10.1929 27.02.1930–18.06.1931	34	77 (cumulating MoC with Prime Minister)
Paul TSCHOFFEN	Catholic	19.10.1929–24.12.1929 23.05.1932–13.11.1934	21	0

(*continued*)

TABLE 1 *(continued)*

Name	Political Party	Dates of Beginning and Ending of Mandate	Number of Months in Office as Minister before Becoming Minister of Colonies	Number of Months in Office as Minister after or While Being Minister of Colonies
Paul CHARLES	Extra-parliamentary (Catholic)	18.05.1931–16.08.1931 20.11.1934–25.03.1935	0	0
Paul CROKAERT	Catholic	06.06.1931–25.05.1932	0	5
Edmond RUBBENS	Catholic	25.03.1935–27.04.1938	4	0 (deceased when in office)
Albert DE VLEESCHAUWER	Catholic	15.05.1938–22.02.1939 16.04.1939–31.01.1945	0	38
Gaston HEENEN	Extra-parliamentary (Catholic)	21.02.1939–16.04.1939	0	0
Edgar DE BRUYNE	Catholic	12.02.1945–16.06.1945	0	0
Robert GODDING	Liberal	02.08.1945–18.02.1946 31.03.1946–11.03.1947	0	0
Lode CRAEYBECKX	Socialist	13.03.1946–20.03.1946	0	0
Pierre WIGNY	Christian-democrat	20.03.1947–12.08.1950	0	62
André (Dries) DEQUAE	Christian-democrat	15.08.1950–12.04.1954	2	58
Auguste BUISSERET	Liberal	23.04.1954–02.06.1958	29	0
Léo PETILLON	Extra-parliamentary (Christian-democrat)	05.07.1958–06.11.1958	0	0
Maurice VAN HEMELRIJCK	Christian-democrat	06.11.1958–02.09.1959	4	0

Annex

Name	Political Party	Dates of Beginning and Ending of Mandate	Number of Months in Office as Minister before Becoming Minister of Colonies	Number of Months in Office as Minister after or While Being Minister of Colonies
August DE SCHRYVER	Christian-democrat	03.09.1959–02.09.1960	63	0
Raymond SCHEYVEN	Christian-democrat	17.11.1959–02.09.1960	4	41
Walter GANSHOF van der MEERSCH	Extra-parliamentary	16.05.1960–20.07.1960	0	0
Harold d'ASPREMONT LYNDEN	Christian-democrat	02.09.1960–27.03.1961	0	0

Remarks: M. Van Hemelrijck and A. De Schryver were "Minister of the Belgian Congo and Ruanda-Urundi" and the latter was "Minister of African Affairs" as from 30 June 1960; R. Scheyven was "Minister without portfolio charged with the economic and financial affairs of the Belgian Congo and Ruanda-Urundi"; W. Ganshof van der Meersch was "Minister without portfolio, charged with general affairs in Africa"; H. d'Aspremont Lynden was "Minister of African Affairs".
"MoC"= Minister of Colonies
This table was compiled with the biographical data in P. Van Molle, *Le Parlement belge 1894–1972* (Antwerp, 1972).

TABLE 2. *Foreign Trade between Belgium and the Congo (1889–1960)*

	Import from the Congo (Value) with Index 1913=100	Import from the Congo in Percentage of Total Import	Export to the Congo (Value) with Index 1913=100	Export to the Congo in Percentage of Total Export
1889	4.1	0.12	7.6	0.14
1890	7.4	0.21	27.2	0.51
1891	14.0	0.37	28.2	0.50
1892	16.5	0.52	27.1	0.53
1893	24.9	0.77	32.9	0.65
1894	26.4	0.81	32.1	0.66
1895	28.6	0.83	40.8	0.79
1896	27.8	0.76	56.1	1.03
1897	34.8	0.93	61.9	1.06
1898	43.5	1.03	34.1	0.53
1899	79.4	1.71	34.2	0.47
1900	94.5	2.07	42.6	0.59
1901	87.9	1.92	32.8	0.48
1902	86.4	1.76	26.5	0.37
1903	99.2	1.81	31.9	0.40

(*continued*)

TABLE 2 (continued)

	Import from the Congo (Value) with Index 1913=100	Import from the Congo in Percentage of Total Import	Export to the Congo (Value) with Index 1913=100	Export to the Congo in Percentage of Total Export
1904	109.0	1.90	52.0	0.64
1905	122.2	1.93	42.2	0.49
1906	152.6	2.15	47.4	0.45
1907	120.6	1.55	68.4	0.64
1908	109.5	1.60	60.2	0.64
1909	129.0	1.69	67.5	0.64
1910	162.4	1.85	88.8	0.70
1911	118.4	1.27	98.4	0.74
1912	125.2	1.22	108.4	0.74
1913	100.0	0.96	100.0	0.72
1919	85.7	1.13	19.6	0.32
1920	143.0	1.43	56.7	0.45
1921	81.0	1.00	81.9	1.00
1922	–	–	–	–
1923	51.0	0.70	111.4	1.15
1924	67.3	0.78	166.5	1.36
1925	91.6	1.01	251.1	1.86
1926	68.6	0.87	237.8	1.93
1927	136.6	1.58	274.8	1.92
1928	267.8	2.82	331.0	2.00
1929	414.3	3.93	444.1	2.61
1930	351.0	3.81	370.0	2.65
1931	291.2	4.10	224.3	1.81
1932	182.5	3.77	104.0	1.28
1933	189.1	4.19	79.5	1.04
1934	223.6	5.39	71.5	0.97
1935	269.0	7.28	61.6	1.00
1936	320.5	6.97	89.1	1.18
1937	483.5	8.19	148.1	1.52
1938	409.2	8.38	156.3	1.88
1939	343.2	8.18	141.7	1.69
1945	214.9	11.17	25.1	2.50
1946	522.8	6.54	170.4	2.26
1947	871.4	7.29	363.5	2.33
1948	909.1	7.43	704.1	3.76
1949	852.8	7.45	862.4	4.27
1950	883.3	7.57	659.5	3.70
1951	1203.7	7.92	1132.9	3.97
1952	1166.3	7.95	1518.8	5.76
1953	1076.3	7.45	1386.0	5.70
1954	1173.2	7.72	1313.6	5.30
1955	1388.9	8.19	1390.6	4.65
1956	1442.9	7.40	1487.6	4.37
1957	1124.7	5.49	1476.1	4.28

	Import from the Congo (Value) with Index 1913=100	Import from the Congo in Percentage of Total Import	Export to the Congo (Value) with Index 1913=100	Export to the Congo in Percentage of Total Export
1958	988.4	5.30	1247.1	3.80
1959	1161.2	5.66	942.8	2.66
1960	1574.5	6.67	636.4	1.56

Source: Annuaire statistique de la Belgique (et du Congo belge), 1889–1960.
Remark: Special trade of Belgium (1889–1921) and of the Belgian-Luxemburg Economic Union (1922–1960). The value of import and export in current Belgian francs has been converted in gold francs of 1914.

TABLE 3A. *Some Important Elements of the Balance of Payments of the Belgian Congo (1920–1939) (in million current francs)*

	1	2	3	4	5	6	7	8	9	10
1920	315	238	7	36	49	57	84	8	92	149
1921	218	276	12	14	54	-110	39	47	86	-24
1922	295	269	68	25	61	-78	120	77	197	119
1923	561	390	86	21	81	25	162	-47	115	140
1924	717	490	90	17	112	42	64	121	185	227
1925	885	896	140	41	140	-250	369	170	539	289
1926	1196	1293	211	-6	226	-540	587	450	1037	497
1927	1457	1496	173	-7	311	-530	720	-45	675	145
1928	1834	1625	258	1	361	-409	1614	-84	1530	1121
1929	2353	1943	355	8	406	-343	989	210	1199	856
1930	1950	1581	330	49	372	-284	1236	261	1497	1213
1931	1183	962	159	1	342	-279	736	341	1077	798
1932	735	465	181	–	327	-238	-24	581	577	319
1933	744	389	236	180	376	-77	-108	376	268	191
1934	884	378	276	341	375	186	-3	-326	-329	-133
1935	1393	525	464	289	406	287	-198	-456	-654	-367
1936	1723	725	500	202	482	218	-955	1126	171	389
1937	2586	1137	540	81	453	537	-119	-328	-447	90
1938	1987	1023	400	30	512	82	-78	-204	-282	-200
1939	1917	932	73	51	457	106	-9	109	100	206

1 = Export
2 = Import
3 = Dividends, interests and *tantièmes* paid to other countries by Congolese enterprises
4 = Donations and advances by Belgium to the Congo
5 = Other elements of current account
6 = Balance of the current account (1–2–3+4+5)
7 = Balance of imported (+) and exported (-) private capital
8 = Balance of imported (+) and exported (-) public capital
9 = Balance of (7) and (8)
10 = Total of the balance of payments (6+9)
Source: G. Vandewalle, *De conjuncturele evolutie in Kongo en Ruanda-Urundi van 1920 tot 1939 en van 1949 tot 1958* (Ghent, 1966), p. 77.

TABLE 3B. *Some Important Elements of the Balance of Payments of the Belgian Congo (1948–1958) (in million current francs)*

	1	2	3	4	5	6	7	8	9	10	11	12	13	14
1948	13173	7711	1019	716	1562	2165	531	396	135	4	31	−27	108	2273
1949	12550	9089	1256	1252	947	6	336	681	−345	—	36	−36	−381	−375
1950	15776	8804	1295	1123	1467	3087	876	498	378	2564	7	2557	2935	6022
1951	20210	14358	1316	1814	1361	1361	1252	321	931	230	394	−164	767	2128
1952	22735	18713	1778	2831	1214	−1801	1058	295	763	2576	115	2461	3224	1423
1953	21701	16592	2212	3596	969	−1668	1581	1456	125	2623	21	2602	2727	1059
1954	24133	17202	2459	4583	1867	−1978	1532	1858	−326	2615	100	2515	2189	211
1955	27123	17486	3266	5328	3082	−2039	2685	2549	136	3028	192	2836	2972	933
1956	29949	18584	4411	6409	4406	−3861	2375	2998	−623	4728	402	4326	3703	−158
1957	27615	19865	3569	6873	5136	−7826	3565	3200	365	569	493	76	441	−7385
1958	24951	16562	3476	5445	5038	−5570	2812	2991	−179	6021	556	5465	5268	−302

1 = Export
2 = Import
3 = Dividends, interests and *tantièmes* paid to foreign countries
4 = Insurances and transportation costs
5 = Other elements of the current account
6 = Balance of the current account (1−2−3−4−5)
7 = Long-term private capital entering the Congo
8 = Long-term private capital leaving the Congo
9 = Balance of both previous elements (7−8)
10 = Long-term public capital entering the Congo
11 = Long-term public capital leaving the Congo
12 = Balance of both previous elements (10−11)
13 = Balance of long-term capital flows (9+12)
14 = Total balance of payments (6+13)

Source: *Bulletin de la Banque centrale du Congo belge et du Ruanda-Urundi (BBCCBRU)*, 1952–1959.

278

Annex

TABLE 4. *Number of Belgians in the Congo (1890–1959)*

	1	2	3	4	5	6	7
1890	430	175	40.9				
1891	745	338	45.3				
1892	948	445	46.9				
1893	749	464	61.9				
1894	970	631	65.0				
1895	1076	691	64.2				
1896	1325	839	63.3				
1897	1474	882	59.8				
1898	1678	1060	63.1				
1899	1630	959	58.8				
1900	1958	1187	60.6				
1901	2204	1318	59.8				
1902	2346	1465	62.4				
1903	2365	1417	59.9				
1904	2483	1442	58.0				
1905	2511	1410	56.1				
1906	2635	1501	56.9				
1907	2760	1587	57.5				
1908	2943	1713	58.2				
1909	2938	1722	58.6				
1910	3399	1928	56.7				
1911	4003	2432	60.7				
1912	5464	3307	60.5				
1913	5926	3551	59.9				
1914–18	NA	NA	NA				
1919	6395	3673	57.4				
1920	6991	3615	51.7				
1921	8218	4744	57.7				
1922	9589	5502	57.3				
1923	10.037	5853	58.3				
1924	11.539	6857	59.4				
1925	12.795	7770	60.7	2713	1173	1538	1449
1926	15.240	9638	63.2	3158	1344	1642	1525
1927	18.169	11.898	65.4	3938	1741	1700	1692
1928	20.702	14.147	68.3	4663	2165	2391	1754
1929	23.276	15.900	68.3	5441	2428	2273	1909
1930	25.679	17.676	68.8	6234	2725	2383	2080
1931	25.179	17.432	69.2	6616	2879	2588	2319
1932	22.482	15.034	66.8	6124	2856	2443	2471
1933	18.721	12.045	64.3	5254	2483	2129	2665
1934	17.588	11.423	64.9	4726	2502	1182	2806
1935	17.845	11.815	66.2	5097	2672	1914	2911
1936	18.683	12.654	67.7	5416	2913	1945	3053

(*continued*)

TABLE 4 *(continued)*

	1	2	3	4	5	6	7
1937	20.103	13.760	68.1	5878	3211	1946	3284
1938	23.091	16.041	69.1	6604	3759	2068	3499
1939	25.209	17.536	69.5	7347	4414	2205	3662
1940–4	NA	NA	NA	NA	NA	NA	NA
1945	36.080	23.643	65.5	NA	NA	NA	NA
1946	33.787	23.506	69.5	9116	7963	3287	3837
1947	34.786	24.058	69.1	9779	7324	3160	4162
1948	43.408	31.889	73.4	13.391	10.456	3208	4525
1949	51.639	36.510	70.7	15.643	12.763	2825	4816
1950	52.113	39.006	74.8	16.080	13.729	3860	5072
1951	57.930	44.028	76.0	17.582	16.611	4261	5336
1952	66.078	51.440	77.8	21.375	17.699	5933	5501
1953	76.764	59.978	78.1	23.987	22.050	6200	5741
1954	86.696	67.827	78.2	NA	NA	NA	NA
1955	89.311	69.813	78.1	27.275	27.989	7671	6276
1956	97.371	76.164	78.2	NA	NA	NA	NA
1957	107.413	84.444	78.6	NA	NA	NA	NA
1958	109.457	86.736	79.2	32.155	39.100	3982	7131
1959	112.759	88.913	78.8	NA	NA	8319	7557

1 = Total number of white inhabitants of the Congo
2 = Number of Belgians living in the Congo
3 = Belgians in percent of total white inhabitants
4 = Number of white women
5 = Number of white children under eighteen
6 = Number of civil servants
7 = Number of missionaries

Source: *Annuaire statistique de la Belgique (et du Congo belge)*, 1890–1959. NA = not available. It would of course be possible to find the missing data in other sources, but this research was beyond our reach. The *Annuaire statistique* mentions gender, age and professions as from 1925. The definition of "civil servant" is not clear for the years between 1913 and 1926. The *Annuaire statistique* gives another table with the number and subcategories of civil servants. For 1925 and 1926, these figures are about 600 units higher than the data mentioned in the above table.

Index

Abako, 91, 94
Académie royale des Sciences coloniales, 77, 222. See also Institut royal colonial belge
Accords of Rabat (1989), 222
Administration générale de la Coopération au Développement, 255, 260
Adoula, Cyrille, 203, 214, 215, 216, 218, 219
Agence maritime internationale, 159
Ageron, Charles-Robert, 6, 69
Air Congo, 246
Air Katanga, 211
Albert I, 53, 54, 109, 189
Albert II, 87
Aldrich, Robert, 7
Algeria, 43, 46, 82, 92, 96, 215, 220, 238
Allard l'Olivier, Fernand, 73
Amedeo of Savoy, 88
American Congo Company, 165
Anglo-Belgian India Rubber Company, 148, 150
Angola, 18, 118, 120
Anticolonialism, 41, 47, 48, 49, 75, 139
Antwerp, 37, 63, 69, 78, 86, 144, 145, 148, 187, 188, 190, 191, 198, 275
Arenberg, Stéphane d', 231
Arendt, Hannah, 3
Argentina, 145, 152
Army, 43, 54, 56, 62, 92, 95, 102, 121, 136, 160, 202, 204, 210, 211, 216, 221, 222, 260, 266. See also Force publique; Forces armées zaïroises; Mercenaries
Aspremont Lynden, Gobert d', 92
Aspremont Lynden, Harold d', 91, 97, 211, 275
Association belge des Intérêts en Afrique, 235
Association des Écrivains et Artistes coloniaux belges, 74
Association des Intérêts coloniaux belges, 44, 128
Association des Universitaires catholiques pour l'Aide aux Missions, 68
Association internationale africaine, 19
Association internationale du Congo, 20, 21, 103
Association pour le Perfectionnement du Matériel colonial, 176
Australia, 252
Aviation, 123, 188, 189, 194, 198, 229, 246. See also Air Congo; Air Katanga; Sabena; Sobelair; *Société nationale pour l'Étude des Transports aériens*

Bahr-el-Ghazal, 105
Bakajika law, 247
Balance of payments, 158, 196, 240
Banana, 188
Bancel, Nicolas, 8, 69
Banking, 118, 145, 181, 182, 194. See also Belgolaise; Congolese National Bank; *Société générale de Belgique*; and specific bank names
Banque belge du Travail, 48
Banque centrale du Congo belge, 158, 161, 184
Banque de Bruxelles, 181, 182
Banque de l'Union parisienne, 149, 165
Banque d'Outremer, 182, 188, 189
Banque du Congo belge, 125, 133, 161, 184
Banque nationale de Belgique, 133, 163, 211
Banque nationale du Katanga, 211
Barbanson, Gaston, 169
Baudhuin, Fernand, 184, 196
Baudouin I, 53, 54, 87, 88, 90, 92, 93, 97, 98, 102, 111, 221, 222, 227, 231, 233, 234
Beernaert, Auguste, 36, 37, 38, 39

Belgian Congo
  Administration, 27, 28, 42, 47, 54, 60, 82, 83, 87. *See also* Colonial Charter (1908); Governor-General
  Economy, 29, 31, 138, 163, 253
  Educational policy, 30, 47, 50, 63, 85, 208
  Social policy, 30, 31, 49, 64, 174
Belgian-Congolese community, 84, 85, 87
Belgolaise, 245
Berlin Act (1885). *See* Berlin Conference (1885)
Berlin Conference (1885), 21, 26, 36, 66, 103, 104, 116, 117, 147, 168
Bern, 128
Blaise, Gaston, 244
Blanchard, Pascal, 8, 69
Boma, 28, 105, 173, 188
Bomboko, Justin, 214, 248
Bordeaux, 124
Borneo, 18
Botanical Garden, 77
Bouvier, Jean, 6
Braeckman, Colette, 228
Brasseur, Robert, 255
Brazil, 140
Brazza, 20
Brazzaville, 118, 208
British Empire, 3, 5, 29, 52, 55, 61, 62, 69, 80, 105, 122, 128, 153, 156, 160, 172, 183, 193, 196. *See also* specific names of colonies and dominions
Browne de Tiège, Alexandre de, 148
Brussels, 19, 28, 32, 35, 44, 49, 64, 70, 72, 77, 83, 93, 96, 109, 112, 113, 114, 118, 119, 120, 124, 128, 132, 137, 139, 140, 147, 168, 186, 189, 210, 221, 222, 223, 227, 230, 233, 246, 247, 254, 258, 261, 264
Buch, Pierre, 135
Buelens, Frans, 185
Buisseret, Auguste, 43, 44, 50, 85, 86, 88
Burdon, Richard, 114
Burundi. *See* Urundi

Cacao, 178, 193
Cahen, Alfred, 232
Caillaux, Joseph, 113
Cameroon, 18, 113, 115
Camus, Albert, 74
Canada, 124, 192
Cannadine, David, 52
Capelle, Robert, 128
Capital flows, 159, 160, 164, 165, 197, 242, 265
Cartier de Marchienne, Emile de, 126
Casement, Roger, 26, 27

Catholicism, 44. *See also* Political parties: Catholic party
  Church, 40, 44, 50, 52, 66, 67, 71, 86, 99, 204, 260. *See also* Vatican
  Missions, 1, 15, 16, 30, 37, 44, 47, 49, 50, 60, 62, 63, 64, 65, 66, 67, 68, 70, 73, 77, 80, 85, 260, 263, 265, 268, 280. *See also* specific names of missionary congregations and associations
Cattier, Félicien, 125
Cayen, Alphonse, 58
Chamber of Commerce, 188
Charles, Paul, 44
Charles, prince, 54
Charles VI, 15
Charter of San Francisco (1945), 138
Chiang Kai-Shek, 214
China, 65, 140, 167, 214, 215
Chomé, Jules, 227
Churchill, Winston, 126
CIA, 206, 220
Cobalt, 29, 155, 187, 191, 192
Coffee, 30, 155, 178, 193, 239
Cold War, 55, 102, 134, 136, 141, 206
Colonial Charter (1908), 27, 28, 41, 44, 51, 108, 111, 112, 161
Cominière, 181, 249
Comité d'Action et de Défense des Belges en Afrique, 234
Comité d'Études du Haut-Congo, 19
Comité national du Kivu, 119, 218
Comité spécial du Katanga, 149
Commission d'Interpénétration économique de la Belgique et du Congo belge, 177, 178, 179
Commission du Colonat, 62
Commonwealth, 52, 84
Communist Bloc, 84, 94, 136, 137, 206, 212, 217
Compagnie belge maritime du Congo, 188
Compagnie des Chemins de Fer du Congo supérieur aux Grands Lacs africains, 149, 218
Compagnie des Métaux d'Overpelt-Lommel, Corphalie, 191
Compagnie du Chemin de Fer du Bas-Congo au Katanga, 149, 165
Compagnie du Chemin de Fer du Congo, 37
Compagnie du Congo pour le Commerce et l'Industrie, 37, 148, 181, 251
Compagnie du Katanga, 149, 181, 218
Compagnie gantoise de Navigation, 188
Compagnie industrielle Union, 191

Index

Compagnie maritime belge, 125, 159, 189, 190, 198, 246
Compagnie maritime congolaise, 246
Compagnie maritime du Zaïre, 246
Compagnie maritime zaïroise, 246
Compagnie sucrière congolaise, 244
Conakat, 91, 94, 210
Congo Free State, 9, 10, 17, 18, 19, 21, 22, 23, 24, 25, 27, 29, 36, 37, 38, 39, 41, 42, 49, 53, 56, 57, 60, 63, 65, 66, 75, 77, 99, 103, 104, 105, 106, 108, 113, 118, 144, 145, 146, 147, 148, 149, 150, 152, 160, 165, 166, 180, 181, 187, 188, 270
Congo Reform Association, 26
Congo River, 19, 20, 22, 104, 115, 141, 208, 268
Congolese army, 94, 95, 202, 204, 206, 208, 214, 216, 220, 230, 261
Congolese National Bank, 248, 254
Congolese nationalism, 32, 86, 90, 92, 104. See also Abako; Conakat; *Mouvement national congolais*; Panafrican Congress
Congrégation du Cœur immaculé de Marie, 65
Congrès colonial national, 54, 63, 173
Conklin, Alice, 7
Constitution, 43, 55, 84, 121
Contentieux, 218, 227, 247
Convention of Saint-Germain-en-Laye (1919), 109, 116, 121, 147, 156, 169, 172, 175, 178, 179
Copper, 29, 146, 155, 157, 168, 191, 192, 232, 239, 244, 248, 249, 250, 265
Cooper, Frederick, 2
Cornelis, Hendrik, 44, 90, 165
Cornélus, Henri, 75
Costantini, Dino, 8
Cotton, 30, 155, 177, 193, 239
Crédit général du Congo, 182
Crem, Robert, 250, 251
Crete, 18
Crokaert, Paul, 49
Culture
  Art market, 73
  Arts, 73
  Comic strips, 75
  Film, 72
  Literature, 74
  Monuments, 72
  Museums, 73, 76, 80
  Schools, 58, 68, 71, 78
  Science, 39, 75
  Universities, 64, 77, 85, 234, 260
Cyprus, 18

Damseaux, Jean-Claude & William, 251
Davignon, Etienne, 219, 226, 231
Davister, Pierre, 228
Daye, Pierre, 111
De Beers, 190, 191
De Bruyne, Edgar, 83
De Croo, Herman, 237
de Gaulle, Charles, 122
de Launoit (group), 249
De Merre, Pierre, 251
De Sagher, Emile, 235
de Saint-Moulin, Léon, 24
De Schryver, August, 44, 91, 92, 97, 275
De Smet, Pieter, 65
De Vleeschauwer, Albert, 43, 51, 79, 123, 124, 125, 126, 128, 129, 131, 132, 133, 162
De Voghel, Franz, 163, 195, 217
De Witte, Ludo, 96
Declaration of Sainte-Adresse (1916), 115
Decolonisation, 32, 85, 89, 93, 138, 201, 208, 234, 242, 253, 265, 266. See also Congolese nationalism; Round-table Conference (1960)
Defense. See Army
Delvaux, Paul, 73
Demuyter, Ernest, 84
Dequae, André, 43, 51, 85
Development aid, 163, 208, 210, 211, 236, 251, 254, 256, 257, 258, 265
Devlin, Lawrence, 206
Diamond, 29, 94, 118, 187, 190, 191, 194, 198, 202, 239, 244, 250, 265
Dierikx, Marc, 123
Diplomacy, 3, 11, 12, 14, 17, 18, 21, 22, 27, 36, 71, 81, 89, 98, 101, 103, 104, 109, 111, 112, 113, 115, 116, 117, 118, 119, 122, 128, 134, 136, 137, 140, 146, 166, 197, 200, 202, 208, 211, 212, 213, 214, 215, 216, 219, 220, 221, 222, 223, 224, 225, 227, 228, 229, 231, 232, 233, 261, 262, 266
  Neutrality, 14, 15, 22, 54, 101, 102, 104, 106, 114, 115, 116, 122, 124, 125, 127, 128, 141
Donation royale, 53
Dubois-Pelerin, Jules, 214, 225, 245
Dupriez, Léon H., 174
Dutch empire, 15, 29, 61, 85, 153, 159, 183. See also specific names of colonies

Economic Round-table conference (1960), 93, 217
Egypt, 128

Élisabethville, 84, 86, 87, 210. *See also* Lubumbashi
Emigration, 1, 16, 60, 62, 208, 243, 262
Empain (group), 249
Empain, Edouard, 149, 181
Enterprises, 44, 48, 49, 61, 62, 71, 99, 124, 132, 148, 176, 180, 182, 186, 193, 218, 221, 225, 231, 235, 242, 243, 245, 249, 251, 256, 262. *See also* specific names of enterprises
  Profits, 183, 184
Ethiopia, 9, 18, 56, 88, 130
European Economic Community, 136, 195, 241
Evans, Martin, 7
Exhibitions, 63, 64, 68, 69, 70, 71, 73, 76, 80, 81
Eyskens, Gaston, 88, 89, 90, 91, 97, 98, 111, 211, 212
Eyskens, Mark, 226

Fabiola, queen, 221
Fabrimetal, 180, 239
Fachoda, 105
Falkenhausen, Alexander von, 128
Fédération des Entreprises congolaises, 231
Fédération des Industries belges, 180, 256
Fieldhouse, David K., 193
Fiji Islands, 18
Financial policy, 37, 38, 39, 40, 55, 132, 133, 143, 161, 163, 164, 197, 217, 218, 222, 229, 235, 253. *See also* Money and monetary policy
  Colonial Lottery, 42, 161
Finoutremer (*Compagnie financière européenne d'Outre-Mer*), 251
First World War, 27, 29, 34, 56, 63, 72, 102, 108, 114, 119, 146, 156, 167, 168, 169, 171, 183, 190, 268
Flemish movement. *See* Language problem in Belgium; Political parties: Flemish nationalist party
Fonds du Bien-Être indigène, 31, 161
Force publique, 21, 55, 56, 92, 94, 115, 127, 129, 137, 205, 234
Forced labour, 17, 22, 23, 28, 30, 38, 108, 119
Forces armées zaïroises, 262
Foreign investment, 109, 149, 165, 166, 194
Forminière, 149, 165, 190, 198
Formosa (Taiwan), 18
Forrest, Georges, 251
France, i, 6, 7, 8, 11, 15, 19, 20, 42, 43, 45, 46, 48, 56, 57, 63, 65, 69, 71, 80, 99, 102, 105, 107, 113, 114, 116, 117, 118, 121, 122, 123, 124, 125, 135, 138, 140, 153, 154, 156, 160, 166, 177, 193, 205, 206, 221, 229, 241, 253, 262, 263, 264, 267, 269
Franck, Louis, 43, 110, 111, 112, 173, 174
Freemasonry, 66, 67
French empire, 29, 61, 62, 84, 95, 122, 153, 156, 160, 171, 183, 193, 196. *See also* specific names of colonies
Frère-Orban, Walthère, 36
Front de Libération nationale du Congo, 221
Fuchs, Félix, 44

Ganshof van der Meersch, Walter, 44, 93, 275
Gécamines, 220, 230, 250
Gécomin, 220, 248, 249, 250
Gérard-Libois, Jules, 207
German East Africa, 115, 118
German empire, 9, 113, 117, 119, 123. *See also* specific names of colonies
Germany, 9, 19, 21, 102, 107, 108, 113, 115, 117, 119, 121, 122, 123, 124, 125, 126, 135, 145, 161, 188, 269
Gernaert, Jules, 108
Ghent, 48, 70, 145, 277
Gilson, Arthur, 97
Girardet, Raoul, 6
Girault, René, 6
Gizenga, Antoine, 104
Godding, Robert, 50, 82, 83, 126, 184
Goering, Hermann, 123
Gold, 30, 150, 155, 160, 161, 164, 174, 184, 239, 265, 277. *See also* Kilo Moto goldmines
Gordimer, Nadine, 24
Governor-General, 28, 44, 50, 82, 83, 84, 88, 90, 91, 112, 123, 127, 128, 132, 135, 140, 162, 164, 170, 184
Great Britain, 3, 4, 5, 8, 9, 11, 15, 16, 19, 20, 21, 25, 26, 29, 42, 45, 46, 47, 48, 52, 55, 57, 63, 66, 71, 78, 88, 99, 103, 105, 106, 107, 113, 114, 115, 117, 118, 120, 121, 122, 124, 125, 126, 127, 128, 129, 130, 131, 134, 135, 138, 140, 143, 144, 145, 147, 148, 153, 154, 159, 171, 177, 186, 188, 193, 194, 212, 241, 263, 264, 269, 271
Greece, 180
Grey, Edward, 114
Gryseels, Guido, 76
Guatemala, 16
Guggenheim, Daniel, 165, 168
Guinea (Conakry), 15
Gutt, Camille, 126, 133

Index

Hailey, Malcolm, 127, 130
Halen, Pierre, 74
Hall, Catherine, 4
Hamburg, 187
Harkis, 264
Harmel, Pierre, 215, 221, 223, 226, 233
Hassan II, 232
Haulleville, Alphonse de, 33
Heenen, Gaston, 44
Helmreich, Jonathan, 11
Hemptinne, Félix de, 131
Hergé, 75
Hiroshima, 134
Hitler, Adolf, 120, 129
Hochschild, Adam, 23, 24
Holding companies. *See* Banking
Holy See. *See* Vatican
Horlings, Edwin, 9
Horn, Max, 83, 126, 174
House, Edward, 109
Huileries du Congo belge, 166
Huybrechts, André, 13, 185

Immigration, 63, 263, 267
Independence. *See* Decolonisation
India, 16, 29, 52, 61, 65, 71, 82, 88, 140, 159, 171, 269
Indonesia, 82, 139, 156, 162, 183, 241
Industrial sectors, 145, 146, 155, 177, 180, 181, 183, 186, 191, 192, 194, 196, 239
Institut cartographique militaire, 36, 55
Institut national pour l'Étude agronomique du Congo, 76
Institut pour la Recherche scientifique au Congo, 77, 161
Institut royal colonial belge, 77. *See also* Académie royale des Sciences coloniales
Institute of Tropical Medicine, 76
International Geographic Conference (1876), 19
International Monetary Fund, 102, 222
Ireland, 5
Isiro, 216
Israel, 262
Italian empire, 62
Italy, 9, 57, 62, 118, 119, 128, 129, 130, 153, 214, 263, 269
Ivory, 23, 73, 149, 155, 187

Jadot, Jean, 168
James, Alan, 212
Janssen, Frans, 176, 177
Janssens, Emile, 94
Japan, 177, 177

Jaspar, Henri, 43
Jungers, Eugène, 44

Kabila, Laurent-Désiré, 205, 207
Kalonji Ditunga, Albert, 202
Kamina, 55, 136
Kasai, 94, 190, 202, 203, 244
Kasavubu, Joseph, 91, 94, 95, 104, 203, 204, 219, 220, 230
Katanga, 21, 22, 30, 70, 91, 94, 95, 96, 97, 98, 105, 118, 125, 127, 131, 134, 136, 165, 181, 202, 203, 204, 209, 210, 211, 213, 216, 218, 219, 220, 221, 243, 247, 251, 254, 261. *See also* Shaba
Kerchove de Denterghem, Charles de, 214, 231
Kerremans, Charles, 230, 232
Kigali, 207
Kilo Moto goldmines, 186
Kimba, Evariste, 219
Kimbanguism, 32
Kinshasa, 13, 207, 214, 215, 222, 223, 224, 227, 228, 229, 230, 232, 233, 246, 247, 248, 249, 250, 259, 264. *See also* Léopoldville
Kipling, Rudyard, 74
Kisangani, 20, 216. *See also* Stanleyville
Kitawala, 32
Kitona, 55, 136
Kolwezi, 221
Kuba, 25
Kwango, 105
Kwilu, 203, 215

Lambert (group), 249
Lambert, Henri, 104
Lambert, Léon, 148
Language problem in Belgium, 35, 48, 50
Latin America, 16, 167, 258
Lavigerie, Charles, 65
Le Cour Grandmaison, Olivier, 8
League of Nations, 117, 119, 138
Lebovics, Herman, 7
Leburton, Edmond, 232, 237
Lefèvre, Théo, 98
Lefort, Claude, 175
Lemaire, Sandrine, 8, 69
Leopold I, 15, 16, 34, 53, 102
Leopold II, i, 10, 14, 15, 17, 18, 19, 20, 21, 22, 23, 24, 25, 26, 27, 33, 36, 37, 38, 39, 40, 41, 45, 49, 52, 53, 54, 57, 65, 66, 69, 71, 72, 76, 77, 78, 81, 98, 99, 102, 104, 105, 106, 108, 111, 121, 137, 141, 146, 147, 148, 149, 160, 165, 167, 187, 188, 197, 206, 217, 229, 234, 270

Leopold III, 49, 53, 54, 87, 88, 102, 120, 121, 122, 124, 125, 128, 129
Léopoldville, 22, 28, 37, 82, 83, 84, 85, 89, 91, 94, 95, 104, 112, 118, 123, 125, 129, 132, 138, 189, 203, 204, 210, 211, 213, 214, 215, 218, 219, 229, 231, 233, 247, 254, 257, 261. *See also* Kinshasa
Lever Brothers, 166
Leyniers, Daniel, 49
Liauzu, Claude, 6
Liège, 191
Lievens, Constant, 65
Liliane, princess, 87
Linguistic problem in Belgium, 58, 201
Lippens, Maurice, 44, 50, 112
Liverpool, 187
Lobby groups, 37, 38, 39, 44, 188, 231, 234, 235. *See also* Association belge des Intérêts en Afrique; Association des Intérêts coloniaux belges; Chamber of Commerce; Fabrimetal; *Fédération des Entreprises congolaises*; *Fédération des Industries belges*; Syndicat de Défense des Actionnaires et des Détenteurs de Biens au Zaïre; Syndicat de Défense des Porteurs de la Dette coloniale
London, 101, 106, 118, 120, 122, 125, 126, 127, 128, 129, 130, 131, 133, 139, 161, 187, 190, 191, 212
Louwers, Octave, 27, 128, 149
Lubumbashi, 222. *See also* Élisabethville
Luluaburg, 210
Lumumba, Patrice, 91, 94, 95, 96, 97, 98, 203, 206, 211, 212, 227, 231, 243

Mackenzie, Colonel, 127
MacKenzie, John, 3, 68
Magritte, René, 73
Malaysia, 150
Malou, Jules, 36
Mambour, Auguste, 73
Mandaila, Gisèle, 264
Mandungu, Antoine, 233
Marchal, Jules, 10
Marlière, Louis, 261
Marseille, Jacques, 6, 183, 193
Marshall, Peter James, 5, 194
Martens, Wilfried, 222, 232, 233
Marysse, Stefaan, 240
Matadi, 22, 37, 118, 210
Mercenaries, 211, 216, 217, 220, 233, 261
Mérode Westerloo, Henri de, 39
Miba (*Minière de Bakwanga*), 250
Michel, Louis, 223

Michel, Marc, 8
Milner, Alfred, 117
Minière du Bécéka, 185, 190, 244, 250
Mining, 183
Minister of the Colonies, 28, 43, 44, 45, 50, 78, 79, 83, 85, 88, 89, 110, 111, 112, 115, 123, 124, 126, 131, 132, 134, 162, 166, 169, 173, 184, 273, 275
Ministry of Foreign Affairs, 13, 27, 82, 201, 219, 255
Ministry of the Colonies, 12, 42, 43, 49, 57, 63, 64, 70, 72, 74, 82, 89, 124, 176, 255, 268
Missiebond, 68
Mixed-race children, 63, 64
Mobutu, Joseph-Désiré (Sese Seko), 95, 203, 204, 205, 206, 207, 214, 215, 219, 220, 221, 222, 223, 224, 225, 226, 227, 228, 229, 230, 231, 232, 233, 234, 235, 236, 237, 245, 246, 247, 248, 250, 252, 257, 258, 259, 260, 261, 262, 264
Molokai, 65
Moluccans, 264
Monarchy, 34, 35, 40, 52, 87, 97, 98, 120, 121, 233. *See also* Albert I; Albert II; Baudouin I; Charles, prince; Fabiola, queen, Leopold I; Leopold II; Leopold III; Lilian, princess; Viceroyalty
Money and monetary policy, 156, 170, 171, 172, 174, 196, 197, 254
Mongolia, 65
Monheim, Francis, 228
Morel, Edmund D., 25, 26, 27
Morocco, 18, 113, 205, 221, 222, 232, 263, 267
Mouvement national congolais, 91, 94, 227
Mouvement populaire de la Révolution, 204, 206
Mozambique, 18
Multatuli, 74
Mussolini, Benito, 88

Nagasaki, 134
National identity. *See* Patriotism
NATO, 102, 136, 142, 212
Ndele, Albert, 248
Nendaka, Victor, 214
Netherlands, 9, 15, 35, 52, 61, 139, 148, 153, 156, 159, 241, 263, 264, 269, 271
New Hebrides, 18
NGOs, 236, 260
Nieuwe Afrikaanse Handels Vennootschap, 148
Nigeria, 166, 238
Nile, 18, 22, 104, 105
Nokin, Max, 245
Norway, 60

Office de Coopération au Développement, 255
Orgaman, 251
Ormsby-Gore, William, 120
Orts, Pierre, 103, 110, 115, 117
Ostend Company, 15

Pacific islands, 65
Palm, 30, 155, 193
Panafrican Congress, 63
Panda Farnana, Paul, 63
Pansaerts, Carl, 120
Papua New Guinea, 252
Parliament, 28, 35, 36, 38, 39, 41, 42, 45, 46, 48, 49, 50, 51, 54, 89, 96, 99
Patriotism, 47, 57, 58, 99, 130
Paulis, 204, 216
Peeters, Wim, 167, 194
Pende, 31
Périer, Gilbert, 190
Pétillon, Léo, 44, 84, 88, 89, 163
Petry, Irène, 232
Philippines, 18, 65
Pierlot, Hubert, 126
Piret, Baudouin, 259
Pirotte, Jean, 67
Plesman, Albert, 123
Pointe Noire, 118
Political parties, 35, 39, 40, 41, 45, 46, 47, 52, 89, 95, 99, 234, 237
  Catholic party, 34, 35, 36, 39, 40, 42, 45, 50, 79, 84, 86, 87, 88, 89, 98
  Communist party, 34, 45, 48, 85, 95, 135, 136, 209, 237
  Flemish nationalist party, 34, 48, 237
  Liberal party, 34, 39, 41, 45, 85, 86, 89
  Socialist party, 34, 39, 41, 45, 47, 85, 86, 90, 92, 98, 232, 237
Porter, Bernard, 4, 69
Portfolio, 217, 218, 219, 227
Portugal, 15, 19, 20, 104, 107, 113, 117, 118, 120, 124, 126, 139, 153, 154, 160, 180, 216, 263
Portuguese empire, 29, 105, 117, 120, 153, 160. *See also* specific names of colonies
Potter, Simon, 4
Powis de Tenbossche, J., 230
Press, 38, 39, 41, 49, 57, 83, 87, 89, 107, 175, 204, 225, 227, 228, 233
Primary products. *See* specific names of primary products
Propaganda, 4, 8, 11, 19, 26, 56, 58, 59, 68, 69, 70, 71, 72, 73, 76, 78, 79, 80, 81, 99, 115, 130, 143, 197, 266. *See also* Exhibitions

Protestant missions, 30, 50, 65, 66, 137

Rabat, 207, 222
Red rubber, 9, 25, 27, 41, 65, 66, 107, 108
Reisdorff, Robert, 57
Relecom, Michel, 251
Renders, Luc, 75
Renkin, Jules, 28, 43, 50, 78, 115, 166, 169, 173, 174
Reynaud, Paul, 123
Rhodesia, 115
Rio Nuñez, 15
Rittweger de Moor, Eugène, 232
Rolin, Henri, 208
Rose, Sonya, 4
Rothschild, Robert, 214, 257
Round-table Conference (1960), 92, 93, 95, 100, 208, 217, 227, 230, 243, 254. *See also* Economic Round-table Conference (1960)
Ruanda, 42, 89, 117, 119, 157, 177, 252, 268, 275, 277, 278. *See also* Rwanda
Rubber, 23, 25, 27, 53, 142, 148, 149, 150, 155, 187, 193
Ruscio, Alain, 8
Russia, 145, 152, 167, 206, 216. *See also* Communist Bloc; Soviet Union
Rutten, Martin, 50
Rwanda, 207, 252, 260. *See also* Ruanda
Ryan-Guggenheim, 149, 190
Ryckmans, Pierre, 82, 83, 112, 127, 128, 129, 132, 135, 140, 162, 170, 184

Sabena, 189, 190, 198, 208, 211, 246
Saint Damien, 65
Saint Francis Xavier, 64
Saio, 130
Santo Tomas, 16
Scandinavian countries, 55, 60
Schacht, Hjalmar, 120
Scheldt River, 188
Scheyven, Raymond, 91, 97, 140, 164, 212, 242, 275
Schöller, André, 91
Schramme, Jean, 220
Second World War, 24, 30, 31, 34, 42, 45, 47, 49, 51, 52, 55, 60, 62, 67, 72, 73, 76, 77, 78, 82, 88, 99, 103, 107, 108, 109, 112, 117, 120, 121, 122, 129, 134, 135, 141, 146, 150, 152, 153, 155, 156, 160, 161, 163, 165, 166, 168, 172, 179, 190, 191, 192, 194
Senegal, 258
Sengier, Edgar, 133, 134

Shaba, 205, 221, 228, 230, 232. *See also* Katanga
Sheppard, William, 25
Shinkolobwe, 135
Shipping, 145, 187, 188, 198, 246. *See also* specific names of shipping enterprises
Sicking, Louis, 136
Sierra Leone, 166
Simonet, Henri, 224, 232
Slavery, 7, 19, 22, 65, 70, 147
Sobelair, 190
Social mobility, 62
Société de Crédit au Colonat et à l'Industrie, 62
Société générale de Belgique, 124, 125, 132, 145, 149, 159, 168, 181, 182, 186, 189, 190, 191, 198, 214, 217, 219, 225, 231, 235, 242, 243, 245, 247, 249, 250, 251, 256, 271
Société générale des Minerais, 192, 214, 248, 249
Société générale métallurgique de Hoboken, 191, 198, 250
Société maritime du Congo, 188
Société nationale pour l'Étude des Transports aériens, 189
Solomon Islands, 18
South Africa, 83, 118, 156, 202, 216, 262
Soviet Union, 137, 140. *See also* Communist Bloc; Russia
Sozacom, 250
Spaak, Paul-Henri, 97, 98, 126, 131, 137, 212, 213, 214, 215, 216, 217, 219, 220, 227, 231, 247, 257
Spain, 15
Spirlet, André de, 190, 225, 231, 248
Sri Lanka, 65
Stanard, Matthew, 72
Stanley, Henry Morton, 19, 20, 148
Stanleyville, 95, 203, 204, 216. *See also* Kisangani
Stengers, Jean, v, 10, 18, 25, 37, 143, 144, 162
Stenmans, Alain, 91
Sterkendries, René, 198
Stock market, 182, 186
Stoler, Ann Laura, 2
Sudan, 140
Sûreté de l'État, 206
Syndicat de Défense des Actionnaires et des Détenteurs de Biens au Zaïre, 235
Syndicat de Défense des Porteurs de la Dette coloniale, 235

Tanganyika Concessions Limited, 165
Tempelsman, Maurice, 248

Tervuren, 69, 72, 76
Thèse belge, 140
Thesiger, Wilfred, 26
Thieffry, Edmond, 189
Thobie, Jacques, 6
Thomas, Martin, 7
Thompson, Andrew S., 5, 8, 11, 46, 57, 183, 193, 242, 269
Thys, Albert, 37, 38, 148, 149, 181, 182
Tin, 30, 155, 157, 191, 192
Tindemans, Leo, 221, 224, 230, 232
Tintin au Congo, 75
Trade, 146, 150, 152, 155, 157, 158, 173, 174, 176, 177, 187, 192, 193, 196, 237, 239, 256
 Free trade, 14, 16, 20, 21, 22, 116, 121, 146, 147, 168, 169
 Trade policy, 145, 147, 168, 170, 172, 178
Trade unions, 34, 86, 146, 204
Transport, 22, 40, 91, 145, 151, 158, 181, 182, 185, 187, 189, 190, 192, 197, 198, 239, 240, 251, 265. *See also* specific names of transport enterprises
Treaty of Rome (1958), 135
Truman, Harry, 253
Tshombe, Moïse, 91, 202, 204, 210, 213, 215, 216, 219, 220, 227, 247, 248, 257
Tunisia, 258
Turkey, 263, 267
Turner, Thomas, 220

Umberto of Savoie, 128
Unibra, 251
Union africaine et malgache, 229
Union minière du Haut-Katanga, 30, 96, 125, 127, 133, 134, 149, 165, 166, 185, 186, 202, 210, 213, 214, 216, 218, 220, 230, 231, 243, 244, 247, 249, 251, 262
Union royale belge pour les pays d'Outre-mer, 234
United Nations, 84, 94, 95, 97, 102, 138, 139, 140, 142, 202, 203, 211, 213, 217, 253, 254
United States of America, iv, 1, 10, 84, 95, 97, 102, 116, 117, 124, 126, 130, 131, 132, 134, 135, 137, 138, 156, 158, 165, 168, 190, 192, 203, 204, 205, 206, 212, 213, 214, 215, 226, 229, 232, 241, 262
Uranium, 29, 134, 135, 191, 192, 194
Urundi, 42, 89, 117, 119, 157, 177, 252, 268, 275, 277, 278

Van Acker, Achille, 88
Van Bilsen, A.A.J. (Jef), 86, 215, 230, 255, 258

Index

Van den Bogaert, Ronald, 222, 237
Van Eetvelde, Edmond, 66
Van Eynde, Jos, 233
Van Hemelrijck, Maurice, 89, 90, 91, 275
Van Iseghem, André, 79
Van Meerten, Michelangelo, 194
Van Miert, Karel, 237
Van Zeeland, Paul, 97
Vanaudenhove, Omer, 97
Vanderlinden, Jacques, 135
Vandersmissen, Jan, 17
Vanderstraeten, Louis-Ferdinand, 56
Vandervelde, Émile, 39, 41, 48, 49, 108, 119
Vandewalle, Frédéric, 216, 277
Vandewalle, Gaston, 157
Vangroenweghe, Daniël, 10
Vanlangenhove, Fernand, 110, 140
Vansina, Jan, 24, 25
Vatican, 50, 66
Vaucleroy, Pierre de, 73
Vellut, Jean-Luc, 10, 13, 268

Vergès, Françoise, 8
Verhaegen, Benoît, 71
Viaene, Vincent, 17, 40
Viceroyalty, 87, 88, 90
Vietnam, 18, 82

Wallef, Louis, 231, 243, 244, 248
Welfare state, 34, 35, 47
Wigny, Pierre, 43, 97, 110, 139, 243
Willame, Jean-Claude, 220
Willequet, Jacques, 113
Williams, Georges W., 25
Williams, Robert, 149, 165
Woeste, Charles, 39

Young, Crawford, 220

Zaire, 12, 204, 222, 233, 236, 250, 259
Zaire Committee, 236
Zairisation, 221, 236, 245, 250, 262
Zinc, 146, 155, 191, 192
Zinzen, Walter, 228

Lightning Source UK Ltd.
Milton Keynes UK
UKHW010036081219
354938UK00002B/75/P